SEEKING SANCTUARY

Seeking Sanctuary

Crime, Mercy, and Politics in English Courts, 1400–1550

SHANNON McSHEFFREY

UNIVERSITY PRESS

Great Clarendon Street, Oxford, OX2 6DP,
United Kingdom

Oxford University Press is a department of the University of Oxford.
It furthers the University's objective of excellence in research, scholarship,
and education by publishing worldwide. Oxford is a registered trade mark of
Oxford University Press in the UK and in certain other countries

© Shannon McSheffrey 2017

The moral rights of the author have been asserted

First Edition published in 2017

All rights reserved. No part of this publication may be reproduced, stored in
a retrieval system, or transmitted, in any form or by any means, without the
prior permission in writing of Oxford University Press, or as expressly permitted
by law, by licence or under terms agreed with the appropriate reprographics
rights organization. Enquiries concerning reproduction outside the scope of the
above should be sent to the Rights Department, Oxford University Press, at the
address above

You must not circulate this work in any other form
and you must impose this same condition on any acquirer

Published in the United States of America by Oxford University Press
198 Madison Avenue, New York, NY 10016, United States of America

British Library Cataloguing in Publication Data
Data available

Library of Congress Control Number: 2017932296

ISBN 978–0–19–879814–9

Links to third party websites are provided by Oxford in good faith and
for information only. Oxford disclaims any responsibility for the materials
contained in any third party website referenced in this work.

Acknowledgements

Over the years I've worked on this book, I've incurred many debts, deriving both from chance comments in casual conversations that had significant effects on my thinking and from long-term, ongoing encouragement and support. No scholar works outside the broad structures that allow us to do our work. This includes the staffs at many archives and libraries that were essential for the research for this book. I'd like to thank those working at the Concordia Libraries (particularly the Interlibrary Loans department), London Metropolitan Archives, the National Archives at Kew, and the Westminster Abbey Library and Muniments (especially Christine Reynolds). I could not have written this book without the online resources of British History Online and the Anglo-American Legal Tradition. Similarly, the financial support of the Social Sciences and Humanities Research Council of Canada has been instrumental. Through the years many scholars and colleagues have been generous with advice and references: Elizabeth Allen, John Arnold, Judith Bennett, Christa Canitz, Martha Carlin, Justin Colson, Roisin Cossar, Matthew Davies, Graham Dawson, Charles Donahue, Konrad Eisenbichler, Kouky Fianu, Ian Forrest, Kit French, Peter Gossage, Vanessa Harding, Richard Helmholz, Cynthia Herrup, Nora Jaffary, William Jordan, Krista Kesselring, Maryanne Kowaleski, Margaret McGlynn, Michelle McKinley, Lydia Murdoch, Derek Neal, Derek Parent, Elena Razlogova, Ronald Rudin, David Seipp, Karl Shoemaker, Victor Uribe-Uran, Michael Wasser, and Ellen Wurtzel. Special thanks are due to those who invited me to deliver talks related to this project: Vanessa Harding and Caroline Barron, who arranged twice for me to give papers at the Medieval and Tudor London seminar at the Institute for Historical Research in London; Michael van Dussen for an invitation to the McGill Medievalists; and Cynthia Herrup for an invitation to speak at an early stage in my work on sanctuary to the Early Modern British Seminar at the USC/Huntingdon Library Early Modern Studies Institute. Students in most of my classes over the last decade have had to suffer my bringing sanctuary in whenever I could, and their questions have proved invaluable for cutting through 'received wisdom'. Chris Perrin and Ryan Madden were research assistants on some parts of the project, helping me figure out Hugh Harvey's spending and the boundaries of St Martin's. Evan May worked also as a research assistant at an early stage, when I had not even landed on sanctuary as my focus, but even more valuable than his (invaluable) archive photos were the insights of his 2010 doctoral dissertation on political culture in London. Krista Kesselring and Graham Dawson were especially generous in sharing some of their notes on sanctuary seekers with me, and Kit French has many times answered questions about Westminster in addition to being a great London roommate and academic BFF. Caroline Barron kindly and astutely commented on Chapter 3 in draft, while the generous, perceptive, and helpful comments of two anonymous reviewers for OUP (who were completely unlike Reader #1 and Reader #2 of internet memes) were invaluable in clarifying my argument. At OUP, Stephanie Ireland, Cathryn Steele, Mohana Annamalai, and Kim Allen were unfailingly helpful in the publication process. Eric Reiter read the manuscript in full and as always I was the beneficiary of his masterful red pen and logical mind. Alice Reiter and Anna Reiter both helped with proofreading and reminded me that the world has continued beyond the sixteenth century.

My family has lived with the sanctuary seekers for a long time now, and I cannot emphasize enough how much their support has meant. This one's for all of you.

Contents

List of Figures and Table	ix
Conventions and Abbreviations	xi

1. **Introduction: Richard Southwell Flees to Sanctuary** — 1
   - Seeking Sanctuary in Late Medieval and Tudor England — 5
   - Explaining the Tudor Resurgence of Sanctuary — 11
   - Sanctuary and the Partiality of the Archives — 24

2. **Tavern Brawls, Civil Wars, and Remedies for Tyranny: The Evolution of Sanctuary in England, *c.* 1380–1500** — 27
   - Herman Stokfyssh and his Flight to Westminster: The Development of Chartered Sanctuary *c.* 1400 — 27
   - Sanctuary-seeking 1400–1550: The Numbers — 35
   - Sanctuary and the Wars of the Roses — 44
   - Sanctuary, Mercy, and Redemption — 50
   - Ecclesiastical Liberties as a Weapon against Tyranny: St Edmund and Sheriff Leoffstan — 54

3. **Dean Caudray and the City of London: The Politics of Sanctuary in the Fifteenth Century** — 58
   - The Escape of John Knight — 58
   - St Martin le Grand and the City of London: Liberties, Franchises, and Jurisdictions — 60
   - Dean Caudray and the Events of September 1440 — 65
   - Marshalling Cases — 72
   - The End of Dean Caudray's Days — 77

4. **The Hospitaller's Cloak: Mercy, Justice, Jurisdiction** — 83
   - Richard Pulham, Ralph Toker, and the Hospitaller's Cloak — 83
   - The Hospitaller Order, English Criminal Justice, and Christian Mercy in Action — 87
   - Sanctuary Claims at Hospitaller Properties, 1400–1485 — 90
   - Sanctuary Claims at Hospitaller Properties, 1485–1520 — 94
   - Sanctuary Claims at Hospitaller Properties, 1520–1539 — 106

5. **Francis Woodleke's Window: Stranger Shoemakers, Boundaries, and Sanctuary in London in the 1530s** — 112
   - Living in the Precinct of St Martin Le Grand — 115
   - Governing St Martin's Precinct in the Reign of Henry VIII — 119
   - Stranger Artisans, Sanctuary Men, and the City — 124
   - The Boundaries of St Martin's — 127
   - The Dissolution of St Martin le Grand and Beyond — 137

6. The Sanctuary Town of Knowle: Crime, Local Authorities, and the State in 1530s England ... 140
   The Goat Inn Robber and Sanctuary at Knowle ... 142
   Robbery, Flight, Sanctuary ... 147
   Sanctuary at Knowle and the Administration of Law and Justice in the 1530s ... 156
   The Knowle Sanctuary and Tudor State Formation ... 160

7. Cheshire Feuds: Aristocratic Violence and the Uses of Sanctuary in the Reign of Henry VIII ... 165
   Affrays in St Paul's Churchyard ... 166
   Breaching Sanctuary ... 173
   Sanctuary and Aristocratic Violence in the Reign of Henry VIII ... 180

8. Conclusions: Sanctuary, Law, and Politics ... 189
   The Statute of 1540 and Sanctuary's Precipitous Decline ... 191
   Sanctuary, Law, and Politics in England, 1400–1550 ... 197

Bibliography ... 199
  Archival Sources ... 199
  Printed and Online Primary Sources ... 200
  Secondary Sources ... 203
Index ... 213

List of Figures and Table

Figures

1.1.	Hans Holbein the Younger, *Sir Richard Southwell* (oil), 1536.	4
1.2.	Hans Holbein the Younger, *Sir Richard Southwell* (sketch), 1536.	5
2.1.	Sanctuary Seekers, five-year totals: all kinds of seekers (abjurers and seekers at chartered sanctuaries; felons, debtors, political refugees, etc.), all sources.	36
2.2.	Church-takers and/or abjurers, five-year totals, all sources.	37
2.3.	Seekers at chartered sanctuaries, five-year totals, all sources.	37
2.4.	Church-takers and/or abjurers, five-year totals, King's Bench indictments (KB 9).	39
2.5.	Seekers at chartered sanctuaries, five-year totals, King's Bench indictments (KB 9).	40
2.6.	Seekers in the Durham and Beverley sanctuary registers.	40
2.7.	Sheriff Leoffstan seizing the sanctuary-seeking woman.	56
5.1.	The boundaries of the precinct of St Martin le Grand, *c.* 1536.	113

Table

1.1.	Sanctuary Seekers by Sex, 1390–1557.	19

Conventions and Abbreviations

To aid the non-specialist reader, for whom medieval spellings prove a challenge, I have modernized the spelling of English quotations. Latin quotations are translated in the text and the original language is provided in the accompanying note. In dates, the year is taken to begin 1 January (for contemporaries, the year changed on 25 March).

The following abbreviations are used in the notes:

BL	London, British Library
CCR	A. E. Stamp, et al., eds, *Calendar of Close Rolls*, 47 vols (London, 1900–1963).
CPR	*Calendar of Patent Rolls, 1232–1509*, 53 vols (London, 1891–1961).
HPO	History of Parliament Trust, 'Members, 1509–1558', *The History of Parliament: British Political, Social, and Local History* (London, 1964), http://www.historyofparliamentonline.org/research/members/members-1509–1558.
L&P	J. S. Brewer, James Gairdner, and R. H. Brodie, eds, *Letters and Papers, Foreign and Domestic, of the Reign of Henry VIII*, 21 vols in 35 parts (London, 1862–).
LMA	London Metropolitan Archives
ODNB	H. C. G. Matthew and B. Harrison, eds, *The Oxford Dictionary of National Biography* (Oxford, 2004-), http://www.oxforddnb.com.
PROME	Chris Given-Wilson, ed., *The Parliament Rolls of Medieval England* (London, 2010), http://www.british-history.ac.uk/no-series/parliament-rolls-medieval.
Registrum	London, Westminster Abbey Library and Muniments, Muniment Book 5, Registrum Collegii Sancti Martini Magni, London.
SDSB	*Sanctuarium Dunelmense et Sanctuarium Beverlacense*, Surtees Society 5 (London, 1837).
Seipp	David J. Seipp, 'An Index and Paraphrase of Printed Year Book Reports, 1268–1535' (2008), http://www.bu.edu/law/seipp/index.html.
SR	*The Statutes of the Realm*, 10 vols (London, 1810).
TNA	Kew, The National Archives
WAM	London, Westminster Abbey Library and Muniments
WARB	WAM, Westminster Abbey Register Book.

1

Introduction
Richard Southwell Flees to Sanctuary

On 20 April 1532, near the king's palace at Westminster, two gentlemen, Richard Southwell, esquire, and Sir William Pennington, faced one another in a sword fight, a quarrel that ended in Pennington's death.[1] The slaying came at a sensitive time in Henry VIII's reign: much attention was focused that Spring on 'the King's Great Matter', Henry's divorce of Katherine of Aragon and his projected marriage to Anne Boleyn. Although different versions of events on that day survive, it seems likely that the quarrel was sparked by the smouldering factional disputes on the king's council that Spring. Richard Southwell was a retainer of the duke of Norfolk, Anne Boleyn's uncle, while Pennington was 'chief gentleman' to the duke of Suffolk, the king's brother-in-law and opponent of the Boleyn marriage. A Venetian diplomat, Carlo Capello, reported in a letter that Southwell had lain in wait with thirty men to ambush Pennington near Westminster palace. Southwell's attack, Capello said, was in retaliation for insinuations about Anne Boleyn's virtue uttered by Pennington's patroness, the duchess of Suffolk (sister to the king). In the official version recorded later in the court of King's Bench, both the king's sister and his intended wife were left out of the story, and instead Pennington was said to have challenged Southwell over a slight insult. The account on the court roll indicates that the two met, each with five or six retainers, in an evenly matched sword fight. In both scenarios, Sir William Pennington ended up dead, steps away from the king's palace, at the hand of one of Southwell's brothers. Following Pennington's slaying, Richard Southwell and his men—including his two younger brothers, Robert and Anthony—took sanctuary at Westminster Abbey. There they remained safe both from the duke of Suffolk's revenge and from arrest for the homicide.

When the Southwells sought sanctuary at the abbey, they were calling upon one of the most venerable roles of the Christian church, the duty to shelter those

---

[1] See Kew, The National Archives, KB 9/520, m. 12; KB 27/1087, rex m. 8; C 66/661, m. 5; SP 1/70, fols 165r–166v, calendared in J. S. Brewer, James Gairdner, and R. H. Brodie, eds, *Letters and Papers, Foreign and Domestic, of the Reign of Henry VIII*, 21 vols in 35 parts (London, 1862–), vol. 5, p. 520; Rawdon Lubbock Brown et al., eds, *Calendar of State Papers and Manuscripts Relating to English Affairs, Existing in the Archives and Collections of Venice*, 5 vols (London, 1864), vol. 4, p. 332; 25 Hen VIII c 32, *The Statutes of the Realm*, 10 vols (London, 1810), vol. 3, p. 489. The details of this case are discussed in Shannon McSheffrey, 'The Slaying of Sir William Pennington: Legal Narrative and the Late Medieval English Archive', *Florilegium* 28 (2011): pp 169–203, https://journals.lib.unb.ca/index.php/flor/article/view/21566/25053.

fleeing for their lives.² The idea of sacred spaces as sites of refuge for accused wrongdoers was an ancient one, part of Roman law and integral to the forms of Christianity practised in the Middle Ages. Sanctuary in Christian cultures shared common themes: churches as islands of peace possessing 'immunity' from violence and force, and clergy as mediators between wrongdoers and those who sought to bring them to justice (victims, victims' kin, judicial and governing authorities). Sanctuary was not, however, timeless and unchanging, but developed through the medieval and early modern periods in ways particular to local situations in different parts of Europe and Latin America.³ In running to Westminster Abbey, Richard Southwell and his fellows sought a form of sanctuary specific to the English context in the 1530s, a legal request recognized under English common law and parliamentary statute.⁴

For the Southwells, sanctuary literally saved their necks. In the immediate aftermath Henry VIII was furious both with Suffolk, whose retainer had insulted his intended wife, and with Southwell for the intemperate killing on his very doorstep. He wanted the quarrel ended. He gave the task of making the situation disappear to his chief minister, Thomas Cromwell, who also happened to be a close friend of

---

² See for the *longue durée* history of sanctuary through the medieval period, Karl Shoemaker, *Sanctuary and Crime in the Middle Ages, 400–1500* (New York, 2011).

³ William Chester Jordan, 'A Fresh Look at Medieval Sanctuary', in *Law and the Illicit in Medieval Europe*, ed. Ruth Mazo Karras, Joel Kaye, and E. Ann Matter (Philadelphia, 2010), pp 17–32; R. H. Helmholz, *The Ius Commune in England: Four Studies* (Oxford, 2001), pp 23–6; Victor M. Uribe-Uran, ' "Iglesia Me Llamo": Church Asylum and the Law in Spain and Colonial Spanish America', *Comparative Studies in Society and History* 49 (2007): pp 446–72, doi:10.1017/SOO10417507000552; Michelle A. McKinley, 'Standing on Shaky Ground: Criminal Jurisdiction and Ecclesiastical Immunity in Seventeenth-Century Lima, 1600–1700', *University of California Irvine Law Review* 4 (2014): pp 141–74.

⁴ On English law and sanctuary, see J. H. Baker, 'The English Law of Sanctuary', *Ecclesiastical Law Journal* 2 (1990): pp 8–13, doi:10.1017/S0956618X00000788; J. H. Baker, *An Introduction to English Legal History*, 4th edn (London, 2002), pp 540–51; Helmholz, *Ius Commune*, pp 16–81. On sanctuary in England more generally, see Isobel Thornley, 'The Destruction of Sanctuary', in *Tudor Studies*, ed. R. W. Seton-Watson (London, 1924), pp 182–207; Isobel Thornley, 'Sanctuary in Medieval London', *Journal of the British Archaeological Association* 38 (1932): pp 293–315; Thomas John de'Mazzinghi, *Sanctuaries* (Stafford, 1887); Norman MacLaren Trenholme, *The Right of Sanctuary in England: A Study in Institutional History* (Columbia, 1903); J. Charles Cox, *The Sanctuaries and Sanctuary Seekers of Mediaeval England* (London, 1911); E. W. Ives, 'Crime, Sanctuary, and Royal Authority under Henry VIII: The Exemplary Sufferings of the Savage Family', in *On the Laws and Customs of England*, ed. Morris S. Arnold et al. (Chapel Hill, 1981), pp 296–320; Peter Iver Kaufman, 'Henry VII and Sanctuary', *Church History* 53 (1984): pp 465–76, doi:10.2307/3166117; Peter Iver Kaufman, *The 'Polytyque Churche': Religion and Early Tudor Political Culture, 1485–1516* (Macon, 1986), pp 141–53; Gervase Rosser, 'Sanctuary and Social Negotiation in Medieval England', in *The Cloister and the World: Essays in Medieval History in Honour of Barbara Harvey*, ed. John Blair and Brian Golding (Oxford, 1996), pp 57–79; Krista J. Kesselring, 'Abjuration and its Demise: The Changing Face of Royal Justice in the Tudor Period', *Canadian Journal of History* 34 (1999): pp 345–58, doi:10.3138/cjh.34.3.345; D. M. Loades, 'The Sanctuary', in *Westminster Abbey Reformed: 1540–1640*, ed. C. S. Knighton and Richard Mortimer (Aldershot, 2003), pp 75–93; Jessica Freeman, 'And He Abjured the Realm of England, Never to Return', in *Freedom of Movement in the Middle Ages: Proceedings of the 2003 Harlaxton Symposium*, ed. Peregrine Horden (Donington, 2007), pp 287–304; Shoemaker, *Sanctuary and Crime*; William C. Jordan, *From England to France: Felony and Exile in the High Middle Ages* (Princeton, 2015).

Richard Southwell.⁵ Sanctuary was an important part of the strategy that unfolded. The killers' shelter in the abbey precinct prevented an escalation of the feud between the dukes of Suffolk and Norfolk: Suffolk, reportedly incandescent with rage and bent on avenging his man's death, could not retaliate without breaching the holy space of the abbey and thereby committing a grave sacrilege. Sanctuary also prevented a swift trial and execution for the killing, as the Southwells could not be arrested as long as they were inside the precinct's boundaries.

The accused men stayed in the sanctuary for five or six weeks, enough time for Suffolk to calm down and for Cromwell to broker a deal. It was settled that Southwell and his men would face charges in the court of King's Bench for homicide, on an indictment that put on record a story very different from the one involving Anne Boleyn's sexual reputation. They would admit their guilt, although then they would be granted the king's pardon rather than face the noose. Southwell and his retainers would go free, their felony wiped out by the pardon, and informally Southwell would be levied a huge fine of £1000, payable to the king. Although the whole process including a trial at King's Bench and an act of parliament confirming the pardon took more than a year to unfold, the situation was successfully defused. The king married Anne Boleyn. Suffolk was reconciled with the king. And the Southwells, all young men in their twenties at the time of the killing, went on with their lives, thanks to the tools—sanctuary and pardon—that allowed them to escape both the vengeance of their victim's patron and the full rigour of the king's justice.

This book will explore how sanctuary functioned in English law, politics, culture, and religion in the period between 1400 and 1550. The Southwells are emblematic—if not exactly typical—of the history of sanctuary-seeking in this period in two ways. Although historians have usually thought of sanctuary as a medieval phenomenon, in fleeing to Westminster Abbey in 1532 the Southwells were not taking advantage of an archaic process on its last legs, but one in its full flower. The type of sanctuary they claimed (an asylum unlimited in time, in an ecclesiastical precinct) had developed only in the years around 1400, began to increase in popularity in the 1480s, and hit its high point right around 1530. The Southwells are also exemplary of the privilege's utility for one particular social group under the early Tudor regime: the landed aristocracy. Although most sanctuary seekers were of humble origins, the Southwells were amongst a significant number of high-ranking gentlemen in Henry VIII's reign who used the privilege to avoid the king's capital penalties when their sword fights ended in death.

Sanctuary was useful not only for the Southwells themselves, but also for many others, including the king and arguably even, in a larger sense, the kingdom. The

---

⁵ Southwell had been Cromwell's son's tutor, and he would go on through the 1530s to work closely with Cromwell on the monastic dissolutions. Stanford E. Lehmberg, 'Southwell, Sir Richard (1502/3–1564)', *The Oxford Dictionary of National Biography*, edited by H. C. G. Matthew and B. Harrison (Oxford, 2004–), http://www.oxforddnb.com, doi:10.1093/ref:odnb/26062. As will be discussed below, Cromwell would have been involved in the crown's waiving of the Southwells' technical ineligibility for the privilege (see below, Ch. 7, n.29).

Southwells went on to become key servants of the crown's government: Richard Southwell played a central role in administering the monastic dissolutions in the second half of the 1530s, sat as MP for Norfolk, was knighted in 1540, and went on to serve as privy councillor under both Edward VI and Mary I. Although the pardon in the Pennington affair cost Richard Southwell a significant sum, he more than made up for it in the land grab following the monastic dissolutions, and he died a very wealthy man.[6] In 1537, when he was thirty-three, Hans Holbein painted his portrait, in which the scars from the fight with Pennington are clearly visible on his neck and cheek, perhaps displayed as trophies of the quarrel (Figures 1.1 and 1.2).[7]

His brother Robert likewise went on to a distinguished legal and parliamentary career, including the office of Master of the Rolls in Chancery and a knighthood in 1542.[8] Both men served as sheriffs, Richard Southwell's appointment to the office

Figure 1.1. Hans Holbein the Younger, *Sir Richard Southwell*, 1536.
Royal Collection Trust / © Her Majesty Queen Elizabeth II 2016.

---

[6] Lehmberg, 'Southwell, Sir Richard'.

[7] John Rowlands, *Holbein: The Paintings of Hans Holbein the Younger: Complete Edition* (Oxford, 1985), plate 93 (catalogue, p. 143); K. T. Parker, *The Drawings of Hans Holbein in the Collection of His Majesty the King at Windsor Castle* (Oxford, London, 1945), pp 46–7. For scars as signs of chivalric honour, see Richard W. Kaeuper, *Chivalry and Violence in Medieval Europe* (Oxford, 1999), p. 151.

[8] J. H. Baker, 'Southwell, Sir Robert (c. 1506–1559)', *ODNB* (2004), doi:10.1093/ref:odnb/26063.

Figure 1.2. Hans Holbein the Younger, *Sir Richard Southwell*, 1536.
Uffizi Gallery, inv. 1890 n. 1087. [By permission of the Ministry of Culture of Italy.]

for Norfolk and Suffolk coming in 1534, a mere two years following the homicide. Both also sat as justices of the peace.[9] In these capacities Richard and Robert Southwell were on the front lines of criminal justice processes in England, with responsibilities as sheriffs for arresting indicted felons in their jurisdictions, and as JPs sitting in judgment over the king's subjects charged with homicides and other felonies. Their own encounter with the law from the other side of the judges' bench had surprisingly little effect on their careers. They were amongst a number of Tudor servants of the state who employed sanctuary and other tools of mitigation that English law made available to them, in order to move past the homicide charges that were an occupational hazard of the landed elite.

SEEKING SANCTUARY IN LATE MEDIEVAL AND TUDOR ENGLAND

Sanctuary, which involves monks or priests sheltering fleeing criminals, *seems* like a medieval phenomenon, and from the early twentieth century, historians have

---

[9] *L&P*, vol. 7, p. 558; Lehmberg, 'Southwell, Sir Richard'; Baker, 'Southwell, Sir Robert'.

tended to think that it was outmoded and little used by Henry VIII's reign. When scholars have noticed what they thought were its vestigial survivals in the sixteenth century, they have viewed them as hold-overs from earlier legal arrangements that had survived by accident or through ecclesiastical determination to stem the tide of modernization. Sanctuary made sense, historians have argued, in an earlier, less elaborated political and legal context, when the church's sheltering of fleeing criminals allowed time for kin groups to arrange compensation for wrongs in the place of retaliatory violence. By the fourteenth and fifteenth centuries, however, the king's justice supplanted informal conflict resolution and so the church's peace-making was no longer necessary and indeed, some have contended, became positively pernicious.[10] Having outlived its usefulness, sanctuary should have—and as historians have assumed, must have—withered away, especially after the accession of the Tudors, when England is supposed to have left behind its medieval ways.

This seems reasonable—except that it didn't happen that way. Sanctuary did not wither away under the early Tudors, but instead revived. The years between Henry VII's accession in 1485 and the late 1530s witnessed a resurgence of sanctuary-seeking, as many like the Southwells used sanctuary to avoid capital penalties for felony. The prevalence of sanctuary-seeking in the first fifty years of Tudor rule has until now escaped notice. Historians usually don't look for evidence when they don't expect to find it, and so no one has searched systematically in the English legal records between 1400 and 1550 for sanctuary seekers. I began this apparently quixotic pursuit only after I had stumbled upon what I thought were anomalous reports of resort to sanctuary in the 1530s, after the practice was supposed to have died off.[11] As I found when I began to dig, the legal records for the fifteenth and sixteenth centuries shows something quite different from what the scholarship had led me to expect.[12] The revival of sanctuary from the 1480s indicates that we have to question the premises of the model that sees sanctuary as a 'medieval' phenomenon unsuited to the fifteenth- and sixteenth-century English system of laws. Far from being outmoded, sanctuary was apparently well-adapted to the early Tudor legal context, and thus we must ask what there was about the practice that allowed it to flourish. The answer to that question demands rethinking the relationship between law, politics, and culture in late medieval and Tudor England.

Before addressing these issues, some basic explanations will be useful. Sanctuary was one of a number of options potentially available to a person fleeing from law enforcement, creditors, or political adversaries. In a legal sense, the theory and practice of sanctuary in late medieval and early modern England straddled a number of legal regimes: the canon law of the Church, the law of the royal courts both criminal and civil, statute law, and local customary jurisdictions of manor, town,

---

[10] Thornley and Baker both refer to late medieval sanctuary as an 'evil': Thornley, 'Destruction of Sanctuary', p. 184; J. H. Baker, *An Introduction to English Legal History*, 4th edn (London, 2002), p. 512; Baker, *Oxford History, 1485–1558*, p. 544.
[11] See Baker, *Spelman*, vol. 2, pp 344–5 (intro), and Ives, 'Crime, Sanctuary', both of which influentially argued that sanctuary-seeking effectively ceased in England after about 1520.
[12] See below, Ch. 2, 'Sanctuary-Seeking 1400–1550: The Numbers'.

or city.¹³ By the fifteenth century, sanctuary in England had two main forms recognized under the English common law. The first, often now called abjuration after its final stage, and usually known in contemporary legal records as 'taking church', had roots in the Anglo-Saxon period and solidified in the twelfth and thirteenth centuries, at the same time as the law of felony was being established in the kingdom.¹⁴ This procedure allowed accused criminals to take refuge in any parish church or churchyard, but by common law such refuge was limited in time, usually to forty days.¹⁵ Local constables acting for the king were to set up guard to ensure felons who had 'taken church' did not escape; an onerous task, meaning that those felons were able to slip out in the dead of night alarmingly often.¹⁶ By the end of the forty days, the accused criminal had either to surrender to the king's justice, or to abjure (or foreswear) the realm, that is, to go into exile forever. A felon who had taken church and wished to abjure was to call for the coroner, the crown's local legal representative. When the coroner came to the church, the accused confessed the felony to him in full, and the royal official recorded it on his coroner's roll. The coroner then administered the oath by which the felon solemnly abjured the realm and assigned the abjurer a port from which to leave the kingdom (or, in some cases, the abjurer appears to have been allowed to choose his or her port). Following the oath and the assignment of port, the coroner gave the felon, as a sign of penitence, a large cross made of white cloth to wear on his or her outer clothing and a wooden cross to carry. The abjurer then walked from locality to locality in the company of a relay team of local constables until he or she had reached the port. There the abjurer was to take the first ship available overseas, never to return. Although this was a particularly English form of sanctuary, it used a form of punishment—exile—that was employed frequently by other medieval European polities for crime and treason.¹⁷

The extent of regularization of procedure for abjuration varied over time, particularly for the travel to the port and then the handling of the abjurer at the port. William Chester Jordan has recently argued for systematization of the management of the hundreds of felons abjuring each year in the late thirteenth and first half of the fourteenth century. Jordan found that in this period abjurers all left from Dover and landed in English-occupied France, at Wissant; the amassing of

---

¹³ See especially Helmholz, *Ius Commune*; Baker, 'The English Law of Sanctuary'; Seán Patrick Donlan and Dirk Heirbaut, '"A Patchwork of Accommodations": European Legal Hybridity and Jurisdictional Complexity', in *The Laws' Many Bodies: Studies in Legal Hybridity and Jurisdictional Complexity, c1600–1900*, ed. Seán Patrick Donlan and Dirk Heirbaut (Berlin, 2015), pp 9–34.
¹⁴ On this early period, see Shoemaker, *Sanctuary and Crime*; T. B. Lambert, 'The Evolution of Sanctuary in Medieval England', in *Legalism: Anthropology and History*, ed. Paul Dresch and Hannah Skoda (Oxford, 2012), pp 115–44; Jordan, *From England to France*.
¹⁵ Helmholz, *Ius Commune*, pp 18, 61; Kesselring, 'Abjuration'; Freeman, 'And He Abjured'.
¹⁶ There may have been a particular problem in London in the late thirteenth and early fourteenth centuries with sanctuary seekers escaping from the parish church before the coroner came to administer the oath of abjuration, as Londoners objected to the burden this placed on them to guard the felons in their parish churches and refused to do it. Many instances of sanctuary-seeking recorded in the London coroner's rolls ended with 'afterwards escaped'. See Reginald R. Sharpe, ed., *Calendar of Coroners Rolls of the City of London, A.D. 1300–1378* (London, 1913), *passim*, e.g. pp 38–9.
¹⁷ Jordan, *From England to France*, esp. pp 5, 7, 27.

the perhaps 500 abjurers arriving in Dover each year requiring passage overseas meant that procedures had to be regularized, and it is even possible that the crown hired vessels for the specific purpose of moving the abjurers across the Channel. Jordan contends that this system collapsed in the mid-fourteenth century following the Black Death and key English losses in Normandy in the Hundred Years War.[18]

Certainly by the fifteenth century, the practice was much less uniform, if for no other reason than that the numbers were much lower. As these later records of abjuration show, after 1400 abjurers were assigned at least twenty-five different ports. Dover remained the most popular, but was followed closely by Southampton, and ports in other parts of the kingdom were also assigned—Newcastle on Tyne, Hull, Lynn, Sandwich, and Chester were regularly employed, for instance.[19] In other ways, the handling of abjurers beyond the basic form was probably often ad hoc. The evidence indicates, for instance, that many (if not all) fifteenth- and sixteenth-century abjurers were left to their own devices to find a passage overseas, and not surprisingly some could not find a ship willing to take them on board.[20] By the early sixteenth century the numbers of abjurers had begun to climb again. In response to this increase, several statutes between 1529 and 1536 changed the basis of abjuration, so that abjurers no longer went into exile but instead proceeded to chartered sanctuaries, another form of asylum we will consider just below. Between about 1200 and the early 1530s, for more than three centuries, the abjuration procedure operationalized, within the developing administration of English royal justice, Christian ideas about churches as sacred spaces of peace, where mercy and redemption could be gained.

By the thirteenth century, any parish church in England offered this forty-day asylum. In fleeing to Westminster Abbey, however, the Southwells and their associates looked for a second form of refuge, the chartered sanctuary. This was an asylum unlimited in time, but only available in the precincts of certain religious houses in the realm. Contemporaries did not usually use a specific word that differentiated this form of refuge from flight to any parish church—they called it simply 'sanctuary'—and I refer to it in this book as chartered sanctuary, from the central importance of royal charters in these houses' claims to offer such privileges.[21] Those who sought refuge in a chartered sanctuary such as Westminster Abbey could remain inside the boundaries of the sanctuary precinct as long as they liked,

---

[18] Jordan, *From England to France*.

[19] See Shannon McSheffrey, 'Sanctuary Seekers in England, 1390–1557' (2016), https://shannonmcsheffrey.wordpress.com/research/.

[20] E.g. John Preston alias Westlake (1490), TNA, KB 9/388, mm. 26–29, KB 29/120, m. 30, KB 27/921, rex m. 2d, Baker, *Spelman*, vol. 1, p. 44; Simon Wigmore alias Vincent (1507), TNA, KB 29/138, m. 7d; Henry Danby (1530), TNA, KB 9/519, m. 147, KB 27/1084, rex m. 7, KB 29/165, mm. 1, 10, 19d; J. H. Baker, ed., *The Reports of Sir John Spelman*, Selden Society 93 and 94 (London, 1977), vol. 1, p. 49, vol. 2, pp 278–80.

[21] Scholars have also used other terms: special, private, or permanent sanctuaries. As Baker remarks, the distinction 'common' (for forty-day sanctuary in parish churches) and 'private' (for sanctuary in precincts of religious houses) was made in some readings at the Inns of Court; Baker, *Spelman*, vol. 2, p. 335 (intro); Margaret McGlynn, ed., *The Rights and Liberties of the English Church: Readings from the Pre-Reformation Inns of Court*, Selden Society 129 (London, 2015), pp 109–10.

provided they met the requirements for the privilege. While inside they were immune from arrest by royal, civic, or ecclesiastical officials.

The procedures for admission to this privilege were different from those governing abjuration, as two surviving fifteenth-century sets of regulations detail. Recorded in a cartulary now in the British Library are ordinances, dated 1420, for those seeking refuge at Paris Garden, a manor on the South Bank of the Thames by Southwark belonging to the Knights of St John of Jerusalem (also known as the Hospitallers).[22] The regulations called for those fleeing 'to the said place for their safety' to swear an oath not to bring harm, scandal, or damage to Paris Garden, to be registered with the reason for their flight ('whether it be for debt, because they are aliens,[23] or for felony, or for whatever transgression'), and to pay an entry fee of 4d. Felons, as distinct from debtors or aliens, were to find guarantors for their good fame and governance, and if they committed another felony after they had taken the privilege they would be barred from the sanctuary and handed over to the King's Bench prison nearby. Debtors could leave the jurisdiction, with permission, but if they wanted to return they had to pay the entry fee of 4d each time. A final regulation levied a significant fine (6s 8d) and loss of sanctuary privilege to anyone in Paris Garden who was presented and convicted at the manor court for receiving a prostitute (*meretricem*) or fostering lechery within the manor, perhaps an attempt to prevent or stem the influence of the red light district in the nearby Clink Manor (known as Stewside).

In 1457, the king's council enacted a somewhat more elaborated set of ordinances to govern the sanctuary of St Martin le Grand.[24] Similarly to Paris Garden, those who sought asylum were to be registered upon entry with the reason for seeking sanctuary ('be it treason, felony surmised upon him, or for other causes'); to swear an oath that they would obey all ordinances; and to surrender all weapons and armour, keeping only 'a reasonable knife to carve withal his meat', as long as the knife was 'pointless'. Any notorious or habitual felon was to find surety for their behaviour, and recidivism was not to be tolerated (although the St Martin's regulations were less precise about whether such re-offenders would be handed over to royal officials, instead indicating that they were to be held in prison or ejected from the sanctuary). The gates of the precinct were to be tightly closed at

---

[22] London, British Library, Cotton Nero E VI, Hospitaller Cartulary, fols 59rv. On this manuscript, see Michael Gervers, *The Hospitaller Cartulary in the British Library (Cotton MS Nero E VI)* (Toronto, 1981), pp 7–31.

[23] Alien or stranger were the terms used to designate those born outside the king's realm (what we would call a foreigner). As we will see in Ch. 5 (see 'Stranger Artisans, Sanctuary Men, and the City'), aliens, especially in the London area, were subject to restrictions on their ability to work in artisanal trades and sell their wares at retail, and so used the jurisdictional independence of liberties and sanctuaries to make and sell goods.

[24] The 1457 articles survive in a number of forms. The City of London recorded the articles in London Metropolitan Archives, Letter Book K, fols 298v–299r; a fragment of the regulations is preserved in a document among the Exchequer records (TNA, E 135/23/49); Alfred Kempe transcribes in full a version that likely derives from BL, Lansdowne MS 170 (a later sixteenth-century copy), although Kempe does not give his source (Alfred John Kempe, *Historical Notices of the Collegiate Church or Royal Free Chapel and Sanctuary of St. Martin-Le-Grand, London* [London, 1825], pp 146–51). See below, Ch. 3 at n.81, for a discussion of the context in which these were promulgated.

nine o'clock at night until the first mass the next morning, with all sanctuary seekers securely inside. If a felon fled to the precinct with stolen goods, the dean and his deputies were to restore those goods to the victim. No counterfeiters or forgers were permitted to stay in the sanctuary, and nor were common putours (sexually misbehaving men), strumpets, or bawds to be tolerated. Any such people who claimed sanctuary were to 'be set in open ward', presumably on a pillory or similar, each day 'until shame cause them to depart, or to amend their vicious living'. No 'deceitful games' (dice, bowling, and so on) were allowed. Artisans dwelling within the sanctuary were to keep Sundays and holidays. Other sanctuaries likely had similar regulations: records for St John's Minster at Beverley, for instance, indicate that seekers were to swear an oath upon entry that they would keep peace within the precinct and faithfully observe all curfews, rules, and regulations.[25] As the Paris Garden and St Martin's ordinances indicate, the seekers' names and reason for sanctuary-seeking were often—and likely normally—recorded in registers. Unfortunately, only two such registers survive, for St John's Minster in Beverley and Durham Cathedral.[26]

Once they had entered a chartered sanctuary, felons, political refugees, and debtors had to remain strictly within the geographical bounds of the precinct, or they were liable to be seized by arresting officials, political opponents, or creditors. They were thus obliged to find a place to live and a way to support themselves while in sanctuary. The precincts of the religious houses that hosted the sanctuaries—like many other urban ecclesiastical properties—were crowded with tenements. Lease records that survive for Westminster Abbey and St Martin le Grand show a brisk rental market.[27] Not surprisingly, for some the financial challenges of extended periods of time in the chartered sanctuaries were daunting. Although the fifteenth-century records do not give us good evidence for the sanctuary-seeker population, evidence from Henry VIII's reign indicates that some long-term sanctuary dwellers lived for decades in the precincts. For many, however, and perhaps even a majority, time spent in sanctuary was short, as we will see in more detail in Chapter 2.[28]

The abbots and deans who ruled over these chartered sanctuaries asserted ancient custom as the basis of their privileges, but this rhetoric almost certainly masked a much more recent origin—late fourteenth century—for the particular form of sanctuary at Westminster Abbey that the Southwells requested. As I will detail in Chapter 2, sometime around 1400 certain religious houses began to offer sanctuary to felons, a refuge that was distinct from the time-limited asylum any English

---

[25] *Sanctuarium Dunelmense et Sanctuarium Beverlacense*, Surtees Society 5 (London, 1837), p. 111.

[26] For Durham's and Beverley's registers, see *SDSB*. References to a register at Westminster: A. H. Thomas and Isobel Thornley, eds, *The Great Chronicle of London* (London and Aylesbury, 1938), pp 212–13; Robert Fabyan, *The New Chronicles of England and France*, ed. Henry Ellis (London, 1811), pp 658–9. At Good Easter (a Westminster Abbey dependency), *The Enquirie and Verdite of the Quest Pannel'd of the Death of Richard Hune Wich Was Founde Hanged in Lolars Tower* (Antwerp, 1537), sig. C3r. At Knowle (another Westminster Abbey dependency), TNA, SP 1/130, fol. 179r.

[27] See especially London, Westminster Abbey Library and Muniments, Westminster Abbey Register Books, vols 1 through 3.

[28] See Ch. 2 at n.46.

church offered. The earliest evidence for this form of sanctuary comes from Westminster Abbey and the collegiate church of St Martin le Grand in London, and by some time in the middle of the fifteenth century the first evidence for similar asylum can be seen for Durham cathedral and the abbeys of Beverley, Glastonbury, and Beaulieu. Some of these religious houses, notably Westminster and St Martin le Grand, had already in the fourteenth century sheltered debtors. We can infer, in the absence of direct evidence, that the general principle of ecclesiastical spaces as asylums for wrongdoers, already both a general tenet of Christianity and part of the English common law through abjuration, intersected with the jurisdictional immunities attached to certain ecclesiastical liberties that from about 1300 had protected debtors from arrest.[29] This created a legal practice whereby those who wished to escape prosecution for felony could remain permanently in sanctuary in the precincts of certain monasteries and collegiate churches—just as debtors already could.

This new form of sanctuary was, as far as the records tell us, relatively little used by felons through the first half of the fifteenth century. Similarly, the much more long-standing practice of abjuration also fell off dramatically in the years following the Black Death. Both kinds of sanctuary, however, became more common again in the second half of the fifteenth century, especially the last two decades. As the evidence for sanctuary seekers we will consider in more detail in Chapter 2 shows, the development of the chartered sanctuaries allowed the general idea of sanctuary to adapt successfully to the shifting legal and political landscape in England in the later fifteenth and early sixteenth centuries. Sanctuary thrived and indeed grew under the early Tudor regime—that is, it flourished until fairly abruptly, within less than a decade, it virtually ceased. The records show a distinct decline in resort to sanctuary in the last half of the 1530s, and after 1540, it falls to a trickle.

EXPLAINING THE TUDOR RESURGENCE OF SANCTUARY

These unexpected patterns demand explanation, and those explanations challenge how historians understand the phenomenon of sanctuary in the century and a half under consideration in this book. Much of the scholarship on English sanctuary in this period has been founded on two articles written in 1924 and 1932 by Isobel Thornley.[30] A remarkable scholar, Thornley was nonetheless very much a historian of her age, believing whole-heartedly in the rightness of progress and Protestantism and the concomitant backwardness of medieval Catholicism. For her, sanctuary was an 'evil', and she approached the late medieval and Tudor evidence for the

---

[29] See for an early sixteenth-century legal commentator's explicit connection of franchisal liberties and the sanctuary rights at Westminster and St Martin le Grand, McGlynn, *Rights and Liberties*, pp 109–10.

[30] Thornley, 'Destruction of Sanctuary' and 'Sanctuary in Medieval London'.

privilege from a partisan perspective.[31] Although she admitted that it had had its place in the 'primitive times' of the early Middle Ages when kings were weak or arbitrary,[32] she thought that sanctuary was no longer necessary and indeed contrary to justice in the Tudor era, when a modernizing, centralizing, and (proto-) Protestant royal government freed itself from ecclesiastical influence and worked more comprehensively towards the due prosecution of felony. As she assumed, the continued survival of sanctuary despite its obsolescence must have been opposed by those working with the crown in this modernization project (judges, MPs, and so on). Thornley celebrated especially London's civic leaders, who in her view led the charge against rapacious churchmen who continued to defend this 'hoary privilege'.[33] The 'destruction of sanctuary', as Thornley called her most important article, was thus the triumph of an urban and commercial lay modernity over clerical medievalism.

I dwell upon Thornley's views here, even though they are now close to a century old, because her essays remain widely cited, and her basic conclusions, if not her prejudices and language, underlie most recent examinations of the phenomenon.[34] The patterns of sanctuary-seeking over this period that I have found, however—increasing in the first fifty years of Tudor rule rather than decreasing—indicate that Thornley's interpretation of the evidence, and the assumptions that guided her interpretation, were faulty. Let me lay out here an alternative way to understand the workings of sanctuary that explains the renewed vigour of this privilege under the regimes of Henry VII and Henry VIII. This entails not only a different approach to sanctuary but also a new way of thinking about English law, politics, religion, and culture in the late medieval and early Tudor period.

Sanctuary as Ecclesiastical Privilege and as the King's Law

As several scholars have noted before me, considering sanctuary as a solely ecclesiastical privilege that stood apart from or even in opposition to royal justice is to misunderstand how it worked in England. The English practice of sanctuary, both in its chartered form and in the more longstanding availability of asylum in a church followed by abjuration, developed *within* the English common law and was

---

[31] Thornley, 'Destruction of Sanctuary', pp 182–4, 202–3; 'Sanctuary in Medieval London', p. 315.

[32] Thornley, 'Destruction of Sanctuary', p. 207.

[33] Thornley, 'Destruction of Sanctuary', p. 182. As I will detail below in Chs. 3, 4, and 5, while civic leaders in London and elsewhere did often oppose sanctuary privilege, they did so less because of their modernity than because the sanctuaries competed with the cities' own jurisdictional ambitions.

[34] E.g. Baker, *Spelman*, vol. 2, pp 340–6 (intro); Baker, *Introduction*, esp. p. 512; Baker, *Oxford History, 1485–1558*, esp. p. 544; Ives, 'Crime, Sanctuary'; Paul R. Hyams, *Rancor and Reconciliation in Medieval England* (Ithaca, 2003), p. 95; Barbara H. Rosenwein, *Negotiating Space: Power, Restraint, and Privileges of Immunity in Early Medieval Europe* (Ithaca, 1999), p. 206; Shoemaker, *Sanctuary and Crime*, pp 145–51; Lambert, 'Evolution of Sanctuary'. Helmholz explicitly eschews Thornley's whiggishness, but accepts her argument that sanctuary was ill-suited to early Tudor law (*Ius Commune*, pp 40–1). Conversely, Kaufman, 'Henry VII and Sanctuary'; Rosser, 'Sanctuary and Social Negotiation'; and McGlynn, *Rights and Liberties* have argued for considering sanctuary as a functional process in Tudor law and society, the argument I embrace here.

adjudicated in the common law courts. Developments in the practice of sanctuary between 1200 and 1540 occurred alongside, and indeed were part of, other changes in English laws of felony, trespass, treason, and debt, and in conceptions of royal, civic, and ecclesiastical jurisdiction. As Margaret McGlynn's work shows, by the middle of the fifteenth century, sanctuary in its various manifestations was thoroughly integrated into common law thinking.[35] Although some legal historians such as J. H. Baker have emphasized the status of sanctuaries as territories where 'the king's writ did not run' and thus their independence from royal power, that was neither literally nor figuratively true. In a technical sense the king's writ *did* run there: a felony committed inside a sanctuary was subject to the same process of inquest and indictment as in other parts of the kingdom.[36] While there were exceptions, by and large sanctuary was accepted as part of the legal landscape. Even most of the contemporary criticism was in fact criticism of its abuse, not of the idea of sanctuary itself.[37]

Conversely, as Richard Helmholz has pointed out, the English manifestations of sanctuary did not always accord with church law, even if a number of ecclesiastical institutions (such as Westminster Abbey and St Martin le Grand) defended it enthusiastically.[38] Although in broad terms these advocates of sanctuary emphasized the 'immunity' of churches and the church's duty to protect the life of all Christians, they only rarely invoked canon law in their defences.[39] They relied instead on the specific English context of royal charters, statutes, and precedents in the king's courts. This was of course partly a rhetorical choice—emphasizing royal charters and grants and English legal usage as the basis upon which a religious house exercised its privileges was far more likely to gain traction when an appeal was made to the crown.[40] Conversely but interestingly, as Helmholz has noted, sixteenth-century opponents of sanctuary sometimes borrowed wording and reasoning from canon law discussions, because again to emphasize the practice's ill fit with the church's own law was a useful and resonant argument.[41]

Sanctuary in England was more a common law than a canon law practice, but this is not to say that it had no religious underpinning. Along with other aspects of the administration of common law (including oath-taking in legal processes,

---

[35] McGlynn, *Rights and Liberties*, *passim*; see esp. pp 70, 83, 86, 93–4, 109–12, 128–9, 149–50.

[36] Baker, *An Introduction to English Legal History*, pp 512–13. On integration into legal processes, see for instance TNA, KB 9/327, m. 22; KB 9/353, m. 96; KB 9/417, m. 128; KB 9/467, m. 15; KB 27/1001, rex m. 1d; KB 27/1004, rex m. 15; KB 27/1023, rex m. 1.

[37] A point made in relation to abjuration by Kesselring, 'Abjuration', pp 354–5.

[38] Helmholz, *Ius Commune*, pp 21–2.

[39] Helmholz, *Ius Commune*, thoroughly discusses the relationship between canon law ideas of sanctuary and the English form of it. *Ius Commune*, pp 16–81. He remarks that only rarely are canon law arguments raised in English discussions (an exception being a learned treatise written in the fifteenth century at Westminster Abbey that made arguments for the licitness of sanctuary for debt, making reference both to canon and common law). Ibid., pp 58–78.

[40] See esp. Ch. 3.

[41] Helmholz, *Ius Commune*, pp 75–8; note also that several readers (lecturers) at the Inns of Court argued that only the pope could make a sanctuary, an argument not made by the English ecclesiastical authorities themselves defending their sanctuaries; see McGlynn, *Rights and Liberties*, pp 76, 81, 109–10.

benefit of clergy,[42] and royal pardons), sanctuary was tightly integrated with the practice of Christianity and closely implicated the institutional church. Although this sometimes made for messy and inconsistent practice, as we shall see, and confuses categories (ecclesiastical and secular) that modern historians often think should have been separate, for medieval and early modern people those categories were thoroughly interwoven. To them, it seemed obvious that the exercise of law and justice should be in accordance with God's law as well as the king's, and thus it was no great stretch to see ecclesiastical institutions and churchmen involved in the processes of criminal justice. Sanctuary's increased importance in the later fifteenth century was made possible by the concept's positive valences: sanctuary signalled life-saving succour, redemption, and escape from tyranny. To be sure, fifteenth- and sixteenth-century English people had mixed opinions about it: in some criminal indictments and petitions to parliament, rhetorically the idea of flight to sanctuary sometimes functioned as shorthand for the fostering of crime and a heinous felon's escape from due punishment. More commonly, though, it connoted the unlimited mercy of God and the life-saving protection offered to the unfortunate sinner or the unjustly accused.[43]

In turn, the practice of sanctuary in late medieval England also indicates how thoroughly imbricated were late medieval and early modern conceptions of Christian religion with kingship. Sanctuary seekers' claims invoked the idea of holiness embodied in a church's building and the security of God's saving grace.[44] In the chartered sanctuaries, that idea of holiness in turn was interlaced with those religious houses' status as royally-chartered liberties, areas designated by the crown as independent from all authorities, even in some ways from the crown itself. Although a religious house's possession of a liberty conferred independence from civic and diocesan officials, and some immunity from the ordinary processes of law, the royal grant of such privileges remained fundamental: rights pertaining to liberties were conceded by, and remained strongly connected to, the Christian king and his protection.[45]

Through the fifteenth and early sixteenth centuries—especially from Henry VI's reign through most of Henry VIII's—English kings defended sanctuary. The

---

[42] The benefit of clergy developed through the later fourteenth and fifteenth centuries to be a legal fiction by which any man who was *eligible* to be a priest—that is that he was literate and had been married no more than once and to a woman who also had not previously been married—could claim to be a member of the clergy and thus transferred to the ecclesiastical authorities for punishment following conviction for felony. As the ecclesiastical authorities did not execute offenders, it saved the felon from capital punishment. As women were not eligible to be priests, they could not claim benefit of clergy. See Baker, *Oxford History, 1485–1558*, pp 531–40.

[43] See on these themes Elizabeth Allen's forthcoming article, 'Once and Future King: Sanctuary, Sovereignty, and the Politics of Pity in the Histories of Perkin Warbeck', *Journal of Medieval and Early Modern Studies* (forthcoming 2017).

[44] See, for instance, the equation of sanctuary for felons with both the sacred space around the altar and the salvific force of divine grace in an early fifteenth-century English sermon: Patrick J. Horner, ed., *A Macaronic Sermon Collection from Late Medieval England: Oxford, MS Bodley 649* (Toronto, 2006), pp 326–8.

[45] On the paradox of sanctuary as potentially both enhancement and compromise of royal power (and indeed demonstration of sovereign power *through* its concession), see Allen, 'Once and Future King'.

crown's protection of sanctuaries had its prosaic, strategic aspect. St Martin le Grand's sanctuary, for instance, thrived not only because of the sacrilege that would have been attendant on its breach but because its presence in the midst of London served a useful purpose to the crown in reining in the overweening ambitions of the City. At the same time, however, the king's sponsorship and patronage of the chartered sanctuaries were powerful demonstrations of his royal and Christian mercy, which was at the heart of late medieval and Tudor royal authority.[46] In a symbolic sense, fifteenth- and early sixteenth-century sanctuaries were demonstrations of, rather than challenges to, royal authority and power. Kings from Henry VI to Henry VIII supported the royally-chartered liberties from the same motivations that Barbara Rosenwein has attributed to early medieval kings in granting monasteries immunities: because they affirmed 'royal control over public agents and their jurisdiction' against those, such as the City of London, that might challenge it, and because they announced 'control over the configuration of space'.[47] Sanctuary was thus by no means a purely ecclesiastical privilege set in opposition to secular power. It was, instead, a means by which the crown could demonstrate its commitment to the tempering of justice with mercy, and through which it could balance the complicated jurisdictional ambitions of the king's corporate subjects.

An important strain of rhetoric about sanctuary—its role as safe haven from corruption and arbitrary justice—was augmented particularly by the kingdom's experience of civil war in the second half of the fifteenth century (conflicts romantically named by nineteenth-century novelists as the Wars of the Roses).[48] The repeated regime changes of the second half of the fifteenth century saw frequent resort to chartered sanctuaries by all sides. The neutral spaces of ecclesiastical precincts, into which the despotism of kings and the violence of the wars could not enter, provided much-needed safe zones recognized, with some important exceptions, by both sides in the conflict. The shelter those sanctuaries offered to refugees from the Wars of the Roses also augmented the association of sanctuary with mercy, colouring shelter offered to unfortunate debtors, desperate thieves, or even heinous murderers with the same brush as the life-saving asylum given those fleeing from the cruelty of tyrants.

All this gave the chartered sanctuaries—just beginning to find their feet at the point when the civil wars began—a more secure place in the political and legal structures of the realm, and established a firm association of sanctuary as a remedy for tyranny that continued to resonate even as the dynastic upheavals ended.

---

[46] On the importance of mercy to contemporary kingship, see Kaufman, 'Henry VII and Sanctuary'; Edward Powell, *Kingship, Law, and Society: Criminal Justice in the Reign of Henry V* (Oxford, 1989), pp 229–32; Claude Gauvard, *'De Grâce especial': Crime, état, et société en France à la fin du Moyen Age* (Paris, 1991), esp. pp 895–6; Pat McCune, 'Justice, Mercy, and Late Medieval Governance', *Michigan Law Review* 89 (1991): pp 1661–78, doi:10.2307/1289496; Rosser, 'Sanctuary and Social Negotiation', pp 58–60, 74–6; Krista Kesselring, *Mercy and Authority in the Tudor State* (Cambridge, 2003); Helen Lacey, *The Royal Pardon: Access to Mercy in Fourteenth-Century England* (York, 2009), esp. pp 11–16, 59–81.

[47] Rosenwein, *Negotiating Space*, pp 7–8, 111 (quotation at p. 7).

[48] See Ch. 2, 'Sanctuary and the Wars of the Roses'.

Henry VII and Henry VIII each found it useful to perform magnanimous acts of clemency through support of sanctuary and grants of pardon as an acknowledgement and rejection of the despotism of their predecessors.[49] In the first decade of Henry VIII's rule, for instance, there was a widespread sense that his father's reign had been despotic and arbitrary, and especially that under his regime jury verdicts had been compromised and justice tainted. Henry VIII's liberality in dispensing pardons and supporting sanctuaries showed clearly that he recognized the problems of his father's regime and that he himself intended to take another path. Even for some who themselves would never commit or countenance a felony, sanctuary might appear a necessity in an imperfect world; this was, for instance, the argument that Thomas More made in the 1510s, that sanctuary provided a haven from the arbitrary acts of tyrannical kings.[50]

This larger ideological context for sanctuary also affected the way that sanctuary seekers themselves (or at least some of them) conceptualized their asylum. The idea of sanctuary as manifestation of mercy or as bulwark against tyranny could provide powerful psychological justification for those who sought to use its shelter to avoid the hanging that their actions would otherwise garner them. The English law of felony provided only hanging as the sentence for a guilty verdict on crimes that ranged from vicious premeditated murders to thefts of goods worth 13d. Felons themselves and other subjects of the king sometimes felt that certain crimes, while wrong, did not merit death. Conceptually, sanctuary and other mitigations provided a way to variegate responses to crime when the hard-line law of felony responded only with execution, regardless of the circumstances.[51] While some felons, no doubt, used sanctuary cynically and calculatingly to enable a life of crime with relative impunity, it is likely that for most seekers, their thinking on the subject was a muddied mixture of conviction that the particular crime they had committed was not really their fault; of reliance on mercy and redemption as the gifts of Christ and the king to their people; and of clutching at any straw that might save their necks.

If law and religion were almost reflexively integrated, that does not mean that the relationship between them did not undergo change in this period, both generally and regarding sanctuary in particular. In tandem with a shifting emphasis away from appeals to a universal church and towards the English king as font of Christian justice, over the years between 1400 and the 1530s the rhetoric of sanctuary-seeking emphasized somewhat less 'the immunity and tuition of holy church' and somewhat more sanctuary as 'the king's privilege'.[52] Alongside this swing and no doubt reinforcing it was a laicization of the management of sanctuaries: the deans, canons, and monks who had personally governed and administered the sanctuaries

---

[49] See on the pardon, Kesselring, *Mercy and Authority*.
[50] See Ch. 2 at n.95.   [51] See Ch. 8.
[52] The standard formula for an abjuration indicated that a felon had taken sanctuary in a church 'pro immunitate et tuicione Sancrosancte Romane Ecclesie' or some variation (e.g. TNA, KB 9/201/4, m. 12; KB 9/297, m. 3; KB 9/408, m. 24; KB 27/986, rex m. 6; C 1/226/44). In the 1530s, it was sometimes called the 'king's privilege' (e.g. TNA, KB 27/1112, rex m. 9; SP 1/130, fol. 179r). See Ch. 6 for the emphasis on sanctuary as an aspect of the 'king's law'.

Introduction: Richard Southwell Flees to Sanctuary   17

in the fifteenth century gave way in the sixteenth to laymen acting as stewards and bailiffs, combining those positions with other offices held from other landlords and the king.[53]

Like much of the administration of criminal law (or indeed any kind of law),[54] the law and practice of sanctuary were uneven and unstable, and indeed may have been more than usually fuzzy around the edges. This was the case from the fourteenth century into the 1530s. The list of which religious houses offered permanent asylum was never entirely fixed, for instance, but rather remained undefined and open to interpretation. A series of parliamentary statutes between 1529 and 1536 modified and regularized sanctuary privileges, introducing some standardization and enjoining abjurers to proceed to chartered sanctuaries rather than into exile. Even with the statutes, however, certain aspects remained ambiguous, and notably the statutes did not define which sanctuaries were legitimate or endorsed, resulting in a few anomalies.[55] Thus sanctuary was firmly embedded in English common law and (by the 1530s) statute law, but like many legal processes in late medieval and early modern England, it was imprecisely defined and subject to influence.

Sanctuary, the Crown's Prosecution of Crime, and Aristocratic Felons

The rising number of sanctuary seekers in the last decades of the fifteenth century intersects with the king's law in another way: it reflects a more rigorous prosecution of felony in the royal courts. One significant reason for the low rates of sanctuary-seeking in the first half of the fifteenth century is low felony conviction and execution rates: as Edward Powell's and Philippa Maddern's studies show, relatively few accused felons were hanged in the first decades of the fifteenth century,[56] indicating that there were more effective ways to escape the noose than sanctuary. When a late medieval felon did not need protection from the king's hangman, then that felon was unlikely to seek sanctuary; conversely when felons were more likely to be prosecuted and executed, they were more likely to take refuge in churches. The rise in the numbers of felonious sanctuary seekers in the 1480s likely then reflects the growing importance under the Tudor regime of using the prosecution of crime and the keeping of peace to demonstrate royal power.[57]

Prosecution and punishment became more rigorous from the later fifteenth century: so more felons sought ways to escape. This does not seem unexpected. It is

---

[53] See esp. Ch. 6.
[54] Christine Carpenter, 'Law, Justice and Landowners in Late Medieval England', *Law and History Review* 1 (1983): pp 212–18, doi:10.2307/743850; Penny Tucker, *Law Courts and Lawyers in the City of London, 1300–1550* (Cambridge, 2007), pp 88–9.
[55] On the statutes, see below, Ch. 6 at nn.36 and 73, and for the most significantly anomaly, the sanctuary at the town of Bewdley, see below, Ch. 4 at n.88.
[56] Powell, *Kingship, Law, and Society*, pp 186–9; Philippa Maddern, *Violence and Social Order: East Anglia, 1422–1442* (Oxford, 1992), pp 34, 50. A comment from David Seipp was particularly helpful for my thinking this through.
[57] Penry Williams, *The Tudor Regime* (Oxford, 1979), pp 219–35; Christopher W. Brooks, *Law, Politics and Society in Early Modern England* (Cambridge, 2008), pp 36–40.

important to note, however, that this use of sanctuary and other mitigations to escape the hangman was not, as we might assume, resisted by the Tudor state and judiciary. The use of sanctuary in the late medieval or Tudor period was not (as Thornley thought) an unholy alliance of greedy abbots and heinous criminals intent on stopping the righteous processes of royal justice. As the evidence for the crown's response to sanctuary seeking in its courts and policies shows, kings found it useful to have a way to moderate the workings of their own law of felony, because there were certain kinds of felons the early Tudor monarchs wanted, or needed, to prosecute, but not hang. Most important amongst these were aristocrats who killed one another in gentlemanly quarrels.

The Tudors' determination to prosecute aristocrats represented a change from their predecessors, especially the Lancastrian kings who ruled in the first half of the fifteenth century. Simply put, a man like Richard Southwell would likely not have needed to seek sanctuary a century earlier, as a homicidal quarrel between two gentlemen in the 1430s would almost certainly not have been prosecuted as a felony. As scholars have shown, under Lancastrian rule the crimes of the landed elite, with few exceptions, were handled outside the formal processes of indictment and prosecution. Rather than indictment for felony, violence done to persons and property in aristocratic quarrels was settled by arbitration and litigation (which did not, of course, involve capital penalties).[58] Yet the immunity of aristocrats from criminal indictment in Lancastrian England does not mean that aristocrats were 'lawless', because in fact the local aristocracy *were* the law, their power and authority exercised in significant measure through their offices as sheriffs, justices of the peace, and so on. To some extent their immunity from prosecution reflected a bargain with the crown, which depended on local men of power to establish and enforce royal authority. But it was more than a cynical *quid pro quo*, as Maddern has argued; there was often a thin line between the violence demanded by honour or necessitated by gentry conflicts and the authorized violence those same gentlemen meted out in the exercise of delegated royal power (arrests, imprisonment, execution).[59] Thus through much of the fifteenth century, the immunity of the landed elite from felony prosecution resolved a fundamental contradiction in male aristocratic life—that an aristocrat was compelled by honour to kill another man in response to insults or challenges and at the same time was bound to enforce laws that in theory punished such killings by hanging.[60]

Under Henry VII and Henry VIII, the aristocracy was no longer immune from prosecution, as the early Tudors sought to emphasize that all were subject to royal justice. This created a point of political tension, as the demands of honour had not fundamentally changed: aristocratic power politics still necessitated occasional acts

---

[58] Powell, *Kingship, Law, and Society*, pp 42–3, 70–1, 107–14; Maddern, *Violence and Social Order*, pp 67–110; Carpenter, 'Law, Justice and Landowners'; for a somewhat different argument, see Brooks, *Law, Politics and Society*, pp 278–81.
[59] Maddern, *Violence and Social Order*, pp 11–13, 227–8.
[60] Carpenter, 'Law, Justice and Landowners', esp. p. 216; Maddern, *Violence and Social Order*, pp 11–13, 34–50, 227–32.

of violence.⁶¹ This tension required resolution, for like their predecessors the first two Tudor monarchs continued to depend on the landed elite in the exercise of their own power; moreover both, especially Henry VIII, shared the assumptions of the chivalric culture of honour and so were receptive to arguments that honour-based quarrels were more excusable than those of the base-born.⁶² It was generally inconvenient for the king and perhaps even for the political stability of the realm for deaths in aristocratic affrays to be punished by execution, even if they required prosecution.

This is one of the factors underlying the growing importance of mitigations for capital punishments—sanctuary, benefit of clergy, pardon—in the later fifteenth and early sixteenth centuries: they constituted work-arounds for a crown that required, on the one hand, more comprehensive felony prosecution and, on the other, principled ways to make exceptions. Although these mitigations were by no means entirely confined to the aristocracy, they worked best for those who were educated (and thus could demonstrate the literacy necessary for the benefit of clergy), connected (and thus had the network to arrange a stay in sanctuary or lobby for a pardon), and wealthy (and thus could afford lodgings in sanctuary or to pay for a special pardon). The expansion of sanctuary, benefit of clergy, and pardon—the original developments of which predated, sometimes by many centuries, the accession of Henry VII—resulted more from functional adaptation than from purposive policy. It is important, nonetheless, not to ignore the ideological context that made it beneficial for Henry VII and Henry VIII to follow the footsteps of their Yorkist and Lancastrian predecessors in tying their own roles as founts of mercy and justice to the grant of sanctuary. Ideology and function were mutually reinforcing.

Sanctuary and Gender

In its Tudor flowering, then, sanctuary was a tool of men of power—and I use the collective male noun advisedly. One of the most surprising elements of the accumulation of evidence on individual sanctuary seekers over the period 1400–1550 (more than 1800 cases altogether) is that the overwhelming majority, over 98 per cent, were men (Table 1.1).

Table 1.1. Sanctuary Seekers by Sex, 1390–1557

	Seekers of all kinds		Felons	
Female seekers	29	1.6%	15	1.0%
Male seekers	1798	98.4%	1449	99.0%

Source: McSheffrey, 'Sanctuary Seekers.'

---

[61] See on this tension Williams, *Tudor Regime*, pp 219–35.
[62] See on chivalry and the early Tudors, Susan Brigden, *Thomas Wyatt: The Heart's Forest* (London, 2012), 39–59.

As a significant proportion of the very small number of female sanctuary-seekers were women of royal and aristocratic families who took asylum during the turmoil of the Wars of the Roses, focusing only on those who sought refuge for felony shows the ratio to be even more marked: ninety-nine men for every one woman. It is certainly true that women made up a small minority generally of those who faced felony charges in England in this period, but these numbers are far more imbalanced than even the lowest estimates for female felons.[63] They are also well below the estimate William Chester Jordan has made for women abjurers in the period before the Black Death (10 per cent).[64]

The highly gendered nature of sanctuary-seeking in the fifteenth and sixteenth centuries is not easy to explain. To some extent, at least, it is owed to the construction of the processes of mitigation in ways that simply assumed that the felon was male. This meant that, in structural terms, women found it difficult or impossible to take advantage of these means of escaping the full force of the law.[65] Benefit of clergy—increasingly important through the fifteenth century as a means of mitigation for laymen as well as male religious[66]—was unavailable to women in this period.[67] We can infer from the numbers that sanctuary, in both its forms, worked much more effectively for men than for women, although it is not clear why. For abjurers, if exile overseas might have been a viable option for a man, perhaps general cultural prohibitions against women travelling alone made it more difficult and dangerous for a woman. Even in chartered sanctuaries, the evidence shows that there were very few women who sought the privilege, indicating that they saw there, too, dangers or difficulties finding the basics of life. Women might accompany their husbands into sanctuary, especially in the case of debtors who stayed in sanctuary precincts long-term, but it seems that most sanctuary precincts were overwhelmingly male places. It may be relevant that nunneries did not offer refuge.[68]

---

[63] The lowest estimate I have seen for prosecution of women for felony is the calculation of 4% of the total number prosecuted from two mid-fifteenth-century Yorkshire gaol delivery rolls, in John G. Bellamy, *Strange Inhuman Deaths: Murder in Tudor England* (Stroud, Gloucestershire, 2005), pp 2–3, 201. Krista Kesselring is currently engaged in a project looking at the prosecution of murder over the period 1500–1700. Sampling the records of indictments deposited in the records of King's Bench, she has found for the period 1500–1529 that women made up about 6% of those indicted for homicide (Krista Kesselring, personal communication, 29 March 2014). Women made up higher numbers of those accused of homicide in later decades, especially from the 1560s onwards; see Krista J. Kesselring, 'Bodies of Evidence: Sex and Murder (or Gender and Homicide) in Early Modern England, c.1500–1680', *Gender & History* 27 (2015): p. 256, doi:10.1111/1468-0424.12124.

[64] Jordan, *From England to France*, p. 18.

[65] This is parallel to arguments made by Garthine Walker and Krista Kesselring about the definitions of felonies, especially homicide, that assume a male perpetrator and gendered the processes of prosecution. Garthine Walker, *Crime, Gender and Social Order in Early Modern England* (Cambridge, 2003): pp 113–58; Kesselring, 'Bodies of Evidence'.

[66] See above, n.42.

[67] Women could 'plead the belly' upon being sentenced to execution if they were pregnant, but as this was to save the life of the unborn child, not the mother, unless some other mitigation (such as a pardon) intervened, such women were hanged following the birth. Kesselring, *Mercy and Authority*, pp 212–14.

[68] I am grateful to Vanessa Harding for this point.

Sanctuary worked best for men, and indeed men of a particular kind: those of the landed classes who needed an asylum following the homicides that were often part of aristocratic power struggles. Women of the aristocracy, by contrast, were rarely directly involved in that violence; I have found only one instance of a woman styled 'gentlewoman' who sought sanctuary for felony, although a number of gentle and aristocratic women did take sanctuary for security during the civil wars of the fifteenth century.[69] Like their male counterparts, whether in sanctuary due to political conflict or because of felony, those high-status women could maintain themselves in sanctuary because they had resources to call upon, even in hard times. It could be difficult: the countess of Oxford was said to have been so poor while in sanctuary in the early 1470s that she was forced to take work as a seamstress,[70] but even that source of income was no doubt the result of charity shown to her by her connections. A poor woman who had stolen two shillings from someone's purse before fleeing to a sanctuary would be unlikely to be able to support herself in the same manner as the countess; if she was to escape the noose, she had to find some other way. The apparent unworkability of sanctuary for women felons was not purposeful—there is no indication that women were barred or discouraged per se. Rather it is an intensified effect of the structures of sanctuary-seeking, amongst which was the need to find external means of support while inside the asylum. If resort to a chartered sanctuary was unviable for a poor, unconnected male felon, it was even less likely to be hospitable to a poor, unconnected female felon.

Sanctuary, Liberties, and Jurisdiction

Thornley and other sanctuary scholars have focused almost entirely on how sanctuary related to crime and its prosecution, and there is no doubt that the (male) felon fleeing from arrest into a church was, in contemporary rhetoric as in modern historians' assumptions, the iconic 'sanctuary man'. Discussion of sanctuary in the fifteenth and sixteenth centuries was, however, substantially influenced also by other contexts besides the narrow frame of the administration of criminal justice, especially the complicated issue of jurisdiction. The development of the chartered sanctuaries in the fifteenth century was tightly connected to the liberties Westminster Abbey, St Martin le Grand, and the other houses possessed—that is, their freedom from the governance of civic authorities in labour regulations and the buying and selling of goods; the protection from debt litigation they offered those who stayed within their bounds; and the refuge they provided for political asylum seekers, to name but three. The evolution of sanctuary in the fifteenth and sixteenth century was

---

[69] The Beverley sanctuary register recorded that Robert Beawmont, 'litteratus', and Elizabeth Beauwmont, gentlewoman, sought sanctuary on 26 Sept. 1480 for the death of Thomas Aldirlay of Almondbury, killed by them on 5 Oct. 1479. The relationship between the two Beawmonts is not stated, but as they were said to be resident in two different places, they were likely not married; mother and son? I have not found anything further about this case. *SDSB*, p. 162.

[70] Norman Davis, ed., *The Paston Letters and Papers of the Fifteenth Century* (Oxford, 1971), vol. 1, p. 449; Fabyan, *New Chronicles*, p. 663.

tightly connected with these other prerogatives. As James Simpson has argued, jurisdiction was a key cultural question in this period: a fundamental shift in England between 1400 and 1550 was the move from a kingdom characterized by 'a complex set of adjacent, interdependent, and competing jurisdictions' to an (incompletely) centralized and unitary authority represented by the crown, a change that affected not only law and politics but literature and other arts.[71]

In the course of the fifteenth century, the right of a religious house to offer refuge for an unlimited time to a felon fleeing from arrest came to be accepted in the royal courts as part of the liberties attached to certain religious houses in the realm. Sanctuary and other kinds of privileges, such as markets independent of local urban governments, were equated with one another: each was probative of the other, so that a shoemaker's right within a sanctuary precinct to make and sell his shoes outside a city's guild structures was both reflection and proof of the sanctuary privileges. This created points of conflict between certain sanctuaries located near or within cities and those cities' governments, as the ecclesiastical liberties' economic jurisdiction competed with the ambitions of urban guilds and corporations. In particular, the geographical juxtaposition with the City of London of two of the kingdom's most notable sanctuaries, Westminster Abbey nearby and St Martin le Grand within the City walls, constituted a constant irritant for the kingdom's most important urban government. This irritation was no doubt aggravated when Henry VII granted St Martin's and its properties to Westminster Abbey in 1503, an appropriation that did nothing to interrupt St Martin's status as a sanctuary and liberty.[72] Intermittently through the fifteenth and early sixteenth centuries, and more concertedly in the 1520s and 1530s, the City of London attacked the sanctuary claims of St Martin le Grand. They did so, as I will argue especially in Chapter 5, not primarily because of the mayor's and aldermen's objection to the sheltering of felons in St Martin's (indeed, it seems likely that St Martin's hosted relatively few felonious sanctuary seekers), but instead because of the hundreds of stranger craftsmen, Dutch shoemakers and French leather dressers, who lived and worked inside the precinct. Those immigrant artisans were not permitted to work within two miles of the jurisdiction of the City of London—with the exception, royally granted and repeatedly confirmed, that they were permitted to work in the

[71] James Simpson, *Reform and Cultural Revolution: 1350–1547* (Oxford, 2004), *passim* (quotation at p. 559); see also Bradin Cormack, *A Power to Do Justice: Jurisdiction, English Literature, and the Rise of Common Law* (Chicago, 2009); Tom Johnson, 'Law, Space, and Local Knowledge in Late-Medieval England' (PhD, Birkbeck College, University of London, 2014); Seán Patrick Donlan and Dirk Heirbaut, eds, *The Laws' Many Bodies: Studies in Legal Hybridity and Jurisdictional Complexity, c1600–1900* (Berlin, 2015), especially Anthony Musson's essay 'Jurisdictional Complexity: The Survival of Private Jurisdictions in England', pp 109–26; R. A. Houston, 'People, Space, and Law in Late Medieval and Early Modern Britain and Ireland', *Past & Present* 230 (2016): pp 47–89, doi:10.1093/pastj/gtv057; Richard Jeffrey Ross and Lauren A. Benton, eds, *Legal Pluralism and Empires, 1500–1850* (New York, 2013).
[72] Minnie Reddan, 'The Collegiate Church of St. Martin Le Grand', in *The Religious Houses of London and Middlesex*, ed. Caroline M. Barron and Matthew Davies, Victoria County Histories (London, 2007), pp 203–4.

liberty of St Martin's.⁷³ Yet when the City attacked St Martin's privileges as a zone outside guild supervision of labour and production, they focused as much or more on the harbouring of murderers and thieves in the 'pretensed sanctuary' and the danger to the City that such a refuge for felons posed as they did on artisan work outside the guild system—not because such felons were numerous in St Martin's, but because it was useful tactically to tie those who sought to work outside the guilds with dangerous criminals. Similarly, both the sanctuary's officials and the immigrant artisans themselves associated their ability to work in St Martin's with the precinct's ecclesiastical immunities and protections. The rhetoric surrounding the legal, political, and at times physical conflict between the City of London and St Martin's saw both sides repeatedly intertwining St Martin's rights as a royal liberty, jurisdictionally separate from the City, with its sanctuary privileges.

While many religious houses had liberties of one kind or another, the sanctuary privileges of some houses became more established than others, and many others did not claim or apparently wish to possess those rights at all, even though they had other jurisdictional privileges. There are few clear patterns in the religious houses that became major sanctuaries: Westminster and Glastonbury Abbey were Benedictine houses; Beaulieu was a Cistercian abbey; St Martin le Grand and St John's Beverley were collegiate churches; Durham was a cathedral. No nunneries appear to have offered sanctuary, with the lone exception of one 1529 abjurer who took church at Wilton Abbey and claimed what was described in the record of abjuration as 'the degree of St. Edith', Wilton's most famous nun; this formulation intriguingly suggests a more developed tradition there than the surviving records of sanctuary-seeking indicate.⁷⁴ Why some religious houses claimed this function and not others is obscure to us now—the differences lie, no doubt, in risks and benefits weighed (for clearly there were many downsides as well as upsides to offering havens to thieves, murderers, and debtors), and in opportunities seized or passed by. Those opportunities were seized at Westminster, Beverley, Durham, and St Martin le Grand. Other houses or orders (notably the Hospitaller Order, as we will see in Chapter 4) made apparent attempts to establish sanctuary privileges at particular moments and were either beaten down or themselves decided to abandon the attempts.

Sanctuary's Sudden Death

In view of sanctuary's successful adaptation to the legal and political context of the early Tudor regime, how can we explain its quite sudden collapse in the second half of the 1530s? The model that viewed sanctuary as an anachronism in the Tudor era did not have to search hard for an explanation for its cessation by the end of Henry VIII's reign: as a dinosaur that had accidentally survived into the next era, its unsuitability to the new environment had doomed it, and the final defeat of medieval ecclesiastical power in the English Reformation dealt the final blow

⁷³ See below, Ch. 5 at n.60. ⁷⁴ TNA, KB 9/1065, m. 129; KB 27/1104, rex m. 8.

to an already dying organism. The pattern I have found—that sanctuary in its evolved state was healthy and indeed apparently growing into the early 1530s, when quite suddenly, within half a decade, it virtually ceased—is at first glance more difficult to explain.

The difficulty recedes, however, if we posit an exogenous rather than endogenous cause for its demise. In other words, sanctuary did not die off because it could not survive in the new climate of Tudor governance, but rather because it was hit by an asteroid: the monastic dissolutions. As I discuss below, the operation of the sanctuaries had become largely abstracted from the administration of the religious houses themselves by the 1530s, delegated to lay bailiffs, stewards, and keepers.[75] Yet despite secularization and the integration of the management of sanctuaries into the mainstream of Tudor office-holding by the 1530s, sanctuary could not survive the reorganization of English religious life in the Reformation as did another of the formerly ecclesiastical mitigations, benefit of clergy. Although sanctuary-seeking had adapted to respond to new circumstances in late medieval and Tudor England, it had evolved always with a fundamental dependency on the religious houses, and in particular their complex of franchises and liberties. With the monasteries dissolved and their franchises ended or dispersed, the sanctuaries had no home.

As I discuss in Chapter 8, there was an attempt to respond to this problem: the 1540 Sanctuaries Act, often depicted as having shut them down, in fact attempted to replace the refuges in ecclesiastical precincts with a new system of secularized sanctuaries in cities (including one at Westminster).[76] The statute indicates that MPs—several of them former sanctuary-seekers themselves—wanted to maintain the availability of sanctuary as a tool of mitigation. Their act, however, was ill thought-out, and the new plan did not function very well, limping along for a few years before apparently petering out. This was, nonetheless, not a deliberate killing but an accidental death. The demise of this long-standing mitigation meant that felons had different and probably fewer choices than they had had before. In the second half of the sixteenth century pardons became more common and benefit of clergy in some ways more expansive, but so also did the rate of execution increase significantly.[77] The landed elite still found ways to escape the noose, but for most felons the chances of hanging were much greater.

SANCTUARY AND THE PARTIALITY OF THE ARCHIVES

This is a book about a practice that is distinctly non-modern, revealing structures of thought and attitudes towards wrongdoing that are often quite alien to our own.

---

[75] See Ch. 5, 'Governing St Martin's Precinct in the Reign of Henry VIII', and Ch. 6, 'Sanctuary at Knowle and the Administration of Law and Justice in the 1530s'.

[76] See Ch. 8, 'The Statute of 1540 and Sanctuary's Precipitous Decline'.

[77] Kesselring, *Mercy and Authority*, pp 46–73; John G. Bellamy, *The Criminal Trial in Later Medieval England: Felony Before the Courts from Edward I to the Sixteenth Century* (Toronto, 1998), pp 155–6.

It is also a book that could only have been written in the digital age. For both the in-depth case studies and the broader gathering of data for the period 1400–1550, I have been dependent not only on old-fashioned hours combing through documents in the archives, but also on online repositories of archival document photographs (especially the invaluable Anglo-American Legal Tradition website[78]), digitized texts and studies, the power of internet search engines, and the analytical capacities of database and spreadsheet programs. If my conclusions challenge many of the arguments made by previous historians of sanctuary in medieval and Tudor England, this is at least partly because our digital landscape allowed me to find things and make connections that others before me could not have done.

Ironically, historians in the twenty-first century have access to more historical evidence and ways to analyse it than ever before, and yet we are less certain than we have ever been about how well we know the past. The remains of the past are inevitably partial, both in the sense of their incomplete and fragmentary nature, and in the sense of their serving of particular interests. On the one hand, the instances of sanctuary-seeking I uncovered through diligent searching of records clearly represent only a part—and perhaps an atypical portion—of all the instances where men and women sought asylum in late medieval English churches. Gathering all the scattered and fragmentary records together certainly serves a purpose and indeed suggests some interesting and unexpected patterns, but there is no way to know how representative the records are. On the other hand, even those documents that do survive were written in the first place by and for particular interests and thus always bear a less-than-direct relationship to lived reality. In some cases, this is a formal and systemic aspect of the records: for instance, certain legal records (such as coroner's inquest reports) followed specific legal formulae into which the 'facts' of the case were shoe-horned, and those records were filed and survive only in specific kinds of cases. We can only, at best, guess at the 'real' facts of these cases or hypothesize about the relationship of the cases that are in the records to the overall landscape of sanctuary-seeking.

Even beyond the formulaic or administratively systemic bias of the records is another kind of partiality, extending to more conscious and deliberate reshaping of events into written accounts.[79] To state an obvious fact that nonetheless bears repeating, pre-modern people did not write documents and keep archives for the information of historians working five centuries later; they wrote and filed records in order to inscribe for their own presents a specific version of events, which in

---

[78] Robert Palmer, *The Anglo-American Legal Tradition*, http://aalt.law.uh.edu/.
[79] Natalie Zemon Davis, 'Les conteurs de Montaillou', *Annales: économies, sociétés, civilisations* 34 (1979): 69–71, doi:10.3406/ahess.1979.294022; Paul Gewirtz, 'Narrative and Rhetoric in the Law', in *Law's Stories: Narrative and Rhetoric in the Law*, ed. Peter Brooks and Paul Gewirtz (New Haven, 1996), pp 2–13; Peter Brooks, 'Narrative Transactions: Does the Law Need a Narratology?', *Yale Journal of Law and the Humanities* 18 (2006): pp 1–28, http://digitalcommons.law.yale.edu/yjlh/vol18/iss1/1; Gabrielle M. Spiegel, *The Past as Text: The Theory and Practice of Medieval Historiography* (Baltimore, 1997), pp xvii–xxi, 14–27, 44–56; Malcolm Gaskill, *Crime and Mentalities in Early Modern England* (Cambridge, 2000), pp 24–9; Laura Gowing, 'The Haunting of Susan Lay: Servants and Mistresses in Seventeenth-Century England', *Gender & History* 14 (2002): pp 183–201, doi:10.1111/1468-0424.00262.

some cases was significantly massaged in order to make a particular point. Sometimes we see that massaging—and sometimes we do not, seduced (as we were meant to be) by the sleight of hand the document's composer performed. This means that we must always keep the partial nature of our records in mind as we analyse them, and that we must accept that we will never know precisely what happened.

The question of how sanctuary worked in England in the fifteenth and sixteenth centuries necessarily raises questions about the evidence we might bring to bear on it: the surviving documents that record the seeking of sanctuary in one way or another are patchy, inconsistent, and each in their own ways anomalous. The documents are like individual puzzle pieces for an immense jigsaw for which most of the pieces are missing. We can infer what the whole picture looks like from those surviving pieces, but we work with considerable handicaps: we don't know how many pieces there were originally (is it a 100-piece or a 5000-piece puzzle?); we're not sure which way the pieces are meant to go; we're not sure if we seem to have so many blue pieces because the picture was mostly sky or because only the pieces from one part of the puzzle survive. And perhaps we are interpreting those blue pieces incorrectly: they may be the blue on a dress or the surface of a calm lake rather than a cloudless sky. The difficulties of the evidence for sanctuary in the late medieval and Tudor period are not especially unusual: all historians, especially of premodern periods, must become masters of inference, at guessing what lies between the isolated puzzle pieces that survive. None of those pieces even in their isolated survival are clear and obvious either: there are no pure and value-free forms of historical evidence that give us unmediated access to 'what happened' in the past. The investigation of sanctuary that follows will make use of thousands of puzzle pieces, assembled into the arrangement that makes the most sense to me.

2

Tavern Brawls, Civil Wars, and Remedies for Tyranny

The Evolution of Sanctuary in England, c. 1380–1500

HERMAN STOKFYSSH AND HIS FLIGHT TO WESTMINSTER: THE DEVELOPMENT OF CHARTERED SANCTUARY c. 1400

On 30 November 1394, after sundown, three men were amongst a large group drinking in the King's Head tavern near London bridge. Two, Herman Stokfyssh and Nicholas Clarebount, were 'Doche', a word late medieval English people applied to anyone coming from the lower Rhineland area that now includes the Netherlands, Belgium, and north-western Germany. The third, Angelo Lettere, was probably Italian. Lettere threw a crust of bread in the face of a certain 'frowe' (a Doche woman), and as a result Lettere and Clarebount exchanged 'contumelious and argumentative words'. Lettere punched Clarebount in the throat, and the two moved into the street and began to fight in earnest. Stokfyssh followed them out and attacked Clarebount, too, pulling out a dagger. He stabbed Clarebount in the right side, so deeply that it reached his heart. Clarebount staggered several streets over to the parish of St Martin Orgar in Candlewick street, where he soon after died. Stokfyssh immediately fled from the scene of the quarrel to the sanctuary of Westminster Abbey, taking his dagger with him, and (as the coroner's inquest jurors put it) 'for fear' of arrest he remained there. The sheriffs of London were ordered to take him, if he could be found outside the sanctuary. About five months later, in May 1395, the King's Bench records indicate that Stokfyssh surrendered himself to the officials of the court of King's Bench; he pleaded not guilty to the charge of homicide and (as usual) was taken into custody. As he presumably knew or at least hoped would happen, however—and this explains his exit from the sanctuary and surrender to authorities—before his trial proceeded further he received a pardon from the king for the felony, and in June he presented it to the justices and was released *sine die* ('without day', meaning that the court did not assign any further dates in the case, effectively ending it).[1]

This indictment of Herman Stokfyssh for the murder of Nicholas Clarebount is amongst the earliest pieces of evidence that survive for the seeking of what appears

---

[1] TNA, KB 9/173/2, mm 32–33; KB 27/536, rex m. 20d.

to be a permanent form of sanctuary at one of the great religious houses. As we saw in Chapter 1, from about 1200 felons had been able to flee to parish churches before abjuring, and it is not always clear in the records whether a felon's resort to a place of sanctuary was meant to be a prelude to abjuration or something qualitatively different. What is particularly suggestive, however, of a shift to chartered sanctuary—which we can detect in small numbers of cases in the 1380s and 1390s—is the flight of accused felons like Stokfyssh to Westminster Abbey from murder scenes inside the walls of the City of London. In similar cases earlier in the fourteenth century, a man killing another in a tavern brawl and intending to take sanctuary in a church prior to abjuration would usually flee to the nearest parish church. The London coroners' inquest rolls for the half century before the Black Death are replete with such cases, while conversely not a single London sanctuary seeker during this period was noted as having fled to Westminster Abbey.[2] By contrast, when Herman Stokfyssh ran to the abbey he bypassed a dozen and more parish churches on the three-kilometre route between London Bridge and Westminster. This implies that the sanctuary attached to the monastery had some kind of special privilege those parish churches did not.

Surviving evidence indicates that in the 1390s flight to Westminster for permanent sanctuary was a new phenomenon: the earliest references that I have found indicating felons' seeking of such refuge come from the 1380s and 1390s, a finding that confirms Isobel Thornley's consideration of the same question using different sources.[3] As Thornley argued, this form of sanctuary developed through an evolutionary conflation of the various forms of jurisdictional immunity that ecclesiastical liberties had come to develop over the twelfth, thirteenth, and fourteenth centuries.[4] The permanent sanctuary certain churches claimed for felons combined the immunity those ecclesiastical liberties offered debtors, an immunity unlimited in time, with the long-standing concept of ecclesiastical sanctuary, both in its ancient sense as a sanctified space offering respite from violence and retribution and in the more specific English common law procedure of church-taking and abjuration. This development must be inferred as it cannot be demonstrated explicitly from the spotty fourteenth-century evidence. The religious houses themselves by no means acknowledged the recent development of this privilege, or indeed recent development of anything: arguing for evolution or change on such a question was not a legally or culturally permissible strategy. In the rhetoric of any dispute about rights, privileges, and jurisdictions, all the parties' claims were based on 'ancient' precedent, as demanded both by the English rights culture of the day and by the king's law regarding usage from time immemorial (statutorily defined

---

[2] See Sharpe, *Calendar of Coroners Rolls*, passim.

[3] Thornley, 'Destruction of Sanctuary', p. 203. There is an oath for the admission of sanctuary seekers at Westminster Abbey that purports to be early thirteenth century but for which the earliest copy is late fourteenth century. It specifies only debt as a reason for seeking sanctuary, although it does not exclude other causes. It is less specific than the regulations for Paris Garden and St Martin's examined above (Ch. 1 at n.22), although similar in its general tenor regarding good behaviour. Emma Mason, Jennifer Bray, and Desmond J. Murphy, eds, *Westminster Abbey Charters, 1066–c.1214*, London Record Society 25 (London, 1988), pp 195–6.

[4] Thornley, 'Destruction of Sanctuary', p. 203.

as prior to the accession of Richard I on 3 September 1189).[5] These allusions to ancient precedent, however, masked a reality in which the jurisdictional and legal context was constantly adapting.[6]

The adaptations occurred within a fertile environment of ideas and practices of jurisdiction, immunity, and holiness. As English royal authority and common law developed through the high medieval period, so also did the jurisdictional immunities of liberties.[7] Many medieval liberties and peculiars enjoying varying kinds and extents of jurisdictional autonomy were secular, while some of the most powerful—the bishop of Durham's palatinate or the estates of Westminster and the other great abbeys, for instance—were ecclesiastical lordships.[8] The connection of liberties to religious institutions indeed added force to the jurisdictional claims: if, for instance, in some ways the bishop of Durham was a lord like any other, his lordship was never entirely abstracted from his episcopal office. Even when the liberties the bishop exercised were secular in nature, they were rhetorically connected to the peace of God and the saints; as Jean Scammell has noted, the bishop of Durham's broad authority over criminal and civil matters in his lands was powerfully intertwined with a 'divinely-protected immunity', overseen by Durham's great patron St Cuthbert.[9]

Authority over crime and criminals was not the only ingredient in this interlacing development of governance, jurisdiction, and sacrality. Commercial regulation, and civic and guild organization, for instance, grew alongside and within the jurisdictional immunities of liberties in England through the high medieval period and beyond. Particularly important were legal mechanisms of debt litigation, which had barely existed in the eleventh century but which had elaborated in royal and local courts by about 1300.[10] The governors of some independent jurisdictions responded: by the first half of the fourteenth century, debtors could escape their creditors' lawsuits by entering into the precincts of certain liberties. It seems likely that Westminster Abbey and the second great sanctuary in the metropolitan

---

[5] See M. T. Clanchy, *From Memory to Written Record, England 1066–1307*, 2nd edn (Oxford, 1993), p. 152.

[6] See Anthony Musson and W. M. Ormrod, *The Evolution of English Justice: Law, Politics, and Society in the Fourteenth Century* (1999); Anthony Musson, *Medieval Law in Context: The Growth of Legal Consciousness from Magna Carta to the Peasants' Revolt* (Manchester, 2001); Brooks, *Law, Politics and Society*, esp. p. 20.

[7] Thornley, 'Destruction of Sanctuary', pp 186–7. On other ecclesiastical peculiars and liberties, see R. N. Swanson, 'Peculiar Practices: The Jurisdictional Jigsaw of the Pre-Reformation Church', *Midland History* 26 (2001): pp 69–95, doi:10.1179/mdh.2001.26.1.69; Michael Prestwich, ed., *Liberties and Identities in the Medieval British Isles* (Woodbridge, 2008).

[8] R. L. Storey, *Thomas Langley and the Bishopric of Durham, 1406–37* (London, 1961), pp 52–67; Jean Scammell, 'The Origin and Limitations of the Liberty of Durham', *The English Historical Review* 81 (1966): pp 449–73, doi:10.1093/ehr/LXXXI.CCCXX.449; A. J. Pollard, *North-Eastern England During the Wars of the Roses: Lay Society, War, and Politics, 1450–1500* (Oxford, 1990), pp 145–50, 153–4; Tim Thornton, 'Fifteenth-Century Durham and the Problem of Provincial Liberties in England and the Wider Territories of the English Crown', *Transactions of the Royal Historical Society*, Sixth Series, 11 (2001): pp 83–100, doi:10.1017/S0080440101000056.

[9] Cox, *Sanctuaries*, pp 98–105; Scammell, 'Origin and Limitations', pp 452–8 (quotation at p. 454).

[10] Pamela Nightingale, 'Money and Credit in the Economy of Late Medieval England', in *Medieval Money Matters*, ed. Diana Wood (Oxford, 2004), pp 51–71.

area, St Martin le Grand, were precocious amongst the religious houses in the realm to cultivate that privilege; the two houses were named in a 1377 statute regulating the practice as paradigmatic amongst the 'privileged places' in the realm that offered refuge to debtors.[11]

Thus sanctuary evolved in response to and as an integral part of the complex development of legal mechanisms of various kinds in late medieval England. This is not to say, however, that sanctuary was divorced from its specifically Christian roots: the shelter offered to the debtor borrowed conceptually from the spiritual protection offered to the sanctuary-seeking criminal, at the same time as the criminal's sanctuary was assimilated to the debtor's. Permanent asylum for debt offered in certain church precincts was associated with the idea of the holy space of the church protected by ecclesiastical immunity. Sometime in the later years of the fourteenth century, the same kinds of refuge unlimited in time that Westminster and St Martin le Grand had offered to debtors were also offered to the felons 'taking church', who had hitherto been limited by custom and the common law to forty days. Conversely, debtors sheltering from their creditors in the precincts of those religious houses were now said to seek sanctuary, their refuge sacralized as the protection of 'holy church' in the same way as felons seeking to save themselves from the noose through the redemptive powers of Christ. Although these equivalences were likely established by usage rather than legal argument, by the fifteenth century, the crown and its courts came to accept the charters that had outlined the liberties of the religious houses, often dating back to the pre-Conquest or early Norman period, as the legal basis for the permanent sanctuary privileges these houses offered felons. Those charters did not explicitly indicate that these houses had such rights regarding felons (indeed the law of felony had not yet been developed at the time in which these charters were written), but those rights were read by the justices into their broader privileges as liberties, as we will see in Chapter 3 with St Martin's in 1440.[12]

A key moment in the melding of jurisdictional liberties with the broader idea of churches as refuges for accused criminals was the Hawley–Shakell affair of 1378, which saw Westminster Abbey become caught up in a complicated and highly political controversy about royal officers' killing of an asylum seeker in the abbey church. Two esquires, Robert Hawley and John Shakell, had been embroiled in a conflict over custody of a prisoner of war with John of Gaunt, the duke of Lancaster and regent for the boy King Richard II. Hawley and Shakell were thrown into the Tower of London, from which after several months of imprisonment the two escaped, running to take refuge in Westminster Abbey. Sir Alan Buxhill, the constable of the Tower, under orders from the king's council, came to the abbey with fifty armed men to retrieve the escaped prisoners; they were able to seize Shakell outside, but Hawley ran into the abbey church, where a mass was in progress. Buxhill ordered his men to pursue Hawley and when they found him, in the choir of the church, a brawl ensued, in which both Hawley and one of the abbey's servants

---

[11] 50 Edw. III, c. 6, *SR*, vol. 1, p. 398.   [12] See Ch. 3 at n.61.

were slain.[13] As the archbishop of Canterbury later put it when the matter was discussed in parliament, simply the entry into the abbey church of 'a great multitude of armed men, at a time when the priest was singing high mass at the high altar', not to mention the violence that ensued, constituted an enormous 'villainy and injury' to the church and to God himself.[14]

Although this case was important in developing the idea of permanent sanctuary for accused criminals, Hawley and Shakell had not sought sanctuary for felony, but rather refuge for a transgression (private keeping of a prisoner of war) that was framed, at least in discussions afterwards, as debt relating to the ransom sought for the prisoner.[15] Both before and after the Hawley–Shakell affair, there were debates in parliament about the immunity of debtors within ecclesiastical liberties. Although opponents of the liberties' privileges, including John Wyclif, made arguments in parliament drawn from canon law that religious houses could not use their immunities to protect debtors, trespassers, or other misdoers not facing capital penalties, those arguments did not carry the day.[16] Two statutes (one in 1377 and the other in 1379) recognized that Westminster, St Martin le Grand, and other such ecclesiastical liberties could offer refuge to debtors who honestly sought time to make restitution, as distinct from fraudsters who abused the privileges.[17] The statutes themselves embraced the relationship between the special kinds of franchises and liberties possessed by ecclesiastical liberties, 'Places of Holy Church privileged', and the sacral character of the refuge they offered to the unfortunate. Debtors continued to take refuge—or sanctuary, as that refuge was increasingly termed—in the precincts of certain religious houses and other liberties for several centuries, even well after English religious houses were dissolved in the sixteenth century. Sanctuary for debt survived in 'Alsatia', for instance, the former Whitefriars convent, into the eighteenth century.[18]

If Westminster, St Martin le Grand, and other unspecified 'privileged places' were thus offering permanent asylum to debtors from the mid-fourteenth century, a privilege that was statutorily recognized by the 1370s, there is no clear evidence that the same refuge was, as yet, being offered to felons—although perhaps it was. Karl Shoemaker has noted some theoretical claims made for such a privilege in an undated earlier fourteenth-century legal submission from St Peter's Abbey in York,

---

[13] See Nigel Saul, *Richard II* (New Haven, 1997), pp 36–8; Elizabeth Allen, '"As Mote in at a Munster Dor": Sanctuary and Love of This World', *Philological Quarterly* 87, no. 1/2 (2008): pp 108–19.

[14] Chris Given-Wilson, ed., *The Parliament Rolls of Medieval England* (London, 2010), Parl. Oct. 1378, ¶27.

[15] *PROME*, Parl. Oct. 1378, ¶28.

[16] *PROME*, Parl. Oct. 1378, ¶8; Saul, *Richard II*, pp 37–8; Allen, '"As Mote in at a Munster Dor"', pp 108–19. Helmholz notes that the question on debt was not, in fact, clear in the canon law on the subject. *Ius Commune*, pp 70–2.

[17] 50 Edw. III, c. 6; 2 Ric. II, Stat. 2, c. 3 (*SR*, vol. 1, p. 398; vol. 2, p. 12). Cf. a different reading of these statutes in Shoemaker, *Sanctuary and Crime*, pp 167, 234.

[18] Nigel Stirk, 'Arresting Ambiguity: The Shifting Geographies of a London Debtors' Sanctuary in the Eighteenth Century', *Social History* 25 (2000): pp 316–29, doi:10.1080/03071020050143347; John Levin, 'Alsatia: The Debtor Sanctuaries of London', http://alsatia.org.uk/site/.

although there is no evidence that it was actually exercised.[19] From the early fourteenth century, Westminster cartularies included a number of writs from its abbots dating from the early Norman period, some of them in badly-transcribed Old English, certifying to sheriffs the presence of sanctuary seekers in the abbey; leaving aside precisely what this meant in the eleventh and twelfth centuries, in the fourteenth century the copying of such records was clearly meant to indicate the antiquity of Westminster's sanctuary rights.[20] More intriguingly, a 1355 discussion amongst King's Bench justices recorded in the Year Book indicated that the justices all agreed that the Westminster charters showed that any felon fleeing was to have impunity of limb and life once he had 'entered the same holy place of Westminster', agreeing in fact that this applied only to felons and not to debtors.[21] This would *seem* to indicate something different from taking church prior to abjuration; and it certainly does show that ideas about refuge, asylum, franchise, and sacral spaces were intertwined in discussions both about felons and about debtors.

Another notorious sanctuary seeker at Westminster in 1388 is difficult to classify and the significance of the rejection of his sanctuary claim hard to assess: in the midst of the political crisis in 1387–1388 caused by the attempted seizure of power from Richard II by the Lords Appellant, Chief Justice Robert Tresilian claimed the sanctuary of Westminster Abbey when he was arrested for treason. Although his claim was summarily denied and he was soon after executed, he may well not actually have been in the sanctuary precinct when seized; it is thus not clear if it was the effectiveness of the sanctuary privilege itself that was denied or Tresilian's assertion that he had been within the precinct's bounds. The *Westminster Chronicle*, however, does tell us that this heinous breach of sanctuary (as the monk of Westminster Abbey who wrote the chronicle termed it) occasioned a discussion amongst the king, the chancellor, and several other close advisors regarding the evidence for Westminster's sanctuary privileges. According to the chronicler, the king decisively confirmed the abbey's ability to shelter those guilty of any offence, treason, felony, or debt. It is hard to know what to make of such a partisan source, but it is also not impossible that Richard II would make such a declaration at this moment, as it cast his enemies as sacrilegious sanctuary breachers.[22] It is possible, then, that one of the spin-off consequences of this particular crisis in Richard II's reign in the spring of 1388 was the firmer entrenchment of the sanctuary rights Westminster Abbey had begun, relatively recently, to assert. Or perhaps conversely Tresilian's own straw-clutching sanctuary claim was a reflection of a new function for the abbey. In any case, it was in the years around 1390 that clearer (if still somewhat ambiguous) evidence for instances of fleeing felons seeking and finding permanent refuge at Westminster begins to be found in the King's Bench records.

---

[19] Shoemaker, *Sanctuary and Crime*, pp 148–9.
[20] Mason, Bray, and Murphy, eds., *Westminster Abbey Charters*, pp 110–11, 116, 135–6, 138.
[21] David J. Seipp, 'An Index and Paraphrase of Printed Year Book Reports, 1268–1535', 2008, http://www.bu.edu/law/seipp/index.html, Seipp 1355.212ass.
[22] L. C. Hector and Barbara F. Harvey, eds., *The Westminster Chronicle, 1381–1394* (Oxford, 1982), pp 310–13, 324–5; John L. Leland, 'Tresilian, Sir Robert (d. 1388)', *ODNB* (2004), doi:10.1093/ref:odnb/27715.

In the ensuing decade, Westminster Abbey may have been joined by another London-area church, the College of St Martin le Grand. In 1402, a Commons petition in parliament complained about 'murderers, traitors, thieves, robbers, felons and malefactors' taking refuge in St Martin's, against whom

> neither justice nor execution of the law has been effective in the past because of certain liberties claimed by the said college, to the great destruction of our said lord the king's lieges, and the undermining of the good laws of the realm.[23]

Even assuming some rhetorical hyperbole about the scope of such sanctuary-seeking at St Martin's, this petition addresses something different from such felons taking church and abjuring—and it ties the sheltering of the criminals to the collegiate church's liberties. How far back such practices went is obscured by poor records. As Herman Stokfyssh's case shows, on the one hand, when we begin to see in the last decades of the fourteenth century indications in the indictment files of King's Bench that felons were being granted permanent sanctuary, the practice appears established and part of the legal process, suggesting that Stokfyssh was not the first accused felon to have sought some kind of unlimited asylum in Westminster.[24] On the other hand, however, such cases are scattered very thinly over late fourteenth- and early fifteenth-century documents.[25]

This leaves us without a straightforward indication of whether the resort to religious houses for permanent asylum was in fact common or relatively rare around 1400—although rare seems the more likely answer. As we will see in more detail in the next section, the number of felons tried and convicted in the first part of the fifteenth century was very low, and thus relatively few needed the refuge from the noose that sanctuary provided. Nonetheless, some did, and in the first half of the fifteenth century, other religious houses besides Westminster and St Martin's— Durham Cathedral, St John's Minster at Beverley, houses pertaining to the Hospitaller Order (as we will see in Chapter 4), and the abbeys at Beaulieu, Glastonbury, and St John's Colchester—began to provide the sanctuary felons sought, claiming the privilege as part of the houses' liberties and franchises. For instance, the sanctuary of St Cuthbert, an intensified version of the immunities

---

[23] *PROME*, Parl. Sept. 1402, ¶70; Thornley, 'Sanctuary in Medieval London', pp 301–2, 308–12.

[24] I have found two cases from the 1380s of flights to Westminster Abbey after killings in Westminster itself or the vicinity, making the kind of refuge the felon sought ambiguous: TNA, JUST 2/96, m. 4 (1381 or 1382); TNA, JUST 2/97A, m. 4 (1386—from St Mary le Strand). In 1388, a man who allegedly committed a homicide in Islington 'fugit et evasit in sanctuarium Westm' [fled and escaped into the sanctuary of Westminster]', TNA, JUST 2/97B, m. 1—in that case, like Stokfyssh's, there were a significant number of parish churches much closer to Islington than the monastery. In another case from 1385 reference is made to a felon lying in wait 'apud portam sanctuarii predicti propter feloniam predictam ibidem faciendi causa ad capiendum et optinendum refugium et libertatem de eodem sanctuario postquam ipse feloniam predictam fecisset [at the gate of the sanctuary of the Blackfriars' church, in order to commit the aforesaid felony there and to take refuge and liberty of that sanctuary after having committed the felony]'. TNA, KB 9/167, mm 42–43. London Blackfriars, although a liberty, was not to go on to claim status as a chartered sanctuary, and it is unclear in this early case whether the jurors meant that Northorp expected to claim permanent sanctuary there, or a temporary refuge prior to abjuration. Note, however, the linking again of concepts of 'sanctuary', 'refuge', and 'liberty'.

[25] See McSheffrey, 'Sanctuary Seekers', for figures.

attached to the bishop of Durham's authority, had been available in the cathedral church itself and its immediate precinct[26] from at least the twelfth century, but as far as the meagre evidence indicates, through the fourteenth century asylum seekers in the cathedral precinct received only the time-limited sanctuary privileges they could obtain in any parish church, prior to abjuration made before the bishop's coroner.[27] The shift towards permanent sanctuary took place sometime in the fifteenth century, at the latest by the 1460s, when the cathedral officials began to register sanctuary seekers in the bishop's records.[28]

The other great northern sanctuary, at St John's, Beverley, had similarly in the twelfth century pivoted from the holiness associated with St John of Beverley to jurisdictional and specifically sanctuary claims that radiated the considerable distance of a mile from the door of the Beverley Minster church in which St John's body lay. Those privileges in the twelfth century were limited to thirty days,[29] but by the fifteenth century Beverley, too, provided permanent refuge to sanctuary seekers.[30] Beverley town ordinances in the 1420s regulating how 'grithmen', or sanctuary men, were to fit into the town's guild structure suggest an evolving situation in the town, as previously transient seekers were supplanted or (more likely) augmented by permanent settlers.[31] In comparison to Durham (the only other sanctuary for which we have a register), Beverley had a significantly higher proportion of debtors, perhaps reflecting the town's market and its willingness to facilitate debtors' ability to work in their trades and thus eventually pay off their debts.[32]

In 1440, during the flurry of argumentation submitted in a controversy about St Martin's sanctuary privileges that we will examine in more detail in Chapter 3, Durham, Beverley, Glastonbury, and Westminster were cited as places in the English realm that offered seekers permanent sanctuary.[33] Glastonbury was not to go on to become one of the great sanctuaries—there is not a single example in the records of a felon or debtor taking refuge there. That list of houses offering sanctuary would be expanded (if never clearly delimited) into the sixteenth century, as we will see in Chapter 4. Ambitious ecclesiastical administrators increasingly saw the assertion of sanctuary privilege as both extension and defence of the broader jurisdictional rights of their houses, perhaps borrowing initially from the strategies

---

[26] Although all the bishop of Durham's properties—the modern county of Durham—were St Cuthbert's lands, a liberty and immunity under his protection, this did not make all his lands a sanctuary. This point is misunderstood in Michael A. Hicks, 'The Yorkshire Rebellion of 1489 Reconsidered', *Northern History* 22 (1986): 54–5, doi:10.1179/174587009X391411.

[27] Scammell, 'Origin and Limitations', p. 455.

[28] *SDSB*, p. 1.   [29] *SDSB*, p. 100; Cox, *Sanctuaries*, pp 130–8.

[30] See *SDSB* for Beverley's register, dating from 1478.

[31] Arthur Francis Leach, *Report on the Manuscripts of the Corporation of Beverley*, Royal Commission on Historical Manuscripts (London, 1900), pp 37, 44–6, 75, 78.

[32] 45% of those who entered Beverley's sanctuary did so as debtors, in comparison to 6% of those who took sanctuary at Durham. See the data for Durham and Beverley (drawn from *SDSB*) and reason for seeking sanctuary in McSheffrey, 'Sanctuary Seekers'.

[33] This must have been a very recent development at Durham, judging by the total lack of attention to the issue of sanctuary in R. L. Storey's detailed examination of Bishop Thomas Langley's defence of his liberties in the diocese of Durham in the first half of the fifteenth century: Storey, *Thomas Langley*.

successfully employed by the abbot of Westminster. If this development had its origins in the years around 1400, long-standing rhetoric intertwining jurisdiction, immunity of the church, and the protection of saints made it a natural evolution from earlier centuries.

SANCTUARY-SEEKING 1400–1550: THE NUMBERS

For this book I examined as many of the surviving records documenting sanctuary seekers between 1400 and 1550 as I reasonably could, finding more than 1800 individual seekers.[34] Most of the scholarship on English sanctuary, both those works written in the first part of the twentieth century and more recent publications, has followed a rise and a fall narrative: sanctuary was in its heyday in the thirteenth century and in decline in the late medieval and Tudor period.[35] As indicated by the graphs in Figures 2.1, 2.2, and 2.3 drawn from that data, however, the evidence shows something quite different.[36]

As Figures 2.1 through 2.3 show, church-taking and abjuration, on the one hand, and resort to chartered sanctuaries, on the other, have somewhat different patterns, although neither fits the rise-and-fall profile.[37] If one considered a different slice of time from the one on which I have focused, say the period 1200–1450, abjuration would indeed seem to flourish and then collapse. This is the argument of William Chester Jordan's recent book: we first see abjuration in the twelfth century, and by the end of the thirteenth century extrapolations from the evidence suggest that hundreds of felons abjured the realm each year. Fourteenth-century records prior to the Black Death indicate continued steady use, but as Jordan contends, both the demographic collapse of the Black Death and the loss in the 1360s in the Hundred Years War of some key English-held ports on the French coast

---

[34] I looked systematically through the King's Bench indictment files (KB 9) from the 1380s through the 1540s, following many, but not all, of those cases through the controlment rolls (KB 29) and the *coram rege* rolls (KB 27). In addition, I used the sanctuary registers from Beverley and Durham (*SDSB*), and examined any evidence about sanctuary seeking in the calendared patent rolls, close rolls, and state papers, and in cases where sanctuary came up in searches through the online catalogue of the National Archives, as for instance in Chancery bills (C 1), Star Chamber (STAC), Exchequer (E), Requests (REQ), etc. See McSheffrey, 'Sanctuary Seekers', for details and references.

[35] See the works cited in Ch. 1, n.4; notably this chronological arc underpins the arguments of the two important recent studies by Shoemaker and Jordan.

[36] See McSheffrey, 'Sanctuary Seekers', for the data on which the graphs below are based. For a broader demographic context, it would be helpful to note here that although population estimates in this period are always hypothetical due to evidence problems, most scholars believe that the English population, decimated by the recurrent plague epidemics that began with the Black Death in 1348–1349, remained largely stagnant from the early fifteenth century until sometime in the second quarter of the sixteenth century, when it began to rise again. This was subject to regional variation, as in some parts of England the population began to climb earlier. Altogether, though, increases in the overall population are unlikely to explain the rise in the number of sanctuary seekers. E. A. Wrigley and Roger S. Schofield, *The Population History of England: 1541–1871: A Reconstruction* (London, 1981), pp 563–9.

[37] As of the 1531 statute 22 Hen. VIII, c. 14 (see below, this chapter, n.40), abjurers proceeded to chartered sanctuaries. Although those seekers are only counted once in Figure 2.1, after 1531 those seekers appear both as abjurers and as seekers at chartered sanctuaries in Figures 2.2, 2.3, 2.4, and 2.5.

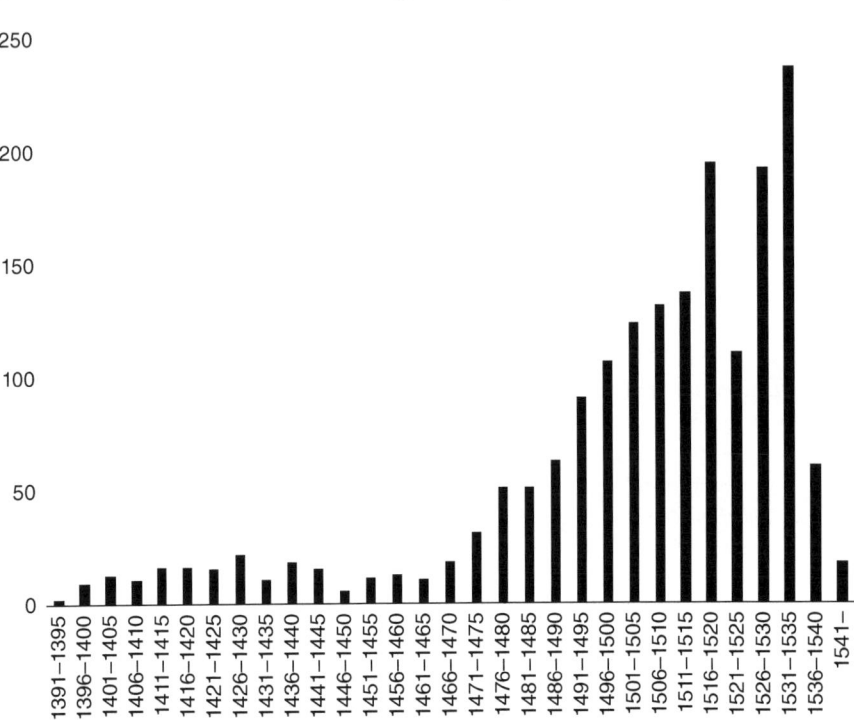

Figure 2.1. Sanctuary Seekers, five-year totals: all kinds of seekers (abjurers and seekers at chartered sanctuaries; felons, debtors, political refugees, etc.), all sources.
Source: McSheffrey, 'Sanctuary Seekers'.

deeply disrupted the abjuration system.[38] The evidence I found for the first part of the fifteenth century indeed shows low numbers,[39] but—in contrast to the argument

---

[38] Jordan, *From England to France*, pp 136–41.
[39] Records for 1400–1499 show 87 abjurations and another 74 who took church but for whom an abjuration is not recorded (see McSheffrey, 'Sanctuary Seekers'); it is impossible to know what proportion of the total these cases constituted, but it is hard to argue from this evidence that hundreds were abjuring per year (although cf. Freeman, 'And He Abjured', pp 301–2). Two important books considering law and crime in the first half of the fifteenth century do not even mention sanctuary, presumably because it did not come up in the detailed research underpinning the books: see Powell, *Kingship, Law, and Society*; Maddern, *Violence and Social Order*. The rarity of references to abjuration in surviving fifteenth-century coroners' rolls is also telling: the fourteenth-century London rolls, which end in 1378, for instance, show significant numbers of sanctuary-seekers and abjurers for the period before the Black Death, but amongst a range of coroners' rolls I consulted from the late fourteenth and early fifteenth century from various parts of the kingdom, I found very few references to abjuration, especially after 1400. For the London coroner's rolls, see Sharpe, *Calendar of Coroners Rolls*. I looked at the following late fourteenth/early fifteenth century coroners' rolls (after which the rolls do not survive until past our period): TNA, JUST 2/61 (3 abjurations over 20 years); JUST 2/96 (no abjurations; one flight to Westminster over 7 years); JUST 2/97A (no abjurations; one flight to Westminster over 4 years); JUST 2/97B (no abjurations; one flight to Westminster over 3 years); JUST 2/119C (one abjuration over 10 years); JUST 2/167 (one abjuration over 14 years); JUST 2/236 (three abjurations over 16 years); and no cases of abjuration or flight to a chartered sanctuary in JUST 2/98, 2/99, 2/100, 2/101, 2/169, 2/240, and 2/244.

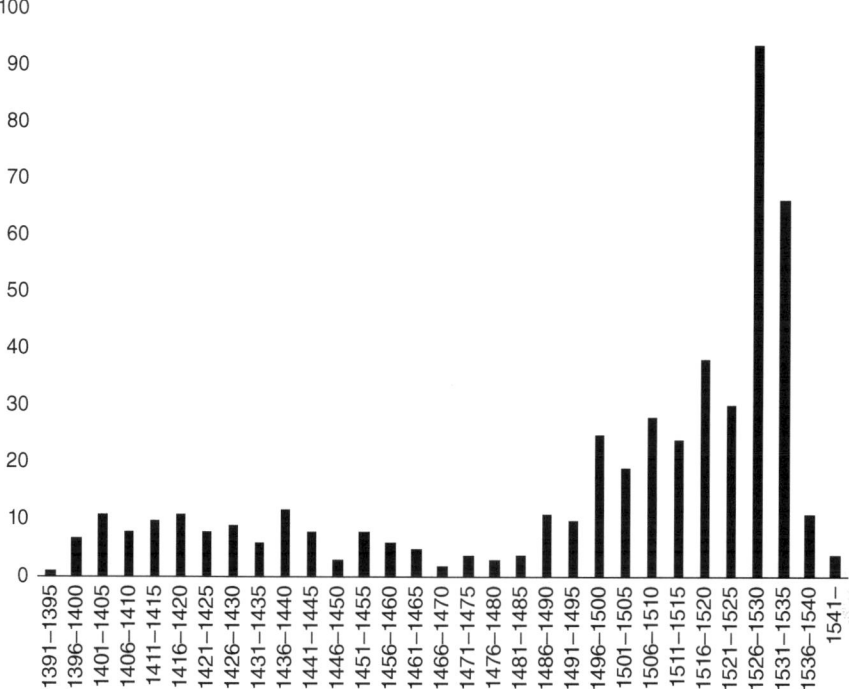

Figure 2.2. Church-takers and/or abjurers, five-year totals, all sources.
Source: McSheffrey, 'Sanctuary Seekers'.

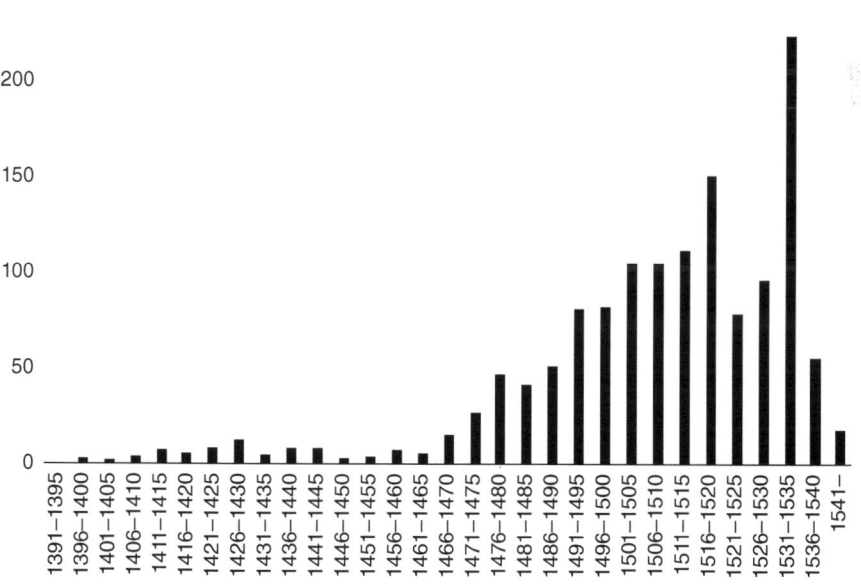

Figure 2.3. Seekers at chartered sanctuaries, five-year totals, all sources.
Source: McSheffrey, 'Sanctuary Seekers'.

for continued decline—from the last years of the fifteenth century the numbers begin to increase again and then continue to rise through Henry VII's later years and the reign of Henry VIII, up until the 1530s. The highest numbers of abjurers in the post-Black Death records, in fact, fall in the period between 1520 and 1535. This increase did not continue: after 1535, the numbers of abjurers fairly suddenly fall off. There was an important statutory change to abjuration in 1531, after which abjurers were no longer to go into exile but instead were to proceed to chartered sanctuaries and remain there permanently.[40] This change may have played a role in the downturn: perhaps many abjurers found this unattractive or impracticable because of the expense of staying in sanctuary. To summarize, then, the pattern for records of abjuration shows a deep post-Black Death dip followed by an uptick in the Tudor period until a sharp decline, although not complete cessation, by the end of the 1530s.

Resort to chartered sanctuaries (Figure 2.3) has a different arc, especially if we stretch our time period under consideration back to 1200. As far as records indicate, no churches, monasteries, or religious houses offered permanent asylum to felons in the thirteenth century or through most of the fourteenth. The first evidentiary traces of this form of sanctuary, as we have seen, appear only in the last years of the fourteenth century and references are quite thinly dispersed through much of the fifteenth century. Like church-taking and abjuration, however, evidence for the seeking of permanent asylum is considerably more plentiful in the reigns of Henry VII and Henry VIII than in the decades before, growing steadily until the 1530s. By the middle of the fifteenth century, communities of 'sanctuary men' (only very rarely 'sanctuary women', as we saw in Chapter 1) had developed in a number of religious houses scattered around the kingdom, although we know most about them in the sixteenth century both because the records are better and because the seekers were almost certainly much more numerous then.

The patterns of surviving *evidence* for sanctuary-seeking and the patterns of *actual* sanctuary-seeking may well be two different things altogether. The uncertainty about an origin point for the chartered sanctuaries stems largely from record survival, along with the contingencies that caused a person's resort to sanctuary to be written down in the first place. Even into the sixteenth century, for the most part felonious sanctuary seekers only entered into the legal records that survive when their cases were to be considered by the court of King's Bench (the only criminal court for which extensive records have survived for the period 1400–1550).[41] Records of sanctuary seekers were filed at King's Bench for a number of reasons: because the seekers were arrested outside the sanctuary; because they had received a pardon and came to present it in court; because they had been dragged out of the sanctuary by force and 'pleaded sanctuary' at their trial, that is, asked the court to

---

[40] 22 Hen. VIII, c. 14, *SR*, vol. 3, pp 332–4.

[41] The Court of King's Bench had jurisdiction in all the counties of England except the palatine counties of Durham, Lancashire, and Cheshire (on which see Baker, *Oxford History, 1483–1558*, pp 293–300). I did not examine the records of felony prosecution in those palatine jurisdictions, although there is a good deal of evidence about Durham and Lancashire seekers in the registers for Beverley and especially Durham (*SDSB*).

rule the seizure illegal and restore them to their asylum; because another person was tried for the same felony and the seeker's flight to sanctuary was incidentally recorded in the record of the accomplice's process. A sanctuary seeker who requested asylum, received it, and stayed there only rarely left evidentiary traces outside the sanctuary registers, especially in the kinds of records we have for the period before the mid-fifteenth century. The indictments filed at King's Bench are nonetheless the most consistent administrative documents for sanctuary-seeking in the period between 1400 and 1550, and thus it is significant—even given all the caveats about the evidence—that the same general pattern of sanctuary-seeking obtains in the KB 9 series as in the other forms of evidence (Figures 2.4 and 2.5).

Other data also corroborate the general pattern. The sanctuary registers from Durham and Beverley, the first dating from 1464 to 1524, the second from 1478 to 1539, both also indicate a quickening of sanctuary-seeking through the reigns of Henry VII and the early decades of Henry VIII (Figure 2.6).[42] The Durham numbers cut off in the mid-1520s when the register book itself ends while the Beverley numbers dwindle in the later 1530s in a similar way to the King's Bench records.

The data—from different kinds of sources, with different biases—thus all point in the same direction. Sanctuary-seeking was not particularly common in the century or so following the Black Death, at least partly because (as we saw in

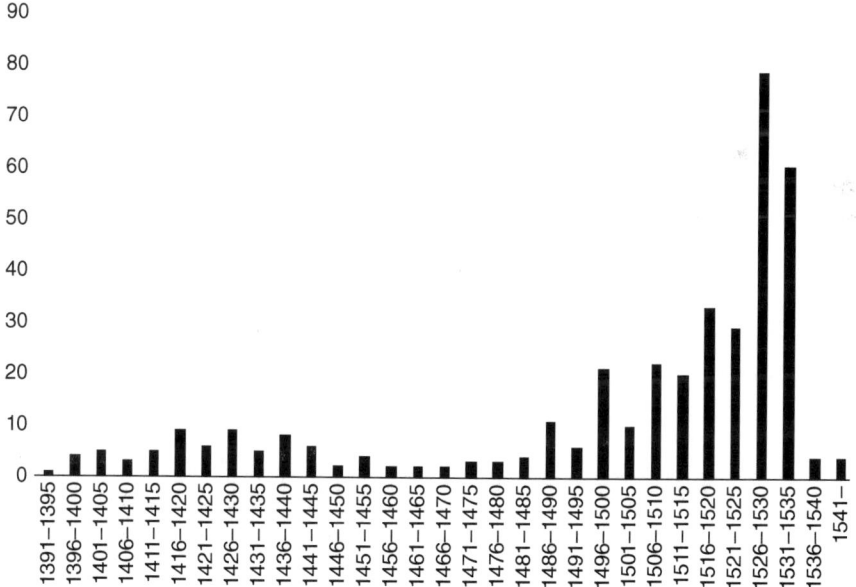

Figure 2.4. Church-takers and/or abjurers, five-year totals, King's Bench indictments (KB 9).
Source: McSheffrey, 'Sanctuary Seekers'.

[42] SDSB.

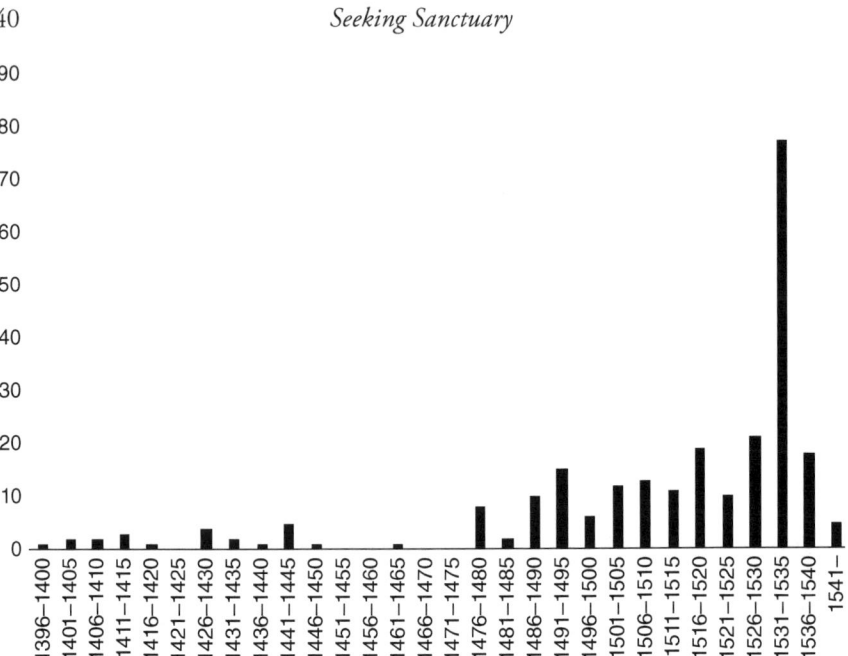

Figure 2.5. Seekers at chartered sanctuaries, five-year totals, King's Bench indictments (KB 9).
Source: McSheffrey, 'Sanctuary Seekers'.

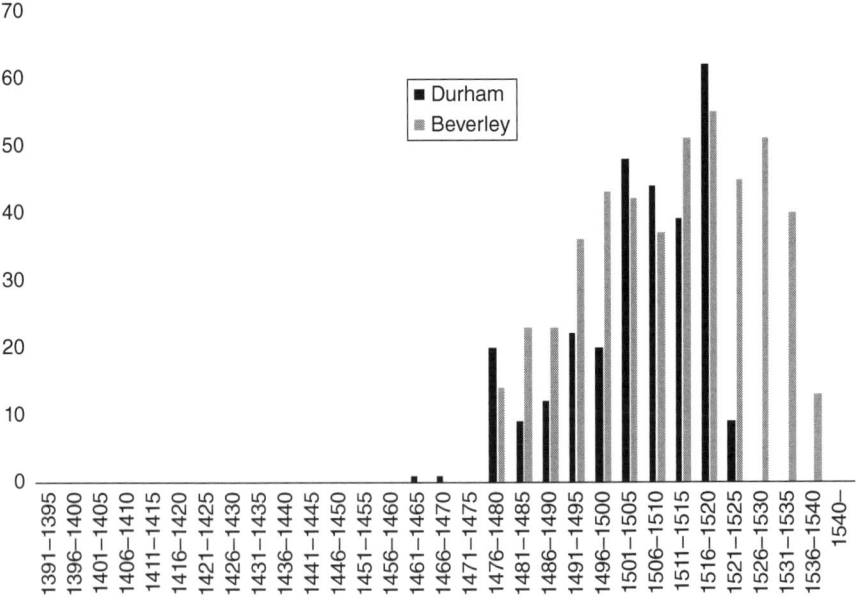

Figure 2.6. Seekers in the Durham and Beverley sanctuary registers.
Source: McSheffrey, 'Sanctuary Seekers'.

Chapter 1) felony prosecution was not particularly robust and even those brought to court were unlikely to suffer execution. Yet during this period, various factors converged that allowed for the development of a new form of sanctuary—permanent asylum within an ecclesiastical precinct—and ultimately also for the revival of church-taking and abjuration of the realm. Both became much more common in the later fifteenth and early sixteenth centuries, but the fifteenth century established the preconditions for that development.

The surviving records, it must be said, are unlikely to constitute a straightforward reflection of the actual incidence of sanctuary-taking: they constitute the visible part of a sanctuary-seeker iceberg, the underwater section of which is of unknown size. At times stray documents or casual references hint that the numbers of seekers and the number of asylums at which they sought refuge might have been much greater than we know. For instance, very few records before the 1530s show resort of felons to the collegiate church at Ripon, Yorkshire, yet it may have had a substantial population of sanctuary seekers. In 1458, six sanctuary men—out of an unknown total population of sanctuary seekers—were chastised by the collegiate chapter for not participating in the Rogation procession. One of the men explained that he had not dared to come out of his house 'because of the fear of creditors', indicating that he was a debtor, as they all might have been.[43] In 1486, a man named John Slingsby petitioned parliament complaining of an unjust private prosecution of murder launched against him after he had been attacked by a band of sixty ruffians, many of whom were sanctuary men and at least one (the man he was accused of murdering) privileged at Ripon.[44] It is hard to know what to make of this evidence: perhaps Ripon had a large and unruly population of felonious sanctuary seekers in the fifteenth century, or perhaps we should assume that Slingsby's petition was typically hyperbolic about numbers and that Ripon's privileges were mostly employed for debtors rather than felons. Between 1400 and 1530 I have found only one King's Bench indictment, in 1507, that indicates a felon's flight to Ripon as sanctuary. Yet in the 1530s, when by statute coroners began to assign specific chartered sanctuaries to which abjurers were to proceed, Ripon was used at least six times by coroners in different counties.[45] Had Ripon only rarely been used before the 1530s as a resort for felons, or for some reason had its regular employment simply remained below the documentary radar?

It is almost certain that the portion of the iceberg above the water is greater for the sixteenth century than the fifteenth. There are simply more records in the sixteenth century of all kinds than in the fifteenth, thus more incidents of sanctuary-seeking are found because more records survive in general. More specifically in relation to sanctuary, there were a greater number of records because there were more diligent attempts, especially in the reign of Henry VIII, to effectively track those who sought sanctuary or used other mitigations such as benefit of clergy.

---

[43] Joseph Thomas Fowler, ed., *Acts of Chapter of the Collegiate Church of SS. Peter and Wilfrid, Ripon, A. D. 1452 to A. D. 1506*, Surtees Society 64 (Durham, 1875), pp 72–3.
[44] *PROME*, Parl. Oct. 1495, ¶34.
[45] For references, see McSheffrey, 'Sanctuary Seekers', searching 'Ripon' under column 'Sanctuary'.

Although it seems highly likely that both general survival of records and more diligence in recording instances of sanctuary affect the difference in numbers of sanctuary seekers found in the sixteenth century as opposed to the fifteenth, it is impossible to know to what extent. At the very least, in any case, it would be difficult in the face of the data to maintain the argument that resort to sanctuary was falling off during the reigns of Henry VII or Henry VIII: there simply is no evidence to support that contention, and much that goes against it. Most telling, perhaps, is the fact that all the different kinds of evidentiary indication—each source with significant, but different biases and limitations—points in the same direction, towards more, rather than fewer, people claiming sanctuary privilege during the reigns of Henry VII and Henry VIII. Qualitative evidence that will be discussed throughout this book confirms the general impression the quantitative evidence gives, which is that sanctuary became ever better established as an option for an accused felon, up until the mid-1530s.

Although it appears that more felons were seeking sanctuary in the first part of the sixteenth century than had in the fifteenth, for many the stay in sanctuary was likely short, sometimes very short, even though it was not technically limited in the way that forty-day sanctuary in parish churches was. The most vivid evidence for this comes from a 1533 census of sanctuary men and women at Westminster Abbey, which recorded how long each inhabitant had had the privilege of the sanctuary.[46] Westminster was by no means normative or characteristic of other sanctuaries—in fact, as far as we can tell, each sanctuary developed its own patterns. Certainly by the 1530s, and likely right from 1400, however, Westminster had the largest number of people requesting sanctuary privilege, perhaps by a significant margin, and if anything its dominance was increasing in Henry VIII's reign. Whether the numbers in the 1533 census are characteristic of Westminster diachronically is difficult to say: the only other surviving census comes from 1532 and it is almost certainly missing its second page, and so cannot be directly compared.[47] It is also possible that the patterns for sanctuary-seeking at Westminster and elsewhere had undergone a significant shift just before the census with the passage of the 1531 statute that directed abjurers to chartered sanctuaries rather than into exile.[48] This may well have increased the number of sanctuary-seekers at Westminster, perhaps substantially.

Nonetheless, the evidence of the 1533 Westminster census is worth a close look. On 1 June 1533, eighty-five men and three women had the privilege of the Westminster sanctuary.[49] This includes four men who were labelled as 'clerks convict' or 'clerks attaint' and were imprisoned in the 'convict house'—that is, they were men who had pleaded benefit of clergy in court and had been handed over to the abbot of Westminster for indefinite imprisonment rather than hanging. For seventy-eight of the eighty-eight people listed, the document notes the length of time since the grant of their sanctuary privilege. The range was from John Gon,

---

[46] TNA, SP 1/238, fols 72–73.
[47] TNA, SP 1/70, fol. 133. Another possible census of those privileged for sanctuary at St Martin le Grand in 1525 lists twelve persons: TNA, SP 1/33, fol. 148 (*L&P*, vol. 4, pt. 1, p. 473).
[48] See above, this chapter at n.39.   [49] TNA, SP 1/238, fols 72–73.

'for murder, twenty years and more past', to several men who had sought asylum the previous day. The average time in sanctuary was 23 months, but the median was much shorter: 6 months. About two-thirds (64 per cent) of those privileged had been there for less than a year. Perhaps most significantly, twenty people—more than a quarter—had sought sanctuary over the previous week. This last number is astonishing, and it is hard to know what to make of it. If that had been a typical week, this could mean that more than a thousand people a year registered in the Westminster sanctuary—a number that is hard to credit, although perhaps much larger numbers of people in one way or another claimed sanctuary, if only briefly, than any other sources have given us reason to believe. In any case, it seems that many of those who came to Westminster in the early 1530s must then have departed soon after arriving, so that fewer than a hundred were resident at any one time. While many cycled in and then out again, there was a core of long-term sanctuary men: twenty-two had lived there for three years or more. As a 1537 enquiry into the conduct of William Webbe, the keeper of the Westminster sanctuary, indicated incidentally, long-term sanctuary dwellers gossiped, had dinner parties, and mixed with both sanctuary functionaries and the townspeople of Westminster.[50]

Others clearly did not become so well-established, staying in some cases presumably only days. Why would these asylum-seekers' stays have been so short? A number of different reasons suggest themselves. Some who ran to sanctuary after a violent altercation later found out that the person whom they thought they had killed had not died after all; homicide was a felony punishable by death, but assault was much less serious and did not require sanctuary.[51] Some no longer needed sanctuary after they were able to find a way past a felony indictment or had been able to arrange for a pardon; in some cases, for those with connections, obtaining a pardon could be a swift process, a matter of two months or so.[52] Perhaps most commonly, however, many asylum seekers likely could not find the wherewithal to support themselves in the sanctuary precinct and were forced to leave. Rents inside the precinct were high and paid work was scarce; unless a sanctuary seeker had financial support from relatives or patrons outside, it would not be possible for them to stay for long. The scribe William Ebesham wrote to his patron Sir John Paston in 1468, for instance, complaining about the 'great cost' of living in sanctuary, 'amongst right unreasonable askers'.[53] His grievance was echoed by the father of a 1530s sanctuary seeker, Thomas Frognall, who had been forced to go to Westminster in 1532 to escape a felony charge; when he was there, his father claimed, 'he was brought into such a miserable estate that he consumed and spent up all that ever he had or could make in this world', making him vulnerable, then,

---

[50] TNA, SP 1/125, fols 40r–43v; see for this enquiry (and its afterlife in popular culture), Shannon McSheffrey, 'William Webbe's Wench: Henry VIII, History, and Popular Culture', in *The Middle Ages on Television: Critical Essays*, ed. Meriem Pagès and Karolyn Kinane (Jefferson NC, 2015), pp 53–77.

[51] In 1527, for instance, John Watson ran to Westminster sanctuary after he thought he had killed his wife Isabel; when she recovered, he left the sanctuary. TNA, SP 1/42, fols 126–128.

[52] The Southwells (see Ch. 1 at n. 1) are a good example; their pardon was dated about eight weeks after the homicide (TNA, C 66/661, m. 5; *L&P*, vol. 5, pp 507–8). Similarly, in 1538 sanctuary seeker Edward Wolfe was able to obtain a pardon about eight weeks after he killed a man. TNA, SP 3/14 (*L&P*, vol. 13, pt. 1, p. 265; KB 27/1107, rex m. 4).

[53] Davis, *Paston Letters*, vol. 2, p. 387.

to extortioners who (allegedly) forced him to surrender his inheritance rights in his father's lands.[54] If the seeker who was forced by poverty to abandon the precinct was lucky, he or she was able to slip out of the precinct undetected, having used the sanctuary to evade a quick arrest and then moving off elsewhere to start life again. This must have happened with considerable frequency, with or without a short stay in sanctuary, judging by the numbers of people who were outlawed. Others were not so fortunate and, after being forced to leave the safety of sanctuary, were arrested, tried, convicted, and hanged.

The Westminster census numbers for 1533 highlight an important point: that resort to the chartered sanctuaries was far more likely to be an effective strategy for people with means and connections than for those without rich and powerful friends. For poorer felons, abjuration was in many cases a better bet, at least before the key statutory change in 1531 that mandated removal to a chartered sanctuary: they would be in the parish church for a few days, they might well be given food and drink as alms while there, and then, assuming they fulfilled their oath of abjuration and went into exile, they had a new start in a new land. Abjuration worked for a man who could (or needed to) pull up stakes and start again from scratch. It conversely was a very poor choice for a man building a career on connections, perquisites, offices, and landholding—for that sort of man, it was impossible to disappear anonymously without severe loss of status and wealth. For them, it was more important to find a way around the felony indictment, not to flee as an outlaw or to abjure, but to find a way to wipe it out or move past it. For this, the chartered sanctuary was highly useful as a means to prevent a quick trial and execution while a longer-term solution could be found, ideally a pardon or, even better, a not guilty verdict or the quashing of an indictment. Both the stay in the sanctuary and the arrangement of a way around the felony indictment were obviously more available for the elite or those connected to them. It is possible that the patterns were different in other sanctuaries: the register for Durham in particular indicates that many of the sanctuary seekers were likely men of low status (committing homicides with agricultural implements, for instance), but it is unclear how long they stayed or how they supported themselves within the Durham cathedral precinct. And lastly, as I discussed in the introduction, sanctuary appears not to have been an attractive or practical option for women: very few women sought sanctuary, according to the surviving records, and most who did were aristocratic and royal wives, widows, and daughters who fled to ecclesiastical precincts during the civil wars of the fifteenth century. Different kinds of sanctuary thus suited different kinds of people; and for some people it did not suit at all.

SANCTUARY AND THE WARS OF THE ROSES

Claims for sanctuary privilege show the complex intertwining of the redemptive powers of Christianity, the sacralized spaces of church properties and precincts,

---

[54] TNA, C 1/1218/49; *L&P*, vol. 8, pp 160, 361.

and the evocation of royal mercy as an indispensable part of the king's justice. As a number of historians have demonstrated, late medieval and early modern kings used their powers of mercy and clemency to enhance and justify their royal power and to connect that power to divine authority.[55] A royal proclamation issued in the name of Henry VI in 1470, in the midst of the most serious struggles of the Wars of the Roses, integrated the reverence due to the 'holy places of sanctuaries of Westminster and Saint Martin's' with the importance of observing the 'sovereign lord's laws and his peace'.[56] We will see in more detail in Chapters 3 and 4 the establishment of sanctuary rights in the first half of the fifteenth century in the London sanctuary of St Martin le Grand and in properties belonging to the Knights of St John, also known as the Hospitaller Order. Here we will consider more generally how sanctuary was affected by the broader political landscape of that century, and in particular the civil wars into which the kingdom plunged in the second half of the fifteenth century.

Between 1399 and 1485, most notably between the 1450s and the 1480s, the crown changed hands several times, a situation that only augmented for the unstable regimes the importance of emphasizing the crown's demonstration of mercy and justice through its protection and observance of sanctuaries. As a result, sanctuary's political, social, and legal role became more established over this period. At each turn of the tide in the civil war, key players in the losing party fled to a convenient nearby sanctuary. Sanctuary provided breathing space for political opponents of a new regime and a chance for a sovereign's sober second thought to prevail over immediate rage: as Polydore Vergil put it, Lancastrian Thomas Dymmok fled to Westminster in 1470, 'meaning there to tarry until the king's ire should be assuaged'.[57] Both Yorkists and Lancastrians took advantage: Edward IV's own wife, Queen Elizabeth, had fled 'secretly by night…unto Westminster, and there registered her and such as to her belonged as sanctuary folks' in October 1470, when Edward was forced to flee into exile with the Lancastrian resurgence. She gave birth to their oldest son while there.[58] As the Yorkist forces rallied in the spring of 1471, the Lancastrians in turn sought asylum: Henry Holland, duke of Exeter, went into sanctuary after the decisive battle at Barnet, and Henry VI's wife Margaret of Anjou and their son the prince Edward took sanctuary at Beaulieu

---

[55] See esp. Lacey, *Royal Pardon*; Kesselring, *Mercy and Authority*; McCune, 'Justice, Mercy, and Late Medieval Governance'; Powell, *Kingship, Law, and Society*, p. 89; and for France, Gauvard, *De grâce especial*, pp 895–6; Natalie Zemon Davis, *Fiction in the Archives: Pardon Tales and Their Tellers in Sixteenth-Century France* (Stanford, 1987); Marie-Sylvie Dupont-Bouchat, 'Guilt and Individual Consciousness: The Individual, the Church and the State in the Modern Era, Sixteenth-Seventeenth Centuries', in *The Individual in Political Theory and Practice*, ed. Janet Coleman (Oxford, 1996), pp 123–48.

[56] Cora L. Scofield, 'Elizabeth Wydevile in the Sanctuary at Westminster, 1470', *The English Historical Review* 24 (1909): pp 90–1, doi:10.1093/ehr/XXIV.XCIII.90. Gauvard also notes the connection between God's peace and French conceptions of royal mercy: *De grâce especial*, pp 940–1, 951–2.

[57] Polydore Vergil, *Three Books of Polydore Vergil's English History*, ed. Henry Ellis (London, 1844), p. 127.

[58] Thomas and Thornley, *Great Chronicle*, pp 212–13; Fabyan, *New Chronicles*, pp 658–9.

Abbey in Sussex as a safe haven while regrouping before the battle of Tewkesbury.[59] Substantial numbers of the most prominent players in the civil war, from both sides, at one point or another went into sanctuaries: St Martin Le Grand offered refuge to Anne Neville, daughter of Warwick the Kingmaker and later wife of Richard III; to the Countess of Oxford; and to John Morton, Bishop of Ely.[60] Even the dean of St Martin's himself, Robert Stillington, an ardent Yorkist, was forced to take sanctuary in his own precinct during Henry VI's readeption in 1470–1471,[61] while John Howard, future duke of Norfolk, took sanctuary at St John's Abbey in Colchester in the spring of 1471.[62] Others, both great and small, took the privilege of sanctuary, most frequently at Westminster, St Martin le Grand, and Beaulieu.[63]

For the most part, the kings observed sanctuary privilege, allowing a regime's enemies to remain unmolested in sanctuary precincts, especially if they were women, children, or clergy. But this was not always true. As we will examine in more detail in Chapter 3, Henry VI considered breaches of sanctuary in the cases of traitors William Cayme and William Oldhall in 1450 and 1451,[64] and in 1454 the duke of York extracted Henry Holland, duke of Exeter, from Westminster sanctuary.[65] York's son Edward IV, following the battle of Tewkesbury in 1471, committed perhaps the most notorious sanctuary breach of the period. According to 'Warkworth's Chronicle', written in the early 1480s, fifteen men who made up the leadership core of the defeated Lancastrian army, including Edmund Beaufort, the duke of Somerset, fled to Tewkesbury abbey following the battle. Edward IV 'came with his sword into the church', but a priest there saying mass, with 'the sacrament in his hands', required the king out of respect for the eucharistic host to pardon those men. The king did so, and the men thus trusting to the king's word stayed in the church rather than fleeing elsewhere to safety. Two days later, however, Edward's forces came and seized them, and by Edward's orders all fifteen were

---

[59] Vergil, *Three Books*, pp 133, 147, 148.

[60] Nicholas Pronay and John Cox, eds, *The Crowland Chronicle Continuations: 1459–1486* (London, 1986), p. 133; Davis, *Paston Letters*, vol. 1, pp 449, 564. During the reign of Richard III, Edward IV's widow Elizabeth Woodville went into sanctuary at Westminster for the second time; Fabyan, *New Chronicles,* pp 658–9, 668; Vergil, *Three Books*, pp 175–8, 210.

[61] Michael A. Hicks, 'Stillington, Robert (d. 1491)', *ODNB* (2004), doi:10.1093/ref:odnb/26528. Stillington, one of the major supporters of Richard III's regime, was deprived of the deanery of St Martin's upon Henry VII's succession. He was, however, pardoned, but then appears to have been implicated in the Lambert Simnel affair in 1488. At that point he claimed a form of sanctuary at Oxford University in the later 1480s; the University refused to surrender him to the king to face treason charges on the basis of its independent jurisdiction, although ultimately they did give him up and he was put into prison, where he died in 1491.

[62] John Ashdown-Hill, *Richard III's 'Beloved Cousyn': John Howard and the House of York* (Stroud, 2012), p. 16.

[63] E.g. a chaplain and servant to Archbishop Bourchier, during the readeption (TNA, C 1/46/163); William Brandon, during Richard III's reign (*PROME*, Parl. Nov. 1485, ¶23[28]).

[64] See below, Ch. 3, at n.69.

[65] G. L. Harriss and M. A. Harriss, eds, 'John Benet's Chronicle for the Years 1400 to 1462', in *Camden Miscellany*, Camden Fourth Series 9 (London, 1972), p. 212; Michael M. N. Stansfield, 'The Hollands, Dukes of Exeter, Earls of Kent and Huntingdon, 1352–1475', (PhD, Oxford University, 1987), pp 242–3.

summarily beheaded.⁶⁶ Edward IV's sacrilege—a betrayal of his word, compounded by its being made in church, at mass, in the presence of the sacrament—may have been justified at that particular moment as a clear indication that traitors to his renewed regime should expect no quarter. His ability to cross that line was no doubt shaped by the political exigencies of the moment, but it was not to be a harbinger of a more general repudiation of sanctuary during his second reign. As the realm returned to ordinary time in the later 1470s and early 1480s, the records begin to show somewhat increased numbers of people seeking sanctuary for felony, particularly in chartered sanctuaries.⁶⁷

When Edward's brother Richard came to the throne in questionable circumstances in 1483, according to the chroniclers many fled to sanctuaries 'because of fear', as the Crowland chronicler put it.⁶⁸ For Richard III, however, seizing opponents from sanctuaries was not an option, because unlike his brother in 1471, he had little political capital to expend. Edward IV's widow, Queen Elizabeth, went into Westminster sanctuary again, just as she had in 1470–1471, along with her children, although the two princes, Edward and Richard, were soon surrendered to their uncle Richard III and put into the Tower.⁶⁹ For Richard, the sanctuary of the queen and her daughters at Westminster was potentially a threat: the Crowland chronicler indicates that it was bruited about that the daughters would be spirited abroad in case their brothers met with a desperate fate. Rather than seizing them, however, Richard put guards on the monastic precinct to prevent their escape, the chronicler said.

> Men of the greatest strictness...watched all entrances and exits of the monastery so that no one inside could get out and no one from outside could get in without [the captain's] permission. [As a result,] the sacred church of the monks of Westminster and the whole neighbourhood took on the appearance of a castle and a fortress.⁷⁰

Yet, tempting as it must have been, Richard did not actually breach Westminster sanctuary to seize the queen and her daughters; even in the case of the more direct danger to his rule that the younger prince, Richard duke of York, constituted, he reportedly negotiated a surrender rather than a breach.⁷¹ To do otherwise would presumably cost more for the fragile moral authority of his regime than any advantage a seizure would bring.

The use Richard's opponents made of sanctuaries, and his reluctance to violate them, augmented the sense that sanctuaries were a positive good, sites of merciful and sanctified protection against tyranny. This is how Henry VII chose at his accession to portray them: sanctuary was situated in the discourse of the regime change

---

⁶⁶ Lister M. Matheson, ed., '"Warkworth's" Chronicle: The Chronicle Attributed to John Warkworth, Master of Peterhouse, Cambridge', in *Death and Dissent: Two Fifteenth-Century Chronicles* (Rochester, NY, 1999), pp 113–14.
⁶⁷ See data in McSheffrey, 'Sanctuary Seekers'.
⁶⁸ Pronay and Cox, *Crowland Continuations*, p. 163, also p. 165.
⁶⁹ Vergil, *Three Books*, pp 175–8, 210; Fabyan, *New Chronicles*, p. 668.
⁷⁰ Pronay and Cox, *Crowland Continuations*, p. 163.
⁷¹ Fabyan, *New Chronicles*, p. 668 (Vergil, *Three Books*, p. 178, on the other hand indicates that the attempt to negotiate a surrender failed and the child was seized).

as a crucial safe haven for supporters of the new king, after a dark night of oppression and danger. Henry granted Piers Curteys, for instance, the office of keeper of the king's privy palace and wardrobe, 'in consideration of his true heart and service and of the great persecution, dangers and losses of goods, sustained by him in the king's cause, he having kept sanctuary at Westminster long time in sadness, punishment, and fear, awaiting the king's arrival'.[72] Chroniclers emphasized both that many took sanctuary during Richard's reign, and that upon Henry's landing in England in the summer of 1485 men poured out of the 'sundry sanctuaries' in which they had been hiding.[73]

Despite this rhetoric, it was of course highly inconvenient for an unstable new regime to tolerate the sheltering of dangerous opponents, and thus Henry VII was keen both to indicate his determination as a godly king to recognize these asylums and yet to find exceptions that would justify taking a traitor out, at least in egregious circumstances.[74] He was able to find such loopholes in at least two situations. In 1486, Richard III loyalist Humphrey Stafford sought sanctuary at Culham, a manor in Oxfordshire held by the abbey of Abingdon. The manor had been used as a sanctuary for debt in the fourteenth century and by this time claims were evidently being made for its sheltering of other misdoers as well, as was also the case with other dependent properties of religious houses around this time.[75] This was Stafford's second sanctuary-taking after Bosworth: he had fled along with Francis, Viscount Lovell to St John's Abbey in Colchester after the battle, and both were attainted for treason by parliament in the fall of 1485. The two men left their refuge in the spring of 1486, however, and raised an unsuccessful revolt against the king. Following that, Humphrey Stafford fled along with his younger brother Thomas to Culham and the two took the privilege there. Soon after, however, they were seized and taken into custody. At King's Bench Humphrey pleaded sanctuary, but after the abbot at Abingdon was unable to show any written evidence that it had previously been able to shelter traitors, the judges held that although Culham had sanctuary privileges, including for felony, it was not privileged specifically for treason. Thus Stafford was given the traitor's death of drawing, hanging, and quartering, although according to Polydore Vergil his younger brother Thomas was pardoned by the king.[76] Similarly, in 1487, Henry wrote a letter to Archbishop Rotherham of York, gently reminding him that although as king he was keen to see the 'privilege and franchise' of the archbishop's lordship of Hexham observed, two men who had sought asylum there, Thomas and Herbert Redshawe, had been arraigned and convicted of high

---

[72] *Calendar of Patent Rolls, 1232–1509*, 53 vols (London, 1891–1961), *1485–94*, p. 26.
[73] E.g. Fabyan, *New Chronicles*, 672; Pronay and Cox, *Crowland Continuations*, p. 165.
[74] Kaufman, 'Henry VII and Sanctuary', p. 469.
[75] See Ch. 4, 'Sanctuary claims at Hospitaller Properties, 1485–1520', and ch. 6.
[76] TNA, KB 27/900, rex m. 8; TNA, KB 15/42, fol 151r–155v; Seipp 1486.044 and 1486.048; Polydore Vergil, *The Anglica Historia of Polydore Vergil, A.D. 1485–1537*, ed. Denys Hay, Camden Series 74 (London, 1950), pp 11–13; C. H. Williams, 'The Rebellion of Humphrey Stafford in 1486', *The English Historical Review* 43 (1928): pp 181–9, doi:10.1093/ehr/XLIII.CLXX.181; S. B. Chrimes, *Henry VII* (London, 1972), p. 71; Kaufman, 'Henry VII and Sanctuary', p. 469.

treason, 'not upon no petty treason nor felony', and that handing them over would be no derogation to the archbishop's franchise.[77]

If the royal and legal opinions seemed to be strong that traitors could not find asylum at Culham or Hexham, both were acknowledged to be privileged for felony.[78] Nor were these decisions regarding treason and sanctuary at Culham and Hexham applicable generally, as traitors were able successfully to take sanctuary elsewhere. Several who participated in Perkin Warbeck's rebellions in the 1490s, for instance, took sanctuary after the particular episode in which they participated, including Warbeck himself, who spent some time at Beaulieu Abbey.[79] In one important case, four men—Thomas Bagnall, John Heth, John Skotte, and John Kenyngton—were accused of using the sanctuary of St Martin le Grand as a base from which to write and disseminate treasonous bills in support of Perkin Warbeck and against the king. The four were brought before King's Bench on charges of treason. Heth, Skotte, and Kenyngton pleaded not guilty, but were found guilty and sentenced to a traitor's death. Bagnall, on the other hand, pleaded sanctuary (his plea recorded in English):

> He saieth that he is a sanctuary man of St. Martin's, the sanctuary place beside Cheap, and was taken out of St. Martin's on Ash Wednesday against his will by Master Sampson and others and Master Digby being present, and prayeth thereto to be remitted [and] restored, and acknowledges the treason whereof he is arraigned.[80]

Bagnall's plea evidently succeeded.[81] At least two other rebels associated with Perkin Warbeck, men named Seyntbarbe and Bland, became fixtures in St Martin le Grand, both living there for some twenty years.[82] In other words, none of these rules were hard and fast: as in other issues connected to the legal status of sanctuary, the procedures were contingent rather than absolute, even as regards what might seem a straightforward issue, whether sanctuary extended to traitors as

---

[77] Eric E. Barker, ed., *The Register of Thomas Rotherham, Archbishop of York, 1480–1500*, Canterbury and York Society 69 (Torquay, Devon, 1976), vol. 1, p. 220; similar assurances regarding recognition of the bishop of Durham's franchise followed the arrest of a traitor at Hartlepool in 1491, James Gairdner, ed., *L&P Illustrative of the Reigns of Richard III and Henry VII*, Rolls Series (London, 1861), vol. 1, pp 98–100.

[78] Cases of sanctuary seekers at Culham: TNA, KB 9/449, m. 46 and KB 9/452, mm 1–2 (1507); KB 9/517, m. 90 (1531); KB 27/1089, rex m. 4 (1532). On the other hand, despite Henry's confirmation of Hexham's privileges for felony in his letter to the archbishop, I have not found cases of sanctuary seekers there, while a number of sanctuary seekers from Hexham sought sanctuary at the Durham cathedral: *SDSB*, pp 8, 14, 26, 29–30, 54, 83.

[79] Thomas and Thornley, *Great Chronicle*, p. 282.

[80] KB 9/78, m. 19; see also KB 9/78, mm 8–9; 20–21; KB 27/931, rex m. 6. In the original accusation, a fifth man, Alexander Synger, was also named as participant in the plots being carried out from St Martin's, but disappears from the records after that.

[81] On the King's Bench *coram rege* roll, no judgment is recorded (TNA, KB 27/931, rex m. 6; see also Thomas and Thornley, *Great Chronicle*, p. 250), but in a later legal discussion of the case recorded by John Port, Chief Justice Hussey remarks that the men from St Martin's who were beheaded were executed because they had not pleaded sanctuary, whereas the one who 'pray[ed] the protection of the place' had it. This must refer to Bagnall and his associates. John H. Baker, ed., *The Notebook of Sir John Port*, Selden Society 102 (London, 1986), p. 32; cf. Thornley, 'Destruction of Sanctuary', p. 199 n.86.

[82] TNA, C 24/3, 'Abbas', mm 15–16, 16–17; STAC 2/20/323, mm 19–23.

well as felons.[83] By the later years of Henry VII's reign, sanctuary was nonetheless well-entrenched in the English legal landscape, even if its boundaries would continue to be imprecise and contested into the 1530s.

SANCTUARY, MERCY, AND REDEMPTION

Mercy and royal authority were key underpinnings of the idea of sanctuary, both during the civil wars and after. Those ideas worked not only because kings employed them, but also because they were consonant with late medieval English Christianity more generally and the dominant mode of conceptualizing the relationship of Christian mercy to law, crime, and sin. The existence of sanctuaries was, it is true, incompatible with a strict discourse of due punishment for crime, as it allowed murderers and even sometimes traitors to escape their just deserts: certainly jurisdictional rivals, especially urban governments, employed that rhetoric when challenging the franchises of local religious houses, as we will see in Chapters 3, 4, and 5.

But that discourse was not the only, or indeed even the majority, point of view in the later fifteenth century. Despite what the anti-sanctuary rhetoric would suggest, many late medieval English people, and arguably most, had little difficulty in accommodating the seeming contradiction of the church's protection of criminals.[84] Mercy and charity towards the most despicable of sinners was a central pillar of late medieval Christianity, a reflection of the redemptive powers of Christ, just as the condemned criminal stood for the redeemer in the pageantry of execution.[85] The embrace rather than rejection of the felon in late medieval religious life is particularly illustrated by the late medieval popularity of the seven works of corporal mercy, active demonstrations of Christian piety derived from the gospel of Matthew (25:31–46). Christians were urged to feed the hungry, to give drink to the thirsty, to receive strangers, to clothe the naked, to visit the sick, to bury the dead—and to visit prisoners. The Seven Works of Mercy were found in popular devotional treatises and were a frequent subject of church wall paintings, with prisoners placed alongside the hungry, thirsty, the naked poor, and the sick and dying as deserving recipients of Christian alms. The

---

[83] Few cases involving traitors and sanctuary came up in the following decades, a situation that at least partly derived from relative civil peace in the realm in comparison to the fifteenth century, at least until the 1530s. John Cowley's odd case in 1518 involved charges of treason and heresy; when he pleaded that he had been seized from St Martin le Grand's sanctuary, the judges ruled that his plea was insufficient in law due to the heresy charge (a heretic, it was ruled, could not have any ecclesiastical asylum as he held opinions repugnant to the church), and he was sentenced immediately to execution without his case being put to a jury, although he had not entered a plea to the treason and heresy charges (possibly a church court had found him guilty of heresy?). TNA, KB 9/475/2; KB 27/1047, rex m. 8; John H. Baker, ed., *Reports of Cases by John Caryll*, Selden Society 115–16 (London, 1999), vol. 2, pp 693–5; John G. Bellamy, *The Tudor Law of Treason: An Introduction* (Toronto, 1979), pp 92–3. It was not until 1534 that traitors were definitively excluded from the privilege by statute. 26 Hen. VIII, c. 13 (*SR*, vol. 3, pp 508–9); Bellamy, *Tudor Law of Treason*, pp 92–3.

[84] Kesselring, *Mercy and Authority*, p. 17.

[85] Mitchell Merback, *The Thief, the Cross and the Wheel: Pain and the Spectacle of Punishment in Medieval and Renaissance Europe* (London, 1999), pp 126–57.

Seven Works also shaped late medieval English charity: common bequests in the wills of late medieval London citizens, for instance, were donations to prisoners in local gaols.[86]

In at least one case, a felon saved from the gallows by sanctuary went on to dedicate himself to God as a hermit, living out the promise of redemption that sanctuary symbolized. In 1537, London butcher George Isotson told a story of a man named Robert who some decades before had escaped from the Marshalsea prison in Southwark and then had run to St Martin le Grand for sanctuary. Afterward, Isotson said, Robert became a hermit in Islington. This is likely the same man as Robert Baker of the order of St Paul the Hermit, to whom the prior of St John of Jerusalem in Clerkenwell granted a property in Islington in 1511 for a hermitage.[87] According to Isotson, Robert was still in his hermitage in 1537, and his life story and the lessons about rehabilitation and redemption that it conveyed were also still being told twenty-five years later.

The Christian duty to succour the poor, the defenceless, and the imprisoned also fit well with contemporary suspicions about the sometimes arbitrary nature of politics and the courts of law.[88] Christian stories, including the 'legal' but unjust executions of the redeemer himself and the early martyrs, invited some scepticism about state judicial processes.[89] In the parish church in Pickering, North Yorkshire, for instance, a parishioner might easily notice that the image of the prisoner being visited as a work of mercy was virtually identical to the scene on another wall of the church where the martyr Katherine of Alexandria was imprisoned prior to her dreadful death.[90] The civil wars only augmented these suspicions that not all 'justice' was just, creating a complex and nuanced attitude towards legal process and due punishment rather than one marked by hard categories.

In contemporary rhetoric, those resorting to crime were connected conceptually to the unfortunate more generally, a connection made even stronger by the inclusion of debtors amongst the body of sanctuary seekers: a thin line separated the righteous and prosperous from those who through the turn of fortune's wheel lost all their goods or committed a desperate act of theft or violence.[91] Richard Caudray,

---

[86] See Matt. 25:36–44; Wynkyn de Worde, *The Crafte to Lyue Well* (Westminster, 1505), fol. 36r; Phillip Lindley, Miriam Gill, and Alex Moseley, *Seven Deadly Sins and Seven Corporal Works of Mercy*, 2001, http://www.le.ac.uk/arthistory/seedcorn/contents.html (2 Dec. 2008); Eamon Duffy, *The Stripping of the Altars: Traditional Religion in England 1400–1580* (New Haven, 1992), p. 360; Megan Cassidy-Welch, *Imprisonment in the Medieval Religious Imagination, c.1150–1400* (Basingstoke, 2011), pp 36–57.

[87] TNA, STAC 2/20/323, mm 29–30; BL, Cotton Nero E VI, Hospitaller Cartulary, fol. 93r, transcribed in Thomas Edlyne Tomlins, *Yseldon: A Perambulation of Islington* (London, 1858), pp 143–5. He could possibly also be the same Robert Baker who received a pardon in the general pardon of 1509: *L&P*, vol. 1, p. 204. On the order of St Paul the Hermit, see Virginia Davis, 'The Rule of Saint Paul, the First Hermit, in Late Medieval England', *Studies in Church History* 22 (1985): pp 203–14, doi:10.1017/S0424208400007956.

[88] Kesselring, 'Abjuration', pp 346, 357; Rosser, 'Sanctuary and Social Negotiation'.

[89] Merback, *The Thief, the Cross, and the Wheel*, pp 148–9.

[90] See Anne Marshall, 'The Life of St. Catherine, Pickering', and 'The Seven Works of Mercy, Pickering', 2002, http://paintedchurch.org/pickcat.htm, and http://paintedchurch.org/picker7w.htm.

[91] Amy Appleford, *Learning to Die in London, 1380–1540* (Philadelphia, 2015), p. 66.

dean of St Martin's, evoked the porousness of the line between the fortunate and the unfortunate when he argued in 1440 that

> Many of the aldermen, sheriffs, officers, and worshipful commoners of the said City [of London] have many times rejoiced and had the tuition and immunity of the said sanctuary [of St Martin le Grand], and namely for debt and trespass,... three hundred and more within a few years.[92]

Although this is probably an exaggerated number, we know that in the fifteenth century a number of prominent London merchants availed themselves of St Martin's and Westminster to flee from creditors.[93] As I will explore in Chapter 7, in the Tudor period sanctuary also increasingly became enmeshed in aristocratic feud strategies, heightening for the realm's most powerful decision-makers a sense of identification with the sanctuary seekers.

The most influential modern writing on sanctuary, however, has assumed a much more black and white attitude towards crime and sanctuary, a view most explicitly voiced by Isobel Thornley, who wrote that 'all sensible laymen'[94] must have deplored sanctuary and that it was only because of the undue power of ecclesiastical authorities that it survived into the Tudor period. The premise that no 'sensible' men supported sanctuary has led to misreadings of several oft-quoted passages from Thomas More's *Historie of kyng Rychard the thirde*. More wrote his *Historie* in the mid-1510s, but it was printed only after his death.[95] In one scene in this dramatic narrative of Richard III's reign, one of the source-texts for Shakespeare's later play, the king's councillors debate the nature of sanctuary privilege. Although Cardinal Bourchier defends the absolute inviolability of sanctuary—'God forbid that any man should, for any thing earthly, enterprise to break the immunity and liberty of that sacred sanctuary, that hath been the safeguard of so many a good man's life'—the duke of Buckingham opines that 'good men' could 'without sin' breach sanctuary in certain circumstances. Buckingham goes on to outline at some length the abuses of sanctuary. Although he admits that there were some for whom sanctuary is a positive benefit (debtors who have lost all their goods at sea or who are pursued by 'cruel creditors', or those caught on one side or the other of the civil wars), for the most part sanctuaries are populated by much less deserving recipients of mercy, 'a rabble of thieves, murderers, and malicious heinous traitors', along with men who cannot manage their money and abused wives who run away with their husbands' plate. Indeed, sanctuary provided for thieves and murderers the opportunity to continue to commit their crimes with impunity, sallying out repeatedly from sanctuary to kill or steal and then running back to the shelter of the privilege.[96]

[92] Westminster Abbey Library and Muniments, Muniment Book 5, *Registrum Collegii Sancti Martini Magni, London*, fol. 49r.
[93] TNA, C 49/68/21; Reginald R. Sharpe, ed., *Calendar of Letter-Books, Letter Book K (1422–1460)* (London, 1911), pp 241–3; Thomas and Thornley, *Great Chronicle*, p. 195.
[94] Thornley, 'Destruction of Sanctuary', p. 186.
[95] On the date of composition, see Seymour Baker House, 'More, Sir Thomas', *ODNB* (2004), doi:10.1093/ref:odnb/19191.
[96] Thomas More, *The History of King Richard the Third*, Complete Works 2 (New Haven, 1963), pp 27–30.

Thornley and others (including me) have cited Buckingham's speech as an illustration of objections of many laymen to the practice of sanctuary, equating the sentiments Buckingham expresses with More's own opinion on the subject.[97] Such a reading seems best described, however, as the result of what scientists call 'confirmation bias': (mis)interpreting one's data to confirm an a priori assumption, in this case that the 'sensible' Thomas More could not have supported sanctuary.[98] As literary scholars have noted, this interpretation neither takes into account Buckingham's full speech, nor its place within the narrative of the *Historie*.[99] Buckingham's purpose in giving this oration to the king's council was to convince the councillors that, if necessary, they should breach Westminster sanctuary to seize the duke of York, the younger of Edward IV's two sons. King Richard already had custody of the older brother, the young King Edward V, and he sought custody of the younger prince in order, of course, to carry out his nefarious plot to kill his nephews. Buckingham was, at this stage in the narrative, Richard's partner and, read in context, his speech is clearly manipulative and mendacious. Sanctuary, Buckingham argued, was not generally necessary, for surely anyone who needed protection would be accorded it by his king; and certainly it was not specifically necessary for the duke of York, who had no need to fear what would happen to him were he to leave its confines. Buckingham is able by this speech to convince the councillors that it is right and just to demand that the dowager queen release her son from sanctuary; the dowager queen herself, seeing no choice and gambling that cooperation will be best for her child, does so. And of course the prince goes from sanctuary to his death, at the order of the king whom the duke of Buckingham had promised he had no need to fear.[100]

It is thus hard to see Buckingham's strident attack on sanctuary—delivered by a villain, and instrumental in Richard III's evil plot to kill the princes—as a straightforward reflection of More's own view. Buckingham's argument that sanctuary is not necessary is belied by the prince's fate; indeed, More seems to be arguing here for the necessity of such asylums in the face of tyranny, rather than the opposite. Aspects of Buckingham's case against sanctuary may indeed have reflected arguments made in canon law treatises[101] and more generally in urban governments' attacks on the privilege, but based on how sanctuary was employed in his narrative in *The Historie of Richard the Third*, More's own point of view in the mid-1510s

---

[97] E.g. Thornley, 'Destruction of Sanctuary', p. 186; Kaufman, 'Henry VII and Sanctuary', pp 470–1; Loades, 'The Sanctuary', p. 87; Baker, *Oxford History, 1485–1558*, p. 545; Shannon McSheffrey, 'Sanctuary and the Legal Topography of Pre-Reformation London', *Law and History Review* 27 (2009): p. 513, doi:10.1017/S0738248000003886.

[98] Thornley, 'Destruction of Sanctuary', p. 186. Although some might argue that More was not particularly sensible, this is Thornley's adjective.

[99] E.g. Arthur Noel Kincaid, 'The Dramatic Structure of Sir Thomas More's History of King Richard III', *Studies in English Literature, 1500–1900* 12 (1972): pp 233–5, doi:10.2307/449891; Elizabeth Story Donno, 'Thomas More and Richard III', *Renaissance Quarterly* 35 (1982): pp 430–2, doi:10.2307/2861062; Alan Clarke Shepard, '"Female Perversity", Male Entitlement: The Agency of Gender in More's The History of Richard III', *Sixteenth Century Journal* 26 (1995): pp 324–7, doi:10.2307/2542793; Allen, 'Once and Future King'.

[100] More, *History*, pp 34–42.

[101] As Thornley pointed out ('Destruction of Sanctuary', p. 186; and as Helmholz details (*Ius Commune*, pp 75–6).

was at best equivocal. As we will see in the pages that follow, by the evidence of the seeking of sanctuary in the first third of the sixteenth century, and the way the courts handled those sanctuary claims, More was not alone. The attitude of More and his contemporaries in the 1510s towards sanctuary was likely coloured by the still-recent experience of regime change and indeed of tyranny, a tyranny that made the mercy and protection of sanctuaries a necessity rather than an evil.

ECCLESIASTICAL LIBERTIES AS A WEAPON AGAINST TYRANNY: ST EDMUND AND SHERIFF LEOFFSTAN

By the early sixteenth century, then, amongst the conditions that allowed for the expansion of sanctuary as ideology and practice was concern with corruption and tyranny, for which sanctuary was seen by some to provide a necessary remedy. This anxiety about tyranny was of course nothing new, and to take us back to the first half of the fifteenth century, where our next chapter starts, let us look at a saint's life that features a sanctuary miracle. This tale serves as an effective bridge, because it offers the protection of the church's franchises and liberties—of which sanctuary was a potent exemplar—as a solution to the problem of tyranny. *The Life of St. Edmund, King and Martyr* was written in the mid-1430s by the English poet John Lydgate, monk at the Benedictine abbey at Bury St Edmunds.[102] The work was almost certainly made at the request of Lydgate's abbot, William Curteys, for presentation to the young King Henry VI, in commemoration of a lengthy stay Henry had made at the abbey in 1433–1434, when he was about twelve.[103] The lavishly illustrated presentation copy made for the king, rightly called one of the most remarkable manuscripts of its age, is now in the British Library.[104] St Edmund had, like the young Henry VI, been a king, ruling over the East Angles during the ninth century. He valiantly fought against the invading Danes and died as a martyr. Edmund's shrine in the monastery at Bury became a popular pilgrimage site as early as the tenth century. In presenting a modern version of Edmund's life to Henry VI, the abbot (and Lydgate) hoped to cement an enduring tie between the abbey and their monarch.

Lydgate's 'translation', as he called it, was for much of the work more adaptation than strict rendering from Latin sources.[105] As we will see in Chapter 3, it is no surprise in the context of the 1430s that Lydgate's story of a sanctuary miracle

---

[102] John Lydgate, *John Lydgate's 'Lives of Ss Edmund & Fremund' and the 'Extra Miracles of St Edmund'*, ed. Anthony Bale and A. S. G. Edwards, Middle English Texts 41 (Heidelberg, 2009). On Lydgate, see Douglas Gray, 'Lydgate, John (c. 1370–1449/50?)', *ODNB* (2004), doi:10.1093/ref:odnb/17238.
[103] See A. S. G. Edwards, 'Introduction', in *The Life of St. Edmund, King and Martyr: John Lydgate's Illustrated Verse Life, Presented to Henry VI*, by John Lydgate (London, 2004).
[104] British Library, Harley MS 2278 (http://www.bl.uk/manuscripts/FullDisplay.aspx?ref=Harley_MS_2278); see also the facsimile edition: Lydgate, *Life of St. Edmund, King and Martyr*.
[105] Edwards, 'Introduction', pp 6–7.

worked by St Edmund was one that plucked particular notes, particularly those emphasizing and equating 'sanctuary' and 'franchise'.[106] Lydgate begins this tale with the general lesson the example would impart: that no 'tyrant' dared to try to break St Edmund's franchise without being punished soon after. His example was the story of the sheriff Leoffstan, who had no devotion to St Edmund and cared little for the saint's miracles. Indifferent as he was to Edmund, Leoffstan had no hesitation in arresting within the abbey church a guilty woman who had taken refuge at St Edmund's shrine 'for dread of death'. Lydgate here followed his exemplar in using a woman as the sanctuary seeker; although female seekers, as we have seen, were rare indeed in this period, if anything her plight as victim of the rapacious sheriff was augmented by her gender. Finding her in the church, the sheriff seized the woman with 'force and violence, unto the saint doing no reverence' (see Figure. 2.7). Clerks who were there hearing divine service resisted, 'defending the franchise' of Edmund's church, but the sheriffs' officers, 'ravenous like hounds', could not be stopped. The woman cried out so that all could hear: 'Help, blessed Edmund!... for but thou help, I shall in haste be dead. Keep and conserve thy jurisdiction from this tyrant, or this day I shall die'. Leoffstan, however, would not 'obey', and insisted on entering the church to sit in judgment on her, with 'no reverence done to the sanctuary'. With violence his officers carried the woman forth, and there and then within the abbey itself her case was put before importuned jurors, who found against her. The sheriff, as judge, proceeded to judgment and execution. The woman died, but true justice nonetheless prevailed: afterward, by St Edmund's reluctant but necessary retribution, a fiend took possession of the 'tyrant' sheriff, and after suffering extreme torments all over his body he was soon dead.

This tale fits into the 'well, they would say that, wouldn't they?' category: it is no surprise that a saint's life written by a monk at the behest of an abbot would include a miracle that emphasized so strongly the evil attendant on breaching the sanctuary of a religious house.[107] There are several things about this story that are of interest nonetheless. First, the timing: Lydgate translated and shaped this anecdote in the later 1430s. As we will see in Chapter 3, this was a moment when issues relating to sanctuary had heated up, both because religious houses, such as St Martin le Grand, were making stronger claims about their franchisal liberties in general and sanctuary in particular, and because other authorities, such as the

---

[106] Lydgate, *John Lydgate's 'Lives of Ss Edmund & Fremund'*, pp 121–3. As editors Bale and Edwards note (ibid., p. 170), Lydgate's rendering of this story was based on a late fourteenth-century Latin life of Edmund, now Oxford, Bodleian Library, Bodley MS 240 (see Carl Horstmann, ed., *Nova Legenda Anglie* [Oxford, 1901], vol. 2, p. 593). It is similar to Lydgate's version, but it emphasizes sacrilege rather than the breaking of franchise, and the woman is able to escape back into her asylum as the sheriff writhed in the agony of demonic possession.

[107] A sermon likely dating from *c.* 1420, written by a Benedictine at Oxford, equates sanctuary breaches to seize felons with breaking God's commandments; as the sermon's editor, Patrick J. Horner, comments, the sermons in this cycle were part of 'an evolving ecclesiastical strategy for defending the privileges of the church', tying defence of the church to support for the Lancastrian kings and opposition to the Lollards. This is a standpoint similar to that of the Benedictines at Bury. Horner, *Macaronic Sermons*, pp 1, 328.

Figure 2.7. Sheriff Leoffstan seizing the sanctuary-seeking woman.
© The British Library Board, Harley MS 2278, fol. 106r.

sheriffs in the City of London, resisted this encroachment on their jurisdiction (or the space or action they hoped to make their jurisdiction). Lydgate highlights precisely what the dean of St Martin's, Richard Caudray, would emphasize a few years later in 1440, repeatedly linking the sheriff's sanctuary breach with his attack on the 'franchise' and 'jurisdiction' of St Edmund and his abbey. The sacral space of the shrine and the legal rights and liberties of the abbey's franchise were the same.

Although Lydgate's arguments tying together the sacred space of the shrine and the sacrilege attendant on breaching the abbey's franchises were what one would expect from a monastic writer, we should not assume that those arguments about the intersection of sacrality, justice, and jurisdiction did not resonate more broadly. Lydgate's arguments also had a clearly political edge to them: at the same time as he maintains the theme in his source text of sacrilege leading to demonic possession and death, his emphasis is less on sacrilege as such than on the tyranny such a breach constituted. And the tyrant in question was not one of Henry VI's illustrious progenitors as king, but instead the fifteenth-century epitome of the petty local tyrant, a sheriff.[108] Instead of attributing debates over ecclesiastical franchise to divisions between the church and secular authorities, Lydgate emphasizes that the franchise's defence came from Henry's royal predecessor. The saintly King Edmund—reluctant though he was to 'make affray', as Lydgate put it—was forced to deliver a terrible sanction to one who would ignore 'his' franchise. This is what a godly king does: he protects his franchises and his sanctuaries against the Leoffstans of the present day. By doing so, the king aligns himself against tyranny and with true justice, which all too often diverged from the kind of justice earthly courts dispensed.

Lydgate's message would have appealed not only to Henry VI, who as we will see acted in Edmund-like fashion in his defence of sanctuary, but also to his successors. With a few exceptions, the privileged sanctuaries were protected by fifteenth- and early sixteenth-century English kings as demonstrations of, rather than challenges to, royal authority. As we will see in our examination of particular disputes in Chapters 3, 4, and 5, Henry VI, Edward IV, Richard III, Henry VII, and Henry VIII supported sanctuaries at least partly because they served to demonstrate to the urban governments that challenged the privileges and franchises of religious houses that the king was the final authority. This was more than political gamesmanship, however; observing sanctuary not only emphasized limitations on the powers of local civic officials and sheriffs, but also aligned that royal power with the mercy and justice of God.

From the earliest examples of wrongdoers seeking permanent asylum in English ecclesiastical precincts at the end of the fourteenth century to the reign of Henry VII, sanctuary became an established feature of the English legal and cultural landscape. As the century ended, increasing numbers of felons took advantage of the centuries-old practice of church-taking and abjuration. Even more strikingly, a new form of sanctuary—asylum unlimited in time within the boundaries of certain ecclesiastical precincts—had developed over the century or so after 1380. Borrowing conceptually from the refuge ecclesiastical powers such as Westminster Abbey offered to debtors, increasingly over the fifteenth century the franchises certain religious houses possessed came to include the right to shelter felons and even, in some cases, traitors. Sanctuary was conceptually tied to mercy and to the succour the church offered to any in need of protection; the regime changes of the civil wars of the second half of the fifteenth century augmented an already established link. As Lydgate's *Life of St. Edmund* illustrates, the protection of ecclesiastical franchise as bulwark against judicial corruption also resonated. We will turn in Chapter 3 to consider in detail how a fifteenth-century churchman could wield those ideas in the defence of sanctuary privilege.

---

[108] On sheriffs as especially corruptible both in 'real life' and in the assumptions of fifteenth-century literature including and beyond the Robin Hood tales, Carpenter, 'Law, Justice and Landowners', pp 218, 231–2.

3

Dean Caudray and the City of London
The Politics of Sanctuary in the Fifteenth Century

THE ESCAPE OF JOHN KNIGHT

While he was in Cambridge in early September 1440, Richard Caudray, dean of the royal free chapel of St Martin le Grand in London, received an urgent letter from his canons.[1] After a hurried address—'Full reverent Master, we recommend us entirely unto you'—the canons launched directly into an account of recent and frightening events in St Martin's. The day before, 1 September, a sheriff's servant was leading a prisoner, a soldier named John Knight, from Newgate gaol to the London Guildhall, where he was to stand trial that afternoon. As Knight and the sheriff's servant walked past the butchers' shops in the Shambles, four of the soldier's companions suddenly burst out of an alley, 'with daggers drawn'.[2] They seized Knight away from the custody of his guard and fled with him to the door of the nearby St Martin le Grand church. There all five claimed sanctuary. Soon after the sheriffs, the alderman of the ward,[3] and the City's chamberlain, together with a 'great multitude of people', came into the church and demanded that the dean's deputy give up the prisoner and his rescuers to their custody. The deputy, however, refused to surrender them without the commandment of the absent dean. After some blustering on both sides, the canons and the City representatives agreed the sanctuary seekers would be double-fettered with irons lent by the London sheriffs and locked into the dean's own prison, awaiting his return.

The sheriffs, aldermen, and chamberlain left St Martin's precinct and, as the canons' letter indicates, the St Martin's clergy thought the situation had been

---

[1] *Registrum*, fols 41rv, and the aftermath fols 41v–58r. The episode has been described in Kempe, *Historical Notices*, pp 116–32; Thornley, 'Destruction of Sanctuary', pp 190–1; Caroline M. Barron, 'The Government of London and Its Relations with the Crown 1400–1450', (PhD, University of London, 1970), pp 397–401. My reading differs from these previous interpretations in its speculations about the sequence of events and in its more sceptical approach especially to the civic records. See also more generally for St Martin's, Reddan, 'Collegiate Church'.

[2] *Registrum*, fols 41r, 43r, 44r, 45v; LMA, Letter Book K, fol. 189r, calendared in Sharpe, *Cal. Letter Book K*, 242; A. E. Stamp, et al., eds, *Calendar of Close Rolls*, 47 vols (London, 1900–1963), *1435–41*, p. 392. Sources differ on the number of men who attacked the sheriff's servant, although four seems to be the correct number.

[3] Although the alderman was not named, the City considered St Martin's to be in Aldersgate ward, the alderman of which was John Sutton in 1440. Alfred B. Beaven, *The Aldermen of the City of London, Temp. Henry III—1908* (London, 1908), p. 2.

defused. But then 'suddenly' at supper time the unwitting canons were beset by the sheriffs, the undersheriffs, and (again) a 'great multitude of people', who demanded once more that Knight and his four confederates be delivered into their custody. The dean's deputy again valiantly refused, but the unarmed canons were no match for the sheriffs and their henchmen, who forcibly dragged Knight and the others out of the sanctuary. The canons ended their letter to the dean by saying that they did not know what would transpire in this case, although they feared the worst. Just before they wrote their letter on the day following the incident, the canons had seen the prisoners being led from Newgate. Dressed only in their linen undergarments, they were chained two by two by the neck and manacled 'as traitors'. The sheriffs' servants led them right by the gate of St Martin's, as if to mock the sanctuary. 'As we be informed', the canons lamented, they 'be like to be dead in all haste'. They beseeched the dean to send them instructions as soon as possible on how to deal with this crisis and, if possible, to return himself 'in all the haste that ye may'. They signed off: 'Written at London with heavy hearts, the second day of September'. This letter was written into a remarkable account of the ensuing conflict over the seizure of Knight and his fellows that Dean Caudray assembled, preserving (and likely embroidering) a record of what he considered to be a crucial encounter with the City. As we will see in this chapter, the City's version of what happened that day was rather different, although perhaps even more embroidered than the dean's account.

The sheriffs' seizure of John Knight and his fellows from St Martin le Grand on 1 September 1440 precipitated a legal and political conflict between the City of London and the collegiate church of St Martin le Grand over the nature and extent of St Martin's sanctuary privileges. That battle brought in the king, his council, and leading churchmen and legal thinkers. The 1440 clash was an early and important episode in a conflict between the City and St Martin's that would last well beyond the medieval period, and in many ways it established for both sides the legal and rhetorical premises on which the battle would be fought over at least the subsequent century. When the dean of St Martin's and the mayor and aldermen of London each appealed to the crown, they raised a host of issues about the late medieval polity; they each also left behind abundant archival remains from the conflict that both enrich and complicate our ability to understand how those issues played out. Those records show us at an unusual level of detail how the heads of religious houses and their strategists constructed claims for sanctuary privilege, and how other bodies—especially civic authorities—responded when they found those privileges encroached on their own developing ideas about jurisdiction. Sanctuary privileges expanded and shifted over the course of the fifteenth century, as both longstanding concepts and contingent circumstances affected the way sanctuary-seeking developed: the broader ideological importance of the church's liberties and immunities in the preservation of peace and the demonstration of mercy converged with the personality of the monarch and the tactics that best suited a period of civil war and frequent regime change.

ST MARTIN LE GRAND AND THE CITY OF LONDON: LIBERTIES, FRANCHISES, AND JURISDICTIONS

Key both to the dispute in 1440, and the other contests waged between the church and the City through the fifteenth century and the first half of the sixteenth, was St Martin's status as an ecclesiastical liberty—a small territory possessing a considerable measure of juridical and political autonomy from other civil and ecclesiastical authorities. St Martin le Grand was a royal free chapel founded in Anglo-Saxon times, before 1503 governed by the dean and canons of the College of St Martin, after 1503 absorbed into the lands attached to Westminster Abbey and ruled by the abbot.[4] St Martin le Grand church stood less than 200 metres north of St Paul's cathedral. Its precinct, comprised of properties in the close surrounding the church and on both sides of St Martin's Lane, was a bit more than a hectare, about the size of the grassy area inside a modern 400-metre athletics track. Despite being within the walls of the City of London, indeed steps away from the Guildhall—the seat of London's civic government—and from St Paul's—the home church of the bishop of London—St Martin's claimed to be independent of both. In arguing for the right of John Knight and his rescuers to take asylum in his church, Dean Caudray contended that, as an aspect of its status as a liberty, the royal free chapel of St Martin le Grand could offer unlimited sanctuary along with manifold other privileges and immunities. Indeed, they had done so, he said, for centuries, even from before the Conquest, a claim the dean 'proved' with a charter granted by William the Conqueror confirming those privileges, written in Old English, a copy of which he helpfully provided in his submission to the crown. The City of London, conversely, argued that St Martin le Grand had no particular privileges at all, and had never had, but was and had always been entirely under the City's governance and purview, such that London's sheriffs had every right to seize and drag away any fugitive found within the chapel's precinct.

Neither of these contentions, however, was well founded. The City's claim was clearly contrary to fact: St Martin le Grand had long been a liberty outside the City's jurisdiction, and in any case the forcible seizure of a sanctuary seeker from any church, within the City or not, was indefensible. Conversely, despite the long-standing basis of many of its liberties and privileges, St Martin le Grand's particular claim to offer sanctuary to felons for a period unlimited in time did not go back anywhere near as far as the Anglo-Saxon period. Although we cannot say with certainty when St Martin le Grand or any other English religious house began to offer a permanent form of sanctuary to felons, as we have seen, the surviving evidence indicates that such a practice likely went back only about fifty years before John Knight's request.

[4] On St Martin Le Grand, see Kempe, *Historical Notices*; Reddan, 'Collegiate Church'; Thornley, 'Sanctuary in Medieval London'; Thornley, 'Destruction of Sanctuary'; Marjorie B. Honeybourne, 'The Sanctuary Boundaries and Environs of Westminster Abbey and the College of St. Martin-Le-Grand', *Journal of the British Archaeological Association* 38 (1932): pp 316–34; Caroline M. Barron, *London in the Later Middle Ages: Government and People 1200–1500* (Oxford, 2004), pp 36–7.

If the broad sanctuary claims of certain religious houses grew from their long-standing privileges as liberties, so also did much of the opposition to their exercise of those sanctuary claims intertwine with antipathy to their liberty status. Town and city authorities in particular—in many cases themselves flexing and extending their own jurisdictional muscles in this period—resisted and challenged both the sanctuary claims and other franchisal liberties of local religious houses.[5] Their attacks revealingly conflated franchisal disputes, such as the right to hold assizes of bread, with the right to shelter felons fleeing from arrest.[6] And London was, not surprisingly, at the forefront, both because of its powerful and precocious development as an urban government, and because of the host of liberties and peculiars within and just beyond its boundaries. The kingdom's largest urban centre constituted a patchwork quilt of legal jurisdictions, very much to the chagrin of the City itself. Although the mayor and aldermen of London were wont to say that the 'chief and most commodious place of the City of London' constituted 'one whole County and one whole Jurisdiction and liberty' over which its citizens ruled, saving only the authority of the king himself,[7] this confident assertion of the City's authority over the metropolitan square mile was constantly belied by the presence of these liberties.

The liberties in London were territories set apart—as its dean Richard Caudray put it, St Martin Le Grand was located in a space both 'in and yet not of the City'.[8] St Martin's privileges were more extensive than the other liberties in late medieval London, but it was by no means alone as a peculiar jurisdiction within the City limits or in its immediate outskirts. The monasteries, nunneries, and hospitals that dotted the City, some with relatively extensive precincts with tenements leased to lay residents, had varying liberties and immunities, especially as concerned guild regulation. They thus often contained, as St Martin's had developed by the mid-fifteenth century, considerable populations of debtors and immigrant artisans who were unable to work within City jurisdiction.[9] Similarly, some non-ecclesiastical territories were outside the City jurisdictionally, if within it geographically: such was the case with the manor of Blanchappleton, a privately-held manor in (but not of) Aldgate ward until the City was able to bring it at least partially under its jurisdiction in the 1470s, and two of the law inns (where common lawyers trained, worked, and often lived) within the City boundaries, Barnard's Inn and Thavie's Inn. All of these privileged areas disrupted the City's authority simply by their

---

[5] See below, Chs 4 and 5.

[6] H. Carrel, 'Disputing Legal Privilege: Civic Relations with the Church in Late Medieval England', *Journal of Medieval History* 35 (2009): pp 279–96, doi:10.1016/j.jmedhist.2009.06.001; Peter Fleming, 'Conflict and Urban Government in Later Medieval England: St Augustine's Abbey and Bristol', *Urban History* 27 (2000): pp 325–43, doi:10.1017/S0963926800000316.

[7] E.g. LMA, Journal 13, fol. 467r; TNA, STAC, 2/20/324, m. 5. As Tom Johnson has noted, late medieval English towns and cities often employed this rhetoric of entirety in reference to their jurisdictions, but it is important to recognize these assertions as political claims rather than legal facts. Johnson, 'Law, Space, and Local Knowledge', p. 87.

[8] *Registrum*, fol. 57v; Henry VI repeated this locution in a writ (ibid., fol. 70r), and it was used in a neutral way as an example of the difference between the prepositions 'in' and 'of' at the court of Common Pleas in 1475; Seipp 1475.052.

[9] See Ch. 5 at n.13.

presence, and some were depicted in civic records as havens of wrongdoers fleeing City jurisdiction. By the City's rhetoric, Blanchappleton harboured illegal workers and permitted sexual immorality; the precincts of the hospitals of St Katherine by the Tower and of St Mary Spital, both on the eastern limits of the City, and the Clink manor across the river in Southwark were notorious for fostering prostitutes and thieves. St Katherine's moreover served as a sanctuary for debtors being sued in London's courts. Although they did not have the same sanctuary status for felony as claimed by St Martin's and Westminster, their residents nonetheless were able to profit from their status as territories in or immediately neighbouring the City, and yet outside the reach of London's sheriffs, mayor, aldermen, and their courts and guilds.[10]

The mayor and aldermen felt that St Martin le Grand especially, with its capacious privileges, directly challenged their authority, and from the early fifteenth century to the mid-sixteenth century they engaged in a running battle, both legal and political, with the ecclesiastical authorities who governed the sanctuary. That campaign was particularly active in the period between the 1420s and 1450s, when the City was at its zenith of self-confidence. Civic leaders like mayor Richard Whittington and common clerk John Carpenter developed expansive ideas about the lay elite's governance of the city, a governance that encompassed both secular and spiritual responsibilities. As part of their extension of what they considered their proper authority, the City challenged other jurisdictions, especially ecclesiastical rights-holders such as the bishop of London and the dean of St Martin's.[11] As we have seen, St Martin's had been offering sanctuary to debtors from at least the 1370s, and by the evidence of the 1402 Londoners' petition to parliament decrying its sheltering of thieves, murderers, and other wrongdoers, it had begun by the turn of the century also to offer asylum to felons.[12] This apparent expansion of the privileges of St Martin's rankled the City of London. In the 1410s and 1420s, London citizens and St Martin le Grand engaged in legal tussles heard in the court of Common Pleas over the London sheriffs' ability to seize debtors who had taken sanctuary there, and over who had the right to recover stolen goods brought into the sanctuary by thieves taking asylum in St Martin's.[13]

---

[10] Mary S. Lobel, 'The Wards c. 1520, including extra-parochial areas', in *The City of London from Prehistoric Times to C. 1520* (Oxford, 1989); Barron, 'Government of London', p. 396; Barron, *London*, pp 35–6; Tucker, *Law Courts*, pp 43–5.

[11] See Barron, *London*, pp 10, 305–6; Caroline M. Barron and Marie-Hélène Rousseau, 'Cathedral, City and State', in *St. Paul's: The Cathedral Church of London, 604–2004*, ed. Derek Keene, Andrew Saint, and Arthur Burns (New Haven, 2004), pp 34–5; Appleford, *Learning to Die*, pp 6, 11, 55–97.

[12] *PROME*, Parl. Sept. 1402, ¶70. A King's Bench indictment for later that decade, 1407, is the first I have located showing a felon fleeing to St Martin le Grand for long-term asylum (rather than prelude to abjuration). TNA, KB/9/201/3, mm 34–35. There is a case in 1324 that shows a sanctuary seeker in St Martin le Grand calling for a coroner to abjure. Sharpe, *Calendar of Coroners Rolls*, p. 80. The City cited this case as part of its case in 1440: *Registrum*, fol. 52v.

[13] Richard Caudray transcribed (or had transcribed) entries related to several cases from Common Pleas, which he argued supported his claims for St Martin's privileges (see below at n.58 for discussion of his use of the cases). See *Registrum*, fols 37v–39r, 63v–64v. For instance, Edmund Chymbeham v. Simon Floure and William Gerveys, canons of St Martin le Grand, over recovered stolen goods surrendered on entry into the sanctuary. This case continued from 1419 to at least 1426—without a clear resolution that I have located. TNA, CP 40/634, rot. 452, CP 40/647, rot. 111d; TNA, CP 40/654,

A 1430 case involving two apostate canons from the Augustinian priory at Waltham, Essex, who had fled their life in religion for reasons the record does not reveal, is the first to leave behind a more substantial record. The case was not, however, definitive, as it evidently ended without any declaration by the king's council one way or the other regarding whether St Martin's could shelter the fugitive canons.[14] The argumentative strategies the two sides employed in their submissions to the crown about the matter are nonetheless significant. The dean of St Martin le Grand, Thomas Bourchier, a young aristocrat whose tenure as dean was prelude to a stellar career in ecclesiastical and royal service,[15] appealed specifically to the grounding of the collegiate church's privileges in royal grant dating as far back as the Conquest, while also gesturing towards the particular harm to the king's peace by violence done in his churches. The City's claims conversely did not admit of any privileges or liberties for St Martin's at all. Each made arguments that those who crafted them must have known were exaggerated, if not outright misleading. Neither side addressed directly the legal question that might have occupied the commission of the king's council—whether sanctuary was available for the offence of apostasy, a legal anomaly sitting at the juncture between ecclesiastical and common law.[16] For the City to address the question would be to allow that St Martin's had some kinds of sanctuary rights, if perhaps not this one; for St Martin's to address it would be to concede that there might be limitations on its privileges.

---

rot. 391. The latter two entries are indexed in Jonathan Mackman and Matthew Stevens, 'Court of Common Pleas: The National Archives, CP40, 1399–1500', *British History Online*, 2010, http://www.british-history.ac.uk/no-series/common-pleas/1399-1500. See also *John and Joyce Shenefeld and Rose Barnet v John Cavendyssh*, a debt case, TNA, CP 40/653, rot. 104 (indexed in Mackman and Stevens, 'Court of Common Pleas'); CP 40/673, rots. 318 and 391; and *John and Ellen Portyngton v William Rosselyn*, another debt case, TNA, CP 40/654, rot. 318.

[14] *Registrum*, fols 35r–36v; LMA, Letter Book K, fol. 72r, 120r–123r. No record survives of a determination made by the royal councilors deputed to hear the matter, and neither the City nor St Martin's introduced the case as a precedent for their arguments in later disputes, suggesting that both sides failed to achieve a clear statement of their rights from the council. Although both Reginald R. Sharpe and Isobel Thornley argue that the king's council clearly confirmed the City's assertions in this dispute, this is based on a misreading of a record related to this dispute in the City's Letter Book K; they read the entry as showing that the king's council endorsed the City's claims that St Martin's had no privileges of any kind, but the entry in question does not actually indicate that the Council 'certified' the City's claims (as Sharpe translated it), but rather only that the City *made* the claims to the Council: '…sicut docebatur expresse coram certis dominis de consilio Regis ad hoc audiendum assignatis [as it was expressly *argued* before certain lords of the king's council assigned to hear it]'. LMA, Letter Book K, fol. 72r; Sharpe, *Cal. Letter Book K*, pp 106–7, 152–4; Thornley, 'Destruction of Sanctuary', p.189.

[15] Bourchier, second son of a highly connected noble family, had been appointed to the position in 1427 at the tender age of about sixteen, and thus in 1430 would have been in his late teens and only recently ordained a subdeacon. Linda Clark, 'Bourchier, Thomas (c.1411–1486), Cardinal and Archbishop of Canterbury', *ODNB* (2004), doi:10.1093/ref:odnb/2993. The young dean may have had help from more experienced canons in shaping St Martin's strategies at this stage, although he was later to show tremendous abilities in his subsequent career as archbishop, cardinal, and chancellor.

[16] See F. Donald Logan, *Runaway Religious in Medieval England, c.1240–1540* (Cambridge, 1996), pp 97–120.

Given that the affair of the canons of Waltham appears to have ended inconclusively, it is not surprising that through the 1430s issues between the City and St Martin's continued to fester.[17] If the deans were resolute in their defence of the privileges of St Martin's, the City's civic leaders were equally determined both to fight against challenges to the City's liberties and to rein in potential threats to order—and the problem of the 'privileged places' within and beside the City epitomized both these dangers. A number of incidents that made their way into the records in the 1430s indicate heightening tensions between the City and the liberties. In the City's view, criminals and murderers were being sheltered in St Martin's and the other liberties in the City, thereby escaping punishment for their felonies.[18] In reaction, as the City records document, the mayor, aldermen, and sheriffs began a campaign to challenge such rights, the mayor himself participating in at least one seizure of a felon and traitor from St Katherine's in 1438.[19] If anything, this situation heated up further in the summer of 1440 as even more concern about sanctuary, crime, and disorder is evident in the City's records. On 22 August 1440—little more than a week before the seizure of John Knight and his fellows from St Martin's—the sheriffs, Robert Marchall and Philip Malpas, seized a debtor named William Foyle from St Bartholomew's Hospital,[20] and in the same month the City issued a proclamation against able-bodied beggars, vagrants, nightwalkers, and rowers in galleys, too many of whom were 'going from day to day up and down from street to street idly within the franchise of this city', disturbing 'the king's people and the peace'.[21] It was in this swirl of concern about disorder and what the City thought were over-mighty claims of privilege by liberties that the issue of an escaped prisoner and his accomplices emerged at the beginning of September 1440.

---

[17] See, for instance, the case of debtor Richard Hertanger, which at least according to the record of the affair kept by St Martin's, was a clear victory for the chapel: a servant of the sheriffs of London had arrested him in the sanctuary in February 1435 to answer to several suits of debt in the London courts. The dean of St Martin's, Thomas Bourchier, immediately petitioned the chancellor, who promptly issued a writ to bring the case into Chancery, where it was found that he had indeed been in the sanctuary and ordered him to be restored. *Registrum*, 39r–40r; TNA, C 1/12/199.

[18] For cases specific to St Martin's, see Thomas Curteys (1435–1437), TNA, KB 9/228/1, mm 26–27; KB 29/69, m. 16; KB 27/705, m. 24; and John Parker alias Gerard (April 1440), TNA, KB 9/232/1, m. 11; KB 29/73, m. 24. The last mention I have found of Parker is an outlawry in 1441. See Barron, 'Government of London', pp 395–7, for cases in the other liberties.

[19] LMA, Journal 3, fols 30v, 171r; Barron, 'Government of London', pp 395–7. Although 1438 mayor William Estfeld was a keen defender of London's liberties and one of the most fervent attackers of these kinds of privileged places, in a sign of how intertwined these networks of influence were, he was also closely connected through friendship and possibly, in the former case, family to two men who were at least briefly deans of St Martin's: William Kynwolmarsh, dean for a few months before his death in 1422; and William Alnwick, who afterwards became bishop of Norwich and then Lincoln. Anne F. Sutton, *The Mercery of London: Trade, Goods and People, 1130–1578* (Aldershot, 2005), pp 531–3; Reddan, 'Collegiate Church', 206.

[20] LMA, Journal 3, fol. 54v. An undated Chancery record (TNA, C 4/49/8) indicates that Foyle was subsequently restored to the sanctuary by the order of the court of King's Bench, as this was deemed a violation of St Bartholomew's privileges. This order may post-date, and derive from, the resolution of the St Martin's affair in the fall of 1440.

[21] LMA, Letter Book K, fol. 188r; parts of this are transcribed in Frank Rexroth, *Deviance and Power in Late Medieval London*, trans. Pamela Eve Selwyn (Cambridge, 2007), pp 358–9.

DEAN CAUDRAY AND THE EVENTS OF SEPTEMBER 1440

Although St Martin's conflict with the City went back some decades, in September 1440 when the sheriffs of London seized John Knight and his fellows from the sanctuary, St Martin le Grand was in the hands of a particularly formidable dean. Richard Caudray had been granted the position in October 1435, succeeding the young aristocrat Thomas Bourchier, who had been consecrated as bishop of Worcester.[22] Richard Caudray was both older and less well born than Bourchier, but he certainly had the experience, the political skills, and the determination to defend and indeed enlarge the privileges of the royal free chapel. When Caudray became dean in 1435, he was in the midst of what seemed an upward trajectory as a clerical star straddling the worlds of royal service and academic administration. From 1421 to 1435, Caudray was clerk of the king's council and at the same time nourished an academic career at Cambridge, becoming warden of King's Hall in 1431 and serving as chancellor of the University from 1433 to 1435.[23] Although his appointment as dean in 1435 might have seemed a prelude to even greater preferment—several of his immediate predecessors went on from the deanery to bishoprics[24]—as it turned out, for Caudray the appointment to the deanery was the end of the road rather than a way station. Caudray remained dean of St Martin le Grand for over two decades, until his death in 1458, a position he held along with the position of warden of King's Hall (until 1448) and a large collection of prebendaries and other benefices. He likely became very wealthy from his various sources of income.[25] In addition to his connections to the university world, ecclesiastical circles, and royal service, by the time he came into the deanship Caudray had also developed an important relationship with an aristocratic patron. Probably through his work on the king's council, by the 1430s Caudray had entered the service of John Holland, earl of Huntingdon and later duke of Exeter. The relationship with the Holland family was to remain important for Caudray for the rest of his life, and it was instrumental in his strategies in the 1440 conflict.[26]

---

[22] *CPR 1429–36*, p. 489.

[23] A. B. Emden, *A Biographical Register of the University of Cambridge to 1500* (Cambridge: Cambridge University Press, 1963), 126–7; Alfred L. Brown, *The Early History of the Clerkship of the Council* (Glasgow: University of Glasgow, 1969), 27–9; R. A. Griffiths, 'Public and Private Bureaucracies in England and Wales in the Fifteenth Century', *Transactions of the Royal Historical Society, Fifth Series* 30 (1980): pp 109–30; doi:10.2307/3679005.

[24] John Stafford, dean 1422–1425, went on to become bishop of Bath and Wells and later archbishop of Canterbury and chancellor; William Alnwick, who held the position in 1426, resigned it that same year to become bishop of Norwich and later bishop of Lincoln; and Thomas Bourchier later became bishop of Worcester, archbishop of Canterbury, cardinal, and chancellor. Reddan, 'Collegiate Church', 206; R. G. Davies, 'Stafford, John (d. 1452)', *ODNB* (2004), doi:10.1093/ref:odnb/; Rosemary C. E. Hayes, 'Alnwick, William (d. 1449)', *ODNB* (2004), doi:10.1093/ref:odnb/421; Clark, 'Bourchier, Thomas'.

[25] In the early 1450s he loaned the crown large sums of money. *CPR, 1446–52*, pp 332, 472.

[26] Stansfield, 'The Hollands', pp 224, 233, 239, 252, 291; S. J. Payling, 'The Ampthill Dispute: A Study in Aristocratic Lawlessness and the Breakdown of Lancastrian Goverment', *The English Historical Review* 104 (1989): pp 905–6, doi:10.1093/ehr/CIV.413.881; Ralph Alan Griffiths, *The*

Caudray was a canny political operator and his long term as dean gave him scope to work hard to promote the fortunes of St Martin le Grand. There is no question that he made his mark on St Martin's—quite literally. The name of 'Dean Caudray' was remembered still in the 1530s when inhabitants of the precinct testified before a royal commission about the sanctuary, because he built a great wall around part of the precinct and engraved his name upon it.[27] Properties in lease books were still identified in the 1520s as having been built by Dean Caudray.[28] As formidable as his role in building walls and properties in the St Martin le Grand precinct was, his role as architect of the liberties and privileges of St Martin le Grand was even more important. As clerk of the king's council, Caudray had presumably seen some of the matters related to the sanctuary at St Martin's discussed, so he was well apprised on the issues. Whatever he had thought, as king's clerk, about the canons of Waltham in 1430, as dean from 1435 his brief was to argue hard, and summon his political resources, for St Martin's privileges.

The most important piece of evidence for Dean Caudray's advocacy on behalf of the royal free chapel of St Martin le Grand surviving today is the book, labelled *Registrum Collegii Sancti Martini Magni* (*The Register of the College of St Martin le Grand*), now held amongst the Westminster Abbey Muniments.[29] In addition to a collection of document transcriptions (charters, letters patent, papal bulls, excerpts from court records) illustrating the privileges and liberties of St Martin le Grand, the Register's heart, about twenty-three folios altogether, is a detailed account of the events of September and October 1440. This account includes further transcriptions of documents—letters, petitions, writs, and the full submissions from both sides made to the crown's commission appointed to hear the case—framed and contextualized by a narrative that takes the reader from one document to the next. It is almost certain that Caudray himself composed the linking narrative and at least supervised the gathering of the documents to be transcribed.[30] In constructing the cartulary, Caudray worked within a recognized genre, especially for religious houses, although he himself used the form in a particularly masterful way.[31] Both Caudray's record of events and the City's own version in its archive are

---

Reign of King Henry VI: The Exercise of Royal Authority, 1422–1461 (Berkeley, 1981), p. 604; TNA, E 13/145B, rot. 78.

[27] Deposition of Piers Peterson, TNA, C 24/3, 'Abbas', m. 2.
[28] WAM, MSS 13318, 13319.   [29] WAM, Muniment Book 5.
[30] *Registrum*. The manuscript is described and a table of contents listed in Lawrence E. Tanner, 'Nature and Use of Westminster Abbey Muniments', *Transactions of the Royal Historical Society*, Fourth Series 19 (1936): p. 80, doi:10.2307/3678686. Westminster Abbey Library holds a typescript calendar of the *Registrum*. The latest date of material in the book is 1479; it may have been bound around then, or possibly in 1503 when the chapel of St Martin le Grand, together with its properties and rights, was granted to Westminster Abbey by Henry VII in 1503 and its archives were transferred to the Abbey.
[31] R. H. Hilton, ed., *The Stoneleigh Leger Book*, Dugdale Society 24 (Oxford, 1960), pp xvii–xxi; Jean-Philippe Genet, 'Cartulaires, registres et histoire: l'exemple anglais', in *Le métier d'historien au moyen âge: études sur l'historiographie médiévale*, ed. Bernard Guenée (Paris, 1977), p. 118. Cf. the strategies (and cartulary) of the head of another London religious house, John Wakeryng, master of St Bartholomew's Hospital: Euan C. Roger, 'Blakberd's Treasure: A Study in Fifteenth-Century Administration at St. Bartholomew's Hospital, London', in *Exploring the Evidence: Commemoration, Administration and the Economy*, ed. Linda Clark (Woodbridge, 2014), pp 81–107.

worth considering in some detail: they reveal a good deal about the strategies employed on the one hand by religious houses and on the other by urban corporations, institutions that would frequently come into conflict over sanctuary in the subsequent century.

Caudray's narrative was skilful and convincing, as he was a natural storyteller with considerable experience in political argument. Caudray began his account of the events of autumn 1440 not with John Knight's escape from custody and his and his accomplices' flight into sanctuary, but rather with a larger frame of reference: the sheriffs' seizure of Knight and his companions was part of the City's larger campaign to 'break' the privileged places in London and bring them under civic control.

> The year of the incarnation of our Lord, 1440, and year of the reign of our sovereign lord king Henry VI, the nineteenth; after Philip Malpas and Robert Marchall, then sheriffs of London, had broken the franchises and privileged places, first of Blanchappelton, then St. Katharine's, and after of St. Bartholomew's in Smithfield, they came with great multitude of the commons of London unto St. Martin's the Grand in London, and broke the immunity and franchise thereof, in manner as it is contained in a letter sent from the canons of the same place, those being present, unto Master Richard Caudray, their dean, then being absent, in wise as followeth:[32]

Caudray followed this *mise-en-scène* with the full text of the canons' letter describing the events of 2 September paraphrased at the beginning of this chapter. The letter is itself a masterly piece of plaintive prose, which moves the plot along like an epistolary novel, suggesting that the version in the *Register* may be an 'improved' version of the original; it is even possible that it was entirely invented by Caudray as a neat form of exposition.

Following the letter explaining the seizure, the dean's account indicates that Caudray returned, in all haste, from Cambridge, some 80 kilometres from London; this was a two-day journey, and so by the time he had received word from his canons and himself made the return trip, it would have been about 5 September.[33] Once back in London, Caudray immediately petitioned the sheriffs, the mayor, and the aldermen to have the prisoners restored to him. The mayor and aldermen, however, put him off, telling him they were too busy to discuss the matter and giving him an appointment the following week. Rather than waiting patiently for the mayor and aldermen to make time to see him, however, Caudray decided to circumvent them by going directly to see the king at Windsor, presenting to him a petition which was transcribed in the register.[34]

---

[32] *Registrum*, fol. 41r.
[33] Travelling 40 kilometres in a day would be a full day's travel on most medieval routes. See Marjorie Nice Boyer, 'A Day's Journey in Mediaeval France', *Speculum* 26 (1951): pp 597–608, doi:10.2307/2853052. In 1511, Erasmus wrote a letter to John Colet discussing his two-day trip from London to Cambridge. Desiderius Erasmus, *Erasmus and Cambridge*, ed. Douglas F. S. Thomson (Toronto, 1963), p. 107.
[34] *Registrum*, fols 42rv. The original submitted to the king survives: TNA SC 8/270/13497. The texts are identical.

Caudray's supplication was written in fifteenth-century petitionary mode, emphasizing the humility of the petitioner ('your simplest dean'), the dastardliness of the supplicant's opponents, and above all the righteous power of the addressee himself, the king. Caudray emphasizes that the sheriffs' sacrilege constituted terrible harm to the king himself—for the king is 'the only lord, founder, protector, and granter of all that is here'. The king to whom Caudray made his petition, Henry VI, had turned eighteen a few days before. He was, as Caudray the former clerk of the king's council would have known well, a remarkably pious young man devoted to his kingly role as protector of the church and as fount of mercy.[35] According at least to Caudray—and not implausibly, given Henry's conceptions of his role as king—Henry VI was sympathetic to the dean's outrage at the breaking of the royally-sanctioned sanctuary of St Martin's. Armed with a signet letter and a writ from the king commanding the City to surrender the prisoners to the Dean,[36] Caudray returned to London.

Caudray himself, however, was not to deliver those documents to the mayor and aldermen; as he indicates in his account, the king had instead designated Lords Huntingdon and Tiptoft[37] to do so on his behalf. On 14 September Huntingdon and Tiptoft summoned the mayor, aldermen, and sheriffs to the royal jurisdiction of the Tower of London to receive the king's letter and writ. What proceeded there, according to Caudray's narrative, was a series of passive-aggressive manoeuvres on the part of the City officials to avoid even reading these documents. First, Huntingdon delivered the king's signet letter, addressed to the mayor, sheriffs, and aldermen of London. The City officials told Lord Huntingdon, however, that they could not open the letters, for they were outside City jurisdiction, and besides, only some of the twenty-four aldermen were present, and they 'dared' not open the letter until all those addressed were in attendance. Lord Huntingdon greatly exhorted them to open and obey the king's letter, but they refused. Presumably somewhat provoked by this point, Lord Huntingdon then pulled out the writ, which was addressed only to the mayor and the sheriffs, all three of whom were present, and he required them 'on the king's behalf, since they would not obey the letter, to obey the writ'. The mayor, aldermen, and sheriffs took the writ, unopened,

---

[35] Griffiths, *Reign of King Henry VI*, esp. 248–9.

[36] The Letter Book transcribes both those documents faithfully, according to the other surviving copies. LMA, Letter Book K, fols 189v–190r; the letter is transcribed and the writ calendared in Sharpe, *Cal. Letter Book K*, pp 243–5. Both documents were also transcribed in the *Registrum* of St Martin le Grand, fols 43rv and 44r, along with the writ. There seem to have been two versions of the writ, the second an 'alias' writ perhaps kept in reserve in case the first writ was not obeyed. They are virtually identical with two differences: one (the City's copy of the writ in the Letter Book) is dated 10 Sept.; the other (the version transcribed in the St Martin's *Registrum*) is dated 12 Sept. There is also one difference in wording: a phrase indicating that the king was bound by his coronation oath to protect the liberties, immunities, and customs of his free chapel was included in the 12 Sept. version but not the 10 Sept. The two different forms of the writs—with the different dates—were also exemplified in crown records; the writ recorded on the crown's close rolls is dated 10 Sept. (and has the phrasing as in the Letter Book), while a copy entered into the patent roll dates it to 12 Sept. and matches the text in the *Registrum*. *CCR, 1435–41*, p. 392 (TNA, C 54/291, m. 43); *CPR, 1436–41*, pp 569–70 (TNA, C 66/450, m. 3.)

[37] Linda Clark, 'Tiptoft, John, First Baron Tiptoft (c. 1378–1443)', *ODNB* (2004), doi:10.1093/ref:odnb/27470. Tiptoft did not have a speaking role in Caudray's narrative.

and left the Tower. They went inside City jurisdiction, into nearby Barking church, and there broke the writ's seal and read it. They sent a delegation back to Lord Huntingdon, asking him for a delay while they considered the matter. The following day, 15 September, they returned to the Tower, and told Lords Huntingdon and Tiptoft that they were unable to obey the writ ordering them to return the prisoners, and instead intended to take the matter up directly with the king.

The Caudray Register's version of events following the seizure of Knight and the others from St Martin's portrays the mayor, aldermen, and sheriffs as both riding roughshod over the rights of the collegiate church and refusing to obey even the king's explicit command. The Register is of course hardly an impartial narrative, but it must be noted that the king's own record corroborates at least the City's refusal to obey the royal writ.[38] The truculence of the mayor and aldermen in the face of the king's commands is somewhat more explicable, however, when one issue strategically omitted from Caudray's account is considered: that the earl of Huntingdon, John Holland, was Caudray's own particular patron and thus hardly a neutral figure. Although in Caudray's narrative he represents the king, no doubt to the mayor and aldermen he instead represented Caudray.

The City's own record of the first weeks of the conflict with Caudray reads rather differently. The dossier related to the seizing of John Knight and his fellows appears in two different sets of City records.[39] They are both much shorter than the account in the Dean's *Register*, and they are much less narrative in their structure. The relatively rough administrative entries recorded in the Journal of the Court of Common Council were likely written more or less on the spot at the meetings of the mayor and aldermen and of the larger Common Council. The City's Letter Book, on the other hand, was a more formal record of the City's business.[40] Their different processes of compilation and their different purposes and intended readership are particularly revealed in the divergences between the accounts of the affair in the two sets of records, which do not line up with one another on the events of September and October 1440.[41]

In the Journal, the initial situation—the seizure of the men from St Martin's—was noted on 1 September, where the record indicates that an alderman was mandated to go to St Martin's to discuss the matter with the canons. Nothing further

---

[38] The entry on the patent rolls in November notes that the writ commanding the mayor and sheriffs to release the prisoners into the dean's custody was delivered to them by John, Lord Huntingdon, and that the mayor and sheriffs did not obey it but continued to detain the prisoners in their custody. TNA, C 66/450, m. 3 (calendared in *CPR 1436–41*, pp 569–70), of which a version was copied into the *Registrum*, fols 57r–58r.

[39] LMA, Journal 3, fols 55v–65v; Letter Book K, fols 189r–190r (calendared in Sharpe, *Cal. Letter Book K*, pp 241–6). In addition, as below, the City prepared an elaborate submission for the commission, but there is no surviving copy of it in the City archives. The first part of the presumed original submitted to the commissioners is now among the Chancery records in the National Archives, and a full (and faithful) copy was entered into St Martin's *Registrum*. TNA, C 49/68/21 (the first membrane of the City's submission); *Registrum*, fols 46rv, 50r–55v.

[40] On the City's records, see Barron, *London*, p. 3.

[41] For how the London mayor and aldermen used their records and archives, see Evan F. May, 'For the Good Order to Be Had Thereby: Civic Archives and the Creation of Conformity in Late Medieval London' (PhD, Concordia University, 2010).

on the matter was recorded in the Journal for the five meetings (three of the court of aldermen, two of the Common Council) in the two weeks that followed. Then on 15 September, the day following the initial meeting with Huntingdon and Tiptoft at the Tower, an entry indicates that the sheriffs appeared before the mayor and aldermen, presenting a petition (which was not transcribed) about the matter at St Martin's.[42] The entries in the Journal contrast with the Letter Book, which includes a copy of a petition from the sheriffs, but dates it to 2 September, the day following the seizure itself, rather than two weeks later, and indicates that it was presented to the full Common Council (the large civic assembly made up of almost 200 men).[43]

The date and venue of the petition's presentation are important, but let us consider first its content. The sheriff's plaint gives a quite different account of the events of 1 September than that described in the canons' letter. As it indicates, sheriff Philip Malpas, presiding on that Thursday over the sheriff's court 'after the custom of the same City', sent John Norburgh, one of the officers of the court, to the king's gaol at Newgate with an order to have John Knight, soldier, then prisoner in the said gaol, brought to the court to answer a plaint for a debt of 11s 6d. As Norburgh was proceeding with the prisoner down the king's road towards the Guildhall, out from St Martin's lane burst four men—named as Richard Morys, John Rede, William Janyver, and Christopher Blakborne—with 'many others which be known for errant and notorious thieves'. All these men had long since hidden in the sanctuary of St Martin's 'for their robberies, felonies, and misgovernances'. They attacked Norburgh, with daggers drawn, and wrested his prisoner from him. Knight and his confederates fled to sanctuary at St Martin's, a flight that was 'expressly both against the common law of this land and against the liberties and franchise of the same City', not to mention the 'great hurt and loss' to the sheriffs themselves. The purpose of the sheriffs' petition was to gain support, political and financial, from London's civic government. Inasmuch as they had been 'grievously menaced' by the dean of St Martin's for this action, and as this was a matter that went beyond their own personal liabilities and was of fundamental concern to the City's franchises and privileges, the sheriffs asked the City to bear the legal costs that would inevitably ensue. They also requested the counsel of John Carpenter, the City's long-time common clerk (by then retired but still active). The sheriffs ended by asking the mayor, aldermen, and Common Council to consider 'that this cause is every freeman's cause, and the good and true keeping and defending of the liberties of this famous City is the welfare of every man that is inhabitant therein'. The Common Council, according to the Letter Book, granted the sheriffs' petition.

The City's record of the affair of John Knight and his fellows, like Caudray's Register, was almost certainly manipulated. There is, for one thing, slippage about the precise wrong that John Knight and his fellows had committed. As the sheriffs' petition indicated, Knight was a small-time debtor, not a felon; moreover, his companions' rescue of him was an ill-defined misdemeanour rarely prosecuted in

---

[42] LMA, Journal 3, fols 55v–58v.
[43] LMA, Letter Book K, fol. 189r; Barron, *London*, p. 132.

English courts in this period.⁴⁴ Yet the City's statements repeatedly referred to them all as the 'thieves of St. Martin's', well known 'for their robberies, felonies, and misgovernances'.⁴⁵ Furthermore, the 2 September entry in the Letter Book of the sheriffs' petition must have been backdated: the sheriffs could not have reported to the Common Council on 2 September that the dean was menacing them about the seizure of Knight and his fellows, as Caudray, who was in Cambridge, would not yet have been informed about the situation. It is thus no surprise that the Journal of the Court of Common Council—drier administrative minutes of the business of the council and of the meetings of the mayor and aldermen without the council—does not report a visit from the sheriffs or indicate any discussion of the St Martin's affair at all at the Common Council meeting on 2 September. In fact, the matter of St Martin's does not arise again in the Journal, despite at least five intervening meetings of either the mayor and aldermen alone or the full Common Council, until the entry on 15 September. On that day, it was noted that the sheriffs presented a petition to the mayor and aldermen (not the large public meeting of the Common Council) and that the smaller executive group agreed that they would support the sheriffs in this dispute. In other words, it seems that the sheriffs' petition was presented two weeks later and before a much less public forum than the Letter Book indicates.⁴⁶

The motive behind this backdating is a bit obscure, although it reflects how London civic governors used their official records in different ways. The more workaday minutes of the meetings of the mayor and aldermen and Common Council in the Journal suggest that for about two weeks following John Knight's escape and subsequent seizure from St Martin's, the mayor and aldermen were either unconcerned about or determined to ignore the situation, for there is no indication that it was discussed. By the middle of the month, however, after Lord Huntingdon had delivered the king's letter and writ, they had to address it. There may well have been divisions amongst the City officials regarding how aggressive they should be towards the liberties—with perhaps sheriffs Malpas and Marchall more willing than others to push the issue⁴⁷—but such differences of opinions

---

⁴⁴ On helping prisoners escape, see Bellamy, *Criminal Trial*, p. 188.

⁴⁵ LMA, Journal 3, fol. 59r.

⁴⁶ LMA, Journal 3, fol. 59r. The Journal further records that on 8 October 1440 sheriff Philip Malpas appeared again before the mayor and aldermen and presented another petition: 'Isto die declaratum fuit per Philippum Malpas que facta fuerunt per ipsum et socium suum in ecclesia sancti Martini Magni et declaravit ut in billa [On this day it was declared by Philip Malpas what was done by him and his associate in the church of St Martin le Grand and he declared [it] as in the bill]'. LMA, Journal 3, fol. 61v. This may well refer to a different document, one of the submissions the City made in the subsequent processes, but it is possible that the 2 September entry in the Letter Book conflates the two separate later occasions, 15 September and 8 October, on which the Journal records that the mayor and aldermen discussed the St Martin's issue with the sheriffs. None of the entries in the Journal indicate that the matter of St Martin's was discussed at the Common Council until 14 October 1440; LMA, Journal 3, fol. 63r.

⁴⁷ Malpas in particular was a difficult man whom others might not have wanted to antagonize. See Anne F. Sutton, 'Malpas, Philip (d. 1469)', *ODNB* (2004), doi:10.1093/ref:odnb/52271; B. Brogden Orridge, 'Some Particulars of Alderman Philip Malpas and Alderman Sir Thomas Cooke', *Transactions of the London and Middlesex Archaeological Society* 3 (September 1865): pp 285–306, https://archive.org/details/transactionsoflo03londuoft.

could not be aired publicly or inscribed in City records.[48] For posterity, it seemed important to someone that the official record of the Letter Book read as if the governors of the City—mayor, aldermen, sheriffs, and indeed the full Common Council—had always been unified and on top of the situation and had discussed it publicly the day after the men were seized: hence the backdating of the Letter Book entry.

MARSHALLING CASES

As both the dean's narrative and the City records noted, a City delegation rode to Waltham to see the king sometime in the week following the encounter with Lord Huntingdon in the Tower. Although according to Caudray the king refused to meet with them, he did mandate a royal commission to look into the matter, headed by the treasurer (Ralph Cromwell, baron Cromwell), the chancellor (John Stafford, archbishop of Canterbury), and Sir Ralph Bottiler.[49] Over the following month, while the five sanctuary seekers remained in Newgate, the two sides assembled submissions to argue their cases.[50] Both submissions survive, at least in part, in the crown's archive and in a transcription in the St Martin's Register; interestingly neither was entered into the City's own records.[51] Each side went far beyond the specifics of the particular case at hand, again addressing the larger question of the nature of the privileges (or lack thereof) of St Martin le Grand. The dean's case in several ways was pitched more successfully than the City's.

The dean made the case for St Martin's privileges in the standard legal form of the era, by presentation of royal charters, letters patent, statutes, and similar records from every king from William the Conqueror forwards, along with papal bulls. The bulls, however, were given a secondary status to the royal charters—no doubt a canny strategic choice when appealing to a king. Although the submission was put together in a professional manner, as one would expect from a clerk with Caudray's training and experience, Caudray made an interesting linguistic choice: the documents he transcribed were reproduced in the original language, but his framing material was written in English, which was at this time an emerging language of law and administration, and one that the young king himself may have preferred.[52] Perhaps, indeed, Caudray's language choice would have seemed cutting edge,[53] particularly so since it was clearly a choice rather than a necessity, as

---

[48] See May, 'For the Good Order to Be Had Thereby'.
[49] *CPR 1436–41*, 570; *Registrum*, fol. 44v; LMA, Journal 3, fol. 63r.
[50] For records of the City's preparation, see LMA, Journal 3, fols 60r, 62v.
[51] TNA, E 135/2/56; C 49/68/21; *Registrum*, 47v–55v. On the City's records, see above, this chapter at n.39.
[52] See Gwilym Dodd, 'The Rise of English, the Decline of French: Supplications to the English Crown, c. 1420–1450', *Speculum* 86 (2011): pp 117–50, doi:10.1017/S0038713410003507.
[53] Dodd points to the late 1430s in particular, the point at which Henry VI assumed personal rule after his minority, as a major turning point in the use of English for supplications to the crown, a genre with which the submissions here have a generic relationship. Dodd, 'Rise of English', pp 129–30, 143–4.

Caudray, an academic luminary and highly experienced clerk, could easily have written in Latin had he wanted to. The City of London, on the other hand, may have been more sensitive to the importance of projecting sophistication and learning, and their submission was thus made entirely in Latin.

Most of the documents transcribed in the submission from St Martin's came from the archives of the chapel itself; some in fact still remain in Westminster Abbey Library and Muniments, where they were transferred when the abbey absorbed St Martin le Grand in 1503. The documents cited included two copies—one in Latin, one 'in the Saxon language'[54]—of a charter from William the Conqueror to the canon Ingelric, confirming the rights and privileges of St Martin le Grand. Although the Latin version would have been much more comprehensible to the councillors and to the justices who later read the submissions, the Saxon charter was important both for the aura of authenticity and antiquity the archaic language signified and for the difficulty that its syntax and vocabulary presented to most fifteenth-century readers. The very opaqueness of its language allowed the dean to interpret its meaning rather broadly. As he explained,

> And also the said words in Saxon import such sentence that the said place should be a sanctuary, franchised, privileged, and have tuition and immunity of all those persons which for treason, felonies, trespasses, debts, or any other cause should flee to the same, or abide therein.[55]

Although the charter itself is authentic, the 'words in Saxon' did not in fact say anything more than the Latin, which confirmed St Martin's jurisdictional liberties without making any mention of sanctuary for felony and so on[56] (for the very good reason that felony had yet to be defined in 1068). The Conqueror's charter was nonetheless clearly the star piece of evidence for the free chapel's case. In general St Martin's arguments laid a good deal of emphasis on charters and other documents dating from before 'time out of mind'. As Caudray bitingly remarked in response to the City's own claims to have jurisdiction over St Martin's, all their pieces of evidence derived from time within memory—only the thirteenth or fourteenth centuries—and thus were worthless novelties in the face of the antiquity of St Martin's claims.[57]

Passing unmentioned in St Martin's submission was the fact that the ancient charters did not (despite his comment on the Saxon charter) specify any particular sanctuary privilege for St Martin's. The omission is hardly surprising, as of course the practice of sanctuary for which St Martin's argued in 1440 assumed an elaborated criminal law and royal court system, as well as a clearly demarcated jurisdiction for the City of London, none of which existed in 1068 when William made his grant to Ingelric. The City's arguments similarly insisted that the mayor, aldermen, and sheriffs had governed the whole and entire territory of the City on behalf of the

---

[54] *Registrum*, fols 9r–10r, 29rv. W. H. Stevenson, 'An Old-English Charter of William the Conqueror in Favour of St. Martin's-Le-Grand, London, A. D. 1068', *The English Historical Review* 11 (1896): pp 731–44, doi:10.1093/ehr/XI.XLIV.731.

[55] *Registrum*, fol. 48r.   [56] See Stevenson, 'An Old-English Charter', pp 736–44.

[57] *Registrum*, fol. 51r.

citizenry from the time of London's foundation by Brutus the Trojan, thus from well before even the time of the Conqueror. Both St Martin's and the City made their arguments as if the legal and forensic structures and the governance of London as they existed in 1440 were always already present.

Caudray, however, did not rest with the presentation of ancient charters from St Martin's own records, but also conducted outside archival research. Amongst the pieces of evidence recorded in the *Register* are records of recent cases in one of the royal courts, the Court of Common Pleas, involving sanctuary claims at St Martin's. The citation of these cases is made, in several instances, from the Common Plea rolls themselves, with archival citations ('rotulo cclxxxii', for instance, for a case that is indeed on membrane 282 for the term indicated).[58] Each of these cases, dating from the 1410s and 1420s, shows the sheriffs of London reporting to the justices of the court of Common Pleas that they could not execute an order to arrest debtors cited to the court because those debtors were inside the boundaries of 'the sanctuary of St. Martin le Grand', and thus outside their jurisdiction. Caudray, of course, prominently featured these cases amongst his collection of evidence for the privileges of St Martin's because they showed 'allowance in eyre' or royal courts' recognition of those privileges. In a larger rhetorical sense they were also useful because these cases showed the sheriffs of London themselves having recently made precisely the argument that Dean Caudray himself adduced in 1440, that St Martin le Grand was a privileged place of sanctuary outside the jurisdiction of the sheriffs of London.

By contrast, the submission of Caudray's opponents, the sheriffs of London, indicated that they intended to 'to show and to prove that the royal free chapel of St. Martin le Grand is of and in the same City, and under its jurisdiction', and had no right to shelter those who sought asylum there. They made this argument, however, with vague allusions to tradition rather than specific and documented evidence. The City, they argued, had possessed its all-encompassing jurisdiction from time out of mind (that is, from before 1189), and indeed had possessed it from the very origins of human government in Britain. London, which was and had always been the chief city of the whole realm of England, had been founded by the illustrious predecessors of the lord king in memory of the great city of Troy, and indeed had long been known as 'Trinovantum', New Troy. Here the London case relied on a civic version of the legend of Brutus, the refugee from the Trojan wars who was thought to have founded Britain; in the London tradition, Brutus was not only the first king of Britain but also established and built the city on the Thames, making the City's rights and privileges coeval with the very foundation of the kingdom

[58] *Registrum*, fols 37v–38r; TNA, CP 40/673, m. 282d. Other citations similarly check out: e.g. *Registrum*, fol. 38v (CP 40/654, rot. 318); *Registrum*, fol. 39r (CP 40/673, rot. 16). In one case, either the scribe or the researcher made a transcription error, as the case cited as falling on 'rotulus ccclii' is instead found on 452: *Registrum*, fol. 63v (CP 40/634, rot. 452). In one case, I have not been able to locate the original: *Registrum*, fol. 38r, 'rotulus cclxxxxvii' is cited, but I have not found anything on any of the membranes with that number on the rolls for that year. Caudray's citation of cases from the records of the central courts was not unique; William Curteys, abbot of Bury St Edmunds, also provided precise references to the Coram Rege roll at King's Bench in his register in an entry written in the 1430s: BL, Add. 14848, Registrum Willielmi Curteys, fols 137r–138r.

itself.[59] Continuing with these general invocations of the past, the statement went on to note—still in an allusive rather than a specific and documented way—that from the time of Edward the Confessor London had been unto itself a whole and undivided county, and that William the Conqueror had granted the City charters confirming its liberties. The charters themselves, however, were not transcribed or directly quoted.[60] The City's more direct evidence that St Martin's had been fully in and of the liberty and jurisdiction of the City came from cases from the reign of Edward I forward (thus well within time of legal memory). Unlike St Martin's, which had a gold-standard piece of legal evidence in the charter from William the Conqueror, the City's evidence was distinctly less impressive.

The councillors deputed by the king to consider the matter did not immediately render a decision; the dean's Register tells us that instead they appealed for legal advice to the chief justices of the courts of King's Bench and Common Pleas. According to Caudray, when the judges considered the documents the parties had submitted, they largely agreed with the dean:

> The said judges said that the general words of the liberties and immunities contained in the said charter of King William, with the use of the same from the time of no mind, be sufficient in law, and ought to be kept in wise as other places privileged in case semblable [similar] keep the privileges, immunities, and franchises granted unto them, rehearsing the privileges of the Archbishop of York for Beverley, the Bishop of Durham, the abbots of Glastonbury and Westminster, which all in effect stand in general words more than in special, but because of those general words and the long continued use before time of mind, they ought to be kept as thing valable [valid] in law. And also they said that the allowance in eyre of the liberties of St. Martin's which they read here was sufficient for as to the allowance of immunity.

That was clearly a vindication for the general arguments that Caudray put forward, particularly as regarded the charter from the Conqueror. Regarding 'other points', however—presumably the specifics of the case of John Knight and his fellows—the justices were not ready to pronounce, and thus prayed for 'greater leisure of other advice' to consider the questions.[61]

Impatient about further delay, and despite a victory at least on the general points at issue if not the particular case, Caudray chose once again to take the matter straight to the top. He directly petitioned the king to order the five men who had

---

[59] Registrum, fol. 50v. See also use of the legend in relation to other jurisdictional rights in the Liber Albus, the City's own record of its rights and jurisdictions, compiled by John Carpenter, who although in retirement advised the City in the 1440 dispute. John Carpenter, *Munimenta Gildhallæ Londoniensis: Liber Albus, Liber Custumarum, et Liber Horn*, ed. Henry Thomas Riley (London, 1860), vol. 1, pp 497–8. On 'New Troy' and London in the fifteenth century, see Sylvia Federico, *New Troy: Fantasies of Empire in the Late Middle Ages* (Minneapolis, 2003).

[60] William's charter of 1067 to London is still extant (LMA, COL/CH/01/001/A), and could have been wielded. It is, however, very unspecific in the rights that it grants Londoners, guaranteeing only that they would be the same as in King Edward's day. See for a translation Reginald R. Sharpe, *London and the Kingdom* (London, 1894), pp 28–9.

[61] *Registrum*, fols 55v–56r; this last passage, implying some doubt about the sanctuary privilege in this case, is scored through by a later hand, likely indicating selective use of, or intention to use, this passage in later arguments for St Martin's sanctuary rights.

been 'taken by the said late sheriffs out of the sanctuary by such violence as is above rehearsed' to be returned immediately to the sanctuary. The sheriffs, moreover, should be duly punished for their disobedience of his original writ in September ordering this return.[62] The king, according at least to Caudray, immediately concurred, and ordered the chancellor to issue a writ of *corpus cum causa* to the sheriffs, commanding that the men be brought from Newgate to have their case heard in Chancery.

Our two sets of sources give somewhat different readings regarding what happened before the chancellor, although in both cases the basic result—the return of Knight and his fellows to sanctuary—was the same. In the dean's record, the sheriffs appeared before the chancellor with the prisoners and capitulated to the royal will, and the chancellor thus ordered that the men should be returned to sanctuary at St Martin's, 'there to abide freely as in a place having plenary franchise, liberty, and immunity, whilst that them liked'.[63] This, then, was in the dean's account, a great victory. As the dean emphasized, 'the which things all done and ministered', the record of the judgment was 'filaced, entered, and enacted in the court of the chancery of record, in the term of St. Michael, the year of our said lord the king the nineteenth, and of the incarnation of our lord, the year 1440'—meaning that it was entered officially into the king's records, onto the patent roll, and, of course, triumphantly recorded in the dean's own account in his Register.[64] The dean had reason to be happy: as the royal records corroborate, he had out-argued the City and emerged from the conflict with a clear confirmation of St Martin's privileges.

The City's records, on the other hand, imply rather that the outcome of the hearing before the chancellor was inconclusive and inconsequential: when the sheriffs answered the Chancellor's *corpus cum causa* writ, they told the chancellor that the original plaintiffs in the debt case against John Knight could not be found. They thus had no case to pursue, they said, conveniently ignoring the escape from custody and the previous rhetoric by which Knight and his confederates were labelled as 'errant and notorious thieves' rather than debtors.[65] With no case, they had no reason to keep the prisoners, they said, and they were therefore indifferent regarding their fate. Then, as the entry continued, the chancellor ordered the prisoners, no longer being prosecuted, to be delivered back to St Martin's, 'as he was certainly permitted to do'. After this 'there was no further process in the aforesaid case'.[66] The City's version of the outcome of the two-month conflict was thus one in which no matters of principle were decided, and no one won, or lost. Given the high rhetoric of the City's records up to this point and the submissions in the case, this is a remarkably anticlimactic ending in a storytelling sense and (by the evidence of the royal records) a misleading record of what happened. The story the City's records tell is not a coherent one: an unwillingness to inscribe certain aspects of

---

[62] *Registrum*, fol. 56r. [63] *Registrum*, fol. 56v.
[64] See *CPR 1436–41*, pp 569–70; the original, TNA, C 66/450, m. 3; and the copy in the Register, fols 57r–58r.
[65] LMA, Letter Book K, fol. 189r.
[66] '...sicut sibi bene licius, et ulterior processus habitus non fuerat in causa supradicta'. LMA, Letter Book K, fol. 190r (Sharpe, *Cal. Letter Book K*, p. 246).

what unfolded created holes in the plot and a dénouement that does not make sense. Dean Caudray's story, by contrast, ties up nicely, a difference that can be traced not only to the generic differences between administrative and narrative sources, but to the happy ending with which the dean's tale finished. This is not to suggest that the dean's presentation of the case was entirely accurate either; his victory was probably not as fore-ordained as the Register pretends, given how hard the dean had to work for it.

THE END OF DEAN CAUDRAY'S DAYS

Dean Caudray's victory in 1440 did not mean that the sanctuary privileges he claimed for St Martin's remained unchallenged over the remainder of his tenure as dean, which lasted until his death in 1458. There was a series of further conflicts with the mayor and aldermen, both over St Martin's economic and fiscal independence from the City,[67] and more specifically regarding the precinct's status as a sanctuary. In all of these, as far as the evidence indicates, the dean won at least qualified victories, although Henry VI's support for Caudray and the chapel was pushed by some difficult treason cases around 1450.

Following Jack Cade's Revolt in that year, one of Cade's 'petty captains', as Caudray put it, William Cayme of Sittingbourne, Kent, fled to St Martin le Grand upon being indicted for treason. According to the dean's own account, Caudray was able to dissuade the king, both with demonstration, again, of the documents proving his privileges and immunities, and by advice from two justices of the court of Common Pleas, from having the traitor seized from the precinct. Caudray agreed that Cayme should be guarded, however, to prevent his escape to do further harm. This lasted only a short time, as soon after the king granted Cayme a pardon.[68] The issue of traitors in the sanctuary arose again about a year later, when Sir William Oldhall, speaker of the House of Commons and chamberlain to the duke of York, likewise sought refuge in St Martin's. The duke of York's pretensions to the throne were becoming manifest about this time, and Oldhall was implicated in 1450 and 1451 in various of the duke's manoeuvres.[69] Although once again Caudray had been able to dissuade the king from ordering Oldhall's seizure from the precinct, in January 1452, supporters of York's main rival the duke of Somerset forcibly seized the accused traitor from the sanctuary. After two days, upon the dean's insistent representation to the king, Oldhall was returned to the sanctuary,

---

[67] Regarding which Caudray requested, and received, a royal confirmation: see the copy in the *Registrum*, fols 75r–82v and the full calendar in *Calendar of the Charter Rolls Preserved in the Public Record Office*, 6 vols (London, 1903), vol. 6, pp 20–2. Cf. Thornley's argument that this charter deliberately omitted sanctuary rights; as those rights had been clearly confirmed in 1440, and would be confirmed again later in the decade, this seems an over-interpretation of the omission. 'Sanctuary in Medieval London', p. 313.

[68] *Registrum*, fols 66rv; Cayme's pardon is recorded 20 May 1451, *CPR 1446–52*, p. 424.

[69] On Oldhall's career generally, see J. S. Roskell, 'Sir William Oldhall, Speaker in the Parliament of 1450–1451', *Nottingham Medieval Studies* 5 (1961): pp 87–112, doi:10.1484/J.NMS.3.13.

although with the proviso that Oldhall was to be kept under royal guard.[70] Oldhall remained in the sanctuary for more than three years, in the meantime being attainted for treason in parliament and indicted for various felonies in King's Bench. He finally left the sanctuary after the Yorkist victory at the battle of St Albans in spring 1455. Later, Oldhall was to argue successfully in King's Bench that during his time in St Martin's he should be regarded as having been in the 'king's prison', as at least up until November 1454 he had been there under the custody of two yeomen of the crown. Thus detained, he had been unable to answer any charges before the king's courts and thus should be absolved of his outlawry, an argument with which the king's attorney concurred.[71] Dean Caudray's sanctuary, at least for the case of this one accused traitor, had survived, but at the cost of its becoming more a prison than an asylum. This case did not, however, become a precedent; by Caudray's account, 'in the end' (perhaps in November 1454, as cited in Oldhall's case) he was able to persuade the king to remove those guards, as they prejudiced the privileges and immunities of St Martin's. With the exception of the security Richard III established in 1483 to ensure his nieces did not escape from Westminster,[72] there is no evidence that guards were mandated for others in coming years who took sanctuary during the civil wars, or later.

From the City's perspective, Dean Caudray's continued success in defending and indeed expanding St Martin's privileges as a sanctuary and liberty must have been highly irritating. Caudray had taken advantage in 1440 and again in the later cases of his connections at court and his understanding of how to appeal personally to Henry VI, on both which accounts the City officials were less successful. One further episode in September and October 1455 could, however, have gone the other way.[73] In the autumn of 1455, the situation seemed more favourable for the City than it had for decades. Henry VI, Caudray's ally, had become incapacitated

---

[70] *Registrum*, fols 70v–71v; Kempe, *Historical Notices*, pp 140–4.

[71] TNA, KB 27/777, rex m. 3. This was formulated in the King's Bench roll not as Oldhall's having been in the sanctuary of St Martin le Grand, but rather that he was in 'prisona domini Regis apud London, videlicet in parrochia sancti Leonardi in warda de Alderichgate [in the prison of the lord king at London, that is in the parish of St Leonard in the ward of Aldersgate]'. Much of St Martin's precinct fell in St Leonard's parish, and as there was no other prison there, it is clearly a circumlocution for the sanctuary.

[72] See above, Ch. 2, at n.70.

[73] TNA, KB 9/291, mm 49–50; KB 27/791, rex m. 6; KB 27/796, rex m. 9; KB 29/88, mm 13, 13d; LMA, Journal 5, fols 263v–266r; Letter Book K, fol. 283v, transcribed in Sharpe, *Cal. Letter Book K*, pp 370–1. Modern commentators on this episode have assumed the City was victorious, not having seen the King's Bench records on the case. See Sharpe's note to the entry in *Cal. Letter Book K*, p. 371; Kempe, *Historical Notices*, pp 145–6; Thornley, 'Destruction of Sanctuary', pp 192–3. Apart from the Letter Book entry, they also refer to chronicler Robert Fabyan's account of this matter, which is very similar to the king's letter in the Letter Book: in fact, so similar, that it seems likely that Fabyan, writing some decades later, fashioned his paragraph on the episode by extrapolating from the Letter Book (in another instance around this same time, he explicitly cited the Letter Book as his source). Fabyan assumed, understandably, that Caudray must have been personally involved in protesting the seizure of the men from the precinct, but this was presumably a guess—as below, n.75 of this chapter, Caudray was not available to make such protests in September 1455. Fabyan's account should thus not be treated as an independent source corroborating the Letter Book. Fabyan, *New Chronicles*, pp 629–30, 633.

for a second time with mental illness and others were likely acting for him.[74] Dean Caudray himself was incarcerated in the Fleet prison for his actions on behalf of Henry Holland, duke of Exeter, regarding a violent seizure of property, and thus not only absent from the scene but in disgrace.[75] Thus when yet another altercation regarding sanctuary men arose in September 1455, the City pushed to take advantage of the moment.

According to a King's Bench indictment, a riot broke out at St Martin's on 18 September 1455 when a victim of theft pressed for the return of his stolen goods from sanctuary men in the precinct. The sanctuary men began to defend the precinct—so the indictment alleged—as if they were at war, climbing the church tower and raining down arrows and lances onto those below, killing two innocent bystanders.[76] Either precipitating the riot or following it, the London sheriffs seized 'divers persons that claimed the immunity' of St Martin's from the precinct.[77] As usual following such a seizure, intense lobbying with the king, or whoever was acting for him at this time, ensued, and once again the matter was put to consideration of the chancellor while the prisoners remained in the City's custody.[78] In preparation for their meeting with the chancellor, the mayor and aldermen brought in for consultation a number of hired-gun canon lawyers,[79] along with other legal minds from the Inns: on this occasion, the City intended to be well-armed with both ecclesiastical and temporal law arguments. It was, however, all for naught. Although the City's records do not indicate the outcome of the meeting with the chancellor, the King's Bench records show that he must have ordered the sanctuary men back to sanctuary, for when they were indicted before the sheriffs and coroner at the Guildhall on 13 October, a week after the scheduled meeting with the Chancellor, they were no longer in the sheriffs' custody.[80] St Martin's privileges

---

[74] Griffiths, *Reign of King Henry VI*, pp 752–5.

[75] Payling, 'Ampthill Dispute', pp 905–6. Caudray was bailed on 15 Oct. 1455, a few days after this situation was resolved. On 6 Oct. Caudray sent a letter to the mayor and alderman about the situation, indicating he was following the affair from his prison. LMA, Journal 5, fol. 266r.

[76] TNA, KB 9/291, mm 49–50; KB 27/791, rex m. 6; KB 27/796, rex m. 9.

[77] LMA, Letter Book K, fol. 283v, transcribed in Sharpe, *Cal. Letter Book K*, pp 370–1.

[78] The entries relating to this affair are at LMA, Journal 5, fols 263v–266r.

[79] The Journal named Drs Aleyn, Styllyngton, Wardale, Lucas, Morton, Ebrall, and Godard. Dr Aleyn was perhaps the canonist John Aleyn; A. B. Emden, *A Biographical Register of the University of Oxford to A. D. 1500* (Oxford, 1957), p. 22. Dr Stillington was Robert Stillington, DCL, future bishop of Bath and Wells and chancellor and, as of 1458, dean of St Martin le Grand (ibid., pp 1777–9). Dr Wardale was John Wardale, DCL (ibid., p. 1981). Dr Morton was likely John Morton, DCL, the future archbishop of Canterbury and chancellor, although it could also have been John Morton, D. Th., who died in 1464 (ibid., pp 1317–18). William Goddard, D.Th., was a Franciscan friar (ibid., p. 776). Thomas Eborall, D.Th., was the Master of Whittington College and rector of All Hallows Honey Lane (ibid., p. 623; see also Appleford, *Learning to Die*, pp 72–3, on his ties to the civic hierarchy). I have not identified a Dr Lucas.

[80] TNA, KB 27/791, rex m 6; TNA, KB 29/88, m. 13, 13d. As far as I have been able to find, only three of the fifteen men who were indicted on that day ever appeared in court to face the charges, and those three men presented pardons and walked free (on three separate occasions, in 1457, 1459, and 1460). By 1460 or so, besides the pardons, processes against four of the fifteen had ceased because they had died, and the remaining eight had not been found and so had been outlawed. Some were still being sought in 1462.

held even when the dean was not there to defend them, a result that must have been deeply disappointing for the mayor and aldermen.

About eighteen months later, on 5 February 1457, the king's council enacted the set of ordinances to govern St Martin's sanctuary examined in some detail in Chapter 2.[81] The precise trigger for this is unknown, although in general it clearly arose from the constant friction between the City and St Martin's. As the preamble indicated, on the one hand the king was desirous to conserve 'the Sanctuary, immunity, privileges, and liberties as appertain to the said chapel', while on the other he was sympathetic to the complaints of the citizens of London over the 'misruled persons' who issued forth from there to commit 'many riots, robberies, manslaughters, and other mischiefs'. Following 'great deliberation and communication' involving consultation with experts in civil, canon, and common law, along with the mayor and aldermen of London and Dean Caudray of St Martin le Grand, the series of ordinances was established.

Isobel Thornley read the promulgation of these ordinances for the governance of St Martin's sanctuary as a triumph for the City, resulting from the pressure the mayor and aldermen had put on the crown to rein in the chaotic situations the sanctuary introduced.[82] It is hard to see, however, that the City would have been very pleased with the these ordinances, for they established clearly, under the king's great seal, precisely what the deans of St Martin's had been contending for decades, and what the City itself had been fighting mightily against: that St Martin's had unquestioned sanctuary privileges for treason, felony, and 'other causes'. One element was likely a victory for the City and may well have come out of the 1455 incident: stolen goods turned over to the dean and his officials were to be returned to the victims, whereas earlier these goods had been claimed as one of the franchisal rights of St Martin's.[83] Otherwise, there is nothing about these ordinances that particularly worked to the dean's disadvantage: surely it was in his interest to have a well-organized and well-behaved population living within the precinct, and clear recognition of the sanctuary was well worth giving up the right to the stolen goods. The ordinances, far from being an indication of weakness for the dean, may have been in fact his greatest triumph for St Martin's.

Dean Caudray died in 1458. Over the course of his long tenure as dean of St Martin's, he was able to use his connections and his political skills to establish firmly St Martin's privileges as a sanctuary for felony and treason as well as for debt. The case that Caudray made in his various representations about St Martin's

---

[81] See above, Ch. 1 at n.24.

[82] Thornley, 'Destruction of Sanctuary', pp 194–5; Thornley, 'Sanctuary in Medieval London', p. 314.

[83] LMA, Letter Book K, fols 298v–299r. See above, n.13 in this chapter, and below Ch. 6 at n.34 for discussion of a similar right in the Westminster abbey manor of Knowle which survived into the 1530s. In the 1455 situation, according to the King's Bench indictment itself (composed by City officials), the clergy at the chapel had been 'well disposed [bene dispositos]' to search for the stolen goods for the victim but had been overrun by the sanctuary men (TNA, KB 9/291, m. 50), suggesting perhaps that by this time St Martin's had already abandoned its claim to confiscated stolen goods, which would have been an obvious irritant and difficult to defend.

privileges was at times bold or even outrageous, but his skilful presentation of his case and his apparently indefatigable determination to achieve clear documented royal sanction for sanctuary were key to his ultimate success. The City, on the other hand, was hampered in the presentation of its case by several factors. One was a poor strategic choice to pursue a much larger agenda—St Martin's status as a liberty outside City jurisdiction—that was very difficult to maintain legally, rather the narrower question of the collegiate church's sanctuary privilege. By wrapping the liberty together with sanctuary in their own attacks on St Martin's privileges, the City effectively accepted the premises of the arguments the dean of St Martin's and the abbot of Westminster had been making for some decades, that the liberty and the sanctuary were conceptually tied together. This could not be a successful strategy for the City, because the evidence for St Martin's franchisal rights derived from the Conqueror's charter and later records was simply too strong. But in any case, the City's direct target was likely the economic privileges attached to the liberty rather than its sanctuary, and thus there would have been little point in focusing only on the sheltering of felons. The City's governors may have thought (with some reason) that the relative novelty of the sheltering of felons and debtors was a weak spot that might bring down the whole edifice of the collegiate church's independent jurisdiction. If so, it backfired, for instead it opened the door for the justices who considered the case of John Knight to read the evidence for St Martin's privileges as a liberty as proof for a sanctuary privilege that went back to time immemorial. If the City's argument was that there was no sanctuary because there was no liberty, then conversely finding that the liberty had long existed became evidence for time-honoured sanctuary privilege. That confirmation of sanctuary in turn intensified rather than diminished the collegiate church's other liberties, and so this was a distinct defeat for the City. This story was not finished: the City continued for the ensuing decades to chafe against St Martin's privileges as a sanctuary and, even more so, as a liberty outside the City's fiscal and guild jurisdiction, as we will see again in Chapter 5.

The battles Dean Caudray fought for St Martin's were uniquely well-documented, but they were characteristic more broadly of contests over franchises, jurisdictions, and the sacralized space of religious houses in the realm. They show how, on the one hand, that sanctuary depended on high principles—the power of kings, the mercy of God, the sacrality of church space. On the other hand, they show that particular contingencies affected the development of the privilege in these crucial decades: the escape of a petty debtor into Caudray's precinct at a moment that the City, or Caudray, or both wanted a test case; the appointment of a highly experienced clerk who had time and ambition as dean of St Martin's to push that house's privileges; the conception of Christian kingship held by the occupant of the throne at the point that the conflicts arose. Although the patchiness of surviving records does not allow us to see precisely how influential these particular cases were in the broader development of sanctuary privilege in decades to come, at a minimum they contributed to a developing argument—rapidly becoming something like an accepted situation—that the jurisdictional liberties attached to many religious houses could include the right to offer permanent sanctuary to those fleeing from felony charges and suits for debt. By the early sixteenth century, legal commentators would remark without controversy that sanctuary rights and franchisal liberties were one and the same.[84] In Chapter 4 we will turn to examine how the strategies of felons and one particular religious order, the Knights of St John of Jerusalem, intersected during the period of expansion of sanctuary rights in the years around 1500.

[84] McGlynn, *Rights and Liberties*, pp 109–10.

4

The Hospitaller's Cloak
Mercy, Justice, Jurisdiction

RICHARD PULHAM, RALPH TOKER, AND THE HOSPITALLER'S CLOAK

On 22 September 1506, two accused felons appeared before the peace sessions at Canterbury.[1] They likely had not met before being held in gaol before their trials; they were charged with different crimes and were brought before the bar separately. Richard Pulham, a harpist from St Mary Hoo, Kent, was indicted for having killed a man named John a Wode of the nearby town of Bobbing the month before. Pulham allegedly hit his victim on the head with a pikestaff, giving him a mortal wound from which he died soon after. When charged with homicide at the Canterbury peace sessions, Pulham pleaded not guilty and asked for his case to be put to a jury, to be summoned for the following day. Also present on 22 September at the peace sessions was a Somerset yeoman named Ralph Toker, an abjurer who had been caught within the realm after he had sworn to go into exile and never to return.[2] At the end of the day's business, neither men's processes having terminated, both Pulham and Toker were returned to the custody of the sheriff to be brought back the following day.

As Pulham and Toker were being led by the sheriffs' men from the peace sessions back to the gaol, they spotted Sir John Rawson, a brother of the crusading order of the Hospital of St John of Jerusalem, commonly known as the Knights Hospitaller.[3] One or both of them apparently had a bright idea. Pulham and Toker placed their hands on Rawson's cloak—Pulham emphasized that he did so 'gently'—and, holding tightly to the Hospitaller's vestments, they claimed 'the sanctuary and privilege of the prior and brothers of St. John of Jerusalem in England' for their separate felonies. They held on to Rawson's cloak until, as Pulham later put it, 'certain malicious men unknown to him violently dragged him away from John Rawson,

---

[1] For Pulham, see TNA, KB 27/984, rex m. 4; for Toker, KB 27/984, rex m. 12.

[2] Toker had in fact abjured twice over the previous six weeks in Kentish churches, for two separate felonies, both burglaries, although the justices of the peace and the coroners for Kent had not yet realized this; at Canterbury he was being tried only on the first abjuration. For other records associated with his processes, see TNA, KB 9/442, mm 17–20; KB 27/993, rex m. 17; KB 29/136, mm 4d, 41d.

[3] Mary Ann Lyons, 'Rawson, John, Viscount Clontarff (1470?–1547?)', *ODNB* (2004), doi:10.1093/ref:odnb/23199.

against his will'.⁴ The two were taken away by the sheriffs' men, spent the night in gaol, and returned to the peace sessions the following day. There they both separately pleaded the sanctuary of the Hospitaller's cloak and asked to be returned to that sanctuary. This may have conjured up in the justices' minds, as it does in ours, the image of two felons indefinitely following Brother John Rawson around, holding his cloak. No doubt, however, they meant, and were understood to mean, that they wished to be put into Rawson's custody and taken to a Hospitaller house.

In Pulham's homicide case, the justices appear simply to have disallowed this ingenious sanctuary claim: they recorded it, and then the record simply skips from his plea to be restored to sanctuary to the jury's consideration of the charge of homicide. The jurors found him guilty of the felony. Pulham then immediately pleaded benefit of clergy, but when given the reading test to prove his eligibility for the benefit, he could not read. Although the king's attorney then sought judgment and execution for him, the judges—for some unrecorded reason—stated that they wished to take the case under advisement and they put him back in prison. In Toker's case, the record is less clear on what happened when he returned to the sessions, but it seems that he refused to answer to the charge of being found in the realm after abjuration, insisting on his sanctuary plea alone. Instead of simply executing him on the abjuration as they could have, however, the justices put Toker, like Pulham, back in prison.⁵

Both men's cases were brought up to the court of King's Bench in Westminster, where they were heard some nine months later, on 26 June 1507. Pulham pleaded clergy again. He was tested once more, and this time he successfully read, perhaps having learned in prison over the intervening months. He was thus delivered over to the custody of the abbot of Westminster, saved from the capital penalty, to be kept in the abbot's convict house or prison.⁶ He disappears from the records after that. As for Toker, he maintained his sanctuary plea, saying still that he wholly refused to respond to the charge related to his abjuration. The court rejected his plea of sanctuary, but suggested he could plead benefit of clergy instead. The crown's attorney objected that he was ineligible (contending he had had it once

---

⁴ Pulham's plea on the King's Bench roll: 'Postquam ipse a curia predicta recessit apud Cantuar' predicta cepit sanctarium et privilegium Prioris et fratrum hospitalis sancti Johannis Jerusalemi in Anglia occasione felonie predicte et pro tuicione et salvacione vite sue, eo quod ipse manus suas super quendam Johannem Raweson militem, unum fratrum hospitalis predicti, tunc ibidem molliter imposuit, et ipsum per vestes suas traxit et tenuit, petendo ab eodem Johanne occasione predicta tuicionem sanctuarii et privilegii hospitalis predicti etc. Et sic ipsum Johannem Raweson in forma predicta tenuit quousque ipse per quosdam malivolos suos ignotos tunc ibidem contra voluntatem suam ab eodem Johanne Raweson violenter abstractus fuit'. TNA, KB 27/984, rex m. 4.

⁵ TNA, KB 27/984, rex m. 12. Several years later, some sanctuary seekers who like Toker refused to plead to the felony and instead insisted only on their sanctuary plea were subjected to *peine forte et dure* (that is they were given a starvation diet and pressed with heavy stones or irons until they pleaded or died); TNA, KB 27/1047, rex m. 8 (1512); KB 27/1008, rex m. 17 (1513). Most who pleaded sanctuary also pleaded to the felony. H. R. T. Summerson, 'The Early Development of the Peine Forte et Dure', in *Law, Litigants and the Legal Profession*, ed. E. W. Ives and A. H. Manchester (London, 1983), pp 116–25. Toker was in a different situation as his abjuration entailed a confession of guilt, and he could simply have been executed without further process.

⁶ TNA, KB 27/984, rex m. 4.

before), and so he was returned to the Marshalsea prison while the matter was investigated. There he stayed until the fall of 1509, when he appeared again before King's Bench, this time to present a pardon from the new king, Henry VIII, for all his felonies. Toker was thus set free.[7]

In neither case, then, was this seemingly strange variety of sanctuary claim accepted by the king's court—yet neither man was hanged for his felony. It is impossible at this remove to see why the justices were reluctant in these cases to impose the ultimate penalty. In this legal system that favoured the wealthy and connected, perhaps each had strings of influence to pull: Pulham was a harpist and as a musician may have made his living in aristocratic households; Toker bore that vague catch-all status, yeoman, and perhaps he also had some patron whose influence made the justices hesitate to send him to the gallows. Whatever the case, there can be no denying that both were given more second and even third chances than strict application of the law would have demanded. Whether or how their appeal to the sanctuary of the Hospitaller's cloak contributed to this mitigation of the final penalty is unclear, but from the point of view of men about to face the hangman, it had certainly been worth a try.

Pulham's and Toker's claim of sanctuary in the Hospitaller's cloak indicates how inventive accused felons could be—an inventiveness born of desperation. If Toker's and Pulham's claims seem far-fetched to us, we should not assume they were as preposterous in the early sixteenth-century context; they were disallowed by the court, but interestingly in Toker's case at least the sanctuary plea was brought up to King's Bench rather than being summarily dismissed at the peace sessions. There is no indication in the record that either John Rawson or the Hospitaller Order supported the sanctuary claim the two men made; we could, in fact, imagine that Rawson recoiled in horror as the two prisoners suddenly darted away from the sheriffs' officials and took tight hold of his cloak. Nonetheless, the justices may have taken the claim more seriously than we would at first assume, because Pulham's and Toker's claim drew upon a number of ideas circulating in early Tudor England both about sanctuary generally and the Hospitallers in particular: the apparent unwillingness of the justices of the peace and at King's Bench to hang these men may have been due to their invocation of the protection of the Hospitaller Order.

The Knights of St John had long had a special role in the processes of English criminal justice, most notably in the order's provision of Christian burial to felons in their churchyards, understood as an act of mercy for the souls of even the most heinous of criminals. This had much in common with the ideology of sanctuary, making the order's association with sanctuary a natural development. Starting slowly in the fifteenth century, in fits and starts, different kinds of sanctuary claims were made at Hospitaller properties. From the mid-1480s, those claims became more expansive and their defence by the order more vigorous. The assertion of broad sanctuary privileges provoked challenges in the courts—which is mostly how we know about it—and defence by the order itself, through the compilation

---

[7] TNA, KB 27/993, rex m. 17.

of cases supporting their claims in a cartulary and the articulation of those claims in legal responses to what it claimed were sanctuary breaches. Although the order did not support Pulham's and Toker's asylum in Brother Rawson's cloak, they did provide highly articulated legal defences of sanctuary claims for other seekers in their properties.

As the Hospitaller sanctuary cases show, however, the expansion of sanctuary claims was not simply due to institutional strategies of religious houses and orders: the actions of the seekers themselves, their invocation of mercy, life-saving protection, and sacred space, often initiated the process by which the boundaries were expanded, both literally and figuratively. The sanctuary seekers' own goals were, of course, not to aid the religious houses or orders, and often enough the seekers' long- or even medium-term goal was not to become a permanent 'sanctuary man'. For seekers, a sanctuary claim was often part of a multifaceted strategy: as in the cases of Pulham and Toker, the sanctuary claims might themselves not have been wholly effective, but they did allow a delay in what otherwise would have been a swift trip from the gaol delivery or peace sessions to the gallows. In that delay, often enough, other more permanent means of escaping execution, pardons, or even a crash course in literacy, were found. The courts themselves were often surprisingly accommodating to this mitigation-shopping, as they were with Pulham and Toker.

A coalescence of forces—the seekers' needs, the order's strategies, the court's and crown's responses, and an ideological context that emphasized a specifically Christian and ecclesiastical role in felony prosecution—allowed for expansive sanctuary privileges in Hospitaller properties in the first three or four decades of the Tudor regime. Parts of this coalescence began to disaggregate in the 1520s, however, for several reasons. To a significant extent, the kind of sanctuary the Hospitallers claimed in the early years of the sixteenth century was too broad and ultimately impracticable: in the arguments they made, as we will see later in this chapter, any dwelling house held from the order could serve as a sanctuary as it shared the sacrality of the order's protection. As the Hospitallers held a great deal of property throughout the realm, it is hard to see how this could have been made to work on a pragmatic level. In other ways, the order made miscalculations, particularly in the terms on which it defended those claims in court. Unlike other ecclesiastical rights-holders, such as St Martin le Grand, in the 1510s especially the Hospitallers downplayed the royal basis of their claims, invoking instead papal grants and the crusading order's own long history in the realm. This was an unfortunate choice. Apart from the obvious poke in the eye to the young king, in a broader sense this was going in the opposite direction from the way sanctuary was shifting in Henry VIII's reign: it was moving away from a universalist ecclesiastical Christianity that the crusading order epitomized towards a more explicitly royal and less emphatically sacralized privilege. The Hospitallers' withdrawal in the 1520s from aggressively cultivating sanctuary-seeking in its properties was not, however, characteristic more generally of the privilege of sanctuary in England: even as the Hospitallers' role in providing asylum fell off, the numbers of sanctuary seekers in other properties continued to expand in the 1520s and early 1530s, as other institutions (perhaps most notably Westminster Abbey) negotiated the changing political and religious climate more successfully.

THE HOSPITALLER ORDER, ENGLISH CRIMINAL JUSTICE, AND CHRISTIAN MERCY IN ACTION

In 1506, when Pulham and Toker seized Brother John Rawson's cloak and claimed sanctuary, the concept of ecclesiastical asylum for felons was well established generally, even if the particular notion of a piece of clothing (or, perhaps, the body of the Hospitaller) as the site of such refuge was problematic. The particular claim the two men made on the Hospitaller's cloak was, however, also framed around the distinctive relationship that religious order had with the English system of criminal justice, one that intersected with the more general ideas about mercy and redemption discussed in the previous chapters.

The Order of the Knights of St John, or to give the more formal name, the Sovereign Military and Hospitaller Order of St John of Jerusalem, Rhodes, and Malta, was founded in the Crusader states in the twelfth century. The Hospitallers, based from the early fourteenth century on the island of Rhodes, held extensive estates throughout western Europe to support their military activities in the eastern Mediterranean. By the late Middle Ages, the Knights of St John were the last of the military orders still active in England. When the Templars were suppressed by the papacy in 1312, the Hospitallers in England, as elsewhere in Europe, became the inheritors of their considerable estates. The English headquarters for the Hospitaller order, the priory of St John of Jerusalem, was at Clerkenwell, just north of the City of London. The Knights of St John, as a military order, were somewhat anomalous in the landscape of late medieval religious life; by this period, the brother knights, usually from gentry or (like Sir John Rawson) occasionally from wealthy mercantile families, were laymen, not clerics, although they swore oaths of celibacy and obedience. By the fifteenth century they were not numerous, perhaps comprising about thirty knights in the English kingdom at any one time; they lived scattered throughout the realm on the order's many 'commanderies' and other estates, often only a single brother (with servants) at a given Hospitaller house.[8]

Despite their small numbers, the order's wealth, the chivalric symbolism and military experience of the brethren, and the Hospitallers' particular role in the ideology of mercy and justice in the realm made the Knights of St John significant figures in England. The Hospitaller prior often played a notable role in the politics of the kingdom; in the fourteenth century, for instance, the Hospitaller priors acted as triers of petitions in parliament and in the fifteenth century sat on the

---

[8] On the order generally, see Helen J. Nicholson, *The Knights Hospitaller* (Woodbridge, 2001); on its establishment in England, Gregory O'Malley, *The Knights Hospitaller of the English Langue, 1460–1565* (Oxford, 2005), pp 28–33.

king's council.⁹ The prior's political importance grew during the reigns of the early Tudors, at least until the order ran up against England's break from Rome. John Kendall (prior 1489–1501) and Thomas Docwra (prior 1501–1527) served as royal councillors, undertook crucial diplomatic missions, and frequently sat as justices of the peace and in other judicial capacities. Although Kendal's and Docwra's terms as prior coincided with crises for the international order—the Hospitaller base on Rhodes was under continual threat from the Turks, ultimately falling in 1522—Simon Phillips has argued that the priorities of the English priors, especially Docwra, were focused on their king rather than on the interests of the international order.¹⁰ The wealth and importance of the Knights of St John in England also meant that, conversely, kings were careful, sometimes arguably overzealous, about overseeing Hospitaller operations; Edward IV notoriously attempted, unsuccessfully, to place one of his Woodville in-laws as prior, for example, and Henry VIII evidently saw the order as a '"finishing school" for naval officers and ambassadors', as Gregory O'Malley has put it, maintaining a firm hand in appointments.¹¹ Indeed, at Docwra's death in 1527, Henry VIII moved to assert his authority over the English Hospitallers and particularly over their estates, briefly sequestering the Clerkenwell priory and Docwra's other properties before re-granting them to the new prior, William Weston, upon payment of a considerable entry fine.¹² The 1530s, of course, posed new challenges, although if in hindsight the order's demise in England appears inevitable in light of England's break with Rome and the dissolution of religious houses, it may not have seemed nearly so foregone a conclusion to those living through that decade. The order's houses were not included in the legislation dissolving religious houses in 1535, or in 1539, and it may have seemed just possible that the anomalous nature of the order—not quite monastic, and yet not quite secular either—might allow it to survive in the new dispensation. This was not to be, however; in 1540, the Hospitaller order in England was dissolved by a separate statute, and the brethren were pensioned off.¹³ According to chronicler Charles Wriothesley, the prior, William Weston, died on the very day of the dissolution, 'of pure grief'.¹⁴

Most importantly for understanding why Toker and Pulham would have understood Brother John Rawson's cloak to have special properties, by the late medieval period the Hospitallers had also come to play an integral role in the process of English justice, a role that highlighted the complex relationship between justice,

⁹ Simon Phillips, *The Prior of the Knights Hospitaller in Late Medieval England* (Woodbridge, 2009), pp 125–32.
¹⁰ Phillips, *Prior of the Knights Hospitaller*, pp 82–8.
¹¹ O'Malley, *Knights Hospitaller*, p. 166.
¹² Henry's reaction to the larger crisis of the Order, now without a base in the eastern Mediterranean and thus without its centuries-long *raison d'être* as defender of Christian states in the Holy Land, was to bruit (but then ultimately to drop) the possibility of converting the English branch of the Order from its international Mediterranean mission to a domestic purpose, as protectors of the English realm from a new base at Calais. O'Malley, *Knights Hospitaller*, pp 178–88.
¹³ 32 Hen VIII, c. 24 (*SR* vol. 3, pp 778–81); O'Malley, *Knights Hospitaller*, pp 1–15, 161–88, 212–25; Phillips, *Prior of the Knights Hospitaller, passim*, esp. pp 154–7.
¹⁴ Charles Wriothesley, *A Chronicle of England During the Reigns of the Tudors, from A.D. 1485 to 1559*, Camden New Series 11, 20 (Westminster, 1875), p. 119; O'Malley, *Knights Hospitaller*, p. 224.

punishment, and Christian mercy. From the thirteenth century, the Knights Hospitaller, as an act of Christian charity, buried the bodies of suicides and convicted felons in their churchyards.[15] The Elizabethan chronicler and urban geographer, John Stow, for instance, explained in the late sixteenth century that in past times the 'Pardon churchyard', next to the Clerkenwell priory, had

> served for burying of such as desperately ended their lives, or were executed for Felonies, who were fetched thither usually in a close cart, bailed over and covered with black, having a plain white Cross thwarting, and at the fore end a Saint John's Cross without, and within a Bell ringing by shaking of the cart, whereby the same might be heard when it passed, and this was called the Fraerie Cart, which belonged to Saint John's.[16]

Other evidence indicates that the 'fraerie cart' was likely brought to peace sessions and gaol deliveries, in readiness for the bodies of executed felons that would normally follow from those processes.[17] Once dead, the hanged bodies were cut down by the Hospitallers (or perhaps more literally, their servants), and taken away in the 'fraerie' or 'St. John's' cart.

So the Hospitaller Knight John Rawson was likely at the Canterbury peace sessions in 1506 in an official capacity, and in holding onto his cloak Pulham and Toker were calling upon a well-established association between the Hospitallers and mercy to criminals. As Pulham and Toker might also have heard, some had even claimed that the St John's cart that carried the hanged criminals to their graves itself functioned as asylum: as Stow put it in the late sixteenth century, the cart 'had the privilege of Sanctuary'.[18] Like many aspects of sanctuary, however, we cannot find this claim earlier than the Tudor period. There were several cases in the thirteenth and fourteenth centuries where felons, having been cut down from the gibbet before they were actually dead, revived while in the 'fraerie' cart and then fled to a nearby church and abjured.[19] In those cases, the cart was not attributed any kind of special protective power or sanctuary status. But the Yearbook for 1486 includes a case where sheriffs' officers were leading a felon, condemned before the justices of the peace at Salisbury, to the gallows; as they proceeded, the wagon of St John, which had a banner attached to it, came near the prisoner. He put his hands on the banner and claimed 'the privilege of St. John's'. Certain 'evilly disposed and riotous persons', as the Yearbook described them, then forcefully seized the prisoner from the custody of the sheriffs' officers and brought him to a church.[20] In the 1486 Yearbook case, the legal question under consideration was not the legitimacy of the cart's sanctuary (which was not commented upon one way or the other), but whether those who rescued the condemned men were subject to criminal prosecution

---

[15] Ralph B. Pugh, 'The Knights Hospitallers of England as Undertakers', *Speculum* 56 (1981): pp 566–74, doi:10.2307/2847742.
[16] John Stow, *A Survey of London*, ed. Charles Lethbridge Kingsford (Oxford, 1908), vol. 2, p. 82.
[17] Pugh, 'Knights Hospitallers as Undertakers', p. 573.
[18] Stow, *A Survey of London*, vol. 2, p. 82.
[19] Pugh, 'Knights Hospitallers as Undertakers', pp 566–8. [20] Seipp 1486.002.

for helping a felon escape.[21] As the earlier fifteenth-century history of sanctuary claims at Hospitaller properties suggests, the cases of the St John's cart and the Hospitaller's cloak belong to that period of enlargement of sanctuary claims, the later fifteenth and early sixteenth century, rather than being a holdover from an earlier custom.

In thinking of the Hospitaller's cloak as a metonym for the mercy associated with the Order of St John of Jerusalem—a mercy that had many of the same valences as the concept of sanctuary—Pulham and Toker invoked a powerful idea, albeit one that could easily fall apart in practical application. Cloaks were strongly associated with divine protection: in the popular late medieval image of the Virgin of Mercy, the mother of God shelters believers beneath her voluminous cloak.[22] Pulham and Toker also invoked more generally the idea that properties associated with the Hospitaller order, movable and immovable, could offer asylum to those who most needed 'protection of their lives'. Although the Hospitallers did not, as far as we know, defend these more tendentious claims to sanctuary privilege represented by their carts or their cloaks, they certainly did vigorously defend their right to offer sanctuary in their immovable properties.

SANCTUARY CLAIMS AT HOSPITALLER PROPERTIES, 1400–1485

The Hospitallers' role in offering succor of various kinds to criminals and prisoners had deep roots in medieval Christian concepts of charity, chivalry, and redemption, but the order's role specifically in offering sanctuary to accused felons seems to have been less elaborated until well into the fifteenth century. As with the sanctuary claims of other kinds of religious houses, those associated with Hospitaller properties show that the privileges were not clearly defined, either in how the courts saw them or in how they worked in practice. Although the sparse evidence for claims on Hospitaller properties in the pre-Tudor period is ambiguous, the cases we have appear to show an uneven and bumpy transition in the course of the fifteenth century from forty-day temporary asylum in Hospitaller properties to

---

[21] Baker, *Spelman*, vol. 2, p. 340 (intro). An interesting Spanish parallel to this case comes from a Fugger family agent who reported in 1579 that a debtor who had taken sanctuary in the parish church of St Ginar outside Seville was persuaded to play the part of Christ in a Corpus Christi drama. The play was to be staged on a cart, and he was promised that as long as he stayed on the cart his creditor could not arrest him. The creditor, however, bribed the actor who was to play Judas to betray Christ by pushing him off the cart as he gave him the kiss. As soon as Christ's feet touched the ground, the creditor had him placed under arrest, but the scene erupted in violence as the actor playing St Peter leaped to Christ's defence. In the ensuing judicial process, Judas was punished as a betrayer, the debtor was forgiven his debts, and the creditor correspondingly forfeited the money owed to him. Victor von Klarwill, ed., *The Fugger News-Letters*, trans. Pauline De Chary (London: Bodley Head, 1928), 37–9. My thanks to Konrad Eisenbichler for alerting me to this example.
[22] Catherine Oakes, *Ora Pro Nobis: The Virgin as Intercessor in Medieval Art and Devotion* (London: Harvey Miller Publishers, 2008), pp 101–28. My thanks to Konrad Eisenbichler and Barbara Wisch for pointing the Virgin of Mercy out to me.

sanctuary unlimited in time of the kind that Westminster and the other chartered sanctuaries offered.

When precisely this shift happened—if indeed there was precise moment, as opposed to inconsistent practice—is unclear. Some evidence suggests a sanctuary privilege at the Hospitaller property of Paris Garden that was very similar to Westminster or St Martin le Grand as early as 1420, while other evidence indicates instead controversy about whether even forty-day sanctuary applied on Hospitaller properties as late as the 1460s. Alongside the shift to claiming chartered sanctuary privileges for Hospitaller properties were several other issues that swirled around through the fifteenth and into the sixteenth century. In particular, sanctuary seekers, or the order, or both, were interpreting the sacral powers of immunity to extend not only to church buildings, or their ambits or precincts, but also to other kinds of properties that we might define as secular (such as residential houses), but which contemporaries may have seen in less categorical ways. This extension to Hospitaller properties more generally showed the conflation of sanctuary with other kinds of jurisdictional rights. By the 1480s, the Knights of St John of Jerusalem were asserting sanctuary privileges as part of a general strategy of promotion of the order's rights and franchises.

First, let us look at the evidence that at least one Hospitaller property was making a claim to offer sanctuary to felons that was of the same kind as the asylum a liberty could offer to debtors or alien workers—in other words, the same kind of sanctuary provided by Westminster and St Martin le Grand. As discussed in Chapter 2, a Hospitaller cartulary now in the British Library recorded a set of sanctuary ordinances, dated 1420, for Paris Garden, a Hospitaller manor in Surrey across the river from the City of London.[23] They represent the earliest known regulations for an English sanctuary; curiously, and perhaps significantly, they were instituted not by the Hospitaller order's officials but by the brother of the king, John, duke of Bedford, to whom the Hospitallers had leased the Paris Garden manor. The tone of the regulations, as we saw in Chapter 2, indicates that Bedford or his agents saw asylum-seekers as a revenue opportunity, perhaps as part of a broader strategy of pursuing a franchisal economy and attracting a residential population of those interested in jurisdictional exemptions.

It is unclear how successful that strategy was. There is scattered evidence in the fifteenth century for sanctuary seekers at Paris Garden, although it is not clear whether these seekers were occasional or frequent, nor whether they took the privilege for felony or for debt. The manorial records for Paris Garden sporadically record entry fees for those taking sanctuary: the constable reported having received fees for two men in 1467; two more in 1468; and from a man and a woman in 1470. Following that there is a long gap until 1490, when a Richard Hyll, gentleman, was said to have violently taken a sanctuary seeker, John Pynchbek, out of Paris Garden, in derogation of the liberties. There is one further record for a sanctuary man's entry in 1492, and in 1500 a tenant on the manor was fined for taking

---

[23] BL, Cotton Nero E VI, Hospitaller Cartulary, fols 59rv.

a sanctuary seeker into his house without reporting it to the constable.[24] In other records I have found only a few references to sanctuary-seeking in Paris Garden: in 1484, Agnes Curteys complained to the chancellor that because of vexatious action of debt against her in the court of the manor of Bermondsey, she was forced to 'take the privilege of Saint John's at Paris Garden'.[25] In 1530, Henry Danby, a London baker and failed abjurer found in the realm and re-arrested, esaped from custody and fled to Paris Garden where he 'took the immunity of St. John', but the constable of Paris Garden immediately handed him over to the Marshal of the Marshalsea and he was ultimately hanged.[26] Danby's flight to Paris Garden was one of the last acts in a tragedy of errors; he had originally abjured in 1530 for homicide and was sent to Portsmouth. The ship he took there was blown back to the port and the sailors put him off the boat and refused to have him back. Following that he wandered around the kingdom for some months, later claiming that he was trying unsuccessfully to find a parish church to abjure anew. The sheriffs of London arrested him and put him in Newgate prison, but he escaped and it was then he ran to Paris Garden. It is not clear whether by this time Paris Garden had ceased to welcome (or never really had welcomed) felonious sanctuary seekers, or whether the constable or his superiors in the Hospitaller order simply did not want to get mixed up in Danby's obviously questionable story.

Certainly there is no evidence that Paris Garden was ever able to achieve status as a chartered sanctuary on a par with Westminster or the other great sanctuaries. There are, moreover, few other records involving sanctuary in Hospitaller properties before the Tudor period, and the cases that do survive focused on a different issue, the extent to which other Hospitaller properties outside the strictly ecclesiastical buildings qualified as sanctuary of the kind offered by any parish church. At the end of the thirteenth century, evidently, a private house held from the Hospitallers in Bristol was deemed not to be sanctuary,[27] but by the early fifteenth century the question was raised again. The Hospitallers' late fifteenth-century cartulary (parts of which were compiled precisely to record the order's sanctuary rights) transcribed a Hampshire gaol delivery record from 1410–1411 in which John Gore pleaded that he had been extracted by force from sanctuary at a certain 'Spitelhous' in Broughton, a possession of the Hospitaller order. He asked to be restored. An attorney for the Hospitaller order appeared before the justices and proffered various proofs that any possession of the order had the same privileges of sanctuary as any church, and that those who breach it are to be excommunicated and anathematized (according to papal bulls, shown to the court). This plea was, the cartulary indicates, put to a jury of worthier men of the county, who found

---

[24] Southwark, Lambeth Archives (Minet Library), Class VI/1, fols. 6r, 6v, 7r, 8r, 14d; Class VI/2, fols 2v, 6v. My thanks to Graham Dawson for generously sharing his notes on the Paris Garden manor court roll with me.
[25] TNA, C 1/64/120; C 1/37/8.
[26] TNA, KB 9/519, m. 147; TNA, KB 27/1084, rex m. 7; KB 29/165, mm 1, 10, 19d; Baker, *Spelman*, vol. 1, p. 49; vol. 2, pp 278–80.
[27] E. A. Fuller, 'Pleas of the Crown at Bristol, 15 Edward I', *Bristol and Gloucestershire Archaeological Society* 22 (1899): pp 163–4, https://archive.org/details/transactionsbris22bris; Jordan, *From England to France*, p. 51.

that from time out of memory this house had indeed served as sanctuary, and that those seized from it by the king's officers had been restored, and that this was so for all the Hospitallers' properties. After conferring with justices of King's Bench and Common Pleas, members of the king's council and other learned men, the justices at gaol delivery restored Gore to the sanctuary.[28]

This suggests not that Hospitaller properties were able to offer asylum akin to Westminster's, but rather that such properties had (it was claimed) the same kinds of privileges belonging to any parish church. This was to some extent based on the general jurisdictional rights of the Hospitallers, but it was also founded on a sacrality that was thought to inhere in Hospitaller properties. A 1421 Yearbook case made clear that, at least at that point, the extent of sacredness in those lands and properties was variegated: a defendant pleaded sanctuary, because he had been taken 'in a field that was of the fee and ancient lordship of St. John, and prayed to be restored'. But in this case the justices answered that it was not sanctuary, as it was a field, and not a church. Houses of St John 'with crosses on their roofs' were held to have the privilege of sanctuary, but not fields.[29] This appears to have meant dwelling houses occupied by tenants as well as more explicitly ecclesiastical buildings, for residential houses on properties leased from the Hospitallers often had crosses on them 'as a sign' (as another Hospitaller cartulary put it) that the tenant held the property from the order.[30]

Thus in a sense all properties belonging to the Hospitallers shared at least a measure of the sacrality of the Order of St John of Jerusalem, and, at least in some circumstances, could also offer that 'immunity of holy church' that ecclesiastical buildings provided. The earlier fifteenth-century cases allowing the broad understanding of sanctuary in Hospitaller properties were confirmed by the crown in 1461. Vincent Hall, a baker and brewer living in St John's Street, a property outside the priory gates at Clerkenwell under the Hospitallers' franchisal jurisdiction, sought refuge in an out-building of the priory complex (thus presumably within the precinct) after he hit a man on the head with a shovel and killed him. An appeal was made to the new king, Edward IV, to determine whether this building had immunity privileges, and the answer came in a writ dated 20 November 1461. The king stated that the building had the same immunity privileges as any church in England, and he mandated the coroner to proceed to the building where Hall had been staying, to hear his confession and administer his abjuration. Hall thus admitted the felony to the coroner, was assigned the port of Sandwich, and was sent on his way with a wooden cross in his hand.[31] This case indicates

---

[28] BL, Cotton Nero E VI, Hospitaller Cartulary, fols 57v–59r.
[29] Seipp 1421.102rog. Similarly, in 1494, it was held that if the felon had been taken 'in the close vicinity' of such a house, then he could have the privilege of sanctuary, in the same way that sanctuary of a parish church extended to the churchyard. Seipp 1494.015.
[30] F. W. Weaver, ed., *A Cartulary of Buckland Priory*, Somerset Record Society 25 (London, 1909), pp 58, 60. In 1489, tenants of the manor of Paris Garden were ordered to put crosses on their houses 'as other tenants of the prior of St. John of Jerusalem in England were accustomed to do'. Howard Roberts and Walter H. Godfrey, eds., *Survey of London*, vol. 22, *Bankside* (London, 1950), pp 94–100.
[31] Hall was found in the realm again within the year, but was then granted a royal pardon both for the felony and for the abjuration. TNA, KB 9/297, mm 2–3, 67; KB 29/92, m. 11; *CPR 1461–67*, p. 214.

that although the immunities offered by Hospitaller properties were in some ways more extensive than for parish churches, in that they extended territorially well beyond the church building itself, at least in these non-ecclesiastical buildings they were of a different kind than those offered at Westminster, St Martin's, Beverley, or Durham. Those who took those immunities were expected to abjure the realm. The privileges at Paris Garden may have been broader and equivalent to the chartered sanctuaries, although it is not entirely clear whether in practice asylum there was sought for felony as well as debt. There is, moreover, no evidence one way or another about the strictly ecclesiastical buildings such as the priory at Clerkenwell. In coming decades, sanctuary at Hospitaller properties changed character.

SANCTUARY CLAIMS AT HOSPITALLER PROPERTIES, 1485–1520

In England in the later part of the fifteenth century, resort to sanctuary by felons began to climb, as we saw in the previous chapter. At the same time, in some cases, clearly as a result of the increased numbers of sanctuary seekers, a flurry of claims, challenges, and attempts to regularize sanctuary privileges at religious houses in the realm ensued. Twice in the 1480s and 1490s—in the first case in the last year of Edward IV's reign, and the second time in 1495–1496—Commons petitions were presented in parliament bidding the king to restrain the new 'feigned' sanctuaries and correct their governance. Neither petition, however, went forward.[32] These petitions likely grew out of local conflicts over sanctuary issues in this same period between religious houses and civic authorities in London, Coventry, and Bristol.[33] In the conflict at Bristol, for example, a riot broke out following the forcible seizure by Bristol civic officials of Dominic Arthur, an Irish pouchmaker, from St Austen's Green, to bring him in to the city court to face a trespass plea. The Green was part of the property of St Augustine's monastery just outside the City's boundaries. The attempt to arrest Arthur on the Green came in the context of a wider dispute between the city of Bristol and the monastery over the keeping of shops and other liberties, including sanctuary, that had roiled over the previous half-decade, and had roots back into the fourteenth century. The evidence suggests that the abbey, in imitation of other religious houses in the kingdom such as Westminster, had

---

[32] TNA, C 49/40/10 (a petition to parliament decrying sanctuaries and debtors escaping due punishment, 1482–1483, which was not apparently considered in the 1483 parliament); *PROME*, Parl. Oct. 1495, Appendix (which indicates only that there had been a bill in 1495 against 'feigned sanctuaries' and that it had received no answer from the king); P. R. Cavill, *The English Parliaments of Henry VII 1485–1504* (Oxford, 2009), p. 170.

[33] The connection of the Commons petition to Bristol's quarrel with St Augustine's monastery is closest, as the best evidence we have for the 1495 petition is from a letter written by the abbot of St Augustine to the king in response to the petition: see Elizabeth Ralph, ed., *The Great White Book of Bristol* (Bristol, 1979), pp 42–3. For London and controversies over sanctuary, see the case of Thomas Bagnall (above Ch. 2 at n.79); for Coventry see the case of William Johnson in 1490: TNA, KB 9/1061, m. 50; KB 29/121, m. 9d; KB 27/919, m. 9; KB 27/920, m. 14; KB 27/925, Fines.

begun to fold sanctuary claims in with other jurisdictional liberties, and that this either began or expanded sometime late in the fifteenth century. The monastery's accounts (which survive for only two years) indicate that for 1491–1492 twelve sanctuary-seekers were admitted, which is a surprisingly large number (higher than either Beverley or Durham for the same year), and it is possible that this represented a recent upsurge. By 1511–1512, the number had dropped to five, indicating ongoing resort to the monastery, although beyond that we know nothing more about its employment as a sanctuary.[34]

Around the same time as these conflicts over sanctuary in Bristol and elsewhere arose, a series of challenges to claims on Hospitaller properties in various parts of the kingdom are also found in the records. A 1488 case showed two characteristics that would be common to a number of Hospitaller sanctuary cases heard in the royal courts over the next three decades or so. First, the defendant presented an argument that was framed by the order itself, giving details of the longstanding nature of the order's tenure of the particular property in question and its equally longstanding sanctuary rights. Second, this and many of the other cases that followed show a somewhat surprising refusal by the crown, or the court, or both, to engage on the question of those properties' sanctuary privileges. William Bougham, a labourer of Garway, Herefordshire, appeared at gaol delivery at Hereford Castle in March 1488 on an indictment of burglary. Answering the indictment, he acknowledged that he had committed the felony, but that in late December 1487 'for this felony and for the tuition of his life and his immunity, he fled and entered into a certain house in Wormelow, Herefordshire, called Harry ap Guyllym's house'. That house, he continued, was a part of the possessions of the brothers of the priory and brotherhood of the hospital of St John of Jerusalem in England, and had been from time out of mind. He stayed there, privileged, for a few hours until later that same day when the sheriff of Hereford, armed with swords and staves, dragged him out of that house against his will. An attorney appeared on behalf of the prior and the order and gave further details regarding the sanctuary privileges attached to Harry ap Guyllym's house: that it was, and had been since time out of mind, a property attached to the Dinmore Hospitaller commandery in Herefordshire (more than 20 kilometres distant), and that, again from time immemorial, it had had the liberty and privilege that 'each man or woman, fleeing to any house of the same prior and brethren for any felony and seeking tuition and immunity of his or her life', had that protection 'in that house, and in each of the houses and their ambits, safe and secure from any officers of the king of the realm of England or

---

[34] TNA, KB 9/409, mm 47–48; Ralph, *Great White Book of Bristol*, pp 21–2, 43–67; Fleming, 'Conflict'; William Worcester, *William Worcester: The Topography of Medieval Bristol* (Bristol, 2000), pp 18, 32, 52, 182, 186, 198, 206; Gwen Beachcroft and Arthur Sabin, eds, *Two Compotus Rolls of Saint Augustine's Abbey, Bristol, for 1491–2 and 1511–12* (Bristol, 1938), pp 232–3. It is worth noting again how much record survival affects our knowledge of sanctuary seeking: although seventeen people are recorded as having paid fees to enter the sanctuary at St Augustine's in 1491–1492 and 1511–1512, I have not found any other records of seekers making resort to that monastery beyond those involved in Arthur's case.

from anyone else,... as long as it pleases him or her'.[35] Reginald Pegge, the king's attorney, disputed this plea, although not by challenging sanctuary privileges in the order's properties. Instead, he contended that Harry ap Guyllym's house was not a Hospitaller possession at all but instead was a freehold tenement belonging to John ap Guyllym, Harry's father. The matter went to a jury: they decided that Harry ap Guyllym's house was, in fact, a possession of the Dinmore commandery and thus a Hospitaller property, and they also agreed that it had the sanctuary privileges outlined by the prior's attorney. The jurors also commented that when felons in the past had been extracted from there against their will, they had been restored. Despite the success of his sanctuary plea, Bougham was hanged anyway; the jurors also found, mysteriously, that he had not committed a felony, and thus could not take sanctuary, even though his offence was evidently capital (he had, perhaps, committed treason?).[36] The Hospitallers nevertheless apparently regarded this as a clear confirmation of sanctuary rights, recording it in their cartulary and adducing it in later legal arguments.[37] In another Herefordshire case from a few years later, also documented in the cartulary, the Hospitallers' attorney used the same arguments (indeed, with precisely the same wording) with an even more straightforward result: the jurors found that the house in which the felon had taken sanctuary was Hospitaller property, and that the accused had taken sanctuary there, and thus the sheriffs of Herefordshire were mandated to conduct him back to the house.[38]

The Hospitallers recorded these cases in their cartulary because they were clear recognitions of sanctuary claims in royal courts, and sanctuary claims that were expansive indeed: in both, the seeker was to 'stay [in the house] safe and secure, as long as it pleases him or her'.[39] Some other records from royal courts for Hospitaller claims were less clear-cut, although again they involved participation by the Hospitallers themselves in defence of the accused felon's claim of sanctuary, presenting the same argument made in the Herefordshire cases, although with more elaboration. In 1495, William Toft, a tailor from Derbyshire, pleaded sanctuary before King's Bench in Trinity 1495, claiming that he had been violently taken against his will from a Hospitaller property at Winkburn, Nottinghamshire. His plea included detailed arguments about the nature of the immunities and privileges attached to the Hospitaller lands in Winkburn and their origin: that the lands had been held by Richard Hastyngs, once master of the knights of the Temple of Solomon (the Templars), and that when the Templar order was dissolved in the reign

---

[35] 'Quilibet homo sive femina ad aliquam domum eorundem prioris et fratrum pro aliqua felonia pro tuicione vite sue et immunitate sua fugiens et petens in illa beneficium privilegii domus illius habeat et habere consuevit pro totum tempus predictum in eadem domo et in qualibet earundem domorum et ambitu earum tuicionem et protectionem pro huiusmodi vita sua in eisdem salvo et securo sive gravamine aliquorum officiariorum Regis Regni Anglie seu aliquorum quorumcumque. Et si aliqua persona scilicet homo sive femina sic ad aliquam huiusmodi domum predictorum prioris et fratrum pro tuicione vite sue et immunitate sua fugiens et ab eodum domo per aliquos officiarios Regis Regni Anglie extracta fuisset ipse vel ipsa per totum tempus predictum racione et vigore privilegii predicti ad eandem domum restituta fuit et restitui debuit ibidem salvo et secure expectatur et moram trahere quamdiu sibi placuerit'. BL, Cotton Nero E. VI, Hospitaller Cartulary, fols 54rv.
[36] On sanctuary and treason, see above, Ch. 2 at n.74.   [37] Baker, *Caryll*, p. 714.
[38] BL, Cotton Nero E. VI, Hospitaller Cartulary, fols 60rv.
[39] BL, Cotton Nero E. VI, Hospitaller Cartulary, fols 54rv, 60rv.

of Edward II, those lands, rights, privileges, and immunities had been transferred by statute to the Hospitallers, and were now held by John Kendal, the present prior of St John of Jersualem in England, and so on. Again, as in Herefordshire, the jurors were convinced: at the Nottingham assizes in Lent 1496, they ruled that Toft had indeed taken sanctuary in a privileged place, and that he had been violently taken from there against his will and should be restored. In this case, however, the justices were not willing immediately to accept this verdict, and so returned Toft to prison while they considered the question. There Toft sat, from term to term, as the justices continued to demur. The last entry for Toft's case indicates that he was still in prison in early 1498.[40]

If Toft's outcome does not seem to have been positive, the other sanctuary seekers in Hospitaller properties between the 1480s and about 1515 were more fortunate. In 1510, for instance, Andrew Hardewyn sought sanctuary in a churchless Hospitaller property at Botolphbridge, Huntingdonshire; he was seized from there, but when brought to trial pleaded sanctuary. The king's attorney contested his plea, but (again) not by challenging the sanctuary rights of the property but instead by alleging Hardewyn was at large outside the property when he was taken. The jurors, however, supported Hardewyn's sanctuary plea and he was restored.[41] Two others, William Morsate and Thomas Jones, claimed sanctuary at a 'messuage' at Gloucester pertaining to the Hospitallers, but rather than staying there indefinitely the two men sought the coroner and abjured.[42]

Others used sanctuary successfully without ever pleading their privilege in court, for the value of sanctuary for the seeker did not depend on its being proved there. A resort to sanctuary could provide the opportunity to disappear. Inquest jurors in the decade of the 1510s reported a number of suspects as having fled to sanctuary in Hospitaller properties immediately after a felony, but those who were accused never came before the court and were outlawed, often several years later. They either remained in sanctuary in the Hospitaller properties permanently or (more likely) escaped once attention was diverted elsewhere. In 1508, William Habage, a capper of Taunton, Somerset, fled to the commandery at Minchin Buckland following the homicide of John Williams and was finally outlawed in 1515;[43] in 1510, John Goldyng of Barrow, Lincolnshire, fled to Horkstow, a cell of the commandery of Willoughton, following a murder and was likewise outlawed in 1515;[44] also in 1510, Robert Carre, indicted for homicide, fled to the Hospitaller commandery at Maltby, Lincolnshire, and was outlawed in 1514;[45] in 1517, William Maynard, a stringer, was indicted for killing Richard Dier in Taunton, Somerset, and had fled Minchin Buckland commandery and was later outlawed,

---

[40] TNA, KB 27/936, plea m. 60; Baker, *Oxford History, 1485–1558*, p. 545; Baker, *Port*, pp 31–6; Baker, *Caryll*, pp 285–6.
[41] TNA, KB 27/997, rex . 9; William Page, ed., *A History of the County of Huntingdon*, Victoria County Histories (London, 1926), vol. 3, pp 190–8.
[42] TNA, KB 9/458, mm 80, 81; KB 29/144, m. 3.
[43] TNA, KB 9/960, m. 83; KB 29/138, m. 2d.
[44] TNA, KB 9/455, m. 24; KB 29/142, m. 25; William Page, ed., *A History of the County of Lincoln*, Victoria County Histories (London, 1906), vol. 2, p. 209.
[45] TNA, KB 9/457, m. 76; *History of the County of Lincoln*, vol. 2, p. 209.

in 1521;[46] and in 1518, Robert Parker of Radcliffe on Trent fled to an unspecified Hospitaller house in Nottinghamshire after killing a man and was outlawed the following year.[47]

The tide turned somewhat around 1515, however, as between 1515 and 1520 a cluster of sanctuary breaches from Hospitaller properties occurred which had poor outcomes for the felons. Yet although most of these men were not restored to their sanctuaries when they pleaded sanctuary in court, nor did the courts in these cases rule directly against the sanctuary claims in those properties. In only one case from the 1510s, in fact, does there seem to have been a definitive ruling, and it was a confirmation, rather than rejection of that right. This decision is known only through citation in a later case as a precedent. According to that citation, in 1515, at Newgate gaol delivery, William Anderson claimed that he had been seized from sanctuary in a house in Islington that belonged to the prior of St John's; the jurors' verdict confirmed his plea and he was restored.[48] If this citation is accurate, this was again validation in the royal court of an expansive form of sanctuary privilege: Islington was not, by any reasonable standard, in the 'ambit' of Clerkenwell priory and, as with the Herefordshire cases in the 1480s and the 1510 Hardewyn decision, the right to sanctuary was based on nothing more than that the tenement in question was held from the Hospitaller order.

In other cases in the second half of the decade, however, the legal outcomes were more ambiguous. In 1516, for instance, three Bristol men—John White, labourer; John Johnson, smith; and Edward Fowler, goldsmith—were indicted for the murder of a man on the king's road in the Kingswood forest outside Bristol. When brought before King's Bench several weeks later, they pleaded exactly the same way Toft had done in 1495, in virtually the same words, the only change being the property concerned (in this case the Temple Fee, in Bristol) and the name of the current prior (Thomas Docwra). Their plea was not put to a jury; the king's attorney had the case deferred for six terms until Hillary 1518 before finally offering the argument that the sanctuary plea was insufficient in law. Following that, the justices demurred for each term from Hillary 1518 until Trinity 1522 while the prisoners remained in the Marshalsea. In the midst of these term-by-term appearances of the accused in court, Johnson's name disappears from the record—he had presumably died in prison—and then in mid-1522 the record just ends, undetermined.[49] Similarly, in 1517, David Jones of Bristol, accused before the Bristol peace sessions of having stolen a horse and committed a burglary, pleaded that he also had been forcibly removed from Bristol Temple Fee, while the Bristol chamberlain, acting as king's attorney, disputed that the Temple Fee had any sanctuary privilege. The case was taken up to King's Bench and Jones committed to the Marshalsea prison by Michaelmas 1518, but it was apparently not heard there before Jones died in the

---

[46] TNA, KB 9/476, m. 74; KB 29/150, m. 22.
[47] TNA, KB 9/969, m. 19; R. F. Hunnisett, ed., *Calendar of Nottinghamshire Coroners' Inquests 1485–1558*, Thoroton Society 25 (Nottingham, 1969), pp 34–5.
[48] TNA, KB 27/1020, plea m. 60; Baker, *Caryll*, p. 714.
[49] TNA, KB 27/1020, rex m. 22.

prison, probably in late 1519.⁵⁰ Below in this section I will discuss in more detail another case from this period, the 1516 seizure of Sir John Savage from the Hospitaller liberty of St John's Street, stopping here only to note that it likewise also ended without a definitive decision regarding his sanctuary plea.

It seems, then, that royal justices were reluctant to pronounce on the flurry of sanctuary cases, most of them associated with the Hospitaller order, that they considered between about 1516 and the early 1520s. The royal justices were not the only authorities unwilling to take a stand: the bishop of London was also disinclined to give his considered opinions on the precise parameters of sanctuary privilege when asked to do so, contributing perhaps to the delays in these other cases in King's Bench. The bishop's viewpoint was requested by the justices of King's Bench in the case of three highway robbers who took asylum in St Mary le Strand parish church in early 1516.⁵¹ This sanctuary-taking, for some reason, caused consternation at the highest levels, and after an inconclusive discussion at the king's council about whether the men were eligible for sanctuary,⁵² the seekers were seized from the church. When they appeared before King's Bench on 12 February 1516, they pleaded sanctuary, but the king's attorney argued that they were ineligible for sanctuary because they were 'common and public' thieves, felons, and highway robbers. The justices at King's Bench responded to this sanctuary case as they never had before: they stated that the cognizance of a plea of sanctuary 'belongs to the ecclesiastical forum' rather than to their competency. They would not proceed in the case until Richard Fitzjames, bishop of London, could certify the truth of the law of holy church in this matter to the lord king, 'so that the king will know how to proceed'. For two years following this the King's Bench record states in every term that the bishop had not yet submitted his certification of the law of sanctuary; finally in Michaelmas 1518, the record simply ends.⁵³ It is not known what happened to the three highway-robbing sanctuary seekers; no opinion regarding their right to sanctuary was offered by Bishop Fitzjames, and no ruling on it was made in the king's court.

Judicial and ecclesiastical authorities' refusal to engage on this and other sanctuary cases in the years between 1516 and the early 1520s was likely additionally exacerbated by unresolved questions surrounding another high profile sanctuary case that was also pending at this same time: the plea of sanctuary made by the younger Sir John Savage after he was seized from a Hospitaller property in May

---

⁵⁰ TNA, KB 9/476, m. 11, KB 29/150, m. 34; KB 29/151, m. 35.
⁵¹ TNA, KB 27/1018, rex m. 11.
⁵² BL, Lansdowne MS 639, King's Council in Star Chamber, fols 44v–45r. Perhaps the reason the king's council became so roused against the three sanctuary seekers for their highway robbery related to the history of their co-conspirator, Robert Favell alias Savell, who had not taken sanctuary and remained at large. Favell had made a considerable career from the early years of the sixteenth century of using various kinds of mitigation, including sanctuary, to escape punishment for his crimes. See TNA, KB 29/133, m. 12d; KB 27/1005, rex m 3d; KB 27/1018, rex m. 11; KB 29/147, m. 38.
⁵³ TNA, KB 27/1018, rex m. 11. It might be significant that Fitzjames apparently became debilitatingly ill in the summer of 1518, although Fitzjames had every reason to want to stay out of this debate, which pertained more to the heads of religious houses than to the bishops. S. Thompson, 'Fitzjames, Richard (d. 1522), Bishop of London', *ODNB* (2004), doi:10.1093/ref:odnb/9612.

1516. This is the most prominent Hospitaller sanctuary case, and indeed according to Eric Ives, the most important sanctuary case in the Tudor period.[54] Despite Ives's arguments regarding its significance, however, the Savage case was just as inconclusive as others from this decade. In 1516, two knights of Cheshire and Worcestershire, Sir John Savage the younger and his father, Sir John the elder, became embroiled in a feud with another Worcestershire gentleman, John Pauncefote. As Ives outlines, the Savages were highly connected at court and had a long history of service to the Tudor monarchy, although by the 1510s (and indeed from long before) they had begun to exhibit an unruly independence from royal directives that Henry VIII's chief minister Cardinal Wolsey sought to curb. When the father and son, together with a band of retainers, murdered Pauncefote on 31 March 1516, the opportunity was taken to bring them into line and at least sixty-seven indictments were drawn up against them. Some six weeks after the murder, on 10 May 1516, the younger Sir John took sanctuary in a house where a man named William Hanley lived, in St John's Street, a liberty of the priory of Clerkenwell outside the priory's gate running south towards the City of London. Sir John stayed there for about six weeks, until 20 June 1516, when he was seized from Hanley's house and taken to the Tower and from there faced at King's Bench an appeal of murder (a private prosecution) brought by Pauncefote's widow.[55]

It is important to note that Savage did not take sanctuary inside the Hospitaller priory church or its precinct, but in a residential house in the liberty of St John's Street. Savage's flight to Hanley's house represents another Hospitaller sanctuary claim based on a broad assertion of the privilege, where asylum could be taken in any property held from the order. It is unclear who William Hanley was, although it seems likely that he knew the Savages through Worcestershire connections: the Savages were constables of Hanley Castle, and a gentleman named William Hanley held property near there.[56] At a guess, then, Savage chose to shelter in the house of a connection who happened to have a London residence conveniently within the Hospitaller liberty, arguably inside sanctuary bounds. What is not clear is why Savage would choose to shelter there, as opposed to a more secure location, for instance within the Westminster abbey precinct, although perhaps in the wake of the 1515 confirmation of the sanctuary claim in Islington, Hanley's house might have been regarded as quite safe.[57]

When brought before King's Bench in Trinity term 1516 to respond to Pauncefote's widow's appeal of the murder, Savage asserted that he had been taken against his will from sanctuary in William Hanley's house, and presented long and detailed

---

[54] Ives, 'Crime, Sanctuary'.
[55] TNA, KB 27/1020, plea m. 60; Baker, *Caryll*, p. 714; Ives, 'Crime, Sanctuary'. On criminal appeals, see Christopher Whittick, 'The Role of the Criminal Appeal in the Fifteenth Century', in *Law and Social Change in British History*, ed. J. A. Guy and Hugh Beale (London, 1984), pp 55–72; Powell, *Kingship, Law, and Society*, p. 72.
[56] TNA, C 1/371/51; C 1/373/74.
[57] Anthony Savage, also appealed by Pauncefote's widow and related in some way to the two John Savages, took sanctuary in 1518 for the homicide at Durham cathedral. He was pardoned in 1521, presumably having sheltered there in the meantime. *SDSB*, p. 80; *L&P*, vol. 3, pp 203, 529; Ives, 'Crime, Sanctuary', pp 296, 318.

arguments, presumably provided to him by the Order of the Knights of St John itself, regarding the basis of the sanctuary in Hospitaller properties. These were not the same arguments as had been wielded before, however, either because Savage was a much higher-status seeker than in the other Hospitaller cases, and that thus it was thought impolitic simply to recycle the old arguments, or because those making decisions for the order decided a new approach was needed. That new approach, however, was ill-considered: unlike Dean Richard Caudray's almost exclusive focus on royal charters and grants in his fifteenth-century defence of St Martin's sanctuary privileges, in what was surely a tactical error the arguments made on Savage's behalf emphasized first the papal bulls on which Hospitaller claims rested, and only secondarily royal grants and cases in the royal courts. After several terms of delays and deferrals, the prior of the English Hospitaller order, Thomas Docwra, was summoned to the court to demonstrate, with documents and charters, the claims to sanctuary in the house in St John's Street. Docwra appeared in Michaelmas term, 1518, 'with his charters, writings, and muniments, and at his request (because he says his claim is so diffuse and long that he cannot make certification without greater and further deliberation), the case was adjourned'. Docwra did not reappear and the case continued to drag from term to term. In the end, the case was brought to an end as most private prosecutions of murder were, by a settlement with the victim's kin. In early 1520, Pauncefote's widow withdrew her appeal, leaving Savage with the homicide charge at the king's suit to answer. Savage in turn dropped his sanctuary claim, which was no longer necessary as the settlement offered a more attractive resolution: he pleaded guilty to the murder and then presented a pardon.[58] Although he and his father were both assessed for significant fines by the terms of the pardon and lost royal favour as a result of the incident,[59] the pardon was preferable both to the noose and to a permanent stay in sanctuary.

The case thus resolved without any ruling in court on whether William Hanley's house in St John's Street could serve as a sanctuary. Before Savage presented his pardon, however, the case occasioned, according to the legal reporters (especially John Caryll), significant discussion amongst the king's justices and the king's council regarding the particular issue of immunity in the house in St John's Street and more generally of the basis of sanctuary. Caryll's report indicates that the justices did not agree with one another on the issues discussed. Most frequently cited in modern scholarship on sanctuary have been the views of Chief Justice John Fyneux, who expressed serious reservations about the status of William Hanley's house as sanctuary and suggested how sanctuary claims should be assessed. Fyneux was evidently not entirely friendly to the idea of sanctuary, but the substance of his comments focused on abuse of sanctuary rather than the fundamental principle of it: he raised first how the basis of sanctuary claims, whether by royal or papal grant, should be assessed (favouring the former); second, he noted the problem of sanctuary

---

[58] TNA, KB 27/1020, plea m. 6, transcribed and translated in Baker, *Caryll*, pp 704–14 (quotation at 714).

[59] Tim Thornton, 'Savage Family (per. c. 1369–1528)', *ODNB* (2004), doi:10.1093/ref:odnb/52794.

men who used the sanctuary precinct as a base to commit repeated felonies; and third, he queried how to define the 'ambit' of the sanctuary (whether it should include the secular buildings or not). All of these issues concerned the definition and regulation of sanctuaries, and the curbing of evident abuses, rather than an opinion that sanctuary in principle could not be supported in law. Fyneux indeed stated that sanctuary privileges were secure when certain conditions were met: the sanctuary had to have a royal grant, a papal confirmation of that grant, and use before legal memory, supported by royal confirmation and use since. As he implied, and as his contemporaries would have inferred, the privileges of Westminster Abbey, St Martin le Grand, Beaulieu Abbey, St John's Beverley, and Durham Cathedral met (or, as regarded the use before legal memory, were believed to have met) those conditions, even if William Hanley's house in St John's Street did not.[60]

Fyneux's words have nonetheless been depicted as instituting a 'drastic reinterpretation of the law of sanctuary', as Eric Ives put it.[61] Sir John Baker has also argued that this case marks a watershed in the way the royal courts handled sanctuary cases, indicating that afterwards 'sanctuary pleas were nearly always contested by the crown' and 'regularly rejected by the courts'.[62] These statements, however, exaggerate both the novelty of Fyneux's definition of sanctuary and the effect of his comments on the subsequent handling of sanctuary cases in the royal courts (where sanctuary pleas could still in fact be made successfully).[63] Baker cites three cases between 1517 and 1522 where sanctuary pleas were rejected, over all of which Fyneux presided.[64] A close look, however, indicates that in all these cases there was an irregularity about the plea. In one, an accused pleaded sanctuary on a trespass rather than a felony; in a second, which involved forty-day sanctuary in a churchyard from which he claimed he had been seized against his will, the accused refused to plead to the felony (and moreover, oddly, referred in vague terms to a pardon he had received from the emperor as well as 'the king's grace'); and in a third, which involved a Hospitaller claim, the plea was presented in such vague terms that it is no surprise that it was not accepted. This last case involved William Burbage, a London labourer, who presumably lacked the connections or advice that might have helped him formulate a proper plea. He was privately prosecuted in 1518 by Gerard Hughes, a London goldsmith, over a burglary at St Albans in which Hughes

---

[60] Baker, *Caryll*, pp 707–11. See above, Ch. 3, at n.61, regarding the fifteenth-century justices' acceptance of arguments for use before time immemorial based on evidence of early charters and exercise of liberty jurisdiction; and see below, Ch. 5, at n.112, regarding remarks made by a chief justice, possibly Fyneux, regarding sanctuary at St Martin le Grand.

[61] Ives, 'Crime, Sanctuary', pp 298–9. See also Kaufman's comments on Fyneux ('Henry VII and Sanctuary', p. 476).

[62] Baker, *Oxford History, 1485–1558*, p. 550. Baker argued in the introduction to *Spelman* (vol. 2, p. 344 [intro]) that Fyneux's comments constituted a 'constitutional precedent', but draws back from that claim in *Oxford History*.

[63] In 1520–1521, for instance, Thomas Wrexham pleaded sanctuary after having been dragged from the Westminster sanctuary and was restored. KB 9/483 mm 16–18; KB 27/1040, rex m. 15 (1520–1521). See also a reference to a sanctuary seeker having been restored (1522), TNA, SP 1/24, fol. 55, *L&P*, vol. 3, pt. 2, p. 909. See below, Ch. 6, for sanctuary breaches and pleas in the 1530s.

[64] Baker, *Spelman*, vol. 2, p. 344 (intro).

claimed he had been assaulted and a significant amount of jewellery and other goods stolen from him. When Burbage appeared before King's Bench at Westminster to answer to the charge, his plea was recorded in English: 'I say that on the Thursday after our Lady day before Christmas, I was taken out of Saint John's hold with force of arms and brought to ward again, and more I will not say and so claim the privilege of Saint John's hold'. The expression 'Saint John's hold' designated a property of the Hospitaller order; the term was used in Bristol, for instance, to refer to the Temple Fee,[65] although there is nothing in the record of Burbage's case that indicates to which of the Hospitaller properties in the kingdom he referred. The vagueness of Burbage's claim almost certainly explains why the sanctuary plea was rejected; he was hanged.[66] In all these cases, the pleas were badly formulated—in two, the pleas were recorded on the King's Bench roll in English to underline their amateurishness—and there is no sign that the religious houses or orders were involved in the preparation of the pleas, as they were in other cases. These were not, in other words, the harbingers of the demise generally of sanctuary claims, but rather a rejection of the most tendentious versions of it.

In most of the sanctuary cases from the 1510s and the very early 1520s, in fact, both royal justices and ecclesiastical officials showed a curious refusal to pronounce conclusively on the privilege, leaving many questions regarding sanctuary unanswered. The Savage case thus occurred at a moment when sanctuary issues were certainly being discussed, and some members of the king's council and other opinion makers were keen at least to curb abuses and perhaps to eradicate sanctuary altogether. This latter opinion was, however, almost certainly very much a minority view at this point, rather than the consensus that some historians have posited. And given the buck-passing and ambivalence seen elsewhere regarding sanctuary and its abuses, the argument for a full-frontal assault against sanctuary in this decade does not stand up to evidence. This is not to say, on the other hand, that there were no abuses, nor that there was no concern about them.

If the Savage case was not the watershed that Ives and Baker have claimed, nonetheless it did occur at a moment when there was considerable religious tension, and when there was concern generally about benefit of clergy, sanctuary, pardon, and the workings of the kingdom's judicial and political systems. Much of the province of Canterbury was in the grips of a Lollard scare in the 1510s, in the wake of a royal mandate to the bishops to sweep the kingdom clean of heretics; a series of heresy prosecutions through most of the dioceses south of Humber followed, and there is evidence that both ecclesiastical officials and laypeople feared that secret conventicles of heretics were gathering and threatening to infect the orthodox population with the contagion of Lollard thought.[67] 1514 also saw the climax of

---

[65] The expression was used in Bristol to designate the Hospitaller property there in 1496 (Ralph, *Great White Book of Bristol*, p. 54). See also *Oxford English Dictionary*, http://www.oed.com, s.v. hold n.1(8).
[66] TNA, KB 27/1026, plea m. 27; Baker, *Spelman*, vol. 2, p. 344 (intro).
[67] See for bibliography G. W Bernard, *The Late Medieval English Church: Vitality and Vulnerability Before the Break with Rome* (New Haven, 2012), ch. 9. The tension over heresy is reflected in an unusually high number of defamation suits heard in the lower-level London commissary court where

London's most notorious and enduringly controversial heresy case, the charge against Richard Hunne and his subsequent death in custody.[68] This case involved not only heresy accusations, but questions also about church rights and perquisites (Hunne's case began as a quarrel over a fee for a burial). Benefit of clergy, especially as it pertained to men in religious orders rather than in its broader employment by laymen, was also subject to intense discussion in the 1510s.

At the same time as controversy about religious life, the church, and ecclesiastical rights boiled, the number of sanctuary seekers saw a significant upturn in the 1510s. Although some of this increase may have been due to greater concern about it (generating more records), it is also evident in the sanctuary registers at Beverley and Durham, which were less prone to concern-based variation. Moreover, arguments for sanctuary privilege were being made more and more broadly. Claims in Hospitaller properties were very extensive indeed, for instance—at least as argued by the order in their various submissions, any of their properties could serve as sanctuary. Similar kinds of claims were also being made on the properties of other religious houses, too. Humphrey Stafford's flight in 1486 to Culham, a manor held by the abbey of Abingdon, was disallowed for him as a traitor, but justices at King's Bench found that it was privileged for felony.[69] Similarly, manors held by Westminster Abbey were also employed for sanctuary in the early sixteenth century. When, for instance, the London summoner Charles Joseph, accused in the notorious Hunne case, fled from Lambeth following Hunne's death, he went to the manor of Good Easter, Essex, claimed sanctuary there, and the bailiff of Good Easter registered his name into the register. Although the record does not indicate this, Good Easter was a manor belonging to Westminster Abbey,[70] and the existence of a register at Good Easter indicates that he was not the first to seek sanctuary there. Joseph was in custody by January 1515, but this may have been as a result of a deal, as he was later released, according to Thomas More.[71] There are a few other cases in the 1510s and 1520s where sanctuary seekers sought refuge in manors belonging to Westminster, Beaulieu, and Durham abbeys, including the manor of Knowle in Warwickshire, which will be examined in more detail in Chapter 6.[72]

Londoners alleged that their neighbours had called them 'heretics' or 'Lollards': LMA, DL/C/B/043/MS09064/011, Act Book of the Commissary Court of the Diocese of London, vol. 11, 1511–1516, fols 155r, 156r, 159r, 160r, 170r, 187r–188r.

[68] For references to the voluminous scholarship on the Hunne affair, see Bernard, *Late Medieval English Church*, pp 1–16.

[69] See above, Ch. 2 at n.75.

[70] *Enquirie and Verdite*, sig. C3r; Richard Wunderli, 'Pre-Reformation London Summoners and the Murder of Richard Hunne', *Journal of Ecclesiastical History* 33 (1982): pp 209–24, doi:10.1017/S0022046900029596. A reference in Caryll's report on Standish's case indicates that Joseph took sanctuary at Westminster; Baker, *Caryll*, p. 686. Good Easter had been an estate (with prebendaries) held by the collegiate church of St Martin le Grand; in 1503, Henry VII granted St Martin's and its properties to Westminster Abbey to fund the Abbey's Lady Chapel. Reddan, 'Collegiate Church', p. 203. As both St Martin le Grand and Westminster Abbey were chartered sanctuaries, it is unclear from which of the two Good Easter's sanctuary claims derived.

[71] Wunderli, 'Pre-Reformation London Summoners', p. 224.

[72] TNA, KB 9/457, m. 107 (1510, St Keverne, Cornwall, a dependency of Beaulieu abbey); KB 9/486, m. 36 and KB 9/502, m. 89 (1521 and 1525, Crayke manor, Yorkshire, dependency of

Those particularly elastic sanctuary privileges clearly derived from the conflation of the franchisal rights attached to liberties and the specifically ecclesiastical privileges of church spaces.[73]

Yet although claims to offer sanctuary privileges were apparently expanding in the early Tudor period, clearly not all properties belonging to the Hospitaller order or to religious houses like Westminster Abbey in a practical sense could, or did, function as sanctuaries. In the case of the Hospitallers, for instance, the order held many properties throughout the realm, including substantial holdings in the City of London, and it would simply not have been feasible for each of these properties to exercise the same kinds of sanctuary privileges that the order claimed for some of them. Why or how some of the properties came to exercise, or claim, those privileges is not clear. Could tenants who held houses from the Hospitallers refuse to take in a sanctuary seeker who appeared at their door? The relatively low number of such claims for which we have evidence suggests that in fact the flights to Hospitaller tenancies were not random, but rather (as was presumably the case with William Hanley and Sir John Savage) that the tenant was connected in some way to the sanctuary seeker. And in some instances the religious houses themselves declined the extension of immunity privileges to all their properties. In at least one case the abbot of Westminster chose not to support a sanctuary plea made on one of its manors. In 1506, Hugh Bradbury, a husbandman of Tottenham, Middlesex, was indicted at Buckinghamshire gaol delivery for burglary, and pleaded sanctuary: he had taken refuge on the manor of Hoddesdon, previously belonging to St Martin le Grand and just recently, in 1503, granted along with the collegiate church's other properties to Westminster Abbey. As Bradbury pleaded, Hoddesdon had always provided sanctuary to all traitors, felons, and murderers, and he had, he said, been taken from there against his will. Bradbury's initial plea was elaborate, suggesting some assistance from the abbey itself in its preparation, but when the abbot himself was summoned to King's Bench to show evidence for the claim Bradbury made, the abbot disavowed that the manor in question had ever had any privilege of sanctuary. Bradbury was returned to the Marshalsea prison and the record ends there. Perhaps the abbot thought better of making this questionable claim.[74] The same impulse not to over-extend may also have been at work when a sanctuary claim made by two men in 1513 on the manor of Easterford was not accepted; it was not even spelled out on the record that Easterford was yet another Westminster Abbey manor, and there is no sign that the plea was supported by the abbey.[75]

Durham abbey); KB 9/509, m. 156 (1529, Knowle sanctuary, dependency of Westminster abbey—and see Ch. 6 more generally on Knowle).

[73] The crown itself may have been the originator of the idea that some manors belonging to the religious houses with sanctuary rights could share in those rights: for instance, Edward IV granted to the tenants of Hoddesdon, a Hertfordshire manor belonging to St Martin le Grand, that they could use and enjoy all liberties and 'immunities' that had been granted to St Martin's itself. WAM, MS 13165.

[74] TNA, KB 9/444, m. 22; KB 27/984, rex m. 8; KB 29/136, mm 26, 41d; Baker, *Caryll*, pp 553–5. The abbot was either unaware of the grant from Edward IV to Hoddesdon cited in n.73, or he simply decided that he was not interested in broadening the sanctuary claims in the abbey's manors.

[75] TNA, KB 27/1008, rex m. 17; Thomas Wright, *The History and Topography of Essex* (London, 1836), p. 260.

SANCTUARY CLAIMS AT HOSPITALLER PROPERTIES, 1520–1539

In general, sanctuary-seeking did not by any means cease after 1520, as the records indicate expansion for another decade. Evidence for sanctuary-seeking on Hospitaller properties specifically, however, becomes much less plentiful. This is not to say that it ceases altogether. As Caryll's report on the Savage case shows, Chief Justice Fyneux evidently did not believe that the hospital of St John of Jerusalem held the right to shelter sanctuary-seekers beyond the general forty-day allowance for all churches, but this does not mean that his view held the day or that it constituted binding precedent. Yet the amount of evidence we see for the seeking of sanctuary at Hospitaller sites in the period between the 1480s and the 1510s cannot be found after 1520. This was likely due at least in part to the order's change in tactics, abandoning a legally and politically expensive policy in what was in general a time of retrenchment for the order. This is not the same thing, however, as seeing the discussions on sanctuary that accompanied consideration of the Savage case as killing the privilege altogether, or even disallowing it for Hospitaller properties.

The few cases in the records involving Hospitaller properties after 1520 indicate that felons did continue, at least occasionally, to seek, and apparently receive, sanctuary in the order's possessions. In July 1526, John Bradley, gentleman of Westminster, fled to what a coroner's inquest jury called 'the sanctuary of St. John of Jerusalem by [*iuxta*] St. John's Street'[76] (thus presumably within the priory precinct rather than outside, although this is not entirely clear). Bradley appeared before King's Bench in Easter term 1527, and presented a pardon for his role in the homicide, and he was released.[77] Not only is there no sign that his sanctuary at the priory was challenged, but his sojourn there was registered on the official King's Bench record of his pardon as if it was unproblematically part of the legal process by which his felony charge was forgiven. Statements made both by the order and by the city of Bristol in disputes over Bristol's Temple Fee in the 1530s, discussed in more detail below, imply that the Temple Fee was also still functioning as a sanctuary for felons as late as 1533, although perhaps in somewhat more restricted ways than earlier. As the Hospitallers' own description of their sanctuary rights there indicated, by that point felons were sheltered only in the order's own dwelling houses and churches, as distinct from houses held by tenants, where debtors and trespassers could stay.[78] This may indicate how, for the Hospitallers, the legal questions of the 1510s were settled, with a retreat back to linking sanctuary for felons with explicitly sacral space.

Yet making that distinction between ecclesiastical and secular buildings may be too neat, as one 1527 case, where sanctuary was pleaded following seizure of a felon from a residential house held from the Hospitaller order, again resulted in the

---

[76] TNA, KB 9/501/2, m. 24.

[77] TNA, KB 27/1063, rex m. 3. Bradley's accomplice George Tunstall also later successfully claimed the general pardon of 1529, arguing that the homicide had not been intentional; it seems likely that he had been in Westminster sanctuary in the intervening period. TNA, KB 27/1075, rex m. 2d.

[78] TNA, STAC 2/6, fol. 94r.

same kind of buck-passing and refusal to rule that had characterized many of the 1510s Hospitaller sanctuary pleas. The plea was neither rejected outright, as we would expect if dwelling houses held from the Hospitallers were clearly no longer able to offer the privilege of sanctuary, but nor was the seeker's plea to be restored to his asylum recognized. Robert Markes, a yeoman from Subberton, Hampshire, was indicted in 1527 as an accessory to a string of robberies over the previous two years. At gaol delivery at Winchester, Markes pleaded sanctuary: he had fled to a dwelling house at the commandery at Baddesley, Hampshire, he said, claiming its privilege. The order must have been involved in some way in his defence: he answered using precise wording that other claimants at Hospitaller properties had used going back to the 1490s. Less than three weeks after he had taken sanctuary there, the under-sheriff of Hampshire, along with many other men, seized him from the sanctuary, with force and arms, and against his will, and took him to the king's gaol at Winchester.[79] The justices at gaol delivery sent this case up to King's Bench to deal with in Michaelmas term 1527, but the controlment roll at King's Bench indicates that the justices at Westminster returned the case to Winchester.[80] There, again, in Lent 1528, Markes made the same plea of sanctuary, and the justices again did not rule.[81] Finally in Easter 1529, Markes appeared before King's Bench, presented a pardon, and was released.[82] The pardon neatly avoided the apparently difficult question of whether his sanctuary plea had any merit.

There is even less evidence for sanctuary seeking on Hospitaller properties in the 1530s, although there is some. Probably not too much can be made of the case of Henry Danby mentioned in the section above looking at cases in 1400–1485: he was the failed abjurer of 1530 who, following a picaresque series of adventures ran to Paris Garden, the Hospitaller property by Southwark. Although he claimed that he 'took the immunity of St. John' there, the bailiff of Paris Garden refused to take him and instead handed him over to the Marshalsea prison.[83] Although Danby was not accepted at Paris Garden, as we saw, a dispute between the Knights of St John and the city of Bristol in 1533–1534 implies continued welcoming of felons at the Temple Fee. In Trinity term 1534, the mayor, burgesses, and commonalty of the town of Bristol petitioned the king in Star Chamber regarding a quarrel with Hospitaller Sir Edmund Hussey over jurisdiction in the Temple Fee, making that familiar conflation of franchisal perquisites such as assize of bread with the privilege of sanctuary.[84] As the mayor and burgesses alleged, Hussey was claiming, wrongfully, that Temple Street was an independent liberty (when the city of Bristol claimed that it was under civic jurisdiction) and indeed that it had the same kind of sanctuary as the prior of St John's claimed in all other lands and tenements of

---

[79] 'Quodque domus illa est et a tempore quo non extat memoria fuit parcella possessionum religiosorum virorum prioris et fratrum sancti Johannis Jerusalemi in Anglia ac domus privilegiatus et sanctuarium a toto eodem tempore et quod ipse tunc et ibidem peciit et clamavit libertatum et privilegium, tuicionum et defencionem eiusdem sanctuarii sive domus privilegiatum pro immunitate et tuicione suis'. TNA, KB 9/504, m. 3.
[80] TNA, KB 29/159, m. 22d.   [81] TNA, KB 9/509, mm 3–4.
[82] TNA, KB 29/161, m. 6; KB 27/1071, rex m. 6.   [83] See above, this chapter at n.26.
[84] TNA, STAC 2/6, fol. 93. Hussey was commander of the Hospitaller commandery at Templecombe, Somerset (ibid.).

the priory of St John. The City of Bristol's petition detailed what those claims were: 'that is to say Sanctuary for all manner…committing murder, felonies, also Sanctuary for debt', and the right to hold a court and to take 'waif and straif' (lost property and stray animals). The Hospitallers' false claims of an independent jurisdiction were causing many unsavoury people to gather and unlawful alehouses to proliferate, and Hussey himself tried to intimidate the burgesses with bands of armed retainers. The mayor and burgesses now stood in jeopardy of their lives unless the king intervened.

The prior of the Knights of St John, Sir William Weston, and Sir Edmund Hussey responded to the mayor's petition by claiming that the accusations of armed intimidation had been sinisterly and shamefully devised to vex Weston and Hussey so that they would cease to exercise the liberties they and their predecessors had lawfully enjoyed, from time out of mind, in Temple Street.[85] In the manor of Temple Fee, the prior of St John had long had the view of frankpledge, waif and straif, assize of bread and ale, and the control of the market on the street. Moreover, they said, the prior and his predecessors had had within the Temple Fee manor sanctuary for debt, trespass, and felony, although not treason. The sanctuary men living there were daily 'ordered, corrected, and punished according to the law'.

As usual in the records of adversarial legal processes where the two parties presented mutually incompatible statements, it is difficult to discern from these two claims what was happening in the Temple Fee in the 1530s. It is likely significant, however, that both parties indicated that the Temple Fee was operating up until this point as a sanctuary for (as Hussey and Weston put it) 'any manner offences except Treason'. As few traces of sanctuary seekers at Temple Fee survive—and none, beyond this Star Chamber suit, after the 1510s—we might guess that relatively few felons were seeking refuge there by the 1530s. Instead, the main issue between the town and the Hospitaller order was likely the other kinds of jurisdictional liberties the Hospitallers exercised on the manor, and in particular the control of the market. As David Harris Sacks notes, Temple Fee had developed by this time as an important manufacturing district for Bristol's burgeoning clothing industry, and the city was determined to extend its authority over it.[86] This particular episode ended two years later in 1536 with a ruling that the Temple Fee was not, in fact, a sanctuary for felony and that the town could execute arrests and writs there; the dispute about the other kinds of jurisdictional liberties was left unresolved, at least until the Hospitaller order was dissolved and the city acquired the order's properties in and around Bristol in the 1540s.[87]

The dwindling of claims at Hospitaller properties in the 1520s and 1530s has, for some historians, epitomized the decline of sanctuary privilege itself. Yet it seems that the Hospitallers' experience in these decades was particular to the order, rather than emblematic of general attitudes towards sanctuary. The number of sanctuary

---

[85] TNA, STAC 2/6, fol. 94.
[86] David Harris Sacks, *Trade, Society, and Politics in Bristol, 1500–1640*, 2 vols (New York, 1985), vol. 1, pp 190–1.
[87] Sacks, *Trade*, vol. 1, p. 191.

seekers expanded in those decades, and they were not confined to the tried and true asylums at Westminster Abbey and the other well established ecclesiastical precincts. As we have seen in this chapter and will see in more detail in the examination of the sanctuary town of Knowle in Chapter 6, although the more extenuated versions of Hospitaller claims in its residential properties were more or less abandoned after about 1520, this did not mean that similar claims on properties far from the sacral centres of other monasteries and churches also fell into disuse. Records from the 1520s and 1530s show the successful employment of sanctuary privilege in the dependent manors of Westminster Abbey and Durham cathedral.

Indeed, in one case the jurisdictional liberties of an entirely secular franchise, in the town of Bewdley, were stretched in the 1530s to include sanctuary—and those jurisdictional liberties were even spuriously sacralized. Bewdley was on the border between Shropshire and Worcestershire, and until 1544, when a statute defined it as falling in Worcestershire, the county in which it fell was ambiguous.[88] The town's liminal status, and perhaps the name it shared with the sanctuary at the Hampshire abbey of Beaulieu (pronounced and often spelled Bewley or Bewdley in the sixteenth century),[89] seems to have led to its being used as a sanctuary. In 1536, Rowland Lee, bishop of Coventry and Lichfield and president of the Council in the Marches, wrote to Cromwell to complain about the 'club sanctuaries' (a term that I have not seen anywhere else) of Wigmore[90] and Bewdley, which were being used as sanctuaries even though he thought they had no such privilege. He recommended that Bewdley's shire be declared by parliament, 'for at such time as any of them be indicted in Worcestershire for any riot or unlawful act done within the said town or franchise, then they say their town and franchise is in Shropshire, and in like manner they make answer when any unlawful act is by any of them done there whereof they are indicted in Shropshire'.[91] In 1539, the antiquarian and travel writer John Leland noted in his description of the town that 'there was privilege of sanctuary given to this town, that is now revoked and abrogated',[92] but that abrogation may have been very recent, as there is evidence of its use as late as 1538.[93] Most of the clear references to Bewdley's sanctuary status, in fact, come from the 1530s—and interestingly, most of them come not from tendentious claims made by sanctuary seekers, but instead from coroners' assignment of the town of Bewdley

---

[88] 34 & 35 Hen. VIII, c. 26 (*SR* 3:936); William Page and J. W. Wills-Bund, eds, *A History of the County of Worcester*, Victoria County Histories (London, 1924), vol. 4, pp 297–317.

[89] References to sanctuary at Bewdley and Beaulieu are often confused and confusing because of their having the same name. It is not clear, for instance, which is meant at *SR*, vol. 2, p. 554; *L&P*, vol. 6, pp 391–3; vol. 7, p. 38; or TNA, C 1/863/46. Some records specified Shropshire or Worcestershire, presumably because of this confusion. Here I distinguish by the modern spellings.

[90] Wigmore was in Herefordshire; apart from Lee's complaint about it there is no other evidence that survives of its use as a sanctuary.

[91] TNA, SP 1/102, fol. 10r; *L&P*, vol. 10, p. 94.

[92] John Leland, *The Itinerary of John Leland in or about the Years 1535–1543*, ed. Lucy Toulmin Smith (London, 1907), 2:89. Its privilege for debt, however, was still being observed at least in 1542 (TNA, C 1/980/47), and in the statute placing it firmly in Worcestershire, its rights, privileges, and franchises were explicitly to continue as they had before.

[93] TNA, KB 9/539, m. 100. In 1542, the town was still described as 'privileged for debt', although perhaps significantly the word sanctuary was not used. TNA, C 1/980/47.

as a sanctuary to which an abjurer should proceed following his oath of abjuration. Bewdley was assigned to a burglar by a Huntingdonshire coroner in 1532; by a Yorkshire coroner to a robber in 1534; and by another Yorkshire coroner to a horse thief in 1538.[94] Most interestingly, in 1532 and 1533, one Essex coroner, Thomas Silesden, sent two abjurers to 'the sanctuary of St. John of Bewdley in Shropshire', in the second of those specifying that the St John in question was the Evangelist.[95] As far as I have been able to tell, there was no church or chapel dedicated to any St John in the area,[96] and so this attribution appears to be the coroner's misapprehension—but a telling misapprehension. It suggests that the coroner was trying to fit the square peg that the secular franchise of Bewdley constituted into the round hole of 1530s sanctuary privilege: although its use as a sanctuary appears to have derived entirely from the conjunction of its secular franchises and its liminal status in relation to county jurisdictions, the coroner thought it must have some connection to a church. Although in the 1520s and 1530s there was confusion and inconsistency about where sanctuary privilege could be claimed, if anything those claims were becoming broader rather than narrower.

* * *

The chronological narrative arc of sanctuary claims at Hospitaller houses was rather different from the broader history of sanctuary in the fifteenth and sixteenth centuries: Hospitaller sanctuary claims dwindled in the 1520s as they were increasing elsewhere. The unique context of the Knights of St John—significant property holders (with attendant jurisdictional rights), with simultaneously broad and yet ambiguous claims for sacrality in those properties—made it possible for the order to make ambitious claims to offer sanctuary, but also made it difficult to maintain them. The pattern of sanctuary claims in their holdings reflects the intersection of strategies employed by the order itself and knowledge amongst those who needed to seek sanctuary about where it could be sought. Although the Hospitallers did not support Toker's and Pulham's contention that the very cloaks the Knights of St John wore had the privilege of sanctuary, between the 1490s and the 1510s the order appears to have pursued a very broad—and ultimately impracticable—strategy of sanctuary claims, contending that any house belonging to the order could serve as refuge for a sanctuary seeker.

In making those claims, the order was conflating (just as Westminster, St Martin's, Durham, and Beverley had) the idea of ecclesiastical immunity with the other kinds of jurisdictional liberties that they were able to exercise on at least some of their properties. If, on the one hand, this equated sanctuary with other income-producing

---

[94] TNA, KB 9/527, m. 149; KB 9/529, m. 186; KB 9/539, m. 100; see also KB 9/531, m. 93.

[95] TNA, KB 9/521, m. 77; KB 9/523, m. 52; on the second, the right edge of the membrane is torn, and only the 'B' can be seen on Bewdley, with Shropshire clear on the next line.

[96] Bewdley was in the parish of Ribbesford, Worcestershire, the church of which was dedicated to St Leonard. A chapel in Bewdley itself was dedicated to St Ann; according to a nineteenth-century history of Bewdley 'tradition relates' that sanctuary seekers 'first built the Chapel in the town that they might receive the consolations of religion without going beyond their bounds'. John Richard Burton, *A History of Bewdley; with Concise Accounts of Some Neighbouring Parishes* (London, 1883), 16; Page and Wills-Bund, eds, *A History of the County of Worcester*, vol. 4, pp 297–317. The Cistercian monastery of Beaulieu in Sussex was dedicated to the Virgin Mary.

perquisites that were not inherently spiritual or ecclesiastical in nature, on the other hand the opposite sort of conflation was also occurring: that such rights and franchises, and indeed tenements and houses held from the Knights of St John, with crosses on the roofs, were to a certain extent sacralized. Late medieval English people associated the Knights of St John with the idea of mercy and succour for prisoners as a general religious value (one of the seven works of mercy, as we saw in Chapter 2), which appears then to have extended to an idea of asylum for the safeguard of felons' lives. These themes of the intertwining of a sacralized sheltering of sinners through the church's redemptive power with liberties, franchises, and privileges of ecclesiastical properties continued to resonate, into the 1530s, even at the same time as there was a subtle shift towards sanctuary as the 'king's privilege'[97] rather than or in addition to 'the immunity and tuition of holy church'. We will see these themes come up again in Chapter 5, as we consider a series of renewed conflicts between the City of London and St Martin le Grand during the reign of Henry VIII. The documentary remains of that dispute give us the most detailed evidence we have of how sanctuary precincts functioned in the kingdom's topography.

[97] See Ch. 1, n.52 and further discussion in Ch. 6.

5

Francis Woodleke's Window

Stranger Shoemakers, Boundaries, and Sanctuary in London in the 1530s

In or around 1533, Francis Woodleke, a shoemaker and resident of the precinct of St Martin Le Grand, decided to create a new shop window in the tenement he sublet. Woodleke was an immigrant to the English realm, a 'stranger' or 'alien' in the English parlance of the day. The building in which he lived and worked was on the east side of St Martin's Lane, on the corner where the lane intersected with the street leading to Cheapside. Up to this point, Woodleke's shoe shop opened only into Pouchmaker's Court, inside the walled close of St Martin Le Grand. On its west side the house and shop backed onto a thick wall, built in the middle of the fifteenth century by Dean Richard Caudray. Woodleke, looking for more passing trade, wanted a shop window that opened onto St Martin's Lane instead of into the close. Others before him had done the same: in the early years of the sixteenth century another alien shoemaker named Harry Potts had made a window through the wall further north on the lane, apparently with no adverse effects. In 1516, John Browe, a stranger pouchmaker, whose shop was probably next door to Woodleke's, also had a window that opened out into St Martin's Lane.[1] Despite these precedents, two decades later Woodleke's planned window on St Martin's Lane was far more problematic (Figure 5.1).

On a December afternoon in 1533, between two and three o'clock in the afternoon, Chamberlain George Medley of the City of London together with fourteen or fifteen other people raided Woodleke's shop, as well as the shop of another shoemaker, George Colyn, who lived across from him in St Martin's Lane. Colyn had opened a shoe shop where there had not been one before, in a former back room of a tavern called the Bull Head. From the two shops Medley and his assistants carried away into the custody of the City thirty-nine pairs of shoes and slippers and twenty pairs of boots. Woodleke and Colyn were alien craftsmen and as such, according to

---

[1] WAM, Westminster Abbey Register Book, vol. 2, fols 81v–82r. Browe agreed by his lease to close the windows at the same time that St Martin's great gate was closed and to hand over the keys to the constable until the gate opened again the following day. Browe's tenement could, in fact, have been the same as Woodleke's, but on balance it seems more likely that Woodleke's was the tenement just to the north of this one, in 1516 held by Thomas Feryng alias Frez or Fryse. Woodleke sublet his tenement from Hugh Payne, the precinct's constable (on whom see the section 'Governing St Martin's Precinct in the Reign of Henry VIII' below). Ibid., fols 23rv, 81v–82r, 234r; TNA, PROB 11/29/400, Will of Hugh Payne, 7 Oct. 1542, proved 26 June 1543.

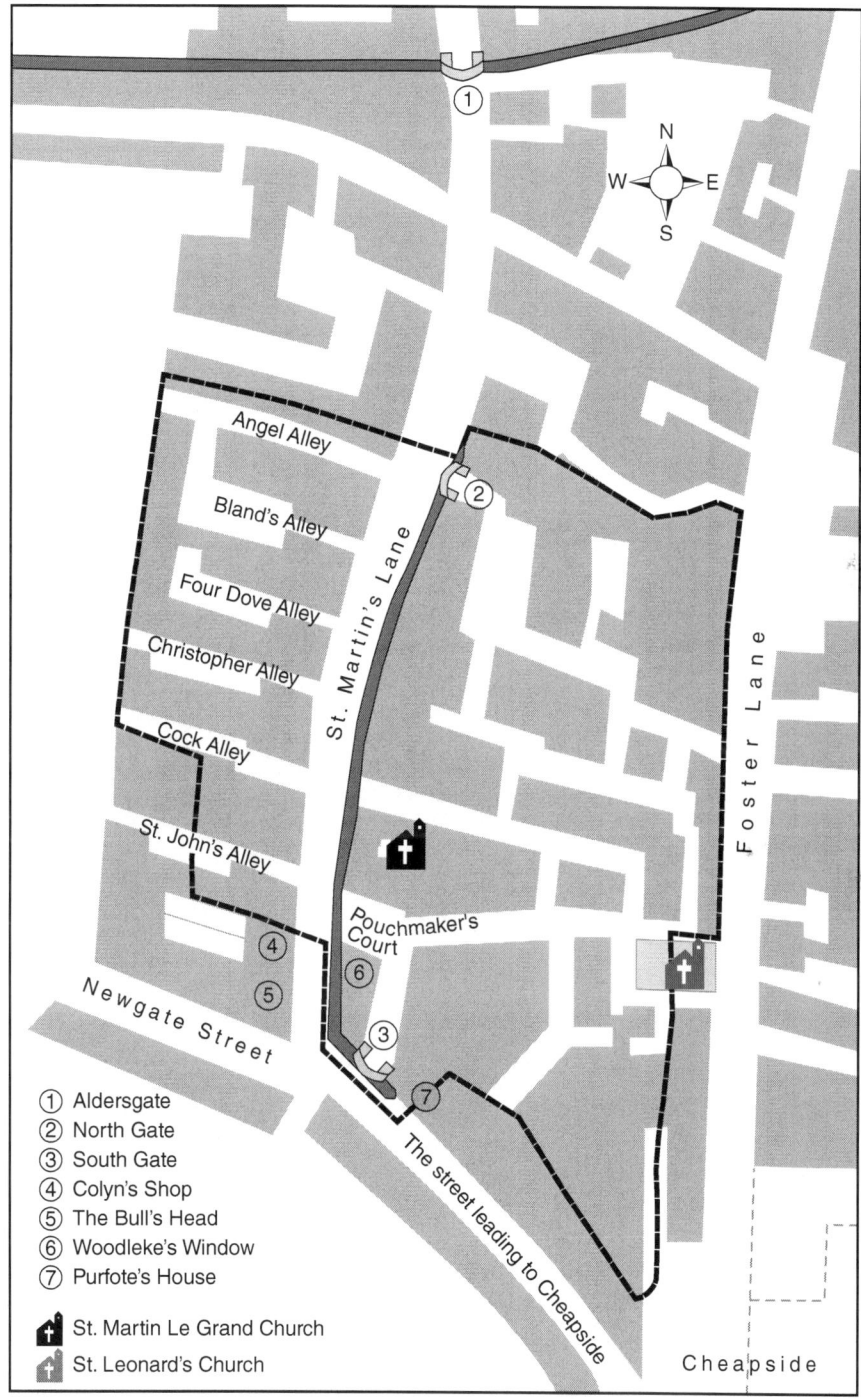

Figure 5.1. The boundaries of the precinct of St Martin le Grand, *c.* 1536.

Chamberlain Medley, they were prohibited from keeping any open shop to offer, buy, or sell any wares or merchandises in the City upon pain of forfeiture. Woodleke and Colyn in response petitioned the king's chief minister, protesting that their shops were in the precinct and liberty of St Martin Le Grand and that the chamberlain thus had no jurisdiction there.

The rival claims of chamberlain Medley and the shoemakers were emblematic of long-standing disputes between the City and St Martin Le Grand about precisely where the boundaries of sanctuary—and thus the liberty—at St Martin's lay and consequently whether shops and tenements on St Martin's Lane were inside or outside City jurisdiction. In the fifteenth century, as we saw in Chapter 3, the collegiate church's dean had vigorously and successfully defended the precinct's privileges, including not only sanctuary but a range of other franchisal rights. In 1503, King Henry VII granted St Martin le Grand and its landed properties in the counties around London to Westminster Abbey to fund the building of a magnificent Lady Chapel in the abbey church, and henceforth St Martin's liberties and privileges were defended by the abbot of Westminster. Those liberties were unchanged at the transition; from the fifteenth century into the reign of Henry VIII, alien craftsmen otherwise unable to work in London had been able to maintain their shops in St Martin's Lane. Their right to do so was protected by the crown both explicitly, through statutory exemptions for St Martin's of London's control of labour and trade in the metropolitan region, and implicitly, through the royal family's at least occasional patronage of St Martin's shops. Some insinuated, for instance, that Harry Potts's boldness in breaking the wall on St Martin's Lane for his shop was due to his being shoemaker to Prince Arthur.[2]

The context in the 1530s was different, however; Woodleke and Colyn had each tried to open or extend their retail space at a particularly sensitive time, when the events of the English Reformation were beginning to unfold and the status of religious houses and their privileges was in some doubt. Although, as we saw in Chapter 2, previous disputes between St Martin's and the City had tended to be resolved in St Martin's favour, in 1533 the City likely thought that it had a much more receptive royal ear and pushed for a decisive statement crushing St Martin both as a sanctuary and a liberty. Responding, if somewhat desultorily, to that demand following the raids on Woodleke's and Colyn's shops, the king mandated a slow-moving royal commission working over several years to establish the boundaries and liberties of St Martin's sanctuary.

As the depositions and statements gathered for that commission show, determining and recognizing the boundaries of special jurisdictions in a dense urban landscape were not straightforward matters.[3] The bounds of St Martin's precinct

---

[2] TNA, STAC 2/20/323, mm 4, 27.
[3] See on these issues Roberta Gilchrist, *Norwich Cathedral Close: The Evolution of the English Cathedral Landscape* (Woodbridge, 2005), esp. ch. 9; Johnson, 'Law, Space, and Local Knowledge', esp. pp 28–34, and ch. 1; Houston, 'People, Space, and Law', pp 53–7, 65–9; and more generally on the complexities of space and law, Lauren A. Benton, *A Search for Sovereignty: Law and Geography in European Empires, 1400–1900* (Cambridge, 2010).

were indicated in some places by walls and gates, as one might expect,[4] but in other places they were marked only by notional, and not surprisingly often disputed, lines in the middle of streets. The limits were established—although always contingently, never definitively—through social practice, its observation, and its recognition. Unlike the sanctuary at Beverley, where the immunity the sanctuary conferred acted as a kind of force-field, strongest near the centre (the shrine of St John of Beverley), less secure at the edges,[5] St Martin Le Grand's urban situation made such gradations of sanctuary impracticable. Immunity at St Martin's was all or nothing: a sanctuary seeker was either in, or out, of sanctuary, and the boundary, although disputed, had to be precise. The meaning of the sanctuary was constituted through claims, counter-claims, and royal confirmations; through precedent and custom; and through how particular kinds of individuals, especially felons and traitors 'privileged' of the sanctuary, inhabited and used a particular territory. Sanctuary men (and, much more rarely, women) lived, walked, stood, and drank—and were seen and remembered to live, walk, stand, and drink—in particular places and not others, and by so doing helped constitute the boundaries.[6] In turn, the sanctuary seekers' walking patterns established rights for the shoemakers and their shops: Francis Woodleke's window was justified, some said, by the immunity of the sanctuary men who frequently strolled past it on the street outside. The commission that ensued from the dispute over Francis Woodleke's window gives us a remarkably high resolution picture of life in St Martin's precinct in the sixteenth century, revealing to us how the high concepts of the immunity of churches and the mercy of Christian kings played out in the social practice and lived experience of fifteenth- and sixteenth-century Londoners.

LIVING IN THE PRECINCT OF ST MARTIN LE GRAND

In the sixteenth century St Martin's precinct was a crowded and diverse place. Its original core was the collegiate church, which had about a dozen or so clergy attached to it.[7] When St Martin le Grand was granted to Westminster Abbey in 1503 the position of dean was abolished, but the canons and vicars remained.[8] In addition to those clerics, there were also four boy choristers who lived and sang in St Martin's.[9] The records that survive tell us little about the clerical life at St Martin's in this period; unlike the fifteenth-century disputes over sanctuary and other liberties in the precinct, in the contests of the sixteenth century the collegiate clergy

[4] Cf. Richard Grafton, *Chronicle or History of England* (London, 1809), vol. 2, p. 225; Kaufman, *Polytyque Church*, pp 151–2.
[5] Cox, *Sanctuaries*, pp 126–7.
[6] This recalls Michel de Certeau's observations on 'pedestrian speech acts', in *The Practice of Everyday Life*, trans. Steven Rendall (Berkeley, 1988), esp. pp 97–9.
[7] There were at most times two canons resident, and about ten or so vicars perpetual who were deputies of the clergy who held the other prebendaries. Reddan, 'Collegiate Church', pp 203–4.
[8] Reddan, 'Collegiate Church', p. 203.
[9] Both the choristers and the collegiate clergy are mentioned in accounts submitted at the college's dissolution in 1542: TNA, E 101/674/4.

appear to have played no role in defending St Martin's privileges, nor in administering the sanctuary. The role of defender was instead taken by the dean's successor, the abbot of Westminster, and the day-to-day management of the precinct was performed by a lay constable deputed by the abbot.

In accordance with the precinct's sanctuary privileges, there were also of course sanctuary men and women, felons and debtors, resident there. It is hard to know how many sanctuary seekers would have lived in St Martin's at any one time, as their sojourn was often temporary. The one extant list of sanctuary seekers in St Martin's—a short report dated 1525 now in the State Papers—may be a representative census, enumerating eleven men and one woman.[10] Three on this list are identified as being in sanctuary for murder, two for felony (which usually meant theft), one for trespass, and one for debt; the other five have only their names listed. The indictments deposited in the court of King's Bench from the early fifteenth century through the first half of the sixteenth century similarly indicate regular, but not particularly frequent, recourse to St Martin's by those accused of felony, treason, or trespass.[11] Felons and debtors in the London area were much more likely to take sanctuary in the precinct of Westminster Abbey (one 1533 census of sanctuary seekers there, as we saw in Chapter 2, recorded eighty-eight people).[12]

The streets, lanes, and courtyards of St Martin's precinct had then perhaps a dozen sanctuary seekers at any one time, and perhaps two dozen clergy, choristers, and other functionaries of the church itself. Most inhabitants of the precinct, however, were neither sanctuary seekers nor clergy, but another group altogether: a host of Dutch, French, and English artisans and their households who leased or sublet their shops and houses from the abbot of Westminster, the ultimate landlord of most of the properties in St Martin's. St Martin's, in fact, had the densest concentration of strangers in the realm, with hundreds crowded into the small precinct.[13] When St Martin's became a particular haven for stranger artisans is obscured by our lack of sources for much of the medieval period,[14] although evidence indicates that alien shoemakers and goldsmiths were living in St Martin's Lane from at least

---

[10] TNA, SP 1/33, fol. 148r; *L&P*, vol. 4, p. 473.

[11] For instance, between 1500 and 1540 I have found references to thirty-five people who sought sanctuary at St Martin's for felony, treason, or trespass, sometimes only briefly; four sought asylum there for debt. See McSheffrey, 'Sanctuary Seekers'.

[12] See TNA, SP 1/238, fol. 72r. Conversely, leases recorded in the Westminster Abbey sanctuary do not show aliens leasing property there as they do for St Martin's. WAM, WARB, vols 2 and 3, *passim*.

[13] Andrew Pettegree, 'The Foreign Population of London in 1549', *Proceedings of the Huguenot Society of London* 24 (1984): p. 144. Although Pettegree notes the density of St Martin's alien population, he underestimates it: see discussion in Shannon McSheffrey, 'Residents of St. Martin-le-Grand, c. 1500–1550', http://shannonmcsheffrey.wordpress.com/research/.

[14] The liberties have been curiously neglected in some of the major scholarship on aliens in later medieval London, omitted, for instance, from Sylvia L. Thrupp, 'Aliens in and around London in the Fifteenth Century', in *Studies in London History Presented to Philip Edmund Jones*, ed. Albert E. J Hollaender and William Kellaway (London, 1969), pp 251–72; J. L Bolton, ed., *The Alien Communities of London in the Fifteenth Century* (Stamford, Lincolnshire, 1998), pp 11–15. Both Archer and Barron comment usefully, if briefly, on the question. Ian W. Archer, 'Responses to Alien Immigrants', in *Le Migrazioni in Europa: Secc. XIII–XVIII*, ed. Simonetta Cavaciocchi (Florence, 1994), pp 755–74; Barron, *London*, pp 35–6.

the 1440s, and likely earlier.[15] The pace of alien settlement in St Martin's may well have quickened in the later fifteenth and early sixteenth century with the general increase in migration from the Continent and the development of more effective City supervision over alien workers, which prompted many to move into areas outside London's jurisdiction.[16] Certainly by Henry VIII's reign—the point at which records allow us to trace more precisely the individual inhabitants—stranger artisans demonstrably made up a significant majority of the precinct population. The precinct did not attract the wealthiest kinds of strangers, the highly-connected international merchants from the Italian city-states, Spain, or the Hanseatic League, but instead the relatively humbler sorts who made shoes and purses. The shoes made in St Martin's Lane were sought after, however, and the goldsmiths, who remained a presence in the precinct into the later sixteenth century, were known for their fine work.[17] Many of those who lived in St Martin's had immigrated to a life of relative prosperity.

Using the evidence of tax records, rent rolls, wills, denization patents, and the records of royal courts, among other materials, it is possible to build a picture of who lived in St Martin's in the first half of the sixteenth century. Working with these sources, I have identified more than 500 residents of the precinct of St Martin le Grand over that period, some of them appearing in many different records.[18] As that evidence indicates, somewhere between eight and nine of every ten inhabitants of the precinct were born overseas. Most strangers in St Martin's were Dutch ('Doche') in the larger fifteenth- and sixteenth-century sense of that word, which stretched to include migrants from the Rhineland areas around Cologne as well as Flanders and the Low Countries.[19] Although much smaller in number, there was also a significant minority in St Martin's born in France.[20] For those who settled in London permanently, we know little about why they chose to move there. The most commonly cited motivation for emigration from the Netherlands in the

---

[15] A list of jurors in the precinct in 1440 includes several with Dutch-sounding names; the mayor and aldermen complained to the king's council in 1446 about the strangers in St Martin's who were refusing to pay 'impositions' to the City 'as they should by authority of parliament'; and provisions were made for aliens in St Martin's in statutes of the 1460s and 1470s. WAM, MS 13191, fol. 1r; Nicholas Harris Nicolas, ed., *Proceedings and Ordinances of the Privy Council of England*, 7 vols (London, 1835), vol. 6, p. 50; 3 Edw. IV, c. 4, 5, and 7; 17 Edw. IV, c. 1, in *SR*, vol. 2, pp 396–402, 452–61.

[16] Archer, 'Responses'.

[17] See Bolton, *Alien Communities*, pp 28–30; Andrew Pettegree, *Foreign Protestant Communities in Sixteenth-Century London* (Oxford, 1986); Derek Keene, 'Du seuil de la cité à la formation d'une économie morale: l'environnement hanséatique à Londres, entre XIIe et XVIIe siècle', in *Les étrangers dans la ville: minorités et espace urbain du bas moyen âge à l'époque moderne*, ed. Jacques Bottin and Donatella Calabi (Paris, 1999), pp 409–24, at p. 410.

[18] For a spreadsheet of this data, see McSheffrey, 'Residents of St. Martin-le-Grand'. For a more detailed discussion of the artisan population, see Shannon McSheffrey, 'Stranger Artisans and the London Sanctuary of St. Martin Le Grand in the Reign of Henry VIII', *Journal of Medieval and Early Modern Studies* 43 (2013): pp 545–71, doi:10.1215/10829636-2338599.

[19] See TNA, C 1/987/32; PROB 11/43/568, Will of Gertrude Myles (1560); PROB 11/70/217, Will of Peter Richardson (1583); William Page, *Letters of Denization and Acts of Naturalization for Aliens in England, 1509–1603* (Nendeln, Liechtenstein, 1969), pp 47, 48, 53, 55, 57, 58, 98–9, 124, 135, 191, 194, 206, 221, 248, 256; *L&P*, vol. 11, p. 209.

[20] Page, *Letters of Denization*, pp 16, 68, 76, 77, 78, 96, 123, 184.

second half of the sixteenth century, religious strife, was not yet a factor, although fifteenth-century political unrest and warfare may have played a part.[21] The chain migration patterns of Dutch immigrants to England in the fifteenth and first half of the sixteenth century suggest that already-existing family and occupational networks tied to the old country were a significant factor in settlement choices.[22] The two dozen wills I have been able to find of those who lived in the precinct show ties of family and friendship among the migrants, as well as maintenance in some cases of property and family ties in the old country. We know that some immigrated as children, probably although not certainly with their parents. The stranger householders often employed a number of their countrymen as servants; indeed, this was a sore point with local journeymen and apprentices.[23]

Dutch and French immigrants came to St Martin's because it was a stranger enclave, but most of all they congregated there because they could practise their trades in the precinct, outside the reach of the London guilds. Perhaps (as their English counterparts claimed) their exemptions from the London guilds gave them a competitive advantage, and certainly prosperity greeted some who settled in the precinct, as the tax assessment rolls indicate. The most common occupations of strangers in St Martin's were cordwainer (shoemaker), pouchmaker, and leatherdyer or leather-seller, with a small but significant number of goldsmiths. It is not clear whether St Martin's was a magnet for immigrants involved in the leather trades, or whether immigrants coming to St Martin's shaped their occupational choices according to the dominance of shoemaking and other leather work there. Probably both factors came into play.

Although London guildsmen often loudly complained about shoddy workmanship among those outside guild supervision, this was likely mere bluster, as goods produced by strangers were evidently popular with consumers and regarded as having a certain cachet.[24] The craftsmen of St Martin's had reason to take pride in their workmanship, and indeed even to regard their expertise as superior to English skills. For perhaps two centuries, St Martin's precinct was evidently the place to buy stylish shoes. In the 1460s, St Martin's shoemakers were exempted from a statutory ban on shoes with fashionably long points; around 1500, as we have seen, Prince Arthur bought his shoes in the precinct; in the 1570s a London shopping guide indicated that St Martin's Lane was still the best place to buy footwear; and in 1661 Samuel Pepys wrote in his diary that he bought his boots in St Martin's.[25]

---

[21] Bolton, *Alien Communities*, pp 33–4; Lien Bich Luu, *Immigrants and the Industries of London, 1500–1700* (Aldershot, 2005), pp 100–12.

[22] See Luu's distinction between individual migration and mass migration and occupational choice. Mass migrations of religious refugees from the Netherlands to London began only in the 1560s. Luu, *Immigrants*, pp 3–4, 13–17.

[23] For references to the wills [search 'will of'], and for servants, see McSheffrey, 'Residents of St. Martin le Grand'; also for servants, see R. G. Lang, ed., *Two Tudor Subsidy Rolls for the City of London, 1541 and 1582* (London, 1993), pp 7–9.

[24] On complaints, see, e.g., LMA, Journal 10, fols 209v–10r; *PROME*, Parl. Apr. 1463, ¶22; 3 Edw. IV, c. 4, *SR*, vol. 2, p. 396; Barron, *London*, pp 35–6. On cachet, see Luu, *Immigrants*, pp 59–61.

[25] 4 Edw. IV, c. 7, *SR*, vol. 2, pp 414–15; TNA, STAC 2/20/323, mm 4, 27; Isabella Whitney, 'The Maner of Her Wyll, & What She Left to London', in *A Sweet Nosgay, or Pleasant Posye*, STC (2nd edn) 25440 (London, 1573), sig. E4v; Samuel Pepys, *The Diary of Samuel Pepys: A New and Complete*

In a similar way, some Dutch goldsmiths working in St Martin's Lane were much sought after, as were other gold workers from the Netherlands working in other liberties in the capital, their skills generally acknowledged to be superior to English work.[26] Although evidently restrictions on their capacity to make and sell their goods affected aliens' work lives, the privileged environment of St Martin's and the relative independence and freedom it conferred were probably more than sufficient compensation.

GOVERNING ST MARTIN'S PRECINCT IN THE REIGN OF HENRY VIII

As a liberty, St Martin's was subject neither to the bishop of London's ecclesiastical courts nor to the City's ward or civic courts, but this did not mean that the precinct had no legal structure at all: as did other liberties, St Martin's had its own spiritual and temporal courts, which dealt with disputes among and discipline over those who lived within its bounds.[27] There are some traces of those courts, although unfortunately very few administrative records of the precinct survive so that we cannot glean much from them about the kinds of interpersonal issues with which the courts dealt.[28] For more serious matters, such as homicides, as with other liberties, the precinct's jurisdiction hooked into the normal processes of royal justice: although the City of London's coroner did not attend suspicious deaths in the precinct, territories held by the abbot of Westminster and thus under his jurisdiction were attended by the coroner for the abbot's liberty. (The same men, in fact, often served as coroner at various times for London and Middlesex, and for the abbot's liberty.[29]) When necessary (and as we will see in the next section, it was necessary fairly often), the abbot's coroner convened a jury of men who lived within the precinct to investigate and report on the circumstances and those reports then led to indictments in the king's courts.

A particularly powerful figure in the first half of the sixteenth century in St Martin's precinct was its constable, a lay official appointed by the abbot. The sanctuary men, the alien artisans, and, in some matters at least, even the clergy of the precinct were subject to his governance. From about 1503 until 1543, one man, Hugh

---

Transcription, ed. Robert Latham and William Matthews, 11 vols (London, 2000), vol. 2, p. 132 (see also vol. 6, p. 332).

[26] Lien Bich Luu, 'Aliens and Their Impact on the Goldsmiths' Craft in London in the Sixteenth Century', in *Goldsmiths, Silversmiths, and Bankers: Innovation and the Transfer of Skill, 1550 to 1750*, ed. David Mitchell (Stroud, 1995), pp 43–52.

[27] See WAM, MSS 13191 and 13294; TNA, C 24/3, 'Abbas', m. 17.

[28] One stray document relating to a defamation in St Martin's heard before the abbot's commissary in 1515 survives as WAM, MS 13294.

[29] See for instance John Elryngton, who wrote many coroner's reports for homicides in the London area for all these jurisdictions between 1486 and 1503. (For a few examples see KB 9/370, m. 55; KB 9/402, mm 102, 103, 104, 105; KB 9/406, m. 20; KB 9/413, m. 48, 51, 52, 53, 54; KB 9/426, m. 63; KB 9/424, m. 24; KB 9/431, m. 110.) On Elryngton see John Hamilton Baker, *The Men of Court 1440 to 1550*, Selden Society, Supplementary Series 18 (London, 2012), pp 632–3.

Payne, held the position, by the 1510s adding the office of rent-gatherer.[30] Payne was originally a citizen leatherseller of London; along with many other men in early Tudor England, he found service to a great landlord to be the path to greater prosperity. As constable, his duties were broad, and seemingly touching on every aspect of the precinct's operations. It was he who formally inscribed the names of the felons and debtors who sought the privileges of St Martin's in a register (which, unfortunately, does not survive). As the primary law enforcement officer of St Martin's, he operated the prison within the precinct. Those who sought sanctuary for felony would be kept there until they had been admitted to the privilege, and those who were accused of misbehaviour of various kinds would be confined there awaiting process before the precinct's steward.[31] Payne's duties extended also to administration of the ecclesiastical side of the precinct. In 1542, as part of the dissolution process, he submitted an account for payments he had made throughout the year. That document shows that he oversaw a broad swathe of administrative tasks, paying out salaries to the collegiate church's clergy, clothing the choristers, purchasing the necessaries for the church ('singing bread', lamp oil, incense, and the like), administering repairs, and generally maintaining the precinct, including payments to the 'gunge farmer' to haul away sixteen tons of human waste over the year.[32]

Over the decades, Payne also came to control much of the property in St Martin's precinct, apparently using his position as rent-gatherer to snap up leases on properties held by Westminster Abbey when they became vacant. The abbot's lease book shows him gradually amassing more and more leases, and many of the Dutch and French artisans who had shops in the precinct (including Francis Woodleke) sublet their properties from him.[33] He also took up leases on some of the abbey's manors in Essex, and a lawsuit in Common Pleas and King's Bench in the mid-1510s shows him trying to acquire other agricultural property in Essex as well. Over the decades he served as constable, he sought to make a transition from artisan pouchmaker and leatherseller to man of property. Already in the suit in Common Pleas in the mid-1510s he was styled (or more likely styled himself) 'gentleman' on the document recording the land sale, although in this suit he was otherwise called 'pouchmaker'. He lived in a large tenement on the north end of the precinct with a garden and stable. When he died in 1543, he left the leases on more than thirty tenements and shops to his widow.[34]

As both constable and major leaseholder, Payne became a dominant force in the precinct, and one who did not hesitate to use his authority as constable to his own

---

[30] WAM, MS 13313. Payne may have been rent-gatherer as early as 1514 (see WAM, MS 13315).
[31] For some evidentiary traces, see TNA, KB 15/42, fols 140v–41r; STAC 2/21/121; C 1/964/24; SP 1/237, fol. 282r; LMA, Repertory 1, fol 97v.
[32] TNA, E 101/674/4. See also *L&P*, vol. 18, pt. 2, p. 118.
[33] WAM, WARB, vol. 2, fols 23rv, 109v–110r, 188v–189r, 234r; TNA, PROB 11/29/400, Will of Hugh Payne; Kempe, *Historical Notices*, pp 205–10.
[34] WAM, WARB, vol. 2, fol. 165rv; vol. 3, fols 84v–85r, 85r–86r, 87v–88r, 90r–91r; TNA, KB 27/1023, plea m. 61 (Payne and other defendants to a suit of trespass had a Common Pleas suit brought to King's Bench on a writ of error); TNA, C 24/3, 'Abbas', *passim*; PROB 11/29/400, Will of Hugh Payne.

personal advantage. In a Chancery bill submitted between 1529 and 1532, the plaintiff Henry Garratson contended that when he and Payne quarrelled over Garratson's lease of a victualling house in the precinct, Payne arrested Garratson on a trumped-up charge. Payne, Garratson alleged, treated him very roughly as he took him into custody, casting him 'flat upon the earth' and beating him. As Garratson put it, 'Hugh Payne useth and behaveth himself as a person not fearing the king nor his laws', avenging himself on the inhabitants of St Martin's 'which will not be obedient unto him after his will and pleasure'.[35] Other complaints similar to Garratson's were made by other Dutch artisans in the 1530s. Although the genre of petitions to Chancery and Star Chamber encouraged rhetorical exaggerations (and indeed Garratson also alleged that Payne had plotted to murder him over the victualling house lease), the patterns of Payne's land acquisitions and the complaints about his exercise of office in the precinct suggest that Payne had indeed become something of a 'Tyrant', as one complaint put it.[36] Although as far as records indicate, there were relatively few resident sanctuary seekers in the precinct, in at least one case Payne seems to have employed as his henchman a man who had taken the privilege: Harry Garretson said that when Hugh Payne roughed him up he was assisted by Henry Coly, sanctuary man.[37] In the 1540s, William Selby, another sanctuary man who had been resident there from the late 1530s, became an assistant to Payne's successor as constable in the precinct, and was also accused of violence and intimidation against residents.[38] Payne's career demonstrates that St Martin's status as a liberty could give rise to manipulation and appropriation of legal authority, although this would hardly have made it an unusual jurisdiction in England in the 1520s and 1530s.

St Martin's was thus densely populated, mostly by stranger artisans whose trade was prosperous, and run as something of a petty fiefdom by its constable. The dominance of artisan households may explain why the precinct's jurisdictional immunities, although allowing stranger artisans to flout the City's labour regulations, did not lead towards the fostering of some other kinds of lawlessness for which other liberties became notorious. The Clink manor in Southwark, for instance, a peculiar governed by the bishop of Winchester, was a red-light district, while the hospital of St Katherine by the Tower was also known as a haven for bawds and whores.[39] There is no evidence that St Martin's had a particular reputation for trade in sex.

Yet a curiously high homicide rate in the precinct indicates that it was not an entirely peaceful place, and the identities of the victims and perpetrators suggest that both the sanctuary men and the immigrant population contributed to the instability. In the reign of Henry VIII, at least seven homicides occurred within

---

[35] TNA, C 1/636/18.   [36] TNA, STAC 2/21/121.   [37] TNA, C 1/636/18.
[38] TNA, C 1/888/11; C 1/946/26, C 1/965/24–25; Kempe, *Historical Notices*, p. 207.
[39] On the Clink manor, see Martha Carlin, *Medieval Southwark* (London, 1996), pp 211–19; Richard M. Wunderli, *London Church Courts and Society on the Eve of the Reformation* (Cambridge, MA, 1981), pp 96–8. Little has been written about the disreputable aspects of St Katherine's Hospital, but see the evidence from a London Consistory Court case in 1491–1492, at Shannon McSheffrey, ed., *Consistory Database*, http://consistory.ca/obj.php?p=973.

the precinct.⁴⁰ One involved a seemingly unlikely victim who was neither sanctuary man nor stranger artisan, but a canon attached to the church. In 1529, Dr Nicholas Myles, doctor of divinity, vicar of the parish of St Bride's Fleet Street, and a canon of St Martin's resident in the College, was found 'murdered and slain in his bed'. Myles was not a young man; he had been ordained by 1487, suggesting that he was at least in his sixties at the time of his death.⁴¹ No details survive regarding the circumstances of his death, which we know about mostly from a letter his nephew William Myles, citizen and grocer of London, sent to the abbot of Westminster disputing the disposition of the deceased canon's goods.⁴² I have not located any records of prosecution for the homicide, but chroniclers reported that in May 1530 Dr Myles's murderer was hanged in chains at Finsbury Field.⁴³ This was a type of execution reserved for particularly notorious crimes, by which the body would not be taken down from the gibbet after the hanging but would instead be left there, suspended by chains, to decompose, as an example to others. John Bellamy notes that normally the order for such an execution was made by the king or his council, as it was in effect an extra-judicial punishment.⁴⁴ Whatever the circumstances of Myles's death, it was evidently seen as an outrageous crime by those of highest status in the realm.

Dr Myles's murder, however shocking, was an isolated one; most of the other recorded homicides in St Martin's occurred more than a decade before and were quite different in nature. Between 1508 and 1517, the precinct experienced a string of a half-dozen violent deaths for which coroner's inquest reports were filed at King's Bench.⁴⁵ In at least one of the cases, Thomas Porter's murder of John Gamlyn on 1 June 1516, the killing resulted from a quarrel between sanctuary men. Both Porter and Gamlyn were privileged of the sanctuary, and they had some kind of tie to Henry VIII: the king's household accounts between 1514 and 1516 record that the king paid £10 a year to the keeper of St Martin's sanctuary for their living expenses. Porter and Gamlyn evidently fell out and Gamlyn ended up dead; Porter himself fled the precinct following the slaying, and the King's Bench records indicate that he was never found. He was outlawed in 1517.⁴⁶

---

⁴⁰ Apart from one homicide in 1508 (TNA, KB 27/1001, rex m. 1d), I have not found any other killings in the precinct before Henry VIII's reign.

⁴¹ Emden, *Biographical Register of the University of Oxford to 1500*, p. 1334.

⁴² WAM, MS 13293; WAM has assigned 'c. 1524' to the undated letter, but Myles's death must postdate his writing of his will, which is dated 10 July 1529. John Richard Magrath, *The Obituary Book of Queen's College, Oxford* (Oxford, 1910), pp 108–10.

⁴³ Charles Lethbridge Kingsford, ed., *Two London Chronicles from the Collections of John Stow*, Camden Third Series 18 (London, 1910), p. 4; Raphael Holinshed, *Chronicles of England, Scotland, and Ireland* (London, 1587), vol. 6, p. 914, http://english.nsms.ox.ac.uk/holinshed/texts.php?text1=1587_7631. The anonymous chronicler edited by Kingsford dates the hanging to May 1529, but (as above in n.42), Myles was still alive in July 1529.

⁴⁴ Bellamy, *Criminal Trial*, p. 154.

⁴⁵ TNA, KB 27/1001, rex m. 1d; KB 9/452, m. 61; KB 9/472, m. 73 (KB 27/1029, rex m. 17); KB 9/472, m. 75; KB 9/472, m. 76 (KB 27/1023, rex m. 1); KB 9/474, m. 61.

⁴⁶ TNA, KB 9/472, m. 73; KB 29/148, m. 48; *L&P*, vol. 2, pp 1466, 1469, 1471. A John Gamlyn was indicted for robbery along with Giles Covert, gentleman of Westminster (who went also by the alias 'Giles Tenysplayer') in 1509. TNA, KB 27/1029, m. 17.

In several of the other homicide cases, one or both of the men involved appear by their names and trades to be stranger artisans: in 1509, Jacob Cay alias Jacob Ruster was killed at St Martin's by Nicholas Strynger, a pouchmaker; a month after Porter's murder of Gamlyn in 1516, a tailor named William Makerell was found dead, and the inquest jurors indicted a shoemaker named Olaf Wilkins alias Williamson for the murder; and in 1517, a leatherseller named John Maydman killed Paul Bugderem, goldsmith.[47] Like Porter, these three accused perpetrators fled and were never found, with two being outlawed and the third dying before the process of outlawry was complete.[48] In two further cases (Thomas Walsshe's alleged killing of Christopher Wilkinson in 1508, and James a Horton's alleged killing of Christopher Trapmell in 1516), it is not clear whether the victim and perpetrator were sanctuary men, stranger artisans, or neither, although in both instances, the jurors found that the homicides had been in self-defence and the defendants were pardoned.[49] All these homicides were committed within the sanctuary, but there is no indication that any of the perpetrators claimed any kind of immunity as a result, which is consistent with the principle that sanctuary could not be claimed for crimes committed within that sanctuary's bounds.

A half-dozen deaths over a decade, in a jurisdiction that likely had a population of about 500 people, made St Martin's an especially violent place. At least in the 1510s it had a homicide rate that would rank it as the murder capital of the world today.[50] The very small population of course tends to skew the statistics[51] and the string of homicides did not continue beyond 1517; apart from Dr Myles's death, the only other homicide I have found in St Martin's occurred in 1538 (the two involved were apparently visitors to the precinct, and the jurors labelled the killing as self-defence and the killer was pardoned).[52] As the indictments do not give us any context for the killings, it is impossible to know whether they were linked, although at least the four deaths that occurred in quick succession in 1516 and 1517 were likely related.[53] It is possible that these homicides intersect in some way with some of the larger currents in the kingdom—they might have contributed, for instance, to the quickening of concern in the courts and the king's council in

---

[47] TNA, KB 9/452, m. 61; KB 9/472, m. 75; KB 9/474, m. 61.

[48] Strynger was outlawed in 1510; KB 29/140, m. 12d; Wilkins was outlawed for his felony more than a decade later, in 1531; KB 29/148, m. 48. Maydman was never arrested but reported dead in 1522; KB 29/149, m. 18. See KB 29/148, m. 48 regarding Thomas Porter's outlawry.

[49] Thomas Walsshe killed Christopher Wilkinson in 1508; TNA, KB 27/1001, m. 1d. In 1516, Christopher Trapmell was killed by James a Horton of London, yeoman; KB 9/472, m. 76; KB 27/1023, rex m. 1.

[50] Counting the six homicides indicted there (and this would be a minimum, as it counts only those where the indictments were filed at King's Bench) between 1508 and 1517, and assuming a population of 500, this makes an annual homicide rate of 120 per 100,000. The highest rate listed on Wikipedia for 2012 is 90 per 100,000; the rate in the United Kingdom was 1.0 per 100,000, for Canada 1.6, for the United States 4.7.

[51] See Robert R. Dykstra, 'Lies, Damned Lies, and Homicide Rates', *Historical Methods* 42 (2009): pp 139–42, doi:10.1080/01615440903259434.

[52] TNA, KB 9/539, m. 39; KB 27/1107, rex m. 4.

[53] The court of King's Bench dealt with the three committed in 1516 together, which may indicate a connection, or may simply result from the records' all being submitted at the same time by the same coroner. See TNA, KB 9/472, mm 73–76; KB 29/148, m. 48.

the mid-teens about sanctuary and crime, discussed in Chapter 4. In addition, possibly those quarrels that involved shoemakers and pouchmakers, at least some of whom seem to have had Dutch names, had their origins in disputes about the making and selling of shoes or pouches in St Martin's Lane such as precipitated the seizure of Francis Woodleke's wares in the early 1530s.

We certainly know that resentment against stranger artisans in St Martin's precinct could cause violence. There were at least three major riots in London against strangers in the second half of the fifteenth century,[54] and in the so-called 'Evil May Day' riot in 1517, hundreds (or, according to some accounts, thousands) of Londoners rose up in the night and attacked the homes and persons of strangers. As a notable enclave of stranger artisans, it is not surprising that the Evil May Day rioters focused their attention on the precinct of St Martin le Grand.[55] From about nine o'clock at night on the eve of May Day, rioters ran through the streets of the City, targeting areas in which stranger artisans and merchants were known to live and work; by three in the morning, the riot had run its course and the City officials had re-established a precarious order. Although a later ballad portrayed Evil or Ill May Day, as the riot came to be known, as a 'Slaughter' of strangers, with the drainage channels in the streets running with blood,[56] all the evidence suggests that no strangers lost their lives in the attacks, damage being limited to assaults and the sacking of houses and shops.[57] The riot was, however, symptomatic of a nexus of xenophobia and resentment against the special status of the liberties, especially St Martin's.

STRANGER ARTISANS, SANCTUARY MEN, AND THE CITY

The City of London and its guildsmen had long harboured considerable antipathy towards the strangers living in the liberties and consistently opposed their rights to work inside the City.[58] The particular status of St Martin's precinct introduced another complication: in both a practical sense and in the conceptual frameworks through which political arguments about its status were articulated, the jurisdictional immunity that allowed stranger artisans to practise their crafts within the St Martin's precinct was intimately intertwined with St Martin's privileges as a sanctuary for felons. Accordingly, the Dutch and French shoemakers and pouchmakers drew their liberties from those granted to felons; and conversely, the crown's support of St Martin's and sanctuary in general through the fifteenth century and

---

[54] Keene, 'Du seuil de la Cité', p. 418.
[55] Polydore Vergil's account makes St Martin's the sole target; for Edward Hall it was primary but not exclusive. Vergil, *Anglica Historia*, p. 245; Edward Hall, *Hall's Chronicle*, ed. Henry Ellis (London, 1809), pp 586–91.
[56] Ambrose Philips, *A Collection of Old Ballads* (London, 1725), vol. 3, p. 58.
[57] Rawdon Brown, ed., *Four Years at the Court of Henry VIII* (London, 1854), vol. 2, pp 70–2; Hall, *Hall's Chronicle*, pp 588–9.
[58] Ian W. Archer, *The Pursuit of Stability: Social Relations in Elizabethan London* (Cambridge, 1991), pp 1–17; cf. Steve Rappaport, *Worlds Within Worlds: Structures of Life in Sixteenth-Century London* (Cambridge, 1989), pp 44–5.

much of the early Tudor period drew at least some of its motivation from the need to restrain the economic and jurisdictional demands of the City of London.

Thus, unlikely bedfellows though they may have been, both stranger artisans and accused murderers and thieves sought the immunity of St Martin's sanctuary space, and the rhetoric used to justify or attack those privileges also shared a good deal. Sanctuary men and women were not numerous in the precinct of St Martin's, but they nonetheless were very important for defining that precinct's privileges. Although the opposition of the City of London to the privileges of St Martin Le Grand was perhaps most inflamed by stranger craftsmen working outside the guilds, the City understood the rhetorical value of invoking 'the enormous enemies of God', the murderers and thieves, that St Martin's privileges fostered, linking the ungodly felons to the suspicious and untrustworthy work of the strangers.[59] And indeed for the alien craftsmen themselves, the few men who lived in St Martin Le Grand as accused felons were the most notable exemplars of their own privileges to make and sell their goods. The safety of a notorious murderer or a conspirator in a plot against the king within the confines of the sanctuary was the most vivid proof in their minds of St Martin's privileges.

The City had made some considerable strides in the later fifteenth and early sixteenth century in its ability to supervise and control immigrant labour. By the end of the fifteenth century, aliens were able to work in the City of London only under guild supervision, but were caught in a double-bind: those born outside England were also denied the possibility of London citizenship or full membership in the guilds. As aliens were thus significantly disadvantaged in the craft associations, many chose to live and work in areas where guild supervision was absent. Escaping the City's jurisdiction was becoming more difficult, however; by statutes from the 1480s into the 1530s, the City gained greater jurisdiction over anyone, especially strangers, working in craft production within a two-mile radius of the City. The restrictions on aliens were significant: they could not sell at retail within two miles of the City and were forbidden to take other strangers as apprentices.[60] If those restrictions had not always been fully enforced,[61] the repertories of the London Court of Aldermen suggest that the City gave them particular attention in the late 1520s and 1530s.[62]

At the same time as the crown appeared to be granting London civic and guild officials significant powers over the metropolitan alien population, however, small but highly significant exceptions were incorporated into the labour statutes. The 1523 statute, for instance, explicitly exempted from its provisions the 'strangers

---

[59] See, for instance, TNA, STAC 2/20/324, mm 3–8 (quotation at m. 5); see also LMA, Journal 13, fol. 467r.

[60] Luu, 'Aliens and Their Impact', pp 44–9; Rappaport, *Worlds Within Worlds*, pp 45–7.

[61] As Archer notes, the London guilds' ability to regulate the work and products of aliens was 'intermittent and faltering', through the Elizabethan period. Archer, *Pursuit of Stability*, pp 138, 140; J. L. Bolton, 'La répartition spatiale de la population étrangère à Londres au XVe siècle', in *Les étrangers dans la ville: minorités et espace urbain du bas moyen âge à l'époque moderne*, ed. Jacques Bottin and Donatella Calabi (Paris, 1999), pp 430–1.

[62] LMA, Repertory 8, fols 1v–4r, 20r, 180v, 237v, 239r; LMA, Repertory 9, fols 26v, 46v, 48r, 51r, 59v, 61v, 62r, 63r, 63v, 85v, 104r, 109v–110r, 135r, 189v.

that now or hereafter shall be…within the sanctuary of St. Martin's le Grand within the City of London', while the 1529 statute only minimally restricted the privileges of the inhabitants of St Martin's, allowing them to hire up to ten servants, English or alien, when aliens elsewhere were confined to two.[63] These statutory exclusions in the 1520s were again nothing new, but reflected similar exemptions made for St Martin's in fifteenth-century statutes.[64]

Yet although the 1529 statute in large measure followed the crown's long-standing policy of exempting St Martin's, a proviso added to the act suggested that there might be a crack in the façade. In April 1529, the king issued a decree in Star Chamber, ratified in the statute, mandating a commission to determine the precise boundaries of the sanctuary of St Martin le Grand. The statute declared that the provisions that spared the stranger artisans of St Martin le Grand were to stand as long as the inhabitants of the precinct conformed to the findings of that commission. In addition to determining the extent of St Martin's sanctuary, the commission was also to consider lowering the number of apprentices and journeymen that craftsmen working in St Martin's should be allowed to employ.[65] In due course the commission received submissions from both parties.[66] The abbot of Westminster outlined in detail the precise boundaries and privileges he claimed for the precinct, while the citizens of London (as they had in the fifteenth century) wholly denied any 'tuition, immunity, or sanctuary' at St Martin's, then or in the past. There is no evidence that the king's council made any decision regarding St Martin's as a result of this enquiry (none survives). The crown's calling of the commission itself, however, was no doubt understood by the City as a sign that the crown's support for St Martin's privileges over the previous century and more might be ready to shift.

The larger context of the 1530s, as that decade unfolded, must have given the City even more hope, as circumstances became dire both for the privileges of religious houses and for strangers. The monastic dissolutions must have seemed to the City like a situation of considerable potential, especially regarding its long-held aspirations to wipe out the liberties and peculiars within its boundaries, mostly associated with religious houses. The larger international politics of the 1530s also increasingly made strangers, particularly those of German and Dutch origin, objects of official suspicion.[67] For the City, the time was ripe to tackle once again the question of St Martin le Grand.

---

[63] 14 and 15 Hen. VIII c. 2; 21 Hen. VIII c. 16; *SR*, vol. 3, pp 208–9, 297–8.

[64] E.g. 3 Edw. IV c. 4, 5; 17 Edw. IV c. 1; *SR*, vol. 2, pp 396–402, 452–61. The only statute governing alien labour in this period that does not exempt St Martin's is 1 Ric. III c. 9; *SR*, vol. 2, pp 489–93.

[65] *SR*, vol. 3, pp 297–301. The letter patent establishing the commission, dated 14 Feb. 1529 and ratified in 21 Hen. VIII, c. 16, was also copied into the Journal of the Court of Common Council: LMA, Journal 13, fols 194rv. Perhaps significantly, the copy in the Journal makes no mention of the provisions exempting artisans in St Martin le Grand.

[66] There was a delay following the initial convening of the commission as one of the commissioners died and had to be replaced. LMA, Journal 13, fols 186v–187r. The records of these submissions survive (as far as I know) only as copied into LMA, Journal 13, fols 195r–196v.

[67] Kevin Sharpe, *Selling the Tudor Monarchy: Authority and Image in Sixteenth-Century England* (New Haven, 2009), pp 55, 67–8, 84–5, 121; Paul L. Hughes and James Francis Larkin, eds, *Tudor Royal Proclamations* (New Haven, 1964), vol. 1, pp 227–8, 272; Irvin Buckwalter Horst, *The Radical Brethren. Anabaptism and the English Reformation to 1558* (Nieuwkoop, 1972), pp 60–2.

In the early 1530s, the City and its guilds began to harass and seize goods from alien craftsmen working within the precinct. In doing so, the City and the guildsmen explicitly acted as if the case they had made ever since the fifteenth-century disputes with the collegiate church had been ratified—that is, that there was no such thing as the sanctuary or liberty of St Martin le Grand, and that those who worked there were fully under the jurisdiction of the City and its guilds.[68] It is likely that this harassment was sporadic rather than concerted, and it may have been driven by the cordwainers' guild specifically; it is also possible that the seizures of goods were meant deliberately to create test cases in the royal courts. Evidence of complaints from St Martin's residents in those courts suggests that both sides, the abbot of Westminster acting for St Martin's and the City, used these cases as an opportunity to rehearse once again the arguments for and against the liberty's privileges.

In late 1533, in the midst of these cases, Chamberlain Medley raided the two shoe shops in St Martin's Lane belonging to stranger shoemakers Francis Woodleke and George Colyn. Over the months that followed the raid on the shops, the Dutch shoemakers and the City made complaint and counter-complaint directly to Thomas Cromwell, by then the king's right-hand man, and in the royal law courts regarding 'the matter of St. Martin's'.[69] The matter dragged on for about eighteen months, until finally the king commissioned another inquiry to examine both the boundaries and the privileges of St Martin's precinct.[70]

THE BOUNDARIES OF ST MARTIN'S

As part of the enquiry commissioned by the king in July 1535 precipitated by Woodleke's breaking of the wall,[71] the City and the Abbot of Westminster each submitted statements of claim, largely repeating what they had submitted earlier in 1529 regarding the same issues. As we have seen, the roots of this quarrel between St Martin's and the City extended back to at least 1400; indeed, the specific claims and the general tone of the City's and the abbot's statements in the 1530s were remarkably similar to the mid-fifteenth-century iteration of the dispute in Dean Caudray's days as well as to the documents produced in 1529 in the context of the more proximate quarrel. This is at least partly because in each case the parties relied on their own archives of documents deriving from the earlier disputes in framing their arguments.[72] In addition to the abbot's and City's claims, more than two dozen men who lived or had lived in the precinct along with London citizens from

---

[68] See, for instance, TNA, C 1/913/66; STAC 3/7/68; STAC 2/29/198 and LMA, Journal 13, fols 195r–196v.
[69] LMA, Repertory 9, fols 46r, 48r, 51r, 63r; Journal 13, fols 410v–414r, 420v–421r.
[70] LMA, Journal 13, fol. 453r; TNA, C 24/3, 'Abbas' (copy in STAC 2/23/266; abbreviated in STAC 2/20/57); STAC 2/20/323; STAC 2/20/324 (cf. LMA, Journal 13, fols 195r–196v).
[71] LMA, Journal 13, fol. 453r; TNA, STAC 2/20/324.
[72] See above, Chapter 2 for references to the earlier documents, and for the late 1520s, LMA, Journal 13, fols 186v–187r; 194r–196v; TNA, STAC 2/29/198 and 3/7/68.

neighbouring parishes were deposed in 1536 and 1537 regarding their knowledge and understanding of the sanctuary's boundaries and privilege. The witnesses, all male, were in many cases quite elderly, in their sixties and seventies, their testimony reaching back half a century and more in some cases.[73] Much of the material I will discuss in the rest of this chapter comes from those depositions, preserved in the records of Chancery and Star Chamber.

The testimony offered in 1536 and 1537 in the Star Chamber enquiry centred on the precise extent of the sanctuary's boundaries. The structure of the testimony of witnesses for both sides suggests that the commissioners[74] read the abbot's statement to the deponents and asked for their comments; the statement the mayor and aldermen had submitted was distinctly less useful for eliciting testimony as it simply flatly denied there was any liberty or sanctuary of any kind (a position that none of the witnesses supported, even those testifying on the city's behalf).[75] In his statement, the abbot had taken his listeners on a verbal walking of the bounds:

> From the said St. Martin's lane at the foresaid Bull Head, turning by a wall that divideth the said tenement of the Bull Head and St. Martin's ground, which wall turneth and extendeth from the east westwards unto the back wall that closeth in St. Martin's ground of the west side, all within the said wall, sanctuary.
>
> Item, along the same back wall that closeth in the west part of St. Martin's ground from the south end of the said wall into the north unto a wall…[76]

Whether agreeing with the abbot's claim or not, the witnesses took the same pedestrian approach to describing the topography of the neighbourhood.[77] For a modern reader, the abbot's and the deponents' descriptions have us reaching for a pad of paper to sketch a map representing the space from a bird's eye perspective. That was not, however, the mental image these men had of their space.[78] For interested parties and observers in the 1530s, a pedestrian perspective was clearly much more precise.

---

[73] Ralph Twyne, for instance, was only fifty years old, but noted that his knowledge of the customs of the precinct derived not only from his experience but also from his apprentice master, a certain Frist, who was in his eighties when Twyne had been apprenticed to him, and thus that his and Frist's accumulated memory went back about a century. TNA, C 24/3, 'Abbas', mm 15–16.

[74] The examiners were Henry Polsted, a servant of Cromwell, and John Croke, a Chancery official. TNA, STAC 2/20/323; C 24/3, 'Abbas', m. 1; *L&P*, vol. 10, pp 93, 432; J. H. Baker, 'Croke, John (1489–1554)', *ODNB* (2004), doi:10.1093/ref:odnb/6732.

[75] TNA, STAC 2/20/324. The witnesses' lack of support for the City's stance is in interesting contrast to the testimony given in an enquiry in 1496 in Bristol regarding the privileges of St Augustine's Abbey, where it was the abbot's positions that the deponents did not support. Fleming, 'Conflict', pp 335–6.

[76] TNA, STAC 2/20/324, m. 2.

[77] See Daniel Lord Smail, *Imaginary Cartographies: Possession and Identity in Late Medieval Marseille* (Ithaca, 2000), esp. pp 1–8.

[78] Although the abbot of Westminster may in fact have ordered such a diagram to be made as part of his submission; John Strype in 1720 reproduced a now-disappeared 'plat' of the precinct, a crude and rather unsuccessful map which he associated with the abbots' submissions in 1536. The map is reproduced in Honeybourne, 'Sanctuary Boundaries', p. 333. See, on other graphic representations of the sanctuary, Honeybourne, 'Sanctuary Boundaries', pp 324–5. Honeybourne herself creates a map based on the abbot's submission, ibid., p. 334.

The boundaries described by the witnesses for both parties were defined by custom, by usage, and in some cases by physical boundary markers such as walls or posts, or remembrance of barriers that had once been there.[79] In the case of a boundary post that had stood by the North Gate of St Martin's close until 'unknown persons' had pulled it down about 1534,[80] for instance, it was the memory of the physical marker that had once been there that for some denoted the northern limit of the sanctuary. Even in cases where the boundaries were marked in a physical sense, though, those walls, posts, or gates did not in the sixteenth century generally function as real barriers to ingress or egress, but as notional borders, generally agreed-upon conventions that on one side lay the City, on the other lay sanctuary, with all the legal, political, and economic implications that accompanied that distinction. The walls, for instance, were often in a state of considerable disrepair, but witnesses were at pains to insist that, despite their crumbling or even having fallen down altogether, the lines they had once followed were still visible and thus they continued to function as clear indications of the boundaries.[81]

The precise limits of the sanctuary were, of course, in dispute. Although there were certain places that many witnesses could not definitively declare to be either sanctuary or not, the main line of division among the witnesses was between those (generally testifying on behalf of the City) who limited sanctuary to the walled close around the church of St Martin, north of the street leading to Cheapside and between St Martin's Lane on the west and Foster Lane on the east; and those who supported the abbot's claim that sanctuary extended to certain tenements leased from the abbey and from the Earl of Northumberland on both sides of St Martin's Lane itself.

The former argument—limiting the privileges to the walled precinct—had both a certain logic and historical precedent behind it. A number of the deponents who testified on behalf of the City in 1536 recalled that in the fifteenth century the area around St Martin's church had been enclosed by a wall, with two or three gates (the number differed according to the deponent) and the west door of St Martin's church as the only points of entry and exit. One witness remembered that the name of the dean who had erected the wall, Richard Caudray, was engraved upon it.[82] The regulations established by the king and council at the tail end of the mid-fifteenth-century dispute between the City and St Martin Le Grand, in 1457,[83] suggest that the sanctuary was indeed at that time confined to the walled area of the close. Those regulations mandated that all gates and postern doors or any other means of egress from the sanctuary be closed and shut nightly at nine o'clock,

---

[79] See more generally on the demarcations of urban space, Gervase Rosser, 'Urban Culture and the Church, 1300–1540', in *Cambridge Urban History of Britain, Volume I: 600–1540*, ed. David M. Palliser (Cambridge, 2000), pp 339–40; Johnson, 'Law, Space and Local Knowledge', ch. 1.

[80] Deposition of Piers Peterson, TNA, C 24/3, 'Abbas', m. 1; STAC 2/23/266, m. 2; this was mentioned by a number of deponents, e.g. C 24/3, 'Abbas', mm 3, 4, 9.

[81] Rowland Johnson deposed, for instance, that 'about St. Leonard's church and so from thence to the said Roger Wright's house [the wall] is down and broken in many places, albeit he saieth that the bound thereof may be well enough perceived'. TNA, C 24/3, 'Abbas', m. 3d.

[82] Deposition of Piers Peterson, TNA, C 24/3, 'Abbas', m. 2.

[83] See Ch. 1, at n.24 and Ch. 3, at n.81.

to remain closed until six o'clock in the morning from All Hallow's Eve until Candlemas (2 February), and in the rest of the year until four in the morning or the beginning of the first mass. All who had fled into the sanctuary 'for treason or felony' were to be within the closure at night-time (implying they were allowed further afield during the day?).

A number of witnesses in 1536 argued that this area within the wall functioned as a kind of natural integral territory, with gates that, of old, had closed at curfew, marking a clear boundary both spatially and temporally between in-sanctuary and out-of-sanctuary. George Isotson told a story of an escaped felon to corroborate his claim that only the area within the close was sanctuary. He knew a man named Robert who had been a prisoner at the Marshalsea prison on the south bank of the Thames. Robert had escaped from the prison (so Isotson had heard) and made his way in the middle of the night to St Martin Le Grand, with irons still upon his legs. Because he could not get in, 'for that the gates were so well kept and shut in, he lay or stood, by report, hard at the South Gate of the said St. Martin's until the morning that the gates were opened and then entered and took sanctuary there'. Robert went on, Isotson said, to become the hermit at Islington whom we met in Chapter 2, and so his story functioned both to show how sanctuary seekers could leave their lives of crime behind to become men of God, and to demonstrate that there was no sanctuary in any part of St Martin's Lane. Robert knew that truly safe sanctuary could only be within the gates.[84]

But even though these witnesses argued that the sanctuary *should* be confined to the close, they virtually all recognized that the tenements and shops on St Martin's Lane—on both sides—were also commonly used and recognized as sanctuary. If the City's witnesses argued that breaking of the sanctuary wall on the east side, such as Woodleke had done, was an illicit innovation of the relatively recent past, the abbot's witnesses could wield the weapon of custom, too: they remembered famous sanctuary-seekers of the fifteenth century living on the west side of St Martin's Lane. John Smith, canon of St Paul's and commissary (judge of the ecclesiastical court) of St Martin Le Grand from the 1480s until 1503, recalled that John Morton, then bishop of Ely and ardent Lancastrian, later Henry VII's cardinal archbishop of Canterbury, took refuge in St Martin Le Grand during the Wars of the Roses. Morton, as Smyth remembered, stayed in Angel Alley.[85] Two deponents remembered that a man named Bland, an associate of Perkin Warbeck, whose rebellion against Henry VII was crushed in 1497, had also lived in St Martin's as a sanctuary man for twenty years, staying in Bland's Alley (perhaps named for him).[86] And, although neither the abbot nor his witnesses raised this point, in the

---

[84] Deposition of George Isotson, TNA, STAC 2/20/323, mm 29–30; see above, Ch. 2 at n.87.

[85] Deposition of John Smith, TNA, C 24/3, m. 17. A 1470 letter from John III Paston to his mother confirms Smyth's memory—'the Bishop of Ely with other bishops are in St. Martin's'—although it is also worth noting that John Smith would have been only about nine years old at the time. Davis, *Paston Letters*, vol. 1, p. 564.

[86] Witness Raff Twynne spoke of 'one Blande which was a Sanctuary man and had continued in sanctuary twenty years and first he dwelt in Cock Alley and afterward in the Broadgate which is now called Bland's Alley'. Deposition of Ralph Twynne, TNA, C 24/3, m 15; see also deposition of William Baylyn in ibid., m. 16. According to Harben's *Dictionary of London* the name 'Bland's Alley' is not

1460s and 1470s Edward IV specifically named both sides of St Martin's Lane as part of the liberty of St Martin Le Grand when he exempted St Martin's from certain pieces of economic legislation in recognition of that status as a liberty.[87] Similarly, the 1525 listing of sanctuary seekers in St Martin's indicated that they all lived in Bland's Alley and Cock's Alley on the west side of St Martin's Lane.[88] Witnesses for the mayor and aldermen, on the other hand, claimed that the west side of St Martin's Lane was fully part of Aldersgate ward, and some witnesses testified that as ward officials they themselves had searched in the lane and assessed its inhabitants in the king's subsidies along with the rest of the ward.[89]

Even the abbot himself, however, did not include the entire length of St Martin's Lane as sanctuary territory,[90] even though there was a good deal of ambiguity about precisely where the dividing line between sanctuary and not-sanctuary lay. The tavern at the southwest corner of the lane, called the Bull Head, was recognized by all as being within the freedom of the City. The status of a small tenement erected on the property behind the tavern, up St Martin's Lane, however, was less clear. By December 1533 the tenement had become a shoemaker's shop, the work and retail space of George Colyn, alien cordwainer, which was raided by London's chamberlain along with Francis Woodleke's shop. This conversion to shoe shop was a relatively recent one; for some time before, according to many witnesses, it had been and was mostly still known as the 'sanctuary parlour', a back drinking room connected to the Bull Head tavern. Piers Peterson, who had lived in sanctuary on the property next door from 1514 but who sided with the City regarding the illegality of Woodleke's and Colyn's shoe shops, argued 'for truth' that the sanctuary parlour was not and never had been sanctuary.[91] He had seen many sanctuary men arrested and taken out of the parlour; moreover, he added, he had heard that a jury had found—presumably in a breach of sanctuary case—that 'the said parlour was no Sanctuary'.[92] A number of witnesses agreed with Peterson,[93] but others suggested that the status of this former drinking parlour was less certain, as indeed Peterson's own story about the number of sanctuary men who drank there suggested: as Cornelius Hobbard said, he had known many sanctuary men to drink in the

---

recorded until 1525, suggesting that the alley may well have been named for this semi-famous inhabitant. Henry A. Harben, *A Dictionary of London* (London, 1918), s.v.

[87] *PROME*, Parl. Apr. 1463, ¶22; see also ¶27, ¶55; Parl. Jan. 1478, ¶27.
[88] TNA, SP 1/33, fol. 148; *L&P*, vol. 4, pt. 1, p. 473.
[89] TNA, STAC 2/20/323, mm 10–16.
[90] TNA, STAC 2/20/324, 'Declarations of the Abbot of Westminster and the Mayor and Aldermen of London regarding the limits of the sanctuary of Saint Martin-le-Grand', m. 2.
[91] WAM, WARB, vol. 2, fol. 64rv; TNA, C 24/3, 'Abbas', m. 2. Peterson had an ambiguous position amongst the stranger artisan community in St Martin's; he had actually participated in the raiding of Colyn's and Woodleke's shops, acting for the City. He was (unusually) later granted the freedom of the City of London for his work undermining the stranger shoemakers' position, although he himself continued to live and work in St Martin's precinct. See LMA, Journal 13, fol. 420v; McSheffrey, 'Stranger Artisans', pp 560–2.
[92] TNA, C 24/3, 'Abbas', m. 2. This may well have been the Griffith case discussed below, this chapter at n.99.
[93] E.g. TNA, C 24/3, 'Abbas', mm 3, 4, 8; Rowland Johnson testified that he had seen a priest who had taken sanctuary for debt in St Martin's arrested there, ibid., m. 3.

parlour, but he had also seen many such sanctuary men arrested there and carried off to prison, so he was not sure whether it was sanctuary or not.[94]

The St Paul's canon John Smith, St Martin's former commissary, offered some intriguing evidence about the sanctuary parlour and how the boundaries could be observed. He testified that although on the whole he did not think that the sanctuary parlour was sanctuary, nonetheless 'he hath seen sanctuary men use to drink in the said parlour and accounted themselves in sanctuary so long as they touched the said wall that parteth the abbot's rents and the Bull Head ground'.[95] At some point this 'home safe' wall-touching seems to have been ruled out of order, however, as by the 1530s only two witnesses unambiguously claimed the sanctuary parlour as sanctuary.[96] The abbot himself implicitly excluded the shop in his own statement regarding the bounds of the precinct[97] and one witness reported that when the abbot had taken an official view of the boundaries of sanctuary in the earlier 1530s, he had given 'monition that the sanctuary men should not resort there but at their peril'.[98]

Witnesses on both sides recalled, usually in vague terms, an episode of a sanctuary man being dragged out of the sanctuary parlour by servants of the sheriffs of London, a story told in greatest detail by deponent John Curteys. He said that 'of late days' a certain man had stolen a silver piece out of the Sun tavern at Cripplegate and then taken sanctuary at St Martin's. Afterwards, Curteys said, he used to resort to the sanctuary parlour. One day, however, officers of the sheriffs of London heard that he was drinking there, and took him out of the parlour and dragged him through the said Bull Head tavern onto Newgate street and thence to Newgate prison. Soon after that, the thief was executed for his felony.[99] This could well have been the same case referenced by the mayor and aldermen in their submission. They said:

> In the time of Sir James Spencer, mayor, anno 20 Henry VIII [1528–1529], judgment was given at Newgate against one Griffith who pleaded sanctuary for that he was forcibly taken out of a house in the lane of St. Martin and the same found no sanctuary by the verdict of twelve men and the prisoner judged to death and hanged.[100]

Knowing where the boundaries lay was literally vital, and cautionary tales such as the seizure and hanging of the Sun tavern thief, perhaps repeated over ale, warned sanctuary men which areas were safe and which not.

It is hardly surprising that the Sun tavern thief would have misunderstood the status of the sanctuary parlour, as the lines that were said to demarcate the sanctuary along the bottom part of St Martin's Lane were unquestionably recondite. The

---

[94] Deposition of Cornelius Hobbard, TNA, C 24/3, 'Abbas', m. 5; see also mm 6, 9, 11.
[95] Deposition of John Smith, 28 Dec. 1536, TNA, C 24/3, 'Abbas', m. 17.
[96] George Hayes testified that the shoemaker's shop 'as far as he knoweth' is sanctuary, for sanctuary men used to drink there when it was a tavern; and Henry Hall more straightforwardly said that it 'hath been ever used as sanctuary'. TNA, C 24/3, 'Abbas', mm 12, 14.
[97] The abbot placed the boundary of the sanctuary north of 'the houses appertaining to the Bull's Head', presumably including the sanctuary parlour. TNA, STAC 2/20/324, m. 2.
[98] TNA, STAC 2/20/323, m. 7.   [99] TNA, STAC 2/20/323, mm 26–27.
[100] TNA, STAC 2/20/324, m. 8.

abbot and those testifying on his behalf argued that while both sides of St Martin's Lane were sanctuary through most of the lane, from the northernmost wall of the Bull Head tenement, the sanctuary bounds ran on a notional line perpendicular to the street up to the drainage channel in the middle of St Martin's Lane and then south to the corner of the lane. Witnesses testified that sanctuary men walking down St Martin's Lane were careful to keep to the east side of the street when they reached its south end. Ralph Twynne noted that Bland, the Perkin Warbeck conspirator, would follow this pattern; when he walked down St Martin's Lane, he sometimes went on one side of the street and sometimes on the other, until he came to the Bull Head ground, 'which was then called the sanctuary parlour', and at that point 'he would always turn over the street and go on the side, that is under Francis Woodleke's said shop window, and would never go on the Bull Head side'.[101]

As Bland's customary walking pattern suggests, one means of delineating the sanctuary and liberty was through remembrance of who walked, stood, leaned, drank, or lived, where. Bartholomew Watson, in arguing that St Martin's Lane had not been considered sanctuary in the years around 1500, testified that about thirty years before he had seen two sanctuary men leaning against the sides of the door of the west end of St Martin's church. They talked with passersby, but they 'durst not step or go any further into the said lane, lest they should have been out of sanctuary'.[102] Derek Tynhof said that he had seen many sanctuary men leaning upon the old post that had stood beneath the north gate, which marked the bounds of the sanctuary.[103] William Mathew testified in 1537 that he had known a man named Seyntbarbe who had been a sanctuary man, a retainer of the Perkin Warbeck conspirator Lord Audeley,[104] who had escaped from the battle at Blackheath field in 1497 to St Martin's. When Mathew was an apprentice, Seyntbarbe would often resort to the shop of his master and stand inside the South Gate of St Martin's close, talking and communing with those who passed by in the street. Neither of these things, 'as the deponent supposeth', could he have done had the area not been sanctuary. Likewise, Mathew's master's house was evidently sanctuary territory because his master had been a 'sanctuary man'; thus he would not, could not 'have dwelled there unless that place had been sanctuary'.[105]

The house in which William Mathew's master lived was on a street apparently with no contemporary name[106] but which the witnesses called 'the street leading to Cheapside', around the corner from Francis Woodleke's shop. On this street stood the South Gate into St Martin's close. Both the marking of the sanctuary bounds outside the gate and the status of Mathew's apprentice-master's house, east of the gate, were at least as complicated as the lower part of St Martin's Lane. Just as with the lane, some witnesses claimed that a line down the middle of the road along the drainage channel marked the boundary on the street leading to Cheapside.

---

[101] TNA, C 24/3, 'Abbas', m. 15.   [102] TNA, STAC 2/20/323, m. 5.
[103] TNA, C 24/3, 'Abbas', m. 11.
[104] Ian Arthurson, 'Tuchet, James, Seventh Baron Audley (c. 1463–1497)', *ODNB* (2004), doi:10.1093/ref:odnb/27576.
[105] TNA, STAC 2/20/323, m. 21.
[106] By 1600 it was called Bladder Street. Stow, *A Survey of London*, p. 313.

This was illustrated most vividly in the minds of many deponents by the spatial organization of proceedings held before the king's justices at St Martin's Gate.

From at least the thirteenth century, the king's justices had held proceedings at St Martin's gate, both in cases where an error in one of the City's higher courts was alleged,[107] and at *nisi prius* (where justices, for convenience, heard proceedings on cases both criminal and civil referred to them by the central royal courts, but did not render judgments).[108] This use of St Martin's for king's court proceedings originated in order to guard the City's privileges against royal encroachment: St Martin's was outside City territory, yet conveniently placed geographically in its midst.[109] But if the justices had to be outside the City's bounds, any accused felons being tried at *nisi prius* could not be within the liberty of St Martin Le Grand, or they could claim sanctuary. In 1440 Dean Caudray had mentioned this as part of his arguments for the precinct's privileges: 'from time that no mind is', he said, the king's justices had sat in the gate, and the persons appeached or indicted of treason or felony were kept by the officers on the other side of the street, so that they could not cross the drainage channel to claim sanctuary.[110] Witnesses in the 1530s testified to the continuity of this practice, Roger Wright recalling that when the king's justices sat at the gate of St Martin's, the gate was shut and a cloth hung over the gate with the justices' seats leaning towards the gate. He saw one Appulton, a barber, arraigned, and at the time of his arraignment Appulton stood on the other side of the street at a bar made there for that purpose.[111] Indeed, one deponent, William Bayly, testified 'that he heard the chief justice say that the half street towards St. Martin's was sanctuary'.[112] The prisoners' bar, about which a number of deponents testified,[113] was presumably erected temporarily, for the purposes of the judicial proceedings. It marked more clearly the boundary that otherwise was indicated only by the drainage channel, and perhaps even served to restrain the prisoners physically from putting their feet over the line.

No deponents referred to any instance of a prisoner being tried before the justices at St Martin's gate making this escape into sanctuary. There had been some notorious cases in the fifteenth century, however, of prisoners being led along Newgate Street to or from Newgate prison escaping through St Martin's gate to

---

[107] Baker, *Oxford History, 1485–1558*, pp 279, 403–7; Tucker, *Law Courts*, pp 39–40.
[108] Baker, *Oxford History, 1485–1558*, pp 256–9.
[109] Reginald R. Sharpe, ed., *Calendar of Letter-Books, Letter Book A (1275–1298)* (London, 1899), p. 213; Reginald R. Sharpe, ed., *Calendar of Letter-Books, Letter Book F (1337–1352)* (London, 1904), pp 59–60, 64, 89, 106; Reginald R. Sharpe, ed., *Calendar of Letter-Books, Letter Book G (1352–1374)* (London, 1905), pp 83, 86; Barron, *London*, p. 37; Baker, *Oxford History, 1485–1558*, p. 279.
[110] *Registrum*, fol. 48r.   [111] TNA, STAC 2/20/323, m. 9.
[112] TNA, STAC 2/20/57, m. 13. Interestingly, that chief justice was possibly Sir John Fyneux, named by another deponent as presiding over proceedings at St Martin's gate (TNA, STAC 2/20/323, m. 22). Fyneux, chief justice of the King's Bench from 1495 until his death in 1525, is often cited as a judicial opponent of sanctuary privileges; J. H. Baker, 'Fyneux [Fenex], Sir John (d. 1525)', *ODNB* (2004), doi:10.1093/ref:odnb/10261; Baker, *Oxford History, 1485–1558*, pp 548–9; Thornley, 'Destruction of Sanctuary', p. 198. As argued above in Ch. 4 at n.60, Fyneux's objection to some sanctuaries may not have extended to St Martin's, as St Martin's met his requirements for a properly constituted sanctuary. Baker, *Caryll*, pp 707–11.
[113] TNA, STAC 2/20/323, m. 22; C 24/3, 'Abbas', mm 2, 4, 8, 13.

safety, including, as we saw in Chapter 3, the escape of John Knight in 1440.[114] As a precaution, and in parallel to the sanctuary men who were careful to walk on the sanctuary side of the street, Roger Newes reported in 1536 that

> all they which come from the Tower to be put to execution at Tyburn and all other prisoners which are brought to or from Newgate been always carried on the further side of the street from the said South Gate, that is to say on the south side of the street for against the same gate.[115]

To further corroborate the importance of keeping the felons away from the north side of the street, deponent Derek Tynholf remembered the aftermath of the 1517 Evil May Day riot which had particularly targeted St Martin's:

> When Ill May Day was, there was a pair of gallows set up at St. Martin's South Gate in the street where one should have been put to execution, which gallows were afterward removed because they stood upon the Sanctuary ground, [and] were set on the further side of the street over right against St. Martin's gate. And the man was hanged.[116]

In yet another twist, the notional line down the middle of the street outside the South Gate did not extend all the way down the road to Cheapside but stopped partway across the tenement on the gate's east side, the house formerly held by William Mathew's apprentice-master and occupied in the 1530s by Roger Wright, a grocer. As many deponents testified, Wright's house had a great post in the middle that marked the sanctuary bounds. One side of the house was sanctuary, the other side, City of London. Wright himself was not a sanctuary man, but a citizen and grocer, and thus the house's status as part-sanctuary was neither here nor there to him.[117] The strange status of Wright's house owed its origins to a previous tenant, Robert Purfote, a London citizen and grocer who had taken sanctuary for debt in the later part of the fifteenth century and had been witness William Mathew's apprentice-master. Mathew testified both in 1536 and 1537 regarding the sanctuary's bounds, and offered his special knowledge of the house from his experience of living in Purfote's household in the 1490s.[118] Purfote became tenant of the house immediately on the east side of the South Gate when he went into sanctuary for debt, sometime in the 1470s or 1480s.[119] The door of the house opened through

---

[114] There are many other examples of escapes into sanctuaries while being transferred to or from a prison. See, for instance, these examples from McSheffrey, 'Sanctuary Seekers': John a Plough (ID #1118); William Johnson (ID #1697); Piers Henrikson (ID #1770); William Smyth alias Chalfunt (ID #1148); and George Brewce (ID #1159), whose case is discussed below in Ch. 7, at n.48.
[115] TNA, C 24/3, 'Abbas', m. 8.   [116] TNA, C 24/3, 'Abbas', mm 10–11.
[117] 'He heard say that the one half of his house, that is to say that part next adjoining to the said gate hath been taken for sanctuary belonging to St. Martin's inasmuch that the old abbot of Westminster about six or seven years passed did view in his own person the said house and diverse other houses in St. Martin's lane, at which time the said abbot said and reported to this deponent and others present that the sanctuary did extend to a great post on the south part of the said house which stood some time in partition within the same house, and which partition did extend northward unto the end of one old wall there yet remaining'. Deposition of Roger Wright, TNA, STAC 2/20/323, m. 6.
[118] Depositions of William Mathew, TNA, C 24/3, 'Abbas', mm 12–13; STAC 2/20/323, mm 19–23.
[119] In 1474, Robert Purfote enrolled a deed in the City's plea and memoranda rolls, so presumably his entry into St Martin's post-dated that time. Philip E. Jones, ed., *Calendar of Plea and Memoranda*

the gate, thus directly into sanctuary. Although, as witness John Marten put it, 'Purfote, because he was a sanctuary man, might not be suffered to open any door into the street', nonetheless 'because he was a freeman he was suffered to open his shop windows into the street' so that he could sell his goods into the City—the customers would be standing in the City of London, the grocer inside the shop, in sanctuary.[120]

In about the late 1480s, according to William Mathew, Purfote was able to discharge his debts and no longer needed sanctuary.[121] He stayed put, however, in the tenement he had leased from the dean of St Martin Le Grand. Soon after, he acquired the tenement next door, which had never been sanctuary territory, and knocked down the wall between the tenements to create a shop of twice the size. He opened up a door into the street, on the east side of the house, and closed up the original door that led into the gate. The western part of the house, however, retained its status as sanctuary, the boundary indicated within the house by a large post standing where the wall dividing the two houses had once been.[122] This anomalous situation continued after Purfote died in 1507 and still held in the mid-1530s, at which time Roger Wright, also a grocer, was the tenant.[123] As Wright himself was not in sanctuary, and he did not have any sanctuary men in his household, the main significance of this sanctuary boundary marker within the house was on the street outside. The notional line marking the sanctuary boundary on the street proceeded from this sanctuary post in Wright's house up to the channel in the middle of the street. From there it ran westward in front of St Martin's Gate, up to the channel in the middle of St Martin's Lane, and then up St Martin's Lane to the end of the Bull Head tenement, after which the sanctuary bounds ran behind the tenements on the western side of St Martin's Lane along the wall that separated lands belonging to St Martin Le Grand from the gardens of the Greyfriars.

* * *

The signals that had been sent by the terms of the inquiry in 1535 had suggested that the winds were finally blowing against the stranger shoemakers, but they seem not to have blown hard enough for the City of London. The immediate outcome of the 1535–1537 commission was maintenance of the status quo. Although once more no decision or outcome of this inquiry from the king's council survives, we can infer from what happened afterward that the commission sided with the abbot of Westminster and St Martin's, or that no decision was made, which had the same effect.[124] For the moment, as of 1537, both the sanctuary and the liberties of

---

Rolls, 1458–1482 (Cambridge, 1961), p. 170. A chancery bill presented 1473–1475, however, indicates that around that time Purfote was heavily in debt to William Dalton, merchant of the Calais staple: TNA, C 1/48/144.

[120] Deposition of John Marten, TNA, C 24/3, 'Abbas', m. 9.

[121] Mathew stated that Purfote was no longer a sanctuary man for the last twenty years of his life, and he died in 1507 or 1508. Deposition of William Mathew, TNA, C 24/3, m. 12; TNA, PROB 11/15/654, will of Robert Purfote, grocer, 1507.

[122] Depositions of William Mathew, TNA, C 24/3, 'Abbas', mm 12–13; STAC 2/20/323, mm 20–21.

[123] In January 1537 Wright himself mentions that he was living in the house six or seven years before. Deposition of Roger Wright, TNA, STAC 2/20/323, m. 6.

[124] I erred on this question in McSheffrey, 'Sanctuary and Legal Topography', p. 506.

St Martin's remained (although the last surviving records of felons taking refuge there date from 1536).[125] George Colyn's shop in the sanctuary parlour was probably closed, but he may simply have moved up the street, as he was living and working as a shoemaker in the precinct of St Martin le Grand, in St Martin's Lane, as late as 1545. Francis Woodleke continued to occupy his shop, with the window opening out into St Martin's Lane, into the 1540s.[126]

In the rhetoric produced by both sides in this legal conflict, St Martin's different privileges, for felons and debtors, on the one hand, and stranger artisans, on the other, were, time and time again, conflated.[127] For those arguing for St Martin's privileges, the right of the shoemakers to sell in St Martin's Lane was anchored in St Martin's ecclesiastical immunities, in its status as a sanctuary.[128] For the City's argument against St Martin's, the 'pretended' sanctuary and its sheltering of heinous criminals had never existed legitimately, and thus the stranger shoemakers could not work and sell there. The City's case could be proved by a series of precedents that mixed cases showing the London sheriffs' arrest of felons in the precinct with others showing the subjection of the 'open shops' in the precinct to the jurisdiction of the City's guilds.[129] Even the very terms of the king's commission for the inquiry intertwined the two ideas of sanctuary and alien labour: the commissioners were asked 'diligently [to] view and try out all and every the bounds and limits of the said Sanctuary', and to examine 'the grants, licences and confirmations' made to the abbot and his predecessors concerning it. Why did the king order this inquiry? 'As we be credibly informed', an alien shoemaker was selling shoes at retail in the lane. A clear report of the usage of the sanctuary was needed in order to determine whether his shoe shop was legal.[130] Yet, as tightly intertwined as the jurisdictional exemptions that allowed strangers to work in St Martin's and felons to stay there free from arrest still were in the 1530s, they would in the following decade separate out again.

THE DISSOLUTION OF ST MARTIN LE GRAND AND BEYOND

Sanctuary at St Martin le Grand was dismantled by the sanctuary statute of 1540[131] and the collegiate church itself was dissolved in 1542, although the estates attached to it were regranted to the new cathedral church of St Peter's, Westminster (that is, the converted abbey). Excepting sanctuary for felons, the liberties that had previously

---

[125] There are two from 1536: John Webbe (TNA, KB 9/1065, m. 116; KB 27/1101, rex m. 4; KB 29/169, m. 27d); and Richard Lloyd (TNA, SP 1/101, fol. 170r; L&P, vol. 10, p. 72).
[126] Lang, *Tudor Subsidy Rolls*, pp 7–9; TNA, E 179/144/123 (1543), m. 5; E 179/145/137 (1545 subsidy), m. 1; PROB 11/29/400, Will of Hugh Payne. Payne's will actually mentioned that Woodleke's tenement opened into St Martin's Lane.
[127] See LMA, Journal 13, fols 186v, 194–196v, 410v–414r, 420v, 453r, 467r–468v; Repertory 9, fols 26v, 46r, 48r, 51r, 59v, 61v, 62r, 63rv, 85v, 104r, 109v–110r, 135r; Repertory 10, fols 9rv, 10r, 31v, 36r, 62r, 88v; TNA, STAC 2/20/324; STAC 2/20/323; C 24/3, 'Abbas'.
[128] TNA, STAC 2/20/324, m. 2. [129] TNA, STAC 2/20/324, mm 5–8.
[130] Copy entered into LMA, Journal 13, fol. 453r.
[131] 32 Hen. VIII, c. 16; *SR*, vol. 3, pp 756–8.

been accorded to the church—its separate status from the City as far as alien craftsmen and debtors were concerned—were to continue. The king delineated precisely where those liberties should be observed: 'within the site of the college of St. Martin and Dean's Court, Pouchmakers' Court, St. Martin's lane, Angel alley, Bell alley, St. John's alley, Cock alley, Christopher alley, Four Doves' alley, and Bland's alley'.[132] In other words, Henry VIII granted that all the territories that had been claimed by the most expansionist versions of the sanctuary were to continue to be acknowledged as a liberty, vindicating much of the abbot's case in the 1520s and 1530s. But, crucially, the liberty now had its basis only in royal grant, not in any holiness inhering in the now churchless site: the imposing church of St Martin le Grand, which had dominated the precinct, was razed in the late 1540s, the site subsequently occupied by the same kinds of tenements that lined much of St Martin's Lane and the other alleys and courts.

It is hard to know to what extent and for how long Londoners might have nonetheless continued to associate the territory's status as a liberty with its former sacrality. In 1558, City of London viewers recorded that an area in the precinct was 'privileged and sanctuary ground',[133] but this was, significantly, during Mary's reign, when it may have been safe or even politic to revive ideas about sacrality and immunity.[134] John Stow, writing his great *Survey of London* around 1600, tells us that after St Martin's church was pulled down, 'a large Wine tavern was built', and many houses were erected and leased to aliens (Stow apparently not realizing that the strangers in St Martin's long predated the dissolution). In practising their trades in the precinct, those aliens, he said, acted as the merchants in the temple mentioned in the twenty-first chapter of Matthew's gospel, in contrast to the canons of old who had served God day and night.[135] Thus the old precinct, on both sides of St Martin's Lane, continued to bear many of the immunities that had been associated with the church for several centuries, retaining its status as a liberty within the City and thus as a haven for alien craftsmen and debtors. St Martin's remained jurisdictionally independent from the City for centuries more, until the early nineteenth century when the precinct was levelled to build the new General Post Office.[136]

Although the witnesses for both the abbot and the City saw the most potent evidence for or against the nature and extent of St Martin's liberties in the daily habits of sanctuary men, the significance of those boundaries was arguably much greater for the hundreds of stranger artisans who lived within the precincts than for the dozen or so sanctuary seekers. The primarily economic jurisdictional exemptions of St Martin's liberty and the sanctuary privileges of collegiate church's precinct had proved to be mutually constitutive: each was bolstered by the other. Of the

---

[132] *L&P*, vol. 17, p. 396.

[133] Janet Senderowitz Loengard, ed., *London Viewers and Their Certificates, 1508–1558: Certificates of the Sworn Viewers of the City of London* (London, 1989), no. 397.

[134] See for instance arguments about Westminster's sanctuary in Mary's reign: Arthur Penrhyn Stanley, *Historical Memorials of Westminster Abbey*, 2nd edn (London, 1868), pp 610–16.

[135] Stow, *A Survey of London*, vol. 1, p. 308.

[136] Kempe, *Historical Notices*; Anthony Paul House, 'The City of London and the Problem of the Liberties, c1540–c1640' (DPhil, Oxford University, 2006), pp 30–1, 183–220.

two, however, it was the economic privileges, ironically likely the crux of the City's antipathy towards St Martin's, that proved more enduring: the precinct of St Martin's became a thoroughly secular place when its church was destroyed, if not before. The desacralization of St Martin's remaining privileges was without doubt accelerated by the Reformation changes, but it was also part of the increasing laicization of the management of sanctuary and its ever greater integration within the processes of England's criminal justice system during the reigns of Henry VII and Henry VIII. Hugh Payne's management of St Martin as a sanctuary and as a liberty was characteristic of other sanctuaries in Henry VIII's reign. These themes will be continued in Chapter 6, which will look closely at how local men in a 'sanctuary town' in Warwickshire handled an escaping felon who sought refuge there in 1537.

6

The Sanctuary Town of Knowle
Crime, Local Authorities, and the State in 1530s England

In late 1537 a man named Hugh Harvey worked as a servant at an inn known as the Goat. The hostelry stood on the Strand, then a road lined by inns and aristocratic residences running along the river between the city of London and the town of Westminster.[1] Harvey later confessed that in November of that year he had robbed one of the guests, although he denied another accusation levelled against him, that he had also stolen from his employer, the Goat's landlord. Immediately following the robbery, he fled to Warwickshire with the pilfered goods. After several days of travelling from place to place in the county, he took refuge in the sanctuary town of Knowle. Attempts by the robbery victim's friends and relatives to arrest Harvey for the theft were rebuffed by the sanctuary's administrators, who asserted that the accused felon had the privilege of sanctuary and thus could not be taken away to face the king's justice. After those who were trying to arrest him realized their attempts were bound to be fruitless, they left. Harvey stayed within the confines of the sanctuary for about two weeks before he, too, departed from Knowle, and disappeared. Hugh Harvey appears to have emerged unscathed from the episode, having used the privilege of sanctuary very much to his benefit. For a poor servant like Harvey, even as late as 1537, sanctuary could work as a temporary stall on the harsh proceedings of English criminal justice until an opportunity to disappear presented itself.

The documents emanating from Hugh Harvey's case show in some detail the ins and outs of the administration of this small sanctuary and more generally the workings of sanctuary privilege in the later 1530s. The episode illustrates further the shift in who managed sanctuaries. In 1440, as we saw in Chapter 3, it was the dean of St Martin le Grand and his canons who handled the sanctuary seekers who came into their precinct. By Henry VIII's reign, the management of this 'ecclesiastical' privilege was much more likely to be undertaken by laymen, working as bailiffs or agents of the religious houses, than by clergy. St Martin's, for instance, as we saw in Chapter 5, was administered by constable Hugh Payne, a leatherseller deputed by the abbot of Westminster not only to handle the rents and keep the peace in the

---

[1] The Goat is mentioned as early as 1519. Richard Yeoman, the landlord mentioned in Harvey's case, was still innholder there in 1544, but died in October 1545. By 1547 the inn had passed out of his widow's hands. TNA, PROB 11/30/572, will of Richard Yoman, innholder, 1545; E 326/6476; E 328/164; *L&P*, vol. 19, pt. 2, p. 319.

precinct but also to register the sanctuary seekers and even to distribute the salaries to the chapel's clergy. The administration of the Knowle sanctuary to which Hugh Harvey fled was similarly conducted by local laymen: more than a dozen men were involved in some way in dealing with Hugh Harvey's request for sanctuary, and only one of those was a member of the clergy, and he played a very minor role.

The records associated with Harvey's case illustrate vividly the laicization of sanctuary administration in Henry VIII's England, when not only day-to-day management but decisions about who was eligible for the privilege were in the hands of laymen, the same men who held local offices of royal administration, sat as jurors, or who otherwise participated in the crown's government of the kingdom. Sanctuary was thoroughly imbricated in the complicated lines of patronage and office-holding in Henrician England, both in its functioning as an income-producing franchise and in its integration into the process of handling felony and felons at the local level. And just as the exercise of some of the offices associated with the king's justice and governing of the kingdom brought with it the opportunity for fees or other profits, so also did the management of the sanctuary at Knowle carry with it financial opportunities for local men.[2]

This means that administering sanctuary was part of the process of state formation in England. Scholars have recently emphasized the importance of the parts played by local men as jurors, constables, churchwardens, and a host of other roles in building the state from below. If early modernists have tended to see the weaving of ecclesiastical administration into the structures of governance and power in the realm as a post-Reformation development, medievalists have shown that lay involvement in ecclesiastical administration and justice dated from the high medieval period.[3] As Ian Forrest points out, laymen's participation in parish management and the church courts was an integral part of the broadening of governance and local elite formation that characterizes the building of the state.[4] By the early sixteenth century, even many aspects of ecclesiastical estate management had come to be taken on by lay administrators.

The interpenetration of ecclesiastical and royal offices generally, and the integration of sanctuary administration into governance by local lay notables, in turn challenges interpretations of the privilege of sanctuary that have focused on it as an 'ecclesiastical' right opposed by a secularizing state. Although, as we have seen, at points there inevitably were conflicts between religious houses as rights-holders and the crown or other secular (especially civic) officials regarding the extent of sanctuary privileges claimed by those houses, it is anachronistic to suppose that those conflicts can easily be reduced to churchmen attempting to shore up their outmoded clerical privileges against the incoming tide of secularized lay modernity. The laymen had

---

[2] On the evolution of Tudor office-holding and its laicization, Williams, *Tudor Regime*, pp 82–5.
[3] See the discussion below, at n.97 in this chapter.
[4] Ian Forrest, 'The Archive of the Official of Stow and the "Machinery" of Church Government in the Late Thirteenth Century', *Historical Research* 84 (2011): pp 1–13, doi:10.1111/j.1468-2281.2009.00528.x; Ian Forrest, 'The Transformation of Visitation in Thirteenth-Century England', *Past & Present* 221 (2013): pp 3–38, doi:10.1093/pastj/gtt013; John Sabapathy, *Officers and Accountability in Medieval England 1170–1300* (Oxford, 2014), pp 236–60; Katherine L. French, *The People of the Parish: Community Life in a Late Medieval English Diocese* (Philadelphia, 2001).

to a great extent taken over sanctuary. And along the way, sanctuary had moved some way towards being desacralized, as the emphasis more and more was laid on its status as a royally-granted privilege that functioned as part of the king's law.

Lastly, the story of Hugh Harvey's sanctuary-seeking at Knowle in 1537 indicates that even at this late date, the privilege of sanctuary—as distinct from Harvey's right to claim it—was entirely uncontroversial. We know that the privilege would collapse, if not immediately die, about three years later, but contemporaries did not know that. Analysis of the evidence for numbers of sanctuary seekers indicates that resort to sanctuaries had begun to decline about two years before Harvey's resort to Knowle, but again it is hard to know if contemporaries noticed. Moreover, by the fall of 1537, the monastic dissolutions were well underway, although the first of the major chartered sanctuaries was not dissolved until 1538 with the closure of Beaulieu Abbey.[5] None of this, however, appears to have entered into the discussion about Hugh Harvey's sanctuary privilege at Knowle in 1537; even as religious houses were shutting down throughout the realm, sanctuary continued to operate there as it had for decades, at least for the time being.

THE GOAT INN ROBBER AND SANCTUARY AT KNOWLE

At the end of March 1538, Henry VIII gave a commission to Sir Anthony Fitzherbert, justice of the Court of Common Pleas, and Reginald Digby, Warwickshire gentleman and servant to the crown, both Justices of the Peace for Warwickshire. Their task was to investigate what had happened to money stolen the previous November from Dr Richard Croke, chaplain to the king. As the terms of the commission stated, one Hugh Harvey had robbed Dr Croke's servant and then fled to the sanctuary of Knowle, in Warwickshire. As the king had been informed, some of the stolen money had made its way into the purses of certain inhabitants of the town of Knowle, while the rest remained in the hands of Hugh Harvey himself. Although the king had sent letters to the officers of the sanctuary 'commanding them by the same to cause restitution to be made to our well-beloved chaplain, Dr. Croke, of all such sums of money' stolen from him, the sanctuary's officers 'have hitherto done little or nothing' about it. Instead, from the 'affection' that they seemed to bear to Harvey, they permitted him to remain in the sanctuary and shielded him from arrest for the crime, notwithstanding that he was indicted not only for the robbery of Dr Croke, but also for robbing his master—a crime for which 'by the laws and statutes of this our Realm' he could not have the privilege of sanctuary.

Seeing all this, the king commanded Fitzherbert and Digby to call before them the officers of the sanctuary and any other inhabitants of the town to find out about Harvey's sanctuary-seeking and what had happened to the money. He asked his commissioners to report back to the king's council a fortnight after Easter, on

---

[5] See Ch. 7, n.43.

6 May.[6] The legal questions in this case were deceptively complicated, accounting perhaps for the lack of response from the sanctuary's officers to the king's previous command to restore the stolen money to Dr Croke. The main issue on which the commission was to focus was not the whereabouts of the felon, but what had happened to the stolen money; that latter question hinged on who held the right to the recovery and redistribution of the stolen goods in the case, which in turn depended on whether Hugh Harvey had been eligible for the privilege of sanctuary at Knowle.

Attached to this commission, now in the State Papers at the National Archives, are most of the papers generated by the enquiry into Hugh Harvey's arrival in Knowle and his seeking of sanctuary privilege. The documents include a list of questions to be posed to witnesses and depositions from fourteen men, supplemented by a number of narrative statements, in several cases apparently hand-written by the witnesses themselves.[7] Altogether, this material extends over thirty-five folios.[8] Fitzherbert's and Digby's final report, presumably delivered to the king's council, was filed separately among the papers of the Court of Requests.[9] The terms of the commission, as above, were by no means neutral in their tone, and thus would seem to have militated towards a particular conclusion (that the sanctuary's officers should deliver Hugh Harvey's ill-gotten gains back to Dr Croke); moreover, one of the commissioners, Reginald Digby, was hardly impartial, as he had already acted for Dr Croke in the case.[10] But if the commission's terms and the appointment of Digby seem to have signalled a particular desired conclusion, Sir Anthony Fitzherbert's appointment as the other commissioner likely mitigated the bias. A senior legal figure in the realm who was about to publish one of the most enduringly influential guides to local legal practice,[11] Fitzherbert was not one to go along blindly with the crown's policies in the 1530s. A legal and religious conservative, it does not seem likely that he was given this commission as a yes-man.[12]

Knowle was not one of Tudor England's better-known sanctuaries—in fact I have found only a handful of references to requests for asylum there between the late fifteenth century and Hugh Harvey's case (and none before 1492).[13] Knowle was a town of between three and four hundred people with a market, encompassed in a manor held by the Abbot of Westminster.[14] It was part of the parish of Hampton, a town some three kilometres from Knowle, but inhabitants of Knowle were permitted

---

[6] TNA, SP 1/130, fol. 154r.
[7] These were by Thomas Trussell, Thomas Haw, Robert Butler, Ralph Marshall, and a joint statement by Robert Croke and William Cull. TNA, SP 1/130, fols 174r–175r, 180rv, 181rv, 182rv, 183r.
[8] TNA, SP 1/130, fols 154r–189v, briefly calendared in *L&P*, vol. 13, pt. 1, p. 228.
[9] TNA, REQ 2/5/115.   [10] TNA, SP 1/130, fols 174v, 175v.
[11] Anthony Fitzherbert, *The Newe Boke of Iustyces of Peas* (London, 1538).
[12] J. H. Baker, 'Fitzherbert, Sir Anthony (c. 1470–1538)', *ODNB* (2004), doi:10.1093/ref:odnb/9602.
[13] TNA, KB 9/397, m. 21 (KB 27/935, rex m. 3d) (1492); TNA, KB 9/509, m. 156 (KB 29/161, m. 1d) (1529); TNA, STAC 2/12/236 (1529); TNA, SP 1/97, fol. 117 (*L&P*, vol. 9, p. 190) (1535).
[14] The commissioners of the chantry survey in 1545–1546 indicated that there were 300 communicants in the 'hamlet' of Knowle. The records of the 1523 subsidy record 64 taxpayers in Knowle; in 1543 there were 70 taxpayers. W. B. Bickley, ed., *The Register of the Guild of Knowle in the County of Warwick, 1451–1535* (Walsall, Staffordshire, 1894), p. xxiii; TNA, E 179/192/139, rot. 4; E 179/192/156, rot. 35–36.

by their bishop to use the College of Knowle, a secular collegiate church with six priests attached to it, as their parish church. The College was home to a guild dedicated to St John the Baptist, St Laurence, and St Anne, which had been very fashionable in the fifteenth and early sixteenth centuries, attracting peers of the realm as guild brothers.[15] The basis of Knowle's privilege as a sanctuary was, however, not directly related to this church, and instead rested on its status as a dependent manor of Westminster Abbey. In other cases in the reign of Henry VIII, as we saw in Chapter 4, felons made claims to sanctuary in dependent properties of Westminster, St Martin le Grand, Beaulieu, the priory of St John of Jerusalem, and the bishop of Durham.[16] In 1525, for instance, coroner's inquest jurors in the city of York reported that Leonard Longstaff had fled following a homicide to the town of Crayke in Yorkshire, 'a part of the liberty and sanctuary of the blessed Cuthbert of Durham' and thereby deriving its privilege from the bishop of Durham's franchise.[17] In some of these cases, these sanctuaries in dependencies of the great chartered sanctuaries were explicitly noted to have registers, indicating a degree of regularization.[18] The somewhat extenuated nature of these sanctuary privileges—attached to church buildings that were sometimes hundreds of kilometres away—may explain why the discussions about Knowle's sanctuary refer to it as a statutory privilege under the king's law, rather than an emanation of the 'immunity of holy church'.

There are scattered pieces of evidence for sanctuary at Knowle before Harvey's case.[19] In 1492, in the earliest reference I have located, two brothers from Worcestershire accused of murder fled 'to the privilege or liberty of the town of Knowle in Warwickshire'. They were ultimately acquitted due to an improperly drafted indictment.[20] In February 1529, coroner's inquest jurors at Rowington, Warwickshire, reported that John Grene, who had killed Robert Orgell of the same town, had fled to Knowle, 'which is a town having the liberty of sanctuary, and thus John could not be taken or extracted from there'. Two years later, Grene was outlawed.[21] In fleeing to Knowle, Grene may have joined a number of other sanctuary seekers who had made the town their home, at least according to a submission to a Star Chamber suit around the same time by Warwickshire gentleman Sir George Throckmorton. Acting on behalf of Cardinal Wolsey, Throckmorton

---

[15] William Page, ed., *A History of the County of Warwick*, Victoria History of the Counties of England (London, 1908), vol. 2, pp 121–3; Bickley, *Register of the Guild of Knowle*, esp. pp xiv, 172.
[16] Search 'dependency' in McSheffrey, 'Sanctuary Seekers', for cases.
[17] TNA, KB 9/502, m. 89; see also KB 9/486, m. 36.   [18] See above, Ch. 1 at n.26.
[19] In addition to the cases cited below, in 1517, Henry Dey alias Johnson of Knowle sought sanctuary at Durham cathedral because he had received thieves in his house (and thus was an accessory to felony). This could indicate a question about Knowle's privileges at a point when sanctuary was somewhat insecure (as in Ch. 4, at n.48), or that the thieves had committed another felony after having taken the privilege, or that only some inhabitants of the town were permitted to take in sanctuary seekers. *SDSB*, p. 76.
[20] '…usque ad privilegium sive libertatem ville de Knolle in comitatu Warr'. TNA, KB 9/397, m. 21; KB 29/123, m. 15d; KB 27/935, rex m. 3d.
[21] 'que est villa libertatem sanctuarii habentem, ita quod extra eadem libertate et sanctuario idem Johannes capi nec extrahi potuit'. TNA, KB 9/509, m. 156; KB 29/161, m. 1d.

said that he had attempted to take possession of a property at Balsall,[22] about seven kilometres from Knowle, but that he was prevented from doing so by the rebellious tenant, who was joined by at least five sanctuary men from Knowle in an armed defence of the manor.[23] By Throckmorton's account, then, Knowle had had at least five sanctuary men in 1529, and on this occasion at least they could be drafted as muscle into the kinds of local land disputes that too often descended into armed conflict.

Two further situations in Knowle in 1535, which may have been related to one another, hint at some of the complications Knowle's sanctuary status brought in its wake. In 1535, a Wiltshire gentleman named William Button complained to Cromwell about a man named Hill who had in the summer of 1535 robbed and tried to kill him before running to sanctuary at Knowle. Button in his letter alleged a mare's nest of corruption surrounding Knowle sanctuary and its administration: Hill, he said, had been using Knowle as a base from which to commit robberies; the bailiff of the sanctuary was complicit in Hill's repeated felonies; Hill, he had heard, would stand trial but only because the sheriff of Warwickshire had received a back-hander to ensure Hill would be acquitted; and (in what was not the most diplomatic of approaches) Button also implied that Cromwell himself and the Chancellor were involved in a deal where the condition of the acquittal was that Hill would join the king's forces fighting rebellion in Ireland.[24] Button's letter may well not have been taken very seriously by Cromwell, as he was a litigious and querulous man.[25] It is also worth noting that although Button alleged corruption and misuse of sanctuary, in his complaint sanctuary was not portrayed as an ecclesiastically-imposed extraneous practice inimical to the way royal justice should be administered, but rather simply as part of the complex of the crown's legal processes that could be (and all too often were) manipulated.

A homicide in Knowle that same summer of 1535 may well relate to the sanctuary seeker Hill, and in any case reveals further local tensions over jurisdiction and the king's law. In early August, Thomas Haw and William Holbache, as coroners for Warwickshire, convened an inquest over the body of William Elliotts of Knowle. Thomas Haw played an important role in the unfolding of Hugh Harvey's sanctuary claim, while William Holbache was likely related to another man involved, Richard Holbache. The jurors reported to the coroners that Elliotts' death had resulted from a brawl that broke out over an attempt to execute 'a certain warrant of the peace of the lord king' in the Knowle liberty. Eight men, including the victim Elliotts himself and two men later involved in Harvey's case, Henry Horley and Thomas Trussell, had joined together to fulfil the warrant (the purport of which the jurors do not explain). In trying to serve it, however, they began 'to

---

[22] Interestingly, the land in question was a Hospitaller property, which itself would, on at least one occasion, be claimed as sanctuary, in 1535. TNA, KB 9/976, m. 55; KB 29/169, m. 2d.
[23] TNA, STAC 2/12/236.   [24] TNA, SP 1/97, fol. 117; L&P, vol. 9, p. 190.
[25] T. F. T. Baker, 'Button, William I (1503–47)', History of Parliament Trust, 'Members, 1509–1558', *The History of Parliament: British Political, Social, and Local History* (London, 1964), http://www.historyofparliamentonline.org/research/members/members-1509-1558.

argue and quarrel and assault one another'. In the course of the fray Elliotts was killed (the accused, a blacksmith named Richard Smyth, acted in self-defence, the jurors argued).[26]

Knowle's status as a sanctuary town, then, dated back to at least the 1490s. Although there were probably not large numbers of sanctuary seekers there, Throckmorton's Star Chamber bill suggests that there may have been half a dozen or so at any one time, although it could have have varied significantly from year to year. The killing of William Elliotts and the affair of Hugh Harvey about two years later reveal that local men had difficulties and disagreements about how the king's law was to be executed in their sanctuary town. Harvey's case shows in detail the general trend in other records, such as those at the court of King's Bench: that the terms under which sanctuary was claimed and allowed in Henry VIII's third decade of rule were often elastic and circumstantial, rather than clearly defined. This remained the case even as a number of statutes in the 1530s attempted to regularize the admission and governance of sanctuary seekers. These statutes introduced complications for those charged with administering the sanctuaries: the individuals involved in Harvey's case differed over whether he was entitled to the privilege under recent parliamentary legislation, and several confessed themselves confused by 'the king's acts'. Yet despite disagreement and confusion, no one questioned that the privilege of sanctuary at Knowle existed for those who qualified: it was not sanctuary itself, or even sanctuary at Knowle, that was controversial, just Harvey's case.

The case of Hugh Harvey and his seeking of sanctuary at Knowle has attracted almost no notice from historians,[27] for the very good reason that the quarrels were petty (at most, Harvey stole about £20, and the amount may have been less than £5) and seemingly of little larger significance. Yet close examination of the material Fitzherbert and Digby gathered sheds considerable light on the workings of sanctuary in the late 1530s. The depositions the witnesses gave before Fitzherbert and Digby are, as one might expect in such a situation, inconsistent and sometimes contradictory. Although we will never be able to establish precisely what happened in this case, the testimony reveals both the difficulties and the opportunities the townspeople of Knowle experienced as a result of their town's status as a sanctuary. The arguments about procedure amongst the local men charged with administering the sanctuary—legal amateurs with their eyes as firmly fixed on the perquisites of office as on their duties—also illustrate the promises and perils of Tudor state formation.

---

[26] TNA, KB 9/535, m. 57; KB 29/169, m. 36. The accused, Richard Smyth, despite the finding of self-defence, fled and was never found; he was outlawed in 1537. It is interesting that the Warwickshire coroners conducted the inquest, even though Knowle was a liberty (and was identified as such in the inquest report); perhaps since it was so far away from Westminster the abbot waived his right to have his own coroner conduct the inquest.

[27] The only reference to this incident in the scholarship that I have seen is Charles Cox's account, apparently closely derived from the short calendar of the State Papers dossier in the *L&P*: Cox, *Sanctuaries*, pp 324–5.

ROBBERY, FLIGHT, SANCTUARY

In November 1537, Dr Croke was staying at the Goat Inn on the Strand, accompanied by a servant, Simon Gelinge. According to the accusations against Hugh Harvey, Gelinge had been carrying a bag of money belonging to Dr Croke when Harvey attacked him. Accounts varied regarding how much money Harvey stole: Dr Croke claimed that Harvey had taken £12 from Gelinge, while the Knowle witnesses indicated Harvey had with him between £4 and £5 when he arrived in their town. It was also alleged—although he denied it—that Harvey had stolen £8 from his master, the innkeeper Richard Yeoman.[28]

In robbing Dr Croke, Harvey chose the wrong victim. Richard Croke was a doctor of divinity, Oxford professor, and pioneer of Greek scholarship in England. An established theologian and humanist scholar by the mid-1520s, he served in 1526 as tutor to the king's illegitimate son, Henry Fitzroy, and in 1529–1530 he traveled to Italy with Thomas Cranmer and others to canvass support among Italian university scholars for Henry's divorce from Katherine of Aragon. Continuing to serve the crown in a number of capacities while he tried to establish his career at Oxford in the 1530s, in early 1537 in particular he worked hard to serve the king's cause by preaching against papal authority in the wake of the Pilgrimage of Grace. As a reward for his service to the crown, around the time of the robbery he was named chaplain to the king.[29]

Although a leading churchman, Croke was not a man inclined to the forgiveness of sins. As J. J. Scarisbrick has put it, he was 'a whining, tiresome man, who seems to have been able to quarrel with anybody'.[30] As royal chaplain and faithful servant to Henry and to Cromwell, he was not reluctant to call upon his contacts when he feared that Harvey would escape punishment. Although Harvey was under a criminal indictment for the robbery,[31] he obviously could not be tried unless he was in custody. Croke probably wanted to see Harvey tried and hanged, but even more than that he seems to have wanted his money back.

Recovery of the stolen money was, however, not a straightforward matter. According to the commission he issued to Digby and Fitzherbert, the king had previously ordered the officers of Knowle sanctuary to return Dr Croke's money to him. By doing so, the king implicitly claimed the right to control the disposal of recovered stolen goods and thus to grant them to the victim, Dr Croke; this was part of the right of felony forfeiture, which also included the crown's seizure

---

[28] For Croke's claim and the allegation of robbing his employer, TNA, SP 1/130, fols 171r, 180r. Several of the Knowle witnesses specified that he had with him exactly 7 marks or £4 13s 4d (ibid., 167r, 173r, 182r). He could, of course, have left some of the money elsewhere.

[29] Jonathan Woolfson, 'Croke, Richard (1489–1558)', *ODNB* (2004), doi:10.1093/ref:odnb/6734; 'Richard Croke', in Peter G. Bietenholz, ed., *Contemporaries of Erasmus: A Biographical Register of the Renaissance and Reformation* (Toronto, 1985). The commission from the king commanding the investigation into the robbery is in fact the first mention of Croke's status as royal chaplain; TNA, SP 1/130, fol. 154r.

[30] J. J Scarisbrick, *Henry VIII* (London, 1968), pp 256–7; quoted in Woolfson, 'Croke, Richard'.

[31] According to the terms of the commission (TNA, SP 1/130, fol. 154r); I have not found any records of criminal process in the case.

of a convicted felon's chattels.³² While in much of the realm the crown held the right to the stolen goods (which could then, by a statute of 1529, be granted back to the victim),³³ in peculiar jurisdictions it was sometimes part of the franchisal rights, and in Knowle the abbot of Westminster claimed confiscated or surrendered stolen goods along with other similar perquisites such as waif and straif (the right to lost property and animals).³⁴ As the testimony in the case suggests, the abbot could have granted restitution of the money to Croke, but apparently did not, and presumably it was ultimately added to the abbey's funds.³⁵

Allied with the question of who held the right to the stolen money held by Hugh Harvey was whether Harvey could claim sanctuary in Knowle; the abbot's right to the money depended on Harvey's eligibility for the privilege of sanctuary. Harvey's right to sanctuary was in question primarily because in addition to the robbery of Dr Croke's servant he had been indicted for stealing money from his employer. By a statute in 1536, any who had committed that particular crime were to be barred from claiming either benefit of clergy or sanctuary.³⁶ This was, however, a badly drafted statute, the terms of which seem to have been drawn up with benefit of clergy in mind rather than sanctuary. The statute assumed that the accused had already been found guilty of the offence when the mitigations were denied. This would work for benefit of clergy, which was usually claimed following a guilty verdict, but sanctuary was normally claimed, of course, before an accused could be taken into custody and indeed its point was to circumvent arrest and trial.³⁷ Although it would be reasonable to read the statute as barring the grant of sanctuary to a felon who confessed theft from an employer, it did not specify a procedure in a case like Harvey's, where the felon had sought sanctuary for another felony and denied the untried allegation of theft from an employer. Although those acting for Dr Croke were to argue that Harvey's sanctuary privilege was invalidated by the indictment for theft from the Goat landlord, legitimizing their taking him away to the king's prison, one might hypothesize that a legal expert like Fitzherbert would question this. He could argue for the application by analogy of the provisions of a 1531 statute addressing a similar question, how to handle an indictment of a person privileged of a sanctuary for having gone out of the sanctuary to commit another felony. By the provisions of that act, four justices of the peace for the county in question or two members of the king's council had to try the allegations first in situ in the sanctuary before an indicted sanctuary

---

³² Krista J. Kesselring, 'Felony Forfeiture and the Profits of Crime in Early Modern England', *The Historical Journal* 53 (2010): pp 271–88, doi:10.1017/S0018246X10000014.

³³ 21 Hen VIII c. 11, *SR*, vol. 3, p. 291; Bellamy, *Criminal Trial*, p. 32.

³⁴ TNA, SP 1/130, fol. 174v. Although it is not clear how common such a right was, St Martin le Grand had also claimed the stolen goods from those who came with them into the precinct in the early fifteenth century, but by the terms of the 1457 regulations of the sanctuary there, the stolen goods had to be restored to the victims. See above, Ch. 3, at nn.13 and 83.

³⁵ TNA, SP 1/130, fol. 174v.   ³⁶ 27 Hen. VIII, c. 17, *SR*, vol. 3, pp 549–50.

³⁷ It is possible that sanctuary was tacked on at the end of the statute as an afterthought. *SR*, vol. 3, pp 549–50; Baker, *Oxford History, 1485–1558*, p. 539.

seeker could be taken from the precinct to stand trial.[38] Hugh Harvey's case did not resolve this legal question, and as far as I know it did not arise in any other case.

It is unlikely, however, that Harvey thought much, if at all, about such legal complications as he fled from London following the robbery (and of course he may have been totally unaware of the allegations of theft from his employer if indeed he was innocent of that crime). He went westward to Warwickshire, staying briefly first in the town of Solihull before moving on, by Friday, 9 November 1537, to the town of Knowle itself, presumably attracted there by its sanctuary privileges. If perhaps not up-to-date on issues of felony forfeiture or the 1536 sanctuary statute, Harvey evidently did understand some of the legal niceties regarding sanctuary, as his actions in the first few days in Knowle indicate that he was trying to have his cake and eat it too. Taking the privilege of the sanctuary would keep him safe from arrest, but it would also entail surrender of the stolen goods he brought with him. Thus for the first few days he did not take the privilege, telling those who asked him that he was not looking for sanctuary but simply passing through. Presumably he hoped that he could get away without undergoing confession, oath, and confiscation of his ill-gotten goods, although he still wanted the safety of being able to request immediately the privilege of sanctuary should the occasion arise (which, as we will see, it did).

Harvey found lodging at the home of Henry Horley, who operated an inn or rooming house in the town. At Horley's house Harvey met up with—or perhaps had all along planned to meet—an old acquaintance also lodging there, Ralph Marshall, a guild priest at the College of Knowle.[39] Harvey asked Marshall to keep some money (seven marks, or £4 13s 4d) in a locked chest in his room, safeguarding it until Harvey went home. As Marshall later testified, he put Harvey's money into his coffer, but gave the money back to Harvey a few days later because a young boy servant at Horley's house had discovered how to pick the lock of his chest and Marshall did not want to be responsible if Harvey's money went missing.[40] It is not clear to what extent Marshall knew or suspected that the money he had been keeping safe for Harvey was ill-gotten. Over the week following Harvey's arrival in Knowle, as Marshall later admitted, the two of them visited a number of local alehouses, drinking on Harvey's money; others alleged (although Marshall denied it) that in those alehouses Harvey waved a piece of gold, boasting to his fellow drinkers, 'lo, we come not hither like no beggars!'[41]

If Hugh Harvey thought he could lie low in Knowle, he underestimated the reach of Dr Croke's friends, who soon learned where he was. Precisely how they knew Hugh Harvey had fled to Knowle is not revealed in the evidence Fitzherbert

---

[38] 22 Hen. VIII, c. 14, *SR*, vol. 3, pp 333–4. This is also fully laid out in Fitzherbert's 1538 *New Boke of Iustyces of Peas*, fols 142r–143v. The point of those statutory provisions in 1531 seems to have been to prevent precisely the kind of spurious accusations to justify sanctuary breaches that I suspect those acting for Dr Croke employed here. See also below, Ch. 7 at n.39.

[39] Marshall still received a pension as a former guild chaplain in the reign of Edward VI, at which point he was aged 42. Bickley, *Register of the Guild of Knowle*, p. xxxii.

[40] TNA, SP 1/130, fols 183r, 185r.

[41] TNA, SP 1/130, fols 156v, 185r. This was an allegation in the interrogatories: none of the witnesses could verify the gold-flashing and boasting. Ibid., fols 165r, 169r, 171r, 177r, 188r.

and Digby collected, although scattered clues give some indication. Harvey himself was apparently not from Warwickshire (he was described as being from another 'country', another part of the kingdom, possibly from nearby Banbury, Oxfordshire, where he apparently kept a horse). He had, however, whether knowingly or not, ended up in an area where Dr Croke had connections. The doctor's brother, Robert Croke, lived in modest circumstances in nearby Coleshill, about 13 kilometres from Solihull and 14 kilometres from Knowle.[42] The lord of the manor of Coleshill, where Robert Croke lived, was Reginald Digby, who advised Dr Croke in the initial stages of the affair and who was later given the commission to investigate it.[43] Robert Croke presumably heard about the robbery and Harvey's presence in his own backyard from Dr Croke's servant, Robert Bury, who had arrived in Warwickshire by mid-November in pursuit of Harvey.

Robert Croke was keen to help Bury pursue the man who had wronged his brother, but he was not quite sure how to go about bringing Harvey to justice, as Knowle's sanctuary status was a complicating factor. On Friday 16 November, Robert Croke travelled to Solihull to consult Thomas Haw, a gentleman with legal experience and training who had served as coroner in the Elliotts homicide in 1535.[44] Croke told Haw that his brother had been done 'a shrewd turn' recently in London, and that the perpetrator had come to Knowle. Could that perpetrator be taken into custody? Haw suggested going 'privily' to Knowle and surprising Harvey so that he could be arrested before he could take the privilege of the sanctuary.[45] Following Haw's advice, Croke, along with his brother's servant Robert Bury and another man, William Cull, went that same day to Knowle, to Harry Horley's house where Harvey was known to be staying, in order to try to arrest him.

Once they arrived at Horley's house on that Friday, a small crowd of men from Knowle gathered to see what the three visitors to the town intended to do, although innkeeper Henry Horley himself, in whose house they gathered, was away from Knowle at the time. The sequence of events was disputed in the depositions taken by Fitzherbert and Digby. In the version Croke, Cull, and Bury later told the commissioners, when they first saw Harvey, Bury immediately put his hand on Harvey and arrested him for robbing his master, the landlord of the Goat Inn, and for robbing Dr Croke.[46] Following this arrest, they said, Harvey asked for sanctuary for both these felonies.[47] A Knowle witness, William Pynnock, described this encounter with small but significant differences. He testified that as soon as he saw the men, Harvey asked for sanctuary, and only afterwards was arrested by

---

[42] Dr Croke is usually seen as having humble origins in London. See 'Richard Croke' in Bietenholz, *Contemporaries of Erasmus*, vol. 1, pp 359–610. As this case suggests, it is also possible that he came from Warwickshire, along with his brother Robert; the obscurity of Robert's status there (I have not found his name in any records beyond this case and his brother's will two decades later) corroborates a humble origin. Richard Croke's will is TNA, PROB 11/40/422, Will of Richard Croke, D.D., 21 Aug. 1558.

[43] Page, *A History of the County of Warwick*, vol. 4, pp 47–57.

[44] Baker, *Men of Court*, pp 839–40; *L&P*, vol. 5, p. 529; John Caley and Joseph Hunter, eds, *Valor Ecclesiasticus Temp. Henr. VIII. Auctoritate Regia Institutus* (London, 1810), vol. 3, p. 67.

[45] TNA, SP 1/130, fol. 180r.   [46] TNA, SP 1/130, fol. 181v.

[47] TNA, SP 1/130, fol. 155r, also 171r.

Bury. (It is not clear to me that the question of which came first, the arrest or the sanctuary claim, was important—certainly felons who had been arrested claimed sanctuary regularly and successfully—although the witnesses treated the distinction as if it was significant.) Pynnock also said that Harvey denied the theft from his master—a much more important distinction, as we have seen.[48] Pynnock's word on this may have carried some weight with the royal commissioners, as he was a man of emerging local importance in the mid-1530s; by this point already he had held a number of positions as receiver, auditor, and collector both for the crown and for a number of religious houses in Warwickshire, and he would go on to be a gentleman usher of the king's chamber and an MP.[49]

Once Harvey asked for sanctuary—whether he did so before or after Bury arrested him—the situation became tricky. William Pynnock, probably the man of highest status there but apparently without any official position in the town, insisted that Croke and Bury could not take the felon away since he had taken sanctuary. Pynnock sent for William Barneshurst of Knowle, deputed to act for the sanctuary's bailiff, who lived in Warwick. When Barneshurst arrived, Pynnock instructed him that, as the bailiff's deputy, his duty was to 'take the confession' of the felon privately, and then to give him the privilege of sanctuary.[50] Croke and Bury, objecting, 'utterly denied' that the felon could have the privilege of the sanctuary because he had been accused of robbing his master. Barneshurst, caught in the middle, was unsure what to do, so he went out into the town to find other officers of the sanctuary. He saw Thomas Trussell, a local gentleman who held the fee-farm of the manor for Westminster Abbey, and called out to him, saying that men had come to arrest 'the fellow with the red cape' who had been staying at Harry Horley's.[51]

Trussell rushed over to Horley's house and found the party gathered in the hall. He addressed Harvey, saying (as he later reported in a somewhat elliptical handwritten statement) that Harvey had said to him just the week before that he was a 'true man' and that he intended shortly to go home to his friends and had no intention of asking for the sanctuary privilege. 'What an errant thief art thou!' Trussell cried, irate that Harvey had first denied any need for sanctuary and was now claiming it. Trussell swore 'a great oath', and declared, in anger, that Harvey would have no succour there. When Croke expostulated that Barneshurst had already given him the privilege, Trussell backtracked and told Croke (perhaps with a sigh) that if Harvey could not have the privilege when he most needed it, then what purpose did the privilege serve. Perhaps to mollify Croke, Trussell promised him that he would do what he could to bring the money to light. Together Trussell and Croke went to question Harry Horley's wife (Horley himself still absent) about whether

---

[48] TNA, SP 1/130, fol. 171r.
[49] Although of humble birth, his abilities and a later astute marriage brought him to these substantial offices. Caley and Hunter, *Valor Ecclesiasticus*, vol. 3, p. 73; *L&P*, vol. 14, pt. 1, p. 160; vol. 17, p. 216; vol. 18, pt. 1, p. 360; vol. 19, pt. 2, p. 82; vol. 20, pt. 1, pp 317, 322, 428; vol. 20, pt. 2, p. 555; vol. 21, pt. 1, p. 632; S. M. Thorpe, 'Pinnock, William (by 1509–1555)', in *HPO*.
[50] TNA, SP 1/130, fol. 181r.   [51] TNA, SP 1/130, fol. 174r.

she knew anything about the money, and she said that she did not.[52] The constable of Knowle, Thomas Avery, arrived and questioned Harvey directly regarding the whereabouts of the money, but Harvey refused to say anything. Croke, Trussell, and Avery all agreed that the felon would be put in safe custody until they could determine the proper course in this situation. Avery put iron fetters on Harvey's ankles and locked him to a post in his house.[53]

The next day, Saturday, Croke came back to Knowle, this time with Thomas Haw of Solihull, the man of law whose advice he had sought earlier. Haw first went to constable Avery's house and asked Avery's wife where the felon was, and she said he was still in bed. Haw said that he wanted to speak with him, and she summoned the felon into the hall, a pair of fetters on his legs and a man guarding him. Haw questioned Harvey about where the money was, but again the accused man refused to say anything. Haw then met with Croke, Avery, Trussell, Pynnock, and a number of other men from Knowle to discuss the legal situation. Before all the men gathered, Haw read from 'a book of statutes' he had brought with him, reciting especially the passage indicating the statute that denied 'the liberty' to anyone who had stolen any goods or chattels from their masters or mistresses, just as they were denied benefit of clergy.[54]

None of the men from Knowle who were present seemed to know quite what to do: those who were responsible for making decisions about granting sanctuary—the bailiff and the steward of the manor and sanctuary—were not at Knowle. Trussell and Avery asked Croke and Bury for respite until Monday so they could send for their bailiff because they themselves, as Avery put it, were 'ignorant of the king's acts'[55] (an ignorance that was excusable, given that through the 1530s procedures for the granting of sanctuary privileges were changed several times by parliamentary statute, as will be discussed in the following section). As a compromise, Croke and Haw offered to bind themselves in obligations of £40 if they were found to have taken the prisoner out of the sanctuary improperly and did not return him when ordered by the king's judges to do so. All the men then agreed that Croke and Haw would come again on Monday with the documents recording the bonds, and with those in hand Avery would release the prisoner to them.[56]

On Monday morning, Robert Croke came back to Knowle, along with three other men, including a bailiff who brought a spare horse with him to conduct the prisoner to Warwick. They called at the house of Avery, the constable, but he was not at home. They waited a while, and at last he arrived—but he told them that he had just returned from seeing 'the high Steward' of Knowle manor, another local gentleman named Richard Archer, and that Archer had 'commanded' Avery not to deliver the prisoner until he, Archer, could come personally to Knowle to deal with the situation. Archer, however, was busy that Monday sitting at Kenilworth 'upon

---

[52] TNA, SP 1/130, fol. 174r.   [53] TNA, SP 1/130, fol. 181r, 182r.
[54] TNA, SP 1/130, fols 180rv. Haw in his own statement wrote that he brought with him a book of statutes from 24 Hen. VIII (1533), although the statute he claimed he recited had in fact been passed in 1536, 27 Hen. VIII, c. 17 (*SR*, vol. 3, pp 549–50). See below this chapter, at n. 73 forward, for further discussion.
[55] TNA, SP 1/130, fols 180v, 188r.   [56] TNA, SP 1/130, fols 174rv.

the king's business', and so could not arrive before the following day. Croke again referred to the statute regarding servants who stole from their masters and 'recited causes why that [Harvey] was not worthy to have the liberty', but still Avery refused to hand the prisoner over.[57] Croke and those with him decided to leave, but 'required' the constable to ensure that Harvey was straitly imprisoned, as it would be on his head if Harvey had disappeared when called upon to make answer 'to the king's laws'. Before they left, Croke and his fellows went again to speak to the prisoner, and this time Harvey told them that he had first given £4 13s 4d to Ralph Marshall, but had received it back again from him, and then had spent some of the money on new clothes. Croke and the others then rode away, leaving 'the felon sitting fettered and locked'.[58]

For whatever reason, Croke and his fellows did not return the following day, but Richard Archer, the steward, did. He later claimed that when he arrived, he was told only that Harvey had been accused of robbing Dr Croke, and that he had requested sanctuary. Archer therefore ordered that his name should be entered into the register of the sanctuary, that he should be given the 'king's badge', signifying his status as a sanctuary man, and that he should be given the liberty of the sanctuary. Sir Richard Morys, priest, entered Harvey's name into the sanctuary register,[59] and William Barneshurst as the bailiff's deputy gave him the badge. Harvey was released from his fetters and permitted to go about at will in the town of Knowle. Archer later claimed that through all this no one told him that Harvey had been accused of stealing from his master in addition to robbing Dr Croke. In fact, he says that he had consulted his understeward Richard Holbache, 'the which is learned',[60] about whether Harvey could take sanctuary in Knowle, and Holbache had replied 'that he might have sanctuary for any felony except that he had robbed his master'. And since Archer knew only that Harvey had robbed Dr Croke, 'he commanded that his irons should be stricken off and be let go at large'.[61]

Once set free, according to Trussell, Harvey handed over to Trussell the money he had originally entrusted to Ralph Marshall, between four and five pounds sterling. This Trussell received as the representative of the abbot; he was, by virtue of his office, as he said, to receive the recovered stolen goods.[62] Trussell in turn used that money to reimburse expenses, distributing it as follows: he gave Richard Archer 3s 4d 'for his pains taking'; Richard Holbache, the understeward, 12d for his writing; William Barneshurst 16d for his expenses in travelling twice to Warwick to try (unsuccessfully) to get the bailiff to come to Knowle to deal with the situation; and Hugh Harvey himself a crown, or 4s 8d. Barneshurst later testified that Trussell gave Harvey the crown 'to the intent to keep him a true man with whilst he was in Sanctuary and that he might therewith send to his friends for succour'.[63] He would not be able to stay in sanctuary indefinitely without some

---

[57] TNA, SP 1/130, fols 174rv, 182r.   [58] TNA, SP 1/130, fol. 182r.
[59] TNA, SP 1/130, fol. 179r. Morys was presumably also associated with Knowle College, although no other evidence about him has been found.
[60] For Holbache as understeward, see TNA, SP 1/130, fol. 179r.
[61] TNA, SP 1/130, fol. 178r.   [62] TNA, SP 1/130, fol. 174v.
[63] TNA, SP 1/130, fol. 169r.

external means of support. Trussell also paid 3s 4d for a meal for the steward and presumably the others involved; as Thomas Avery explained it, it was 'in consideration of such pains as they had taken with the felon before'.[64] Trussell reported that he took the remaining money (£3 10s) to the council of the abbot of Westminster, entitled to the recovered stolen goods.[65] Others reported that earlier Harvey had given 5s to Horley to buy a shirt for him (although Horley claimed he had been unable to do so and returned the money to Harvey); 7s 6d to Thomas Ichener, the bailiff of the neighbouring manor of Packwood, to buy him a coat; and 5s to Horley's son to go to Banbury to convey his horse from there to Knowle.[66]

When Trussell received the money, according to a self-exculpating account of his part in the affair filed along with his deposition taken by Digby and Fitzherbert, he went to Westminster intending to deliver it as recovered stolen goods to the abbot's council. Before going to the abbey, however, he met first with Dr Croke and Reginald Digby, at the Goat Inn, where Dr Croke was apparently still staying. Trussell told them that he had with him part of the money that Harvey had stolen from Dr Croke, and that if they could get him a discharge from the king's council, he would deliver the money to Dr Croke rather than to the abbot's council. He could not do so without the override of the king's council, however, for otherwise he was bound by the seal of the abbey 'to make a true audit of all felons' goods'. If he failed, he would forfeit his office, which he was not willing to do. Otherwise, Trussell suggested, Croke could appeal to the abbot himself for restitution. These negotiations came to nought, and Trussell duly delivered the money to the abbot's council, for which he reported that he was given an acquittance.[67]

Harvey stayed in Knowle for about two weeks after being set free by Archer. In early December, he left, presumably on the horse conveniently fetched for him from Banbury. Most of the witnesses denied knowing anything specific about when or how he left, although the constable Thomas Avery told Fitzherbert and Digby that 'about sixteen days after, he took his leave of divers of the township and went his way'.[68] No one in Knowle had any idea where he went, or so they said. No doubt the inhabitants of Knowle were quite relieved when he departed. Harvey himself, as far as I have been able to uncover, was never caught. If he had indeed originally stolen something like £12 or even £20, he probably still had a tidy sum as he rode off into the sunset.

The story of the money is one aspect of the opportunities and problems a community such as Knowle experienced as a result of its sanctuary privileges. Amongst Croke's accusations was a complaint that the townspeople of Knowle had taken advantage of the situation to make a profit out of other people's crimes. This last

---

[64] TNA, SP 1/130, fol. 188r.   [65] TNA, SP 1/130, fol. 174v.
[66] TNA, SP 1/130, fol. 188r. The sums do not add up. Harvey originally gave Marshall £4 13s 4d. The money that Trussell reports disbursing plus the money he delivered to the abbot adds up to £4 3s 8d, leaving between 9s and 10s unaccounted for. Some of this was presumably spent on the alehouse visits, and Harvey indicates that he paid out a total of 17s 6d for a new shirt and coat, and for the fetching of his horse from Banbury. Trussell also does not report having taken any fee himself for his 'pains' and expenses.
[67] TNA, SP 1/130, fol. 174r–175r.   [68] TNA, SP 1/130, fol. 188r.

allegation the townspeople of Knowle were anxious to refute—although their responses do suggest a nuanced attitude towards the proceeds of the robbery. The arrival of Hugh Harvey in their town provided some cash flow. Ralph Marshall, the guild priest, benefited from Harvey's alehouse largesse, being treated to a number of evenings of drinks. Several other people in the town received remuneration for 'pains taking' in relation to Harvey's stay, and possibly other money, unreported in the depositions, made its way into their pockets. It is impossible at this remove to determine whether the recompense the townspeople received for their expenses and efforts was adequate or represented considerable padding; was the 16d that William Barneshurst received for two trips to Warwick, about 18 kilometres from Knowle (meaning in each case a full day of travel and business) fair, or excessive? It was undoubtedly normal that the payment the steward Richard Archer received for one trip from Tanworth, 11 kilometres from Knowle (3s 4d, more than three times as much as Barneshurst), was much greater than what the others received, as his 'pains' as a local notable were simply worth more than those of someone like Barneshurst.

At what point did the reimbursement of expenses and recompense for trouble shade over into receipt of stolen goods? The interrogatories that shaped the depositions accused the inhabitants of Knowle of finding a good deal of personal advantage in the situation. Henry Horley, for instance, was charged with paying off a debt to a mercer in Coventry and buying barley with money he received from Harvey (an accusation he denied).[69] Thomas Trussell was accused of hosting a meal on the Tuesday when Archer came to town, and paying for it with some of the money confiscated from Harvey; he admitted that he had done so, but indicated that this was simply part of the expenses involved in administering Harvey's case. As Trussell was reported to have said, 'whosoever should have the stolen money, such poor men and others that took pains there should not be put to cost'.[70] After all, why should the townspeople of Knowle have borne the price of hosting sanctuary seekers such as Harvey, especially when their cases involved a good deal of trouble, as Harvey's had?

Indeed, had the people of Knowle done what Dr Croke's agents, his brother Robert and his servant Robert Bury, requested, they would have been put to even more trouble. As they themselves reported, after leaving Knowle on Monday, with the situation still in limbo, Robert Croke and Bury never returned to the town, even though they had been promised a discussion the following day with a man in a position to make clear decisions, the steward of Knowle, Richard Archer.[71] Croke himself implies that he never intended to return to the town—yet, as he testified more than four months after the episode, when Avery refused to deliver Harvey to him on Monday, 19 November, Croke left the constable with the charge 'to keep the felon in sure prison that he might be forth coming as he would make answer to the king and his council when the felon should be called for'.[72] Neither Croke nor anyone else, however, subsequently 'called for' him. One might ask, then,

---

[69] TNA, SP 1/130, fol. 157v, 165r. [70] TNA, SP 1/130, fol. 169r.
[71] TNA, SP 1/130, fol. 175r. [72] TNA, SP 1/130, fol. 181r.

whether Croke expected constable Avery to keep Harvey in custody in his house indefinitely, at the expense of the people of Knowle, on the off chance that someone might eventually come and conduct him to the king's gaol at Warwick? It would not be unreasonable for the people of Knowle to feel that they should not be responsible for Harvey's indefinite imprisonment.

SANCTUARY AT KNOWLE AND THE ADMINISTRATION OF LAW AND JUSTICE IN THE 1530s

The confusion over Harvey's situation and the legality of the attempts made by Dr Croke's agents to arrest him highlights both the general problems in a criminal justice system managed at the ground level by amateurs and the specific difficulties those involved in the administration of sanctuaries had in keeping abreast of the king's laws regarding the privilege. In 1529 and 1530, two statutes changed the basis of abjuration and tidied up ambiguities regarding those who re-offended.[73] In 1534, sanctuary was barred for those accused of high treason.[74] In 1536, parliament passed two acts directly affecting Harvey's situation at Knowle; the first (already mentioned) deprived those who robbed their employers of benefit of clergy and sanctuary,[75] and the second set out more generally the regulations for sanctuaries in order to prevent sanctuary seekers from abusing the privilege, especially through using their refuges as bases from which to commit further crimes. Sanctuary men and women were to wear at all times while out of their lodging a badge of ten inches length and breadth; they could not bear weapons; they could not be out of their lodgings at night; and they were to be subject to the jurisdiction of the 'governor' of the sanctuary or his deputy in discipline cases or in disputes with other inhabitants of the sanctuary.[76] It is notable that many of the regulations imposed on sanctuary men by the 1536 Act—curfews and the like—echoed in detail the regulations established in 1457 regarding sanctuary seekers at St Martin's and thus may have reflected what was already the practice, or supposed to be the practice, at St Martin's and elsewhere.[77]

We get a sense from the testimony regarding Hugh Harvey's case how knowledge concerning parliamentary legislation was passed around and put into practice by those charged with its implementation—and about some of the uncertainties that resulted from the frequent legislative changes of the 1530s. The officers at Knowle were well aware of the badge provision in the 1536 statute; as soon as he had been registered as a sanctuary man, Harvey was given one. They seem to have been somewhat less sure about the other 1536 statute regarding those who robbed their employers, however, and so, as we saw in the previous section, in order to convince the Knowle administrators that Harvey was not eligible for the privilege of sanctuary,

---

[73] 21 Hen. VIII, c. 2; 22 Hen. VIII, c. 14, *SR*, vol. 3, pp 284, 332–4. On this and the other statutes cited below, see Stanford E. Lehmberg, *The Reformation Parliament 1529–1536* (Cambridge, 1970), pp 98, 126, 204, 230.
[74] 26 Hen. VIII, c. 13, *SR*, vol. 3, pp 508–9.   [75] 27 Hen. VIII, c. 17, *SR*, vol. 3, pp 549–50.
[76] 27 Hen. VIII, c. 19, *SR*, vol. 3, p. 551.   [77] See above, Ch. 1, at n.24.

Robert Croke had his legal advisor Thomas Haw read from a 'book of statutes' made 'the twenty-fourth year of our sovereign lord the king that now is'. As Haw himself put it, he read

> the Statute made and ordered for them that embezzle or steal any goods or chattels from their masters or mistresses being put in trust, and showed them that if any servant put in trust by his master or mistress the liberty would not keep them, in like case if any man were attainted for such cause he should be put from his clergy and suffer death as he were no clerk.[78]

The king's statutes from each parliament were printed by the king's printer, Thomas Berthelet,[79] and it is presumably from one of those books of statutes that Haw read, although he was rather oddly mistaken about the regnal year, which should have been the twenty-seventh, rather than the twenty-fourth.[80] Haw's account of the statute was otherwise quite accurate (although the statute specified arraignment rather than attainder). His statement was written apparently in his own hand, and thus could have been written from home with the statute book in front of him. The relevant passage from the statute book printed in 1536 reads:

> That … every such servant, that so shall steal from his said master or mistress … and be found guilty thereof, or of any parcel of the same, according to the law of the land, or upon his arraignment before any Justice confess the same, shall from henceforth be put from his clergy, and be put to execution, as if he were no clerk. And be it further enacted by the authority aforesaid, that every such person or persons, that so shall steal the goods of his said master or mistress, or embezzle that that so to him shall be delivered, as is aforesaid, if the same goods be of the value of 40s. as is aforesaid, shall lose the privilege of all sanctuaries: any use or custom heretofore had or used to the contrary notwithstanding.[81]

As I noted above, the statute did not indicate, however, what was to be done in a case where a sanctuary seeker denied an accusation that he had robbed his employer; was an indictment on that felony to deprive him of the privilege?

Both sides relied on local men with government experience and high-functioning literacy to give them advice. Robert Croke's advisor Thomas Haw had acted as coroner for Warwickshire in 1532 and 1535 and was a commissioner for the Valor Ecclesiasticus, surveying ecclesiastical properties, in 1535.[82] Like most who served

---

[78] TNA, SP 1/130, fol. 180v.

[79] On the printing of statutes, see G. R. Elton, 'The Sessional Printing of Statutes, 1484–1547', in *Wealth and Power in Tudor England*, ed. E. W. Ives, R. J. Knecht, and J. J. Scarisbrick (London, 1978), pp 68–86; Katherine F. Pantzer, 'Printing the English Statutes 1484–1640: Some Historical Implications', in *Books and Society in History*, ed. Kenneth E. Carpenter (New York, 1983), pp 69–114; Baker, *Oxford History, 1485–1558*, pp 505–6; Sebastian Sobecki, *Unwritten Verities: The Making of England's Vernacular Legal Culture, 1463–1549* (Notre Dame, Indiana, 2015), pp 130–3.

[80] There was no statute relating to sanctuary in the parliament held in 24 Hen. VIII. *SR*, vol. 3, pp 417–35; *Anno XXIIII Henrici VIII. Actis Made in the Session of This Present Parlyamente* (London, 1533).

[81] *Anno XXVII Henrici VIII Actes Made in the Session of This Present Parlyament* (London, 1536), fol. 21r.

[82] TNA, KB 9/535, m. 57; *L&P*, vol. 5, p. 529; Caley and Hunter, *Valor Ecclesiasticus*, vol. 3, p. 67.

as coroners, Haw had formal legal training.[83] Richard Archer, the steward of Knowle, consulted Richard Holbache, who was identified as Archer's understeward by the constable Avery, and who had served in the late 1520s as under-sheriff of the county. Holbache is not known to have had any formal legal training, although he seems to have come from a legal family.[84] Likely both for Haw and especially for Holbache, their function as repositories of legal knowledge derived from their practical experience and their general familiarity with the kinds of guides, such as books of statutes and books written for justices of the peace (such as the one Fitzherbert revised and published in 1538), that informed those at the local level who needed to administer the king's justice in its many complicated forms.

Although Knowle's own expert—Holbache—did eventually give roughly accurate advice that sanctuary privilege could be offered to felons but not if they had robbed their masters, the handling of Hugh Harvey by the officials of Knowle sanctuary was inefficient and arguably seriously bungled. Much of the blame for this would have to be placed at the door of those who were the sanctuary's governors, the bailiff and the steward, one of whom, the bailiff, never appeared to deal with the situation, while the other, the steward, appeared late and then acted (apparently) precipitately based on faulty understanding of the charges against the felon.

The appointed bailiff of Knowle was William Webbe, whose office at Knowle apparently proceeded from his position as bailiff of the sanctuary of Westminster Abbey, in which capacity he appears frequently in contemporary records.[85] There never seems to have been any expectation that he would deal directly with this situation. Webbe of Westminster, as he was known in the testimony, had designated another William Webbe, known in the depositions as Webbe of Warwick, as his deputy. They were presumably related to one another, although their precise family tie is unclear. Webbe of Warwick served the crown in Warwick Castle, and several members of the Warwickshire Webbe family were important figures in the royal stable at Westminster through the 1530s and 1540s. Webbe of Warwick would later serve as Warwick's Member of Parliament in 1542.[86] This latter Webbe, already himself a deputy of Webbe of Westminster, in turn deputized a local man of Knowle, his son-in-law or stepson William Barneshurst,[87] to act as his representative in the sanctuary town. Barneshurst was, however, clearly not equal to the complicated situation Harvey's case presented. William Pynnock (another future MP for Warwick) had to instruct Barneshurst on what to do when Harvey asked for sanctuary privilege ('seeing you be the bailiff's deputy, you ought to take the

---

[83] Baker, *Men of Court*, pp 839–40.

[84] TNA, SP 1/130, fol. 188r; TNA, C 1/866/79–82. He may have been related to William Holbache, who was coroner for Warwickshire in 1528, 1535, and 1541 (in 1535 serving with Thomas Haw). TNA, KB 9/506/1, m. 61 (1528); KB 9/535, m. 57; KB 29/174, m. 29 (1541).

[85] TNA, KB 27/1100, rex m. 7; KB 27/1112, rex mm 1, 9; KB 27/1131, rex m. 6; REQ 2/8/254; SP 1/118, fol. 115r; SP 1/124, fol. 204r; SP 1/125, fols 40r–43v; SP 1/127, fol. 201r; McSheffrey, 'William Webbe's Wench'.

[86] S. M. Thorpe, 'Webbe, William III', in *HPO*.

[87] Barneshurst referred to Webbe of Warwick as his 'father in law' (SP 1/130, fol. 169r); in contemporary parlance that could mean stepfather as well as father of one's spouse.

confession of the felon privily, and so to give him the privilege of the sanctuary').[88] At least Barneshurst knew his limitations and tried to get others to take responsibility. He appealed to Thomas Trussell, another local gentleman with high-level literacy and an official role as the fee-farmer for the abbot, but while Trussell did take a role, according to his own account of the events he steadfastly refused to act in an official capacity regarding the sanctuary claim: 'I never would take no charge of the prisoner but ever refused and said, "I am no officer"'.[89] Barneshurst's repeated trips to Warwick to persuade Webbe to come and exercise his office as bailiff directly were similarly unsuccessful.

Instead, Richard Archer, the steward of Knowle manor, came, gave the prisoner his privilege (claiming later that no one told him the full extent of the charges), had his dinner, accepted his fee for his 'pains taking', and presumably went back home again. Archer was a gentleman of the long-established Archers of Tanworth, who had held land in Tanworth from the twelfth century. In usual sixteenth-century gentry fashion, his appointment as steward of the manor of Knowle was only one of a number of such offices he accumulated in his career. He was escheator for Warwickshire and Leicestershire in 1536–1537,[90] and whatever he was doing in Kenilworth on Monday 19 November that kept him from coming to Knowle, it was described as the 'king's business'. Interestingly, in contrast to Trussell and Haw, who submitted statements in their own hands in practised scripts, Archer's signature on his deposition suggests undeveloped writing skills: birth and position could matter more than formal education. Despite what might have been something of a hiccup with this situation, Archer went on to be reconfirmed as steward of Knowle manor in 1541 in the wake of the dissolution of Westminster Abbey, and was named as Esquire of the Body to the king that same year; he also served on several commissions of the peace in Warwickshire through the late 1530s to the mid-1540s.[91] Archer's successful career ran off the rails in about 1544, however, when he was indicted and found guilty of murdering the husband of a local woman with whom he had been committing adultery, and he was hanged.[92]

The outcome of the inquiry undertaken by Sir Anthony Fitzherbert and Reginald Digby into Hugh Harvey's sojourn in Knowle is unclear. As above, Hugh Harvey seems to have gotten away with it. The report made by Fitzherbert and Digby to the king's council, which accompanied the depositions and examinations, indicated that Fitzherbert and Digby had attempted to broker a settlement regarding the stolen money between Dr Croke on the one side and Richard Archer, Thomas Trussell, Henry Horley, Ralph Marshall, and William Barneshurst on the other. We do not know what kind of settlement Fitzherbert and Digby suggested, but they reported that 'Master Archer and his neighbours refused' it.[93] Archer himself

---

[88] TNA, SP 1/130, fol. 181r.   [89] TNA, SP 1/130, fol. 174v.
[90] See TNA, E 136/228/4.
[91] *L&P*, vol. 16, p. 714; vol. 14, pt. 2, p. 221; vol. 17, p. 637; vol. 19, pt. 1, p. 154; vol. 20, pt. 1, p. 318.
[92] TNA, KB 9/560, mm 30–31; KB 27/1132, rex m. 4; KB 29/177, mm 6, 11, 15, 16, 20; *L&P*, vol. 19, pt. 2, p. 317; vol. 21, pt. 1, p. 246.
[93] TNA, REQ 2/5/115.

was by far the least cooperative of the witnesses Digby and Fitzherbert examined, and it may well have been he who primarily refused the settlement. Certainly Trussell, at least according to his statement, had been willing to compromise, and there is no reason to think that he would not have (it was no skin off his nose). Because the people of Knowle were not willing to accept the 'direction and order as we, the said Sir Antony and Reginald, moved unto them', they were ordered to appear before the king's council.[94] What happened at that point we do not know—although those involved seem to have retained their positions at Knowle, and thus perhaps at most they were obliged to cough up the money they had received from Harvey.

THE KNOWLE SANCTUARY AND TUDOR STATE FORMATION

Webbe's and Archer's poor management of the Knowle sanctuary demonstrated a negligent lack of engagement, which may have stemmed from their respective personalities; that lack of engagement was also, however, a structural issue, related to their exercise of office at Knowle from a distance and alongside a number of other responsibilities. The administration of Knowle sanctuary, in short, suffered from what is often cited as a serious problem in the governance of the pre-Reformation church: pluralism. Pluralists were the clergy with status and connections, who gathered as large a number of 'benefices' (income-producing employment positions) as they could, each of which was a rung on the ladder to further advancement. The pluralist clergy deputed the actual duties associated with their multiple benefices to those further down the ecclesiastical hierarchy; the classic case entailed poor chaplains, whose education and skills were not always equal to the task, acting as parish clergy in the stead of more powerful and well-educated pluralists who collected revenues from multiple positions and themselves worked as academics or in royal or aristocratic service. Although conventionally we might see sanctuaries such as Knowle as coming on the 'ecclesiastical' side of the kingdom's complex administrative structure, and thus the pluralism evident at Knowle as exemplary of this widespread problem in church governance, this is not quite what was going on in Knowle. By the 1530s clerics were evidently involved only tangentially in the administration of the Knowle sanctuary: the only cleric who appears to have had any administrative role in this story was Richard Morys, the priest who entered Harvey's name in the sanctuary register after the steward admitted him to the privilege.[95] The name of the warden of Knowle College—Gilbert Fowler—is entirely absent from the documents, suggesting that there was no expectation that he would be involved.[96] The arguments on both sides regarding the privileges of the sanctuary

---

[94] TNA, REQ 2/5/115. [95] TNA, SP 1/130, fol. 163r; 166r; 179r; 186r.
[96] Fowler became warden on 22 Feb. 1537 and was still warden in the next decade. Bickley, *Register of the Guild of Knowle*, p. xii. Note that in the case of the accused felon named Hill in Knowle sanctuary in 1535, there was apparently a letter sent from Cromwell to the warden—then John Townesend—'for the punishment and examination' of the felon, thought then to be in sanctuary. Following

came not from clergy but from laymen, and the decision to give Harvey the privilege was made by a local gentleman who was also a servant of the king.

As the careers of Webbe of Warwick and Richard Archer suggest, no easy caesura can be drawn between 'church' and 'crown' administrators. The 'pluralism' from which the administration of Knowle sanctuary suffered was not an ecclesiastical one, but instead reflective of the standard *cursus honorum* towards successful life as a gentleman. In one common career path, the accumulation of capital, both financial and socio-political, depended on the accumulation of offices, and the offices of steward of Knowle manor and bailiff of Knowle sanctuary were part of the same world as serving as tax collectors, as justices of the peace, and as members of parliament. The amassing of those offices was not always the same as actually performing the duties attached to them, however: when decisions needed to be made or actions taken, the steward and the bailiff were not always at hand. A surprisingly large number of local men, both apparent local notables and those occupying specific offices such as constable, instead had to step in.

The administration of Knowle sanctuary—with its widely-distributed participation by men at various social levels, acting and making decisions for the governance of their town, in the name of the lord and the king—exemplifies in many ways the political culture of late medieval and Tudor England. If for mid-twentieth-century historians such as G. R. Elton, 'political' history was emphatically and exclusively that which concerned and flowed from the court and parliament, scholars have more recently substantially recalibrated thinking about how governance and politics worked in this era.[97] The approach taken especially by historians of the later sixteenth and early seventeenth century allows us to see how what we know about social structures and relations amongst ordinary people contributed to the governance of the society in which they lived, fruitfully linking the concerns of social history with political history in a way that allows fields of scholarship previously

---

this letter, though, it appears that the bailiff was thought to be handling the felon. TNA, SP 1/97, fol. 117r.

[97] For some of this scholarship, see Michael Braddick, 'State Formation and the Historiography of Early Modern England', *History Compass* 2 (2004): pp 1–17, doi:10.1111/j.1478-0542.2004.00074.x; Michael Braddick, *State Formation in Early Modern England, c. 1550–1700* (Cambridge, 2000); Mark Goldie, 'The Unacknowledged Republic: Officeholding in Early Modern England', in *The Politics of the Excluded, c. 1500–1850*, ed. Tim Harris (New York, 2001), pp 153–94; Steve Hindle, *The State and Social Change in Early Modern England, c.1550–1640* (New York, 2000); Ethan H. Shagan, *Popular Politics and the English Reformation* (Cambridge, 2003). Scholars of medieval England have addressed some of the same issues, although not always in the same terms: see Musson and Ormrod, *Evolution of English Justice*; Robert B. Goheen, 'Peasant Politics? Village Community and the Crown in Fifteenth-Century England', *The American Historical Review* 96 (1991): pp 42–62, doi:10.2307/2164017; James Masschaele, *Jury, State, and Society in Medieval England* (New York, 2008); Simpson, *Reform and Cultural Revolution*; Sobecki, *Unwritten Verities*; Forrest, 'Archive of the Official of Stow'; Forrest, 'Transformation of Visitation'. Marjorie McIntosh's work importantly stressed continuities more than ruptures over the late medieval and early modern period. As she argued, her analysis did not support arguments that conceptualized state building as proceeding from the centre out to the peripheries. Marjorie K. McIntosh, *Controlling Misbehavior in England, 1370–1600* (Cambridge, 1998), esp. pp 39–41. See also for wide-ranging scholarship on medieval European state formation the volumes of the European Science Foundation's 'Origins of the Modern State in Europe' series, especially Peter Blickle, ed., *Resistance, Representation, and Community* (Oxford, 1997); and Antonio Padoa Schioppa, ed., *Legislation and Justice* (Oxford, 1997).

hermetically sealed from one another to begin to address the same questions. Those scholars have taught us to understand the multiplicity of directions from which governance was exercised, and that the early modern state developed not just as a result of the focus of authority at the centre, but that it drew its power from the active participation of men of a broad array of sociopolitical positions, from the king's intimates down to the jurors in municipal ward tribunals and manorial courts. This was, as Patrick Collinson once commented, a political culture of substantial 'social depth'.[98]

Thinking about sanctuary administration as part of 'state formation' highlights the need to think about the ways in which governance was multiple rather than monopolistic. Although for some scholars, the idea of the 'state' entails the monopoly of power (and thus any study of the formation of the state would necessarily focus on centralization), it is much more useful, as scholars such as Michael Braddick have suggested, to consider more broadly any governing authorities late medieval and early modern people themselves evidently thought were relevant.[99] Perhaps most important to emphasize is not only the diversity of authorities relevant in late medieval or Tudor England (crown, church, magnate, locality, and household) but also the extent to which those authorities were interlaced, institutionally, ideologically, and rhetorically. In Hugh Harvey's case, the men of Knowle acted on behalf of an ecclesiastical institution, Westminster Abbey, but as part of the machinery of royal criminal justice; they consulted and discussed parliamentary statutes in relation to their actions; whether they knew it or not during their discussions and negotiations, they would later have to answer to crown commissioners as well as to the abbot for what they did. As Braddick has commented regarding the Elizabethan period, local men of note often wore different hats as deputies for king, church, or town, but all their activities were regarded as 'legitimate magisterial activity'[100] reflecting their patriarchal roles; all were, in effect, political.

Such intertwining of 'church' and 'state' is often regarded as a post-Reformation phenomenon, a legacy of the 'triumph of the laity'[101] the Reformation changes were thought to have brought in their wake. Although scholars of the religious

---

[98] Patrick Collinson, 'The Monarchical Republic of Queen Elizabeth I', *Bulletin of the John Rylands Library* 69 (1987): p. 414, doi:io.ioi7/Sooi8246Xo999oo33.

[99] Braddick, *State Formation*, pp 1–14; see also, from a different perspective, Keith Stringer, 'States, Liberties and Communities in Medieval Britain and Ireland (c. 1100–1400)', in *Liberties and Identities in the Medieval British Isles*, ed. Michael Prestwich (Woodbridge Suffolk, 2008), esp. pp 7–9; Rees Davies, 'The Medieval State: The Tyranny of a Concept?', *Journal of Historical Sociology* 16 (2003): pp 280–300, doi:10.1111/1467-6443.00206.

[100] Braddick, *State Formation*, p. 77.

[101] See, for instance, G. R. Elton, *The Tudor Constitution: Documents and Commentary* (1982), p. 336, where he described the later Henrician Reformation as the 'unquestioned triumph of the laity over the clergy'; and the subtitle of Claire Cross, *Church and People, 1450–1660: The Triumph of the Laity in the English Church* (London, 1976). Early modernists who have emphasized the intertwining of the ecclesiastical and civil aspects of the parish as a key government institution, who otherwise would reject Eltonian viewpoints, have nonetheless tended to assume that these lay roles in the parish were a new phenomenon in Elizabeth's reign. See e.g. Keith Wrightson, 'The Politics of the Parish in Early Modern England', in *The Experience of Authority in Early Modern England*, ed. Paul Griffiths, Adam Fox, and Steve Hindle (New York, 1996), pp 10–46; Braddick, *State Formation*, pp 59–60; Hindle, *State and Social Change*, esp. p. 126; Goldie, 'Unacknowledged Republic'.

shifts of the sixteenth century no longer view them as a battle between (medieval) cleric and (modernizing) layman, we still tend to see the pre-Reformation period in particular through that dichotomy of clergy and laity. We are used to thinking about penetration of one form of authority, clerical, into the secular sphere, as bishops and other clergy had long played central roles in royal government. Relatively little attention has been paid to the reverse: lay involvement in ecclesiastical administration and in aspects of church governance. By the early sixteenth century, and indeed in some spheres by the thirteenth century, that lay involvement was quite considerable.[102] Advowsons—that is, the right and duty to appoint parish priests—were often in the hands of individual laypeople or lay organizations (the mayor and aldermen of London, for instance, held the advowson on a number of London parishes); this allowed considerable power to those in the pews to determine who ministered to them.[103] Even in cases where advowsons were in ecclesiastical hands, by the early sixteenth century appointments might well be handled by a lay agent.[104] Ecclesiastical offices and functions, and the practice of Christian religion, were tightly interwoven into the political, social, economic, and cultural relationships that made up English society in this period. Those relationships were in turn governed by a complex amalgam of patronage, favour, corruption, honour, duty, and charity.

The Hugh Harvey case illustrates well the way historians have come to understand Tudor state formation: the 'volunteer' labour of local men, working in the interests of the general governance of the realm (a phenomenon that of course long predated the Tudor period).[105] Such service was in one sense voluntary, but it was not entirely uncompensated. As the men of Knowle argued, there was no reason why 'poor men' in the localities should bear the costs of royal justice, although they were more than happy to share in the trickle-down of its profits. The world of Tudor political governance was remarkably broad and complicated, but one particularly hard boundary must be acknowledged: it was a man's world, and with rare exceptions women partook of it only indirectly. Only two women were mentioned among the dozens of people involved in Hugh Harvey's affair, in both cases as wives (and they enter into the accounts only in the absence of their husbands).

If the political culture of England in the fifteenth and sixteenth centuries distributed power and largesse more broadly, and in a wider range of governance spheres, than a more traditional approach to political history, focused on court and parliament, had understood, it is also important to emphasize that even amongst men the distributions—both in influence and in financial gain—were hardly

---

[102] French, *People of the Parish*; Forrest, 'Archive of the Official of Stow'; Forrest, 'Transformation of Visitation'.

[103] Bernard, *Late Medieval English Church*, pp 77–8. Regarding London, see e.g. Reginald R. Sharpe, ed., *Calendar of Letter-Books, Letter Book I (1400–1422)* (London, 1909), p. 92; LMA, Letter Book M, fol. 109v; Repertory 2, fol. 15r.

[104] See, e.g., the employment by the priory of St Bartholomew in West Smithfield of a lay agent to find suitable candidates for the parish of Theydon Bois, Essex, in 1513. LMA, DL/C/0206, Deposition Book of the Consistory Court of the Diocese of London, 1511–1516, fol. 235r.

[105] There is some disagreement about the 'amateurishness' of this administration of justice. Bellamy, *Criminal Trial*, pp 10–12; Musson and Ormrod, *Evolution of English Justice*, pp 62–74.

equal.¹⁰⁶ The Knowle sanctuary's management demonstrates the crucial part played by men of varying social levels; for those men, participation in local politics both reflected and constituted their socio-political status in the area, along with offering many opportunities for fees, emoluments, and other payments. Both talent and birth affected men's capacities to act: men of somewhat lower social origin like William Pynnock were able to parlay shrewdness and abilities into a significant career, while Richard Archer held his position as the abbot's steward apparently from his inherited stature in the neighbourhood rather than his skills or aptitudes. Gentlemen had far more influence on the unfolding of the process; they were also given higher compensation for their 'pains', as a matter of course. Late medieval and Tudor government worked (and sometimes failed to work) as a remarkably broadly-based and pragmatically ad hoc system in which participation was motivated at least partly by material gains to be amassed. Those material gains not surprisingly themselves shaped decisions and actions; as Krista Kesselring has pointed out, the profit-taking aspects of sixteenth-century processes of criminal law in felony forfeitures and the like gave incentive to local men to see the king's law applied, but 'this did not always mean heightened rigour', but sometimes rather actions and verdicts that benefited the profit-takers.¹⁰⁷

In Knowle, the administration of sanctuary was simply part of this complicated web of service, favour, and political and financial gain. In 1537, the calculations and negotiations around Hugh Harvey's sanctuary claim were conducted fully within that sphere of patronage and service that characterized the king's governance of the realm; this was no church-state battle. It was rather a conflict amongst many different interests—a victim wanting recompense whose representatives may well have embellished the charges to close off a loophole for the perpetrator; local men who saw the sanctuary status of their town as both part of the large machine of the king's justice and as an opportunity to earn some money (although quickly tiring of the bother the felon caused); a thief who similarly played with the rules to try to escape not only the noose but also surrender of the stolen goods. Notable is the absence of argument either for the sacrality of the sanctuary space in the town, or conversely against the idea of sanctuary, which was taken for granted by all involved. In Chapter 7 we will turn towards another way in which sanctuary had become embedded in the socio-politics of Henrician England: its role in solving the conundrum posed by aristocratic violence within the system of felony prosecution.

---

¹⁰⁶ Kesselring, 'Felony Forfeiture and Profits of Crime', pp 273, 283–5; Andy Wood, 'Subordination, Solidarity and the Limits of Popular Agency in a Yorkshire Valley c.1596–1615', *Past & Present* 193 (2006): pp 41–72, doi:10.1093/pastj/gtl011.
¹⁰⁷ Kesselring, 'Felony Forfeiture and Profits of Crime', pp 283–5.

7

Cheshire Feuds
Aristocratic Violence and the Uses of Sanctuary in the Reign of Henry VIII

In early 1539, five men from Cheshire allegedly attacked and killed Richard Cholmeley, a gentleman from the same county, in the churchyard of St Paul's Cathedral. Three months later, another Cheshire man, Ralph Holcroft, was slain in similar circumstances in the same place. Like thousands of others before them, in both cases the perpetrators fled from the scene of their crime to a sanctuary— the most important sanctuary in the realm, Westminster Abbey. For Ralph Holcroft's killers, sanctuary appears to have been as efficacious as it had been for Hugh Harvey: after their initial sheltering there, the accused men were ultimately freed from the homicide charges after an arbitrated settlement with the victim's family. For the slayers of the first homicide victim, Richard Cholmeley, however, the sanctuary privilege failed. Within days of Cholmeley's death, the five accused murderers were seized from the Westminster precinct on the orders of the Lord Privy Seal, Thomas Cromwell, and handed over to stand trial for the homicide. Their sanctuary pleas were disregarded and they were all summarily convicted. Within ten days of Cholmeley's death they were hanged.

How we understand these two outcomes is shaped by our view more generally of the workings of sanctuary in 1539. According to the standard scholarly interpretations of sanctuary in England in the late medieval and Tudor period, one would not expect that anyone would have thought to take sanctuary in a church at that late date: after all, sanctuary is supposed to have fallen into disuse by this time and moreover the monastic dissolutions were well under way. Thus the few scholars who have noticed the court's rejection of the sanctuary pleas in the Cholmeley case have found it unsurprising (while no one has, as far as I know, ever noticed the second case before).[1] As by now readers of this book will realize, however, sanctuary had not yet disappeared in the later 1530s, and so the court's endorsement of the sanctuary breach for Cholmeley's killers is in fact somewhat startling. Conversely, the second and successful employment of sanctuary for Holcroft's

---

[1] G. R. Elton, *Policy and Police: The Enforcement of the Reformation in the Age of Thomas Cromwell* (Cambridge, 1972), p. 290; Baker, *Spelman*, vol. 2, pp 345–6; Tim Thornton, *Cheshire and the Tudor State, 1480–1560* (Woodbridge, 2000), p. 221. Although both Elton and Thornton cite the King's Bench records for the Cholmeley case (as does Baker), they have read the first name of the victim incorrectly: it is clearly Richard, not Roger, in the record.

killers fits the expected pattern, even in 1539. No doubt some at the time thought the seizure and execution of Richard Cholmeley's killers just, but it was not consonant with English law as it stood in 1539, in letter or in practice. This chapter will consider these two Cheshire-related cases in more detail, both to understand why the sanctuary breach was permitted to stand in court, and to reflect more generally on the relationship of aristocratic violence to the politics of sanctuary in this tumultuous decade in England's history.

If sanctuary was still part of English law in 1539, this is not to say that in the second half of the 1530s it was proceeding entirely as it had been for the previous fifty years or so. As we have seen, the number of sanctuary seekers in the records began a significant downturn about 1535.[2] The precise reasons for this decline are not as obvious as it may seem at first. Although clearly in some way it intersects with the complex unfolding of the monastic dissolutions and the Reformation more generally, even as late as 1539 almost all of the religious houses that hosted sanctuary seekers were still operating. Moreover, it remained uncertain that monasticism would be entirely dismantled or whether sanctuary-seeking (more and more abstracted from the internal function of the religious houses) would go with it. We know what had happened by 1541, but those living in the second half of the 1530s did not. Thus we can guess that the decline in sanctuary-seeking from 1535 reflected felons' evaluations that sanctuaries were insecure; moreover, heads of religious houses, especially from 1537 when they were under serious pressure to dissolve voluntarily, may have felt it impolitic to continue to welcome seekers to their precincts. The evidence indicates, however, that some people continued to make resort to sanctuaries, Westminster Abbey predominantly, and that sanctuary continued to figure in strategies of aristocratic feud, as a high proportion of the instances of sanctuary-seeking from the later 1530s involved gentlemanly violence. When the first set of Cheshire gentlemen and their retainers took sanctuary at Westminster in early 1539, they had no cause to think that it was unsafe for them to do so; they could reasonably believe that it would serve for them as it had served for many others before them, as a respite from the noose. It is significant that three months later, even following the seizure of the first gang from the sanctuary precinct and their swift trial and execution, the killers in the second case were to resort to sanctuary again. They emerged with the outcome those involved in aristocratic feuds sought from the various mitigations offered by the Tudor criminal justice system, freedom to continue their political careers unscathed.

AFFRAYS IN ST PAUL'S CHURCHYARD

On 10 February 1539, a London coroner and the two sheriffs of London convened a coroner's inquest over the body of Richard Cholmeley, gentleman, who 'lay dead and feloniously murdered' in the parish of St Gregory, in the shadows of St Paul's

---

[2] See the data in McSheffrey, 'Sanctuary Seekers'.

Cathedral.³ The inquest jurors reported that on the last day of January in 1539, at nine o'clock in the morning, Richard Cholmeley, in God's peace and the king's, entered the churchyard of St Paul's Cathedral in London when suddenly he was beset by five men, named as John Mainwaring, Robert Jones, Thomas Potter, William Edwards, and Hugh Griffith. Attacking Cholmeley with swords, shields, and knives, they gave Cholmeley a wound on the back of his head that penetrated to his brain. Cholmeley fell unconscious and was taken to a nearby house where he languished for more than a week before finally dying on 9 February. In the meantime, the jurors reported, his killers bolted; as later documents in the case reveal, they fled from London to the abbey of Westminster, some three kilometres distant, where they sought, and were granted, the privilege of sanctuary. In addition, the jurors also stated that the five men had not acted of their own accord: the murder had been ordered a week before by a certain Randall Mainwaring, gentleman, of Swanley, Cheshire.⁴ Accused as an accessory to murder, Randall Mainwaring was liable to the same capital penalties meted out to those who actually wielded the knife.

The coroner's inquest, in other words, described an assassination; as we will see, given the history between the Mainwarings and Cholmeley, this is a plausible scenario. It may, however, be significant that when the second Cheshire-related murder happened in St Paul's churchyard three months later, the mayor and aldermen of London issued a strict warning to the coroner and his inquest jury investigating the death in St Paul's churchyard, that they must be impartial in their verdict. This was not a usual or formulaic entry in the civic record, and it implied that the verdict accompanying the first inquest had been false in some way.⁵ Perhaps Cholmeley's killing was a targeted assassination; or perhaps it was a more spontaneous armed encounter in which he was mortally wounded in the fray, as so many other such killings were described in coroner's reports. Either way, Cholmeley was slain by a band of Mainwaring retainers who then sought to escape arrest and trial for the killing by running to sanctuary.

All those involved in this homicide, victim and perpetrators, were either certainly or probably Cheshire men.⁶ This murder was a settling of scores in a violent Cheshire dispute, both factional and personal, that had rumbled for some years between Richard Cholmeley and Randall Mainwaring. Records of various courts show that Cholmeley and Randall Mainwaring had been at loggerheads from at least 1534, a feud that involved also Mainwaring's patron and namesake, Sir

---

³ The details that follow come from the coroner's report and the records of the process at King's Bench, at TNA, KB 9/541, mm 85–87; KB 27/1112, rex m. 9.
⁴ Randall Mainwaring's first name is rendered a number of different ways both in sixteenth-century and modern sources: Randall, Randle, Randolph, Ranulph, Ralph. I will use one form and spelling, Randall, for consistency.
⁵ LMA, Repertory 10, fol. 95r.
⁶ Both Cholmeley himself and the four men charged with the homicide were said in the indictment to be 'of London', but Cholmeley was clearly primarily resident in Cheshire, and the four indicted perpetrators were presumably all either originally from Cheshire or at least connected to the Mainwaring family of Cheshire. TNA, KB 9/541, mm 85–87.

Randall Mainwaring of Over Peover, one of the powers in Cheshire politics.[7] Cholmeley and the Mainwarings were evidently driven by mutual enmity, an antagonism that seems to have been heightened by the fact that they were closely related to one another. This aspect of the dispute is interestingly almost thoroughly occluded in the fairly voluminous paper trail their quarrels left in the legal records, emerging only in sixteenth-century pedigrees and genealogical sources. As those sources show, Randall Mainwaring of Swanley and Kermincham was Richard Cholmeley's brother-in-law, while Sir Randall Mainwaring of Over Peover was Cholmeley's stepfather.[8] Where John Mainwaring—the principal felon in the homicide—fits into the Mainwaring family is unclear, but presumably he came from some junior branch of the family. Rooted though this homicide was in Cheshire politics and family drama, it was, nonetheless, unsurprising that this episode took place in the metropolis. Cheshire gentlemen like Cholmeley and Mainwaring were accustomed to travel to London and Westminster regularly, despite the considerable distance, to conduct their legal and business affairs. Some of those involved also had positions at court: two of Cholmeley's killers were said to have been members of Prince Edward's household.[9]

If it was indeed a targeted killing, it is also possible that the Mainwarings planned the murder in London because their strategy involved the seeking of sanctuary at Westminster following the deed. Such an assassination was risky, but John Mainwaring and his fellows could well have thought the risk worth taking once sanctuary was factored in. As we saw in the introductory chapter with William Pennington's killers in 1532, cases of aristocratic violence often ended with a royal pardon or other mitigation of the capital penalty for felony for the surviving party.

---

[7] On where this dispute fits into Cheshire politics in the 1530s (although some of the names are confused, and the family relationships are not noted), see Thornton, *Cheshire*, ch. 9 and 10, esp. pp 216–21. For records related to the feud, see TNA, C 1/754/46–7; C 1/865/29; C 1/755/27; C 1/771/11–14; STAC 2/8, fols 272–274; STAC 2/24/30; STAC 2/26/294; STAC 2/29/182; SP 1/112, fol. 203; SP 1/128, fol. 125; SP 1/102, fol. 39; *L&P*, vol. 11, p. 530; vol. 13, pt. 1, p. 50; vol. 10, p. 119.

[8] On the family relationships, see TNA, C 1/655/7, C 1/1508-33-34, C 4/17/46; CHES 3/62/9, Inquisition Post Mortem of Richard Cholmeley of Cholmeley, 11 Jan. 1519; CHES 3/69/3, Inquisition Post Mortem for Randall Mainwaring of Kermincham, 1547 (d. 1546); STAC 2/29/182; Robert Glover et al., *The Visitation of Cheshire in the Year 1580*, Harleian Society 18 (London, 1882), pp 63–4. Elizabeth Brereton, Richard Cholmeley's mother and Sir Randall Mainwaring's wife, was the sister of Sir William Brereton, most well known as having been one of the men with whom Anne Boleyn was accused of adultery in 1536. A dominant figure in Cheshire society before his fall from grace, Sir William had ties both to his nephew Richard Cholmeley and to the Mainwarings. Sir William evidently lent his nephew Richard Cholmeley some money in about 1534. Humphrey Mainwaring, Randall Mainwaring's younger brother (and part of his retinue in the 1537 affray with Cholmeley) was bailiff of one of Sir William Brereton's manors from 1529 until at least 1535 and Randall Mainwaring of Swanley and Kermincham himself was his brother's surety for that office. E. W. Ives, ed., *Letters and Accounts of William Brereton of Malpas*, Record Society of Lancashire and Cheshire 116 (Old Woking, Surrey, 1976), pp 55, 93, 163, 183, 202, 252.

[9] The king's heir was customarily named prince of Wales and earl of Chester, and although Edward was himself never formally accorded those titles, men from both Wales and Cheshire served in his household. Thornton, *Cheshire*, pp 224–5. Hall and Wriothesley differ on which were the prince's servants: Hall identifies them as Jones, Potter, and Mainwaring (although in each case he renders their first names incorrectly, as indeed he does for the victim as well), while Wriothesley indicates that it was the other two. Hall, *Hall's Chronicle*, p. 837; Wriothesley, *Chronicle*, vol. 1, p. 93.

Time was needed to make arrangements and, as we will see in the last section of this chapter, the Southwells and the Mainwaring gang were not the only men involved in aristocratic feuds and affrays to use sanctuary as a bolt-hole while a pardon was being pursued. Thus the flight of the Mainwaring gang to the Westminster sanctuary after their attack on Cholmeley followed a recognizable, and often effective, pattern. Cholmeley's five murderers could have expected to wait in sanctuary while their patrons organized their pardon.

Sanctuary did not work for Richard Cholmeley's killers, however, as it had for others. Five days following the coroner's inquest on 10 February 1539, John Mainwaring and his four associates appeared at the prisoners' bar at gaol delivery at Newgate, having been seized from the Westminster sanctuary on the orders of Thomas Cromwell, then Lord Privy Seal and the most powerful man in the kingdom after the king. Asked to respond to the homicide indictment, John Mainwaring pleaded sanctuary—that is, he asked the court to rule that the seizure was illegal and that he should be restored to the 'king's privilege at Westminster'.[10] Although Mainwaring emphasized that he had been taken from the sanctuary against his will, his co-accused Jones, Potter, Edwards, and Griffith tried a different tack: they too indicated they were privileged as sanctuary men but emphasized that they had come voluntarily at the Lord Privy Seal's behest, assuming perhaps that (as had happened in other cases) they would be asked to give evidence to implicate the bigger fish who had ordered the killing before being returned to the sanctuary. Altogether, the Mainwaring gang's plea of sanctuary was 'not obviously bad', as Sir John Baker has put it,[11] and it should have worked, sending them back to the Westminster Abbey precinct.[12]

But it did not work, as John Mainwaring and his fellows must have known as soon as they walked up to the prisoners' bar and faced their judges, for the commission hearing gaol delivery for the City of London on 15 February 1539 included not only, as was usual, the mayor of London and a royal justice, John Hales,[13] but also Sir Richard Rich, a lawyer, civil servant, and Cromwell lackey, and Sir Thomas Cromwell, Lord Privy Seal, himself. Thus Mainwaring's plea that he had been unlawfully seized on the orders of the Lord Privy Seal was to be decided by a panel including, and no doubt dominated by, the Lord Privy Seal. Although Cromwell

---

[10] After Mainwaring had sworn the oath and been admitted to the sanctuary, as it is recorded on the plea roll, 'Their I remayned in godis peace and the kyngis, unto suche tyme that by my lorde pryvyeseales commandement I was fetchyd out, contrary to my wyll. Wherefore I trust to god I am pryvyledgyd man, and desyre that I may have the advauntage of the pryvyledge therof, accordyng to the kyngis graunt their to the monasterye of Westminster'. TNA, KB 27/1112, rex m. 9 (dorse).

[11] Baker, *Spelman*, vol. 2, pp 345–6.

[12] See the Bull and Roo case discussed in the section 'Breaching Sanctuary' below, and the case of James ap Powell, who had escaped from the Tower and taken sanctuary at Westminster in a treason case; in 1531, he was brought out of sanctuary by the abbot to give evidence against his fellows, and when he was finished testifying the abbot 'humbly requested the justices to return' him to sanctuary, which they granted. TNA, KB 27/1075, rex m. 4; Baker, *Spelman*, vol. 1, pp 47–8.

[13] Hales was baron of the court of Exchequer. He was, at the time, about sixty-nine and would retire soon after. He was often employed as a member of the king's council, advising on criminal matters. J. H. Baker, 'Hales, John (1469/70–1540?)', *ODNB* (2004), doi:10.1093/ref:odnb/11912. He may also have been placed on the commission as Cromwell's man.

had sat as a judge in Chancery when he was Master of the Rolls between 1534 and 1536, I have found no other instance of his sitting on a gaol delivery commission, suggesting that this was precisely what it seemed: a parachuting of Cromwell and his sidekick onto the bench to assure the verdict.[14] It is no surprise, therefore, that the case did not go in Mainwaring's favour. His fellows, who insisted that they had come willingly at the Lord Privy Seal's command, may have thought their show of cooperation would work in their favour, but such was not the case. Once the five accused had made their sanctuary pleas, William Whorwode, the solicitor-general,[15] acting for the king, made his statement, which was that each of these pleas was, simply put, insufficient in law.[16] The court concurred, and then moved directly to the sentence, that the accused were to be hanged. They had pleaded not guilty to the felony, but in what can only be called a highly irregular process, neither those pleas nor their sanctuary claims were put to a jury; they were simply summarily convicted. The hangings were sufficiently interesting that they were briefly mentioned in Edward Hall's and Charles Wriothesley's chronicles. Hall and Wriothesley indicate that three of the men were hanged in St Paul's churchyard four days later on 19 February, and the other two in Cheshire soon after.[17] The alleged procurer of Cholmeley's murder, Randall Mainwaring, had better luck than his retainers. He was not arraigned until the summer of 1539, and in late October when the jury heard his case he was acquitted.[18]

In the meantime, another homicide with remarkable similarities had unfolded, this one about ten weeks after Richard Cholmeley's death. Those similarities were not coincidental, as this later affray was almost certainly connected to the Cholmely–Mainwaring feud; one of the main protagonists in the second drama, Sir John Done of Utkinton, was Sir Randall Mainwaring's son-in-law.[19] (His opponent, Thomas Holcroft, on the other hand, was at this time aligned with another faction in Cheshire politics.[20]) There are two different versions of the events surrounding the April homicide. The first, the coroner's inquest report on

---

[14] On Cromwell in Chancery, see Baker, *Oxford History, 1485–1558*, pp 183, 418. As Baker put it in *Spelman*, Cromwell 'arranged a suitably reliable commission of gaol delivery (including himself and Rich) to overrule the [Mainwaring's] not obviously bad plea'; Baker, *Spelman*, vol. 2, p. 346 (intro).

[15] Solicitor-general from 1536 to 1540, and later attorney-general from 1540 until his death in 1545. S. R. Johnson, 'Whorwood (Horwood), William (by 1505–45)', in *HPO*.

[16] 'Willelmus Whorwode armiger, pro domino rege, dicit quod dicta quinque separalia placita modo et forma predictis per ipsos separaliter placitata minus sufficientes in lege existunt et quodlibet placitum predictum minus sufficiens in lege existit, ad quod et cetera'.

[17] Wriothesley, *Chronicle*, vol. 1, p. 93; Hall, *Hall's Chronicle*, p. 827. The two chroniclers disagreed about which was hanged where.

[18] TNA, KB 9/541, mm 85–87; KB 27/1112, rex m. 9.

[19] N. M. Fuidge, 'Done, Sir John (1501/2–61), of Utkinton, Cheshire', in *HPO*. Given that Cholmeley was also related by marriage to both Randall Mainwarings and yet was their mortal enemy, we cannot take for granted that Done was tied to his father-in-law, but he probably was.

[20] Thomas Holcroft was a relative newcomer to Cheshire, as his family had been based in Lancashire. He found opportunities in the county's messy divisions of the 1530s to create a significant career for himself, which flowered in the 1540s. At this point he was tied to the Breretons, while the Mainwarings were tied to Piers Dutton. There was a quarrel in the late 1540s between a Robert Mainwaring and (the recently knighted) Sir Thomas Holcroft, Chester, Cheshire Archives and Local Studies, MS DCH/J/237, accessed through the calendar on A2A, http://discovery.nationalarchives.gov.uk/details/rd/91a6d5b2-2af3-4ca3-bbf7-963ded4cf393.

the victim, said that mid-morning on 12 April 1539 Sir John Done, accompanied by three retainers, had gone to St Paul's Cathedral to meet with one of the duke of Suffolk's servants.[21] Also in the cathedral at that time were Thomas Holcroft and four of his servants. Although Done and Holcroft did not speak together inside the church, as Thomas Holcroft saw Done and his men leave, he and his retinue hastened to exit by another door so that he could confront them outside. When the two parties met on the steps of the main south door to the church, Holcroft challenged Done by throwing down his gown, and an affray ensued. In the course of the fight, Done's man William Ryder gave Holcroft's man, Ralph Holcroft, a mortal wound. Although the inquest jurors found that William Ryder feloniously slew Ralph Holcroft, and that Done and his other servants were accessories, the general tenor of the report cast moral responsibility on Thomas Holcroft for inciting the quarrel. Immediately afterward, Sir John Done and his three retainers fled to the sanctuary of St Peter at Westminster.

The second version of events of that April morning in St Paul's churchyard was written in a bill submitted eight months later in an appeal of murder, a private prosecution by the closest relative of the victim, Ralph Holcroft's brother Geoffrey.[22] The scenario presented in Geoffrey Holcroft's appeal was quite different, and indeed reminiscent of the narrative employed in the indictment of Richard Cholmeley's killers: Done and his men had lain in wait in St Paul's churchyard to assault Ralph Holcroft, who had been in God's peace and the king's when for no reason he was suddenly attacked by Done's gang and stabbed to death by William Ryder.

Clearly we cannot know what precisely happened that morning, whether either, or neither, of these records is reliable. As already mentioned, on the same day as the inquest on Ralph Holcroft's body was convened, an unusual note was inscribed in the records of the court of London Mayor and Aldermen, suggesting that there was some concern about coroner's inquests making suspicious findings, perhaps particularly in homicides that involved Cheshire men in St Paul's churchyard.[23] If the circumstances of Ralph Holcroft's death remain far from certain, it is even less clear what happened immediately afterward, beyond the perpetrators' flight to Westminster. Done at least may not have stayed there long; in July 1539, some three months after Ralph Holcroft's death, both Sir John Done and Thomas Holcroft were confirmed as Justices of the Peace for Cheshire.[24] The continued inclusion of Done on the judicial bench for the county while he had an accessory to homicide charge over his head is especially odd, even assuming he was no longer in sanctuary, and so it seems to indicate that at that time the indictment was not

---

[21] TNA, KB 9/545, mm 87–90. The servant was named as Leonard Veale, who was a member of the duke of Suffolk's household. S. J. Gunn, *Charles Brandon, Duke of Suffolk, c. 1484–1545* (New York, 1988), p. 192.
[22] TNA, KB 27/1115, plea m. 21.
[23] LMA, Repertory 10, fol. 95r. The note reads: 'Item, the matter concerning the murder of one man slain in affray between one Master Done, knight, and one Holcroft in Paul's churchyard and before the whole jury the said matter was rehearsed and monition given unto the coroner and jury that they shall indifferently behave themselves in the same upon the pains that shall fall thereon'.
[24] *L&P*, vol. 14, pt. 1, pp 584–5.

proceeding. In the fall of 1539, however, Ralph Holcroft's brother, Geoffrey, launched his private prosecution of the murder, a process likely orchestrated by Thomas Holcroft himself in frustration with the lack of movement on the crown's felony prosecution. Done and the two other accessories appeared in early 1540 before the court of King's Bench to respond to the appeal and were bailed, while Ryder, the principal felon, was reported to be still at large, perhaps still in sanctuary, or somewhere else safe. The matter was scheduled to be put to a jury on 2 November 1540, but on that day Geoffrey Holcroft failed to appear, thus defaulting on his appeal, and the crown declined to proceed with the prosecution of the felony. Done and his co-accused, including Ryder, were all, then, free to go.[25] As was often the case with appeals, this dropping of charges reflected an out-of-court settlement between the parties. John Done and Thomas Holcroft came to an agreement, arbitrated by the Privy Council, no less, by which Sir John was to pay Holcroft the relatively small amount of 100 marks (£66 13s 4d) 'for amends'.[26] Both Holcroft and Done went on to serve as JPs, MPs, and in other forms of royal service for several decades to come.[27] In the end no one was judicially deemed responsible for Ralph Holcroft's death.

Although we do not know how long Done and his servants stayed in the Westminster sanctuary and how important a role their resort to asylum there played in the ultimate extinction of the felony charges against them, the most interesting thing about their sanctuary-seeking is that it happened at all. Only ten weeks after John Mainwaring and his fellows found that Westminster sanctuary would not keep them safe from arrest, another group of men from Cheshire nonetheless thought it made sense for them to flee to Westminster when a fight ended in a homicide. This could not have been because they were ignorant of the Mainwaring gang's end, for the quarrels were almost certainly related. Their flight to Westminster indicates instead that sanctuary had not yet become an unthinkable response to such a situation.

In both these cases, the process was engineered in order to achieve a desired result; in neither case did those processes accord with a strict (or indeed even relatively loose) interpretation of the law. The parties involved, including the crown, employed the law and the courts, but rigged the outcome when necessary. It is no great surprise to see legal processes massaged by those with power and influence. What is more surprising, and unusual, was the naked inscription of the manipulation in the Mainwaring case onto the official judicial record, with the Lord Privy Seal himself presiding over a highly irregular process. To put these two cases into context, let us turn first to look at sanctuary breaches in general in the reign of Henry VIII, and then to consider the role sanctuary played in strategies of aristocratic violence.

---

[25] TNA, KB 27/1115, plea m. 21.
[26] Nicolas, *Proceedings*, vol. 7, p 87; Whittick, 'Role of the Criminal Appeal', pp 63–4.
[27] See Fuidge, 'Done, Sir John (1501/2–61)', and R. J. W. Swales, 'Holcroft, Sir Thomas (1505/6–58)', in *HPO*.

BREACHING SANCTUARY

If sanctuary had long been in decline under the Tudor regime, it would seem sensible to interpret the seizure of Richard Cholmeley's killers from Westminster sanctuary and the firm rejection of their claim of sanctuary privilege in court as simply a reflection of how far 'opinion had set firmly against the whole principle' of sanctuary by 1539, as G. R. Elton put it in his comment on the case.[28] Although it is true that sanctuary-seeking was waning by the end of the 1530s, that decline had been sharp rather than long-term and gradual, and the privilege remained legal and recognized. Moreover, 'opinion' on sanctuary in 1539 was much more complicated than Elton's formulation implies, in two ways in particular.

First, Cromwell's order to have the Mainwaring gang seized was not a blow struck against Westminster Abbey's privilege. Although the breach may seem at first a forceful or even hostile incursion on a recalcitrant and presumably defensive ecclesiastical establishment, in fact when Cromwell ordered the seizure of the accused felons from the Westminster sanctuary, he almost certainly did so with the cooperation, rather than the opposition, of the abbot. The abbots of Westminster during Henry VIII's reign, John Islip and William Benson, were closely allied to the crown and, in the 1530s, to Thomas Cromwell;[29] they cooperated with the crown when asked to do so regarding sanctuary-seekers, even to the extent of accompanying indicted sanctuary men into court when they were summoned.[30] Cromwell himself was closely associated with the abbey and knew the operations of the sanctuary well: William Benson, the abbot from 1533 (and later dean of the new cathedral in the 1540s), had been appointed through Cromwell's patronage,[31] and in 1534 the abbot in turn appointed Cromwell as steward of the abbey, an office that included authority over the sanctuary.[32] When Cromwell ordered Mainwaring and his gang seized in 1539, it is likely that William Webbe, the sanctuary's keeper, oversaw the order's fulfilment.[33] Those governing Westminster sanctuary had in previous years worked closely with Cromwell and the crown, and no doubt hoped to continue to do so. Thus if Cromwell ordered the surrender of John Mainwaring and the others, the abbot and the sanctuary's keeper were almost certainly willing to fulfil his command, regardless of its technical legality.

---

[28] Quotation from Elton, *Policy and Police*, p. 290; the same argument made (with citation to Elton) by Baker, *Spelman*, vol. 2, pp 345–6 (intro); and by Thornton, *Cheshire*, p. 221. All three in turn cite Thornley, 'Destruction of Sanctuary', and Ives, 'Crime, Sanctuary'.
[29] Barbara F. Harvey and Henry Summerson. 'Islip, John (1464–1532)', *ODNB* (2004), doi:10.1093/ref:odnb/14492; C. S. Knighton, 'Benson [name in Religion Boston], William (d. 1549)', *ODNB* (2004), doi:10.1093/ref:odnb/2146; for Cromwell's involvement generally in monastic elections and other affairs in the 1530s, see Michael Everett, *The Rise of Thomas Cromwell: Power and Politics in the Reign of Henry VIII* (New Haven, 2015), pp 110–19.
[30] See above this chapter, at n.12.   [31] Knighton, 'Benson, William'.
[32] WAM, WARB vol. 2, fols 288rv, 298v; see also 177r, 292rv, 297rv, 299r; Barbara F. Harvey, *Living and Dying in England, 1100–1540: The Monastic Experience* (Oxford, 1993), pp 165–6.
[33] Mainwaring does not indicate who actually forcibly removed him from the sanctuary, but the similar Spencer case about a year later (examined later in this section) names Webbe as the one who carried out Cromwell's command.

Second, although Cromwell could count on the abbot and the keeper of the sanctuary to do what he asked, he could not, conversely, count on the courts to recognize the seizure as valid, because the judiciary was not in fact as hostile towards sanctuary as legal historians have assumed. Mainwaring and his fellows could expect the courts to uphold their sanctuary privilege, because the courts had done so before, and not long before. There had of course been previous violations of sanctuary, and in particular in the 1510s there was a significant number of breaches by a range of different authorities. As I argued in Chapter 4, however, although in that decade impatient authorities (mostly civic governments) strongly challenged the sanctuary claims of ecclesiastical franchises, there were also indications that courts would not, in fact, explicitly support those breaches unless there were technical ineligibilities. For some of the cases, the courts passive-aggressively refused to rule; in others the courts restored the seekers.[34] The 1520s marked the end of this spate of sanctuary pleas in the courts; as the number of sanctuary seekers continued to increase in that decade, this must have been because officials stopped committing the sanctuary breaches that occasioned the sanctuary pleas.[35] Sanctuary seekers appear to have been quite safe in the 1520s. In 1526, for instance, one of Wolsey's servants wrote a letter explaining to the cardinal why he had not been able to take a certain felon into custody as he had been ordered to do; the felon had fled to the house of the Crutched Friars in Colchester, and as the servant put it, he dared 'not enterprise' into the church to seize the man, whose right to sanctuary was vigorously defended by the prior.[36] It was evidently no easy thing to breach a sanctuary in the 1520s, even with Cardinal Wolsey's authority.

A 1532 case likely made it even more difficult in the following decade, as the justices at King's Bench definitively confirmed felons' sanctuary rights. On a Saturday at the end of May 1530, Maurice Bull and Nicholas Roo, both described as yeomen of the town of Westminster, appeared before the court of King's Bench to face charges of felony. According to an indictment brought down by a panel of Middlesex jurors, on 30 August 1529 Bull and Roo had entered into the sanctuary at Westminster Abbey and been registered as 'felons of the lord king'. Three weeks afterwards, however, the indictment continued, Bull and Roo had left the sanctuary to commit a robbery. Asked how they responded to these charges, Bull and Roo stated that they were not guilty of the theft, and that furthermore they pleaded sanctuary, contending that their seizure from Westminster had not been legal. They argued that when they had entered the Westminster sanctuary at the end of August, they had taken the privilege for debt and trespass respectively, not for felony. On 21 September, the day following the theft, however, they changed the status of their sanctuary privilege, registering themselves anew, this time as felons—not for the 'supposed' theft (as they put it) in the present indictment to which they had pleaded not guilty, but coincidentally for previous felonies that they had

---

[34] See Ch. 4 at n.49.
[35] That is, rather than the cessation of sanctuary pleas because they were an unsuccessful legal strategy; cf. Baker, *Spelman*, vol. 2, p. 345 (intro).
[36] TNA, SP 1/39, fol. 41, *L&P*, vol. 4, pt. 2, p. 1065.

committed before coming to the sanctuary. After this new registration, they stayed within the Westminster sanctuary, protected by its privilege, for a month. Then on 21 October 1529, Bull and Roo claimed, they were violently seized by the king's men. Both the accused and the crown asked for the question of the nature and timing of the sanctuary claim to be put to a jury and in the meantime the two accused were returned to the Marshalsea prison. After delays and two jury verdicts—both of which accepted Bull and Roo's version of their double sanctuary registration, referring to details that likely came from the sanctuary register itself—in June 1532 the justices gave their judgment: that their sanctuary plea was good, and thus they were to be restored to Westminster sanctuary. Bull and Roo were both listed among the 'privileged men' in the Westminster sanctuary in the census taken on 1 June 1533.[37] While nothing further is known about Nicholas Roo, Maurice Bull was still a resident of the sanctuary as late as September 1537 when he was a witness in an enquiry ordered by Cromwell.[38]

The success of Bull's and Roo's claim indicated that even in hard cases sanctuary pleas would hold in the king's courts. Intensifying this endorsement of sanctuary (and perhaps contributing to the justices' decision), a 1531 statute had recently defined and confirmed the circumstances under which felons could be seized—and when they could not. The statute of 22 Henry VIII c. 14 allowed for the taking of felons from sanctuary when in some way the felon had abrogated the privilege, usually by the commission of a further offence after admission as felons to sanctuary. At the same time, the statute limited the conditions for seizure even when a sanctuary person was indicted for such a subsequent offence; any privileged persons indicted of a crime alleged to have been committed while they were in sanctuary were not in the first instance to be arrested and taken from the sanctuary for trial. They were instead initially to be examined in the sanctuary by two of the king's council, or four JPs from the shire where the sanctuary was located, and if they could provide an alibi for the time of the alleged felony they were not to be extracted, notwithstanding any indictment. If they could not provide an alibi, such persons could then be taken from the sanctuary, but in court could make a sanctuary plea, which was to be tried before a jury (as they had been before, and as was the case with Bull and Roo). If the allegations of re-offending were found to be true, then they were to have execution of sentence as if they had no privilege of sanctuary; but if the jurors found that they had not in fact re-offended while in sanctuary, then the seeker was to be restored to the same sanctuary from which he or she had been taken.[39] The statute made legal the breaching of sanctuary under certain quite limited circumstances, but in so doing it also clearly recognized that felons who had not committed the offences that legitimated a breach had a statutory right to be there.

---

[37] TNA, SP 1/238, fol. 72r. Neither name appears on a similar census dated 1 June 1532; this document is likely missing one of its pages, but in any case their omission makes sense, as they were both in the Marshalsea prison at that point. TNA, SP 1/70, fol. 133.

[38] TNA, SP 1/124, fol. 204r; SP 1/125, fols 40r–43v.

[39] *SR* vol. 3, pp 332–4; Margaret McGlynn, 'The Use and Abuse of Sanctuary in Henrician England' (presentation at the American Society for Legal History Annual Meeting, Philadelphia, 2010).

Bull and Roo had probably manipulated the sanctuary privilege, yet technically they were entitled to it—the statute clearly indicated that re-offenders had to have held the privilege for felony before the second offence, not for trespass or debt. Both the jurors and the justices at King's Bench ultimately, if somewhat belatedly, upheld their claim. The Bull and Roo case, especially in combination with the 1531 statute, likely ensconced sanctuary even more firmly in English legal processes, so that sanctuary privilege was more secure by the end of 1532 than perhaps it had ever been.

In the immediate aftermath of Bull's and Roo's restoration to the Westminster sanctuary, Cromwell went so far as to work around the court system entirely in one case where sanctuary pleas might have allowed the perpetrators of a notorious crime to escape punishment. In July 1533 John Wolfe, registered as a sanctuary man at Westminster as a debtor, conspired with his wife Alice Wolfe and a number of co-conspirators to rob and murder two Italian merchants, Jerome de George and Charles de Benche, in a boat on the Thames by Westminster.[40] Following the murder, it is likely the Wolfes and their co-conspirators ran back to the Westminster precinct and took sanctuary, Wolfe changing his registration for debt to privilege for felony, exactly as Bull and Roo had done. The murder became an international incident, and the king tasked Cromwell with making sure that John and Alice Wolfe did not escape condign punishment. Cromwell could seize them from sanctuary (and probably did, as they became prisoners in the Tower of London), but if they were arraigned on a felony indictment, they—like Bull and Roo—could plead sanctuary and the courts would restore them. Thus Cromwell employed for them an act of attainder in parliament which stripped them of any rights to claim clergy or sanctuary and condemned them to death.[41] In early April 1534, John and Alice Wolfe were publicly executed in spectacular fashion by being hanged from a tree over the Thames, drowned by the incoming tide. Cromwell could get around sanctuary in the mid-1530s—but he had to take the rather extraordinary path of passing an individual act of attainder in order to do so.

In short, by the 1530s sanctuary was well-entrenched indeed in the English legal system, defined by statute and confirmed by the courts. When in 1536, Rowland Lee, bishop of Coventry and Lichfield and fierce law-and-order president of the Council of the Marches of Wales, wrote Cromwell in 1536 to urge him to seize two 'great rebel[s] and outlaws' from sanctuary in Westminster, he acknowledged

---

[40] For sources on the Wolfe case, see under John Wolfe in McSheffrey, 'Sanctuary Seekers'.

[41] Although this was the first time in the Tudor era a parliamentary attainder was used for felony, they had of course been used before for treason, and perhaps Cromwell's strategy with the Wolfes borrowed from another legal and political problem unfolding at the same time for which he also feared failure in the royal court. This was the case of Elizabeth Barton, the 'holy maid' of Kent, who prophesied King Henry's downfall should he divorce Katherine and marry Anne Boleyn; when Barton began to attract support from other opponents of the divorce, it became politically imperative to crush her and her followers. Cromwell diverted around justices in the royal courts for the prosecution, as the justices were likely to be reluctant to convict her and her confederates for treason (her prophecies did not at that time fit the statutory parameters for treason). Instead, he had them attainted as traitors by an act of parliament. Diane Watt, 'Barton, Elizabeth', *ODNB* (2004), doi:10.1093/ref:odnb/1598; Bellamy, *Tudor Law of Treason*, p. 23.

that if the men pleaded sanctuary, they would have it 'according to the king's laws', but he was sure that a technicality could be found to bar them from it.[42] Lee did not think, in 1536, that even Cromwell could grab whom he wanted from sanctuary without a legal justification that would stand up in court.

Returning to the Mainwaring gang's flight to Westminster in 1539: there was every reason, then, for Cholmeley's five killers to think that their resort to sanctuary would be effective, and even once grabbed from sanctuary on Cromwell's orders, their pleas of sanctuary—the same as made by Bull and Roo—should have worked. By 1539, however, the situation was different than it had been when Cromwell found it necessary to work around sanctuary. Cromwell himself by this time had become especially impatient, or cocky, or both. The progress of the monastic dissolutions was clearly also relevant: although most of the houses hosting the major sanctuaries, including Westminster, were still intact in 1539, the future of monasticism was, at the least, up in the air. Instances of sanctuary-seeking had not ceased, but evidence for them is much sparser in the late years of the decade. Seekers, or religious houses, or both may have felt that sanctuary privilege was unsafe. As the religious changes proceeded, heads of religious houses might not have wanted to push anything that smacked too much of ecclesiastical privilege, and they may have discouraged sanctuary seekers. Felons fleeing the scenes of their crimes may also have thought it too risky.[43]

Although sanctuary-seeking was evidently in decline, that did not mean that the courts no longer recognized sanctuary. The seizure of the Mainwaring gang from Westminster in February 1539 and particularly the blatant disregard for their sanctuary plea in court were not at all characteristic of how sanctuary was treated in the courts up to that point.[44] And it was also not entirely characteristic of the fate of sanctuary seekers in the remainder of 1539, either. Beyond the example of Sir John Done and his men in April, John Caryon of London fled to Westminster following a homicide in July 1539, using his time there to organize a pardon, which he was granted several months later.[45] A petition to Cromwell indicates that another

---

[42] If Lee's contentions were fair—that at least one of them had previously sought sanctuary and then subsequently had 'stolen, burned, and killed without mercy'—then Lee was right that his sanctuary plea would not stand, for a re-offender was barred from sanctuary by 22 Hen. VIII, c. 14. SP 1/101, fol. 18, L&P, vol. 10, p. 12.

[43] This was perhaps particularly true from 1538 when Beaulieu Abbey became the first of the houses hosting major sanctuaries to shut down. It appears that the plan was for the thirty-two sanctuary men resident at the time of the dissolution to be transferred to another sanctuary, but even the king's commissioners who oversaw the institutional dismantling of the abbey thought that was difficult and impracticable. TNA, SP 1/131, fol. 9; SP 1/131, fol. 120; SP 1/78, fol. 140; BL, Cotton Titus MS B I, fol. 465; L&P, vol. 13, pt. 1, pp 254, 295, 296, 322; W. H. St John Hope and Harold Brakspear, 'The Cistercian Abbey of Beaulieu in the County of Southampton', *The Archaeological Journal* 63 (New Series, vol. 13) (1906): pp 129–88, doi:10.1080/00665983.1906.10853026.

[44] See for instance the case of William Walde or Wade, who in 1538 was restored to sanctuary in Suffolk by a jury verdict at the Suffolk peace sessions. TNA, KB 9/548, mm 192–194; KB 27/1116, rex m. 10; KB 29/172, m. 31d; KB 29/173, m. 18d.

[45] John Caryon of London fled to Westminster following a homicide in July 1539; he was pardoned in the autumn of 1539. TNA, KB 9/544, m. 157; KB 9/548, mm 159–160; TNA, KB 27/1113, rex m. 6; KB 29/172, m. 23d. Three men took sanctuary at Beverley in 1539, but for debt. *SDSB*, pp 208, 209, 211.

fugitive from an aristocratic feud, Thomas Foteman, had remained in sanctuary at Westminster from 1537 until October 1539, despite his enemies' fervent entreaties that he be taken out to stand trial. Foteman apparently still found the sanctuary secure enough to stay through most of 1539. It is also notable that Cromwell apparently declined to seize Foteman, perhaps preferring not to get caught up in the particular quarrel in which he was implicated.[46]

There were, however, two other sanctuary breaches that made their way into the courts after the Mainwaring affair, in October and November 1539. These cases are recorded on the King's Bench roll in ways similar to the extraction of the Mainwaring retainers, suggesting that the Mainwaring case served as a kind of precedent.[47] Sanctuary was not yet impossible, as the cases cited just above show, but certainly it had become very risky, perhaps especially if in some way the case came to Cromwell's attention. In the first of these two cases, George Brewce of London, yeoman, was seized from sanctuary at the Hospitaller priory in Clerkenwell after apparently escaping custody. The justices considered his sanctuary plea for a few weeks, but then ruled it inadmissible and sentenced him to hang on the basis of a prior jury verdict on the felony.[48] The evidence for Cromwell's hand in the Brewce case is only circumstantial—the man who dragged Brewce from sanctuary was one of his clients[49]—but indications of his involvement in another case are clear. In early November 1539 Anthony Spencer, yeoman of London, took sanctuary at Westminster for homicide, but two weeks later, as he afterwards pleaded in court, the keeper of the sanctuary William Webbe violently seized him on Cromwell's orders and handed him over to stand trial. As in the case of George Brewce, the justices took his plea of sanctuary under advisement, but they did not quickly return with a judgment as they had with Brewce. Instead the case was passed from one term to the next while Spencer himself remained in custody, from 1540 until 1544.[50] Finally in the Easter term of 1544, Spencer appeared before the court again and once more pleaded sanctuary, and this time there was an about-face. William Whorwood, the same king's attorney as in the Cholmeley case in 1539,

---

[46] TNA, KB 9/541, m. 76; KB 27/1106, plea m. 21; KB 27/1123, plea m. 111; KB 29/172, m. 3d; Baker, *Spelman*, vol. 1, pp 62–3; TNA, SP 1/152, fol. 46; SP 1/154, fol. 53; *L&P*, vol. 14, pt. 1, p. 496; vol. 14, pt. 2, p. 145. The larger quarrel involved Sir John Bridges and Sir John Huddleston. M. M. Norris, 'Brydges, John, First Baron Chandos (1492–1557)', *ODNB* (2004), doi:10.1093/ref:odnb/3807; Sir John Huddleston was the father of the future MP of the same name, and there is some information about him in the latter's biography: D. F. Coros, 'Huddleston, Sir John (1517–57)', in *HPO*.

[47] In addition to the two 1539 cases discussed below, there was another sanctuary breach that year, this one in Surrey, when a husbandman named Thomas Tykmor claimed when arraigned that he had been seized from the parish church in Newdigate. His case was sent up to King's Bench, he was committed to the Marshalsea prison, and I have not been able to find any further records on his case. TNA, KB 9/547, mm 12–13; KB 29/173, mm 16, 22.

[48] TNA, KB 27/1113, rex m. 5; Baker, *Spelman*, vol. 2, pp 345–6 (intro).

[49] Roger Virgoe, 'Amadas, John (by 1489–1554/55)', in *HPO*. Note that Amadas himself had sought sanctuary in Tavistock Abbey in relation to a 1529 quarrel in his home county of Devon (although he may more literally have sought refuge from an attack in the abbey church rather than seeking the legal privilege of sanctuary); TNA, STAC 2/1, fol. 148.

[50] There is no indication on the controlment roll that he was bailed: TNA, KB 29/174, mm 31, 39.

took a directly opposite stance this time, and stated that Spencer's claim that he had been extracted against his will from sanctuary was absolutely true.[51] Spencer was thus returned to the Westminster sanctuary, which was, incidentally, still operational and in fact still had William Webbe as keeper. The coda to the story is that about two months later the king granted Anthony Spencer a pardon for the homicide.[52]

Spencer survived, I think, because of the timing of his case. Extracted in the fall of 1539, by the time his case came to trial in February 1540, Cromwell's own position had become shaky (culminating in his arrest in June and execution in July of that year). It is perhaps not surprising that in February 1540 the justices were reluctant to rule on a sanctuary plea made following a breach ordered by Thomas Cromwell. Putting off decisions until such time as Cromwell's position was clarified might have seemed like the right path. What remains unexplained is the long delay until 1544 before the case was decided, although perhaps nothing more lies behind that than Spencer's own difficulties lining up what he needed for his pardon, as such conclusions were achieved through the pulling of strings, words put in the right ears, and the gathering of resources to pay a fine.

The Mainwaring gang were not as fortunate as Anthony Spencer, primarily because the string-pulling and words-in-ears went against them rather than in their favour. Their trial was a political, rather than a legal, solution to the problem posed by Richard Cholmeley's murder: the escalation of the feud between the Mainwarings and Cholmeley threatened to destabilize the extension of royal authority in the former palatinate of Chester. This was nothing unprecedented: processes and verdicts were frequently manipulated in order to obtain results that suited those with the power to influence them. By 1539, however, Cromwell was willing to be more open about his determination to control the legal process to reach the verdict he needed than earlier in the decade, when such manoeuvres took place behind the scenes.[53] It would be a mistake, however, to assume that Cromwell's disregard for sanctuary was reflective of a more general and natural rejection of the privilege by those on the bench, or those in parliament. There were simply too many such men who—like Sir John Done—themselves had found sanctuary to be useful or even essential in extricating themselves or their servants from inconvenient felony charges.

---

[51] 'Et Willelmus Whorwod, generalis attorn' dicti domini Regis, qui pro ipso domino rege sequitur pro eodem domino rege super relacione et testimonio diversorum fidedignorum hic in Curia presencium, dicit quod ipse non potest dedicere quin predictus Antonius Spencer extractus fuit extra dictum sanctuarium Westm' contra voluntatem ipsius Antonii, modo et forma prout predictus Antonius superius placitando allegavit. Et placitum illud, quoad extraccionem illam, pro dicto domino rege cognovit fore verum. [... on the relation and testimony of many trustworthy men present in the court, he says that he cannot deny that the aforesaid Anthony Spencer was extracted from the aforesaid sanctuary of Westminster against his will, in the manner and form as Anthony, pleading above, alleged. And this plea, as touching the extraction, he recognizes, on behalf of the lord king, to be true]'. TNA, KB 27/1131, rex m. 6.

[52] TNA, C 66/741, m. 27; L&P, vol. 19, pt. 1, p. 636.

[53] This runs counter to the Eltonian view of Cromwell's period of power, which the great Tudor historian saw as an era of greater emphasis on the due process of law (see, e.g., *Policy and Police*, pp 374–5).

SANCTUARY AND ARISTOCRATIC VIOLENCE IN THE REIGN OF HENRY VIII

A certain sector of the English aristocracy during Henry VIII's reign regularly employed physical force, alongside lawsuits, flattery, offices, and cultivation of court contacts, in the progress of their careers. The chivalric culture of the landed elite demanded the masculine defence of honour, if necessary by violence.[54] Many aristocrats seem to have expected fights to break out whenever they went about their business; at least in the scenarios painted in indictments, even gentlemen going about their day 'in God's peace and the king's' always had swords with them. For instance, in the tale told in the coroner's inquest report on Ralph Holcroft's death, Sir John Done and his men were inside St Paul's Cathedral, having a discussion with one of the duke of Suffolk's men, with their swords. Thomas Holcroft and his men, also inside the church at the beginning of the story, also had swords and even shields with them. Thus when Holcroft flung down his cloak in challenge to Done on the steps outside the cathedral's south door, both were ready.[55] Sometimes, it was the aristocrats themselves who fought in affrays with one another, while at other times men of high station delegated the violent deeds to retainers lower down the sociopolitical ladder, as in the Mainwarings' alleged delegation of the Cholmeley killing to John Mainwaring, Jones, Potter, Edwards, and Griffith. In both scenarios, aristocratic feuds were facilitated by sanctuary and other legal and political mechanisms that insulated perpetrators of violence from the full force of legal prosecution and judicial execution to which they might otherwise be subject.

Amongst the aristocrats who took advantage of the availability of sanctuary were Richard Southwell, his brothers Robert and Anthony, and several other retainers who, as we saw at the beginning of this book, immediately sought the privilege of the Westminster sanctuary following their slaying of Sir William Pennington in 1532.[56] Sanctuary was essential in shielding Southwell and his companions from revenge, and the judicial process was managed so that the Southwells received pardons, after Southwell paid a large fine of £1000 (to be compared, incidentally, with Done's fine of 100 marks for Ralph Holcroft's death). In a technical sense, in fact, sanctuary at Westminster should have been barred to the Southwells, as the killing had taken place within the abbey precinct itself, but the political context undoubtedly affected the bending of the rules.[57] For Richard Southwell and his brothers

---

[54] See for explorations of these issues, Kaeuper, *Chivalry and Violence*; Mervyn James, *English Politics and the Concept of Honour 1485–1642* (Oxford, 1978).

[55] TNA, KB 9/545, mm 87–90.

[56] See above, Ch. 1 at n.1. This case is also discussed in more detail in McSheffrey, 'Slaying'.

[57] For obvious reasons one of the bars to the privilege of sanctuary was committing the felony inside the boundaries of the asylum. Helmholz, *Ius Commune*, pp 34, 51–6; Mazzinghi, *Sanctuaries*, p. 29. The abbot's grant of sanctuary privilege coupled with the lack of any legal challenge by the crown indicates that the abbot (who was closely tied to the king) must have been given the signal from the palace to bend the rules and grant the Southwells their request for the privilege. Although a number of others were indicted for homicides inside sanctuary boundaries, in none of the other cases is there any indication of a claim of the privilege within the same sanctuary, although in one case the accused felon fled to another sanctuary. For the latter, see TNA, KB 27/1107, rex m. 4; for examples of other cases of homicide within sanctuary precincts, see KB 9/327, m. 22; KB 9/353, m. 96; KB 9/417, m. 128; KB 9/467, m. 15; KB 27/1001, rex m. 1d; KB 27/1004, rex m. 15; KB 27/1023, rex m. 1.

their shelter in sanctuary was instrumental in escaping both revenge from the duke of Suffolk (who was enraged by the slaying of his man) and a swift legal process that might hang them before someone could intervene. The same was the case for other gentlemen in the 1530s. William Orrell of Yorkshire, for instance, abjured to Westminster sanctuary in 1532, after killing a merchant of Kingston upon Hull named John Lownde; after a stint at Westminster, Orrell was pardoned by the king.[58] Another gentleman, George Cornwall of Herefordshire, sought sanctuary at Westminster in March 1533 following his killing in London of John Ode alias Wode, a serjeant of the mace. Cornwall's road to freedom from the homicide charge was not as swift as most others but ultimately just as secure; he presented his pardon for the homicide at King's Bench in the fall of 1537 after an apparent delay in gathering the sureties he needed (which may well, as with Richard Southwell, have involved the payment of a fine), and he too was free to go.[59]

In some cases, as we have seen, lower-level henchmen performed the actual bloodshed in aristocratic quarrels, and they, too, fled to sanctuary, where they had to be supported by their patrons. A report on 'suspected persons' in various places around London compiled for Cardinal Wolsey in 1519, for instance, indicated that one Henry Hart in the Westminster sanctuary was 'in service with Master Knevet, and William Knevet and George Audelegh payeth for his board'.[60] The king himself had paid for the support of two sanctuary men in St Martin le Grand in the mid 1510s;[61] we can only guess at the services they provided to him.

The case of one Humphrey Eye demonstrates how sanctuary might function to persuade a lower-level member of a retinue to do the dirty deeds his lord wanted without undue risk to his own life. According to an unusually elaborate coroner's inquest report, on 23 March 1534 at five in the morning, Humphrey Eye, a yeoman of the Wiltshire manor of Stock near the town of Great Bedwyn, attacked a man named John Flory. He did so, the inquest found, at the behest of his master, Thomas Essex, a lawyer in his mid-twenties and only son of Tudor courtier and administrator Sir William Essex.[62] Why Essex wanted Flory dead, the jurors do not indicate. Early on the morning of 23 March, Eye shot Flory with a crossbow and a forked arrow (the Tudor equivalent of a hollowpoint bullet), giving him a wound that killed him instantly. After retrieving the arrow from the body (perhaps

---

[58] Lownde's widow appealed his murder, introducing legal conundrums about whether she could appeal an abjurer, and about how the pardon of the abjuration affected the appeal. TNA, KB 9/526, mm 79–80; KB 9/529, mm 57–58; KB 29/166, mm i, 36; KB 29/167, m. 26d; SP 1/238, fols 72–73; Baker, *Spelman*, vol. 1, pp 51, 167; vol. 2, pp 282–3.

[59] Cornwall's pardon was dated about a year after Ode's death, May 1534, but it was only in November 1537 that he was able to obtain the letters close from the king guaranteeing his future good behaviour, which likely had been contingent on his payment of a fine. TNA, KB 9/523, mm 105–106; KB 27/1087, plea m. 17; KB 27/1105, rex m. 2; KB 29/166, mm i, 1; SP 1/238, fols 72–73; SP 1/67, fol. 84 (*L&P*, vol. 5, p. 208).

[60] TNA, SP 1/18, fol. 254.

[61] See above, Ch. 5 at n.46.

[62] Baker, *Men of Court*, vol. 1, p. 645; T. F. T. Baker, 'Essex, Sir William (c. 1470–1548)', in *HPO*. On Stock, see Ralph B. Pugh, ed., *A History of the County of Wiltshire*, Victoria History of the Counties of England (London, 1956), vol. 16, pp 15–16. Property in Great Bedwyn (including the manor of Stock), as well as the manor of Littlecote, referenced below, was held in 1530s by Sir William Essex as part of a wardship (see Baker, 'Essex', in this note).

a messy business, given the fork in the arrowhead), Eye fled from the scene to Essex's manor house at Stock, where he washed the blood from the arrow, put the crossbow and the arrow back where they had been before he took them, had some food and drink, and set out to Berkshire to report to Essex that the deed was done. Upon hearing the news, Essex gave Eye an angel noble (a coin worth 7s 6d), and told him to go to a sanctuary, 'for his safety'; once he had established himself there, Eye was to send word to Essex telling him which sanctuary he had chosen, and Essex would send him more money. Eye made his way some 130 kilometres from Essex's house to the sanctuary of Bewdley in Shropshire, a voyage that must have taken him at least two days. There Eye remained, safe from arrest, protected by the jurisdictional immunities of the Bewdley sanctuary.[63] At a later trial, Thomas Essex, alleged procurer of the killing, was acquitted of the charge of accessory to homicide, and he went on with his successful and prosperous life. Humphrey Eye was outlawed, as he could not be found to face the charge of homicide on which he was indicted. We do not know what happened to him: he may have remained in the sanctuary at Bewdley, where law enforcement officials could not have taken him into custody, until the 1540s; he may have been arrested later and tried in a court for which the records do not survive; or he may simply have disappeared in the dead of night, adopting a new identity in another part of England or even abroad. If events unfolded more or less as the coroner's inquest report indicates, then Thomas Essex was able to procure the murder of the inconvenient John Flory, and Humphrey Eye was able to accomplish the killing, without significant penalty. Influence, connections, and legal know-how may have helped Essex escape justice; for his servant Humphrey Eye, sanctuary was key, even if he only used the safety of Bewdley's jurisdiction in order to gather thoughts and resources together to move on somewhere else.

That relative impunity for the landed elite, and for their henchmen, too, was a common outcome for those involved in aristocratic violence, thanks to sanctuary and other mechanisms that allowed the perpetrators not only to escape punishment but to continue in the progress of their careers. Sir John Done, as we have seen, suffered few after-effects of his indictment for homicide, being appointed as Justice of the Peace for Cheshire a scant three months after Ralph Holcroft's death, while the indictment was still pending. He went on to hold many other offices and perquisites. Ultimately Done was not even prosecuted on the indictment, and thus the lack of injury to his career might seem to reflect a judgment that he was neither morally nor legally culpable in Holcroft's killing. In fact, however, his coming through unscathed is also characteristic of other aristocrats whose guilt was acknowledged in court. For the Southwells, for Orrell, for Cornwall, and for others like them, a homicide indictment followed by a pardon (which acknowledged their guilt in the felony but nonetheless, by the king's grace, forgave the crime), was no encumbrance to future success, a success enabled by their stays in sanctuary. Their rehabilitation was, moreover, in most cases virtually immediate. Orrell, after his pardon, even successfully lobbied the king for recompense for the 'punishment of

---

[63] TNA, KB 9/529, m. 163; KB 27/1100, rex m. 1. On Bewdley, see above Ch. 4 at n.88.

his body' that he had suffered, as well as restoration of his properties and offices; he went on to further royal offices and positions, and by the 1540s he was a gentleman of the king's household.[64] George Cornwall similarly suffered no lasting impediment to his life course as prominent aristocrat: after his killing of John Ode, he went on to serve as MP for Herefordshire in 1539, sheriff for the county in 1547–1548 and 1559–1560, and justice of the peace from 1543; additionally he served the crown in a number of other capacities. He was knighted following the French campaign of 1544.[65] Richard Southwell was already a JP for Norfolk when, in his late twenties, he had his fatal encounter with Sir William Pennington. His name does not appear on the peace commission for Norfolk in 1533, presumably because of the homicide indictment that was pardoned in May of that year, but by the end of 1534 he had entirely regained his place amongst the county gentry, as he was appointed that year as sheriff of Norfolk and Suffolk.[66] Both he and his brother Robert Southwell went on from there to significant, and highly lucrative, careers in royal service. Cromwell appointed both Richard and Robert to positions as receivers in the court of Augmentations in 1536. Richard went on to be a privy councillor during the reigns of Edward VI and Mary, and Robert to be Master of the Rolls of Chancery. Both were also knighted in the 1540s.[67]

It is especially significant that for a number of these former sanctuary men the offices included appointments as sheriffs or justices of the peace, for in those capacities they were directly responsible for overseeing the arrests of felons, the judging of their cases, and their execution—and they did so as convicted (albeit pardoned) felons themselves. Far from being a disqualification for law enforcement or the bench, however, one suspects that such demonstrations of vigorous masculinity may have been a significant boon for the Henrician aristocrat-on-the-make. This may explain why Richard Southwell's Holbein portrait, painted in 1537, shows the scars on his neck and cheek so prominently; the scars could easily have been concealed had Southwell simply faced the other way. Southwell seems to have been proud of his battle wounds, and they may have been an advantage in the (sometimes literally) cut-throat politics of the day.[68]

Thus in the reigns of Henry VII and Henry VIII, at the same time as ecclesiastical holders of franchises were experimenting with offering their precincts as sanctuary for runaway felons as a way of confirming or extending their jurisdictions, aristocrats were looking for ways to shelter from felony indictments. The relationship between one particular gentry family and a monastery—the Raynsfords of Essex and St John's Abbey in Colchester—illustrates how those interests could come together. In February 1512, John Raynsford the younger and Maurice Gryffyn, along with a number of other men, were indicted as principals for the murder the month before of one John Burges of East Greenwich, within the

---

[64] *L&P*, vol. 6, pp 404, 428–9; vol. 11, p. 156; vol. 17, p. 262.
[65] A. J. Edwards, 'Cornwall, George (by 1509–1562)', in *HPO*.
[66] *L&P*, vol. 5, pp 78, 704; vol. 7, p. 558; Diarmaid MacCulloch, *Suffolk and the Tudors: Politics and Religion in an English County, 1500–1600* (Oxford, 1986), pp 409–10, 415.
[67] Lehmberg, 'Southwell, Sir Richard'; Baker, 'Southwell, Sir Robert'.
[68] See Ch. 1, figs 1.1 and 1.2 and n.7.

precinct around the king's palace there. Richard Cornwall, gentleman (1530s sanctuary seeker George Cornwall's father), and William Courtney, esquire, were indicted as accessories for having procured the murder.[69] The accused procurers, Cornwall and Courtney, were gentlemen who served the king in the usual official capacities and would later both serve in parliament and attain knighthoods.[70] Their alleged chief co-conspirator, John Raynsford, was similarly a gentleman of high birth; he was the son of a prominent Essex knight, Sir John Raynsford, knight of the body to Henry VIII and soon to be captain in Henry VIII's French wars of the 1510s. The younger Raynsford was born in the early 1480s, making him about thirty years old at the time, about the same age as Cornwall and Courtney.[71] The identity of the victim John Burges (beyond his name) and the motive for the homicide are not revealed in any records I have found.

Raynsford and his servant Maurice Gryffyn fled following Burges's murder to sanctuary at St John's Abbey in Colchester.[72] All the accused were pardoned in mid-1513.[73] The pardon was granted as forces were being mustered for an English offensive in France in August and September, during which the younger Raynsford served with the king's forces. His father, Sir John, was a captain of the English troops, and it seems that the pardon was timed to allow the son's participation.

Before the pardon, during the fifteen months or so Raynsford and Gryffyn were in sanctuary at St John's Abbey, both were implicated in another murder, allegations concerning which made their way into a series of Star Chamber suits.[74] The records concerning both murders suggest a pattern of influence and manipulation that helped men such as Raynsford, Courtney, and Cornwall escape from serious felony accusations with few lasting effects. Seeing felony up close from the perspectives of both felon and judge was in at least one, and perhaps two, of these men's cases a family affair—as we have seen, Richard Cornwall's son George would seek sanctuary following a homicide in the 1530s and himself go on to sit as JP and MP and so on; and Sir John Raynsford, father of the younger sanctuary-seeking Raynsford and long-established as a major figure in Essex political circles, was accused of covering up a murder committed by one of his servants and of uttering threats to prevent the servant's arrest (an accusation that he denied).[75]

We know about the homicide in the Colchester abbey sanctuary from a series of accusations made by the former bailiff of the sanctuary, Richard Vynes, who sued both John Raynsfords, father and son, in different but apparently interrelated Star Chamber suits. Both suits alleged that the Raynsfords had been able to escape any consequences for their involvement in multiple homicides, due to the influence in Essex of Sir John Raynsford.[76] Vynes's allegations about the homicide in sanctuary

---

[69] TNA, KB 9/458, mm 57–60.
[70] L. M. Kirk and A. D. K. Hawkyard, 'Courtenay, Sir William I (by 1485–1535)', and A. J. Edwards, 'Cornwall, Sir Richard (by 1480–1533)', in *HPO*; *L&P*, vol. 1, pt. 1, p. 549.
[71] D. F. Coros, 'Raynsford (Rainforth), Sir John (by 1482–1559)', in *HPO*.
[72] TNA, KB 9/458, mm 57–60; STAC 2/18/283.
[73] *L&P*, vol. 1, pt. 2, p. 967. [74] TNA, STAC, 2/18/294; STAC, 2/22/216.
[75] TNA, STAC, 2/18/283; 2/18/294.
[76] TNA, STAC 2/18/283, 2/18/294, 2/20/26, 2/20/100, 2/22/216; *CPR 1494–1509*, p. 639; Coros, 'Raynsford'.

tell a vivid story. While in their asylum, according to Vynes, John Raynsford and Maurice Gryffyn were a troublesome pair, constantly quarreling and 'us[ing] themselves in…affrays'. One day, Vynes said, Raynsford had a quarrel with another sanctuary man, Michael Brasebrigge. Brasebrigge was a military man and aristocratic retainer, having been most recently the servant of Sir Henry Marney (a cohort of John Raynsford's father, Sir John). He had taken the privilege for slaying a servant of George Talbot, earl of Shrewsbury and lord steward. Vynes alleged that Raynsford began to quarrel with Brasebrigge over a woman, and as the fight became violent Raynsford, Gryffyn, and one of Sir John Raynsford's servants visiting the precinct, Humphrey Lastell, joined forces to attack Brasebrigge. The fight ended when Gryffyn stabbed Brasebrigge in the back with his sword. Gryffyn immediately fled from St John's to another church in Colchester where he abjured; Lastell also fled to the same church, but escaped before the coroner came. Neither Raynsford nor Lastell, Vynes complained, had been indicted for the murder by a coroner or before the justices of the peace for Essex.[77] (Raynsford, for the record, denied in response that he had been anything but an innocent bystander to the homicide, attempting to keep the king's peace. He claimed, moreover, that Gryffyn had been driven to kill Brasebrigge by the latter's taunting and gloating over his unredeemed slaying of one of Gryffyn's kinsmen, in other words arguing in his submission to the court of Star Chamber that Gryffyn's act had been necessitated by honour.[78])

Vynes may have—as Raynsford's parliamentary biographer D. F. Coros assumed[79]—unfairly accused Raynsford of complicity in the murder of Michael Brasebrigge. Yet even what Raynsford admits (or fails to deny) in his Star Chamber submission suggests a number of interesting things about the Raynsfords and the sanctuary at St John's Abbey in Colchester. From other records we know that Raynsford's father Sir John had a longstanding family relationship with the abbey: in his will, he asked to be buried in the Lady Chapel, as his father had been before him, and made arrangements to continue his father's obit as well as his own.[80] Amongst the services the abbey rendered Sir John was the harbouring of those close to him who required asylum for felonies. This, of course, included his son, John, in sanctuary for the Greenwich homicide, but there were others as well. While in the sanctuary at St John's, John Raynsford was (again, by his own account) in the company of at least three other sanctuary seekers who had connections with him or his father: Raynsford's own servant Maurice Gryffyn, who had come to sanctuary with him fleeing from the same homicide indictment; Raynsford's servant William Baker,[81] who allegedly provided the sword that killed Brasebrigge;

---

[77] TNA, STAC 2/18/283.   [78] TNA, STAC 2/20/26, 2/20/100.
[79] Coros cites only some of the STAC depositions. Coros, 'Raynsford'.
[80] TNA, PROB 11/20/79.
[81] Although Vynes alleged that Baker was an 'unlawful retainer' of Sir John Raynsford, the younger Raynsford said Baker was Sir John's lawful servant, formerly keeper of Greenstead Park (TNA, STAC, 2/20/100), which was just outside Colchester and held by St John's Abbey; Sir John Raynsford may have administered the estate for the abbey, with Baker as his deputy. See n. 80 in this chapter on Raynsford's will, and William Page, ed., *A History of the County of Essex*, Victoria County Histories (London, 1907), vol. 9, pp 382–90.

and the victim Michael Brasebrigge, who had once been the servant of one of Sir John's great friends, Sir Henry Marney. In addition, Vynes also alleged Raynsford's tie to a fourth sanctuary man, 'Black Tom', a tailor who, Vynes claimed, had been in Raynsford's retinue and had both committed crimes on Raynsford's behalf in London and been shielded by Raynsford from prosecution for all of them. (Again, for the record, both Raynsfords denied that Black Tom had ever been in their service.)[82] And lastly, one of those involved in the affray who afterwards fled to a church in Colchester outside the abbey precinct following the homicide, Humphrey Lastell, was also a servant of Sir John Raynsford; he, the younger Raynsford indicates, was visiting the victim, Michael Brasebrigge, in the sanctuary when the skirmish broke out. Vynes complains in his submission that Raynsford and Gryffyn were violent and quarrelsome, difficult for him as bailiff of the sanctuary or for the abbot himself to control. Whether or not Vynes's allegations were just, this was neither the first nor the last such accusation against Raynsford; in another Star Chamber suit, neighbour Henry Wilcokkes accused him of being a dangerous man who delighted in violence and mayhem.[83]

This suggests a situation in the sanctuary in St John's Colchester that must have been difficult for the abbot, the monastic community, and the abbey's staff. The Raynsfords were great benefactors to the abbey, but they expected a good deal in return for their offerings. Like all the other examples we have examined, neither the Greenwich homicide, his time in sanctuary, nor the subsequent allegations regarding the death of Michael Brasebrigge proved obstacles to the younger Raynsford's subsequent career. Raynsford was knighted in 1523, and most years from then until his death in 1559 he served as Justice of the Peace for Essex. He sat as Member of Parliament in 1529, probably in 1536, and perhaps also 1539 and 1542.[84]

Aristocrats' employment of sanctuary as part of the suite of mechanisms that allowed men charged with felony to continue to serve the king, as well as themselves, was not a new thing in Henry VIII's reign. It must also be noted, however, that almost all evidence for the landed elite's employment of sanctuary for felony comes from the Tudor regime, especially from Henry VIII's reign. This probably does not so much reflect growing violence amongst aristocrats as it does an increased tendency for those violent acts to result in felony indictments. In the fifteenth century, aristocratic violence was rarely prosecuted as felony in the king's courts, instead being handled through arbitration and litigation; felony prosecutions, conducted by those same aristocrats as sheriffs and justices of the peace, were for the lower orders.[85] This virtual immunity from prosecution allowed for the sublimation of the paradoxes inherent in aristocratic governance, that on the one hand acts of violence were imperative to maintain power and authority, and on the other such acts of violence were in theory liable to prosecution as capital offences. If this may seem a contradiction to us, Christine Carpenter and Philippa Maddern

---

[82] TNA, STAC 2/18/283, 2/20/26, 2/20/100.
[83] Coros, 'Raynsford'.   [84] Coros, 'Raynsford'.
[85] Carpenter, 'Law, Justice and Landowners'; Powell, *Kingship, Law, and Society*, pp 40–3; Maddern, *Violence and Social Order*, pp 34–50, 74–110, 231–2.

have emphasized how well aristocratic violence dovetailed with the lawkeeping roles of the landed elite: the line between violence as self-interest and violence in the name of the king was a fine one.[86] The growing importance by the end of the fifteenth century of using the prosecution of crime to demonstrate royal power, however, created a point of tension.[87] Aristocratic power politics still required the demonstration of honour, which in turn required the use of violence. Royal justice, by contrast, required the prosecution of felony, even (or perhaps especially) when committed by the landed elite. Yet both the Tudor kings' sharing of the assumptions of the chivalric culture of honour (especially with Henry VIII) and their pragmatic political dependence on the landed elite in the exercise of their own power meant that it was generally inconvenient, for the king as well as the killers, for aristocratic affrays to end in execution; indeed, it was arguably injurious to the political stability of the realm. This is one significant reason why the importance of mitigations for capital punishments—sanctuary, benefit of clergy, pardon—grew in the later fifteenth century, as they represented a solution to this conundrum: the felony could be prosecuted, but the felon need not be hanged. Although those mitigations were by no means entirely confined to the aristocracy, they worked best for those who were connected and wealthy, and it is likely precisely because of the usefulness of the mitigations for the landed elite that they flourished.

Violence remained a way of life for aristocrats in Henry VIII's England, and sanctuary was an important means by which the landed elite was able to escape the full force of the king's capital penalties for felony. If we no longer assume that politics in late medieval and early modern England was always and only about king and court, it nonetheless remains indisputable that the landed elite remained immensely powerful. The workings of power and influence amongst aristocrats depended both on the performance of honour—which necessitated at times the use of violence—and on interactions with the bureaucratic state, including its law enforcement arm. This was true in the fifteenth century, as scholars of that period have emphasized,[88] and the emphasis on honour with the concomitant necessity of violence evolved rather than abruptly ceased in the sixteenth century.[89] The relationship of these complicated and sometimes countervailing streams of power and governance to law was not a simple one: at the same time as the legal processes developed through the intersection of particular contingencies of interests (jurisdiction-expanding religious houses and mitigation-seeking violent aristocrats, for instance), they also rested upon a rhetorically powerful framework of tradition and precedent. That framework was, however, flexible rather than rigid, allowing legal, political, and cultural ideas to adjust to circumstances.

---

[86] Carpenter, 'Law, Justice and Landowners', p. 216; Maddern, *Violence and Social Order*, pp 11–13, 227–8.

[87] Williams, *Tudor Regime*, pp 219–35, notes the tension, but does not discuss mitigations as a solution.

[88] Carpenter, 'Law, Justice and Landowners', esp. pp 225–6; Powell, *Kingship, Law, and Society*, esp. pp 19–20, 42–3; Maddern, *Violence and Social Order*, esp. pp 69–72, 74, 110.

[89] See especially James, *English Politics*; John A. Guy, 'Tudor Monarchy and Political Culture', in *The Oxford Illustrated History of Tudor and Stuart Britain*, ed. John S. Morrill (Oxford, 1996), pp 219–38; Brooks, *Law, Politics and Society*, pp 278–86.

Sanctuary both rested on ancient traditions of Christian succour for the unfortunate and adapted in response to particular and ever-changing political and cultural realities in fifteenth- and sixteenth-century England. Key to its successful adaptation was the service it provided to the politically powerful. Scholars have tended to imagine the sanctuary-seeker as a 'common criminal', a marginal person largely outside the realm of 'political society'; and in some cases this must have been roughly true. A truly marginal criminal, however, would rarely have found especially the chartered sanctuaries their best refuge from the noose, as it would not be possible to remain very long in a sanctuary without some kind of outside means of support. Sanctuary in fact worked best for those who were connected to men of high influence, the men at the very heart of the realm's power structures; for many of them violence, often accomplished by members of retinues, was an inescapable accompaniment of political rivalries. Sanctuary-seeking benefited not just the grasping abbots and small-time criminals on which the early twentieth-century historians focused, but also the political decision-makers of late medieval and Tudor England.

8

Conclusions
Sanctuary, Law, and Politics

The pattern of sanctuary-seeking in the middle years of Henry VIII's reign indicates that sanctuary had not only survived but was evidently expanding. It was not doing so as an anachronism: English sanctuary in 1535 was not the sanctuary of 1300, 1400, or 1450. As I have argued in the previous chapters, the practice of sanctuary evolved over the fifteenth and sixteenth centuries, in concert with and in relation to ideologies of Christianity and kingship, legal processes, jurisdiction, and felons' use of the privilege. Sanctuary had long roots in the traditions of Christianity and western law, and in the twelfth and thirteenth centuries became embedded as a form of judicial exile in the English law of felony. In the century following the Black Death, however, relatively few people sought sanctuary. If the years around 1400 saw perhaps the lowest numbers of sanctuary seekers in England in the medieval common law era, that was nonetheless the origin point for a new form of sanctuary in England. The chartered sanctuary, an asylum unlimited in time based in the precincts of religious houses, probably most precociously at Westminster and St Martin le Grand, was born out of new ways of thinking about jurisdiction, territoriality, and the sacrality of ecclesiastical space.

Relatively little evidence survives for either traditional abjuration or this new mechanism of permanent sanctuary in the first half of the fifteenth century, because low rates of felony prosecution and conviction meant that few needed the protection of sanctuary. With the political turmoil of the civil wars of the mid-fifteenth century, however, the chartered sanctuaries in particular became entrenched in English culture and politics as refuges from conflict and tyranny. From the 1480s, coinciding with the Tudor accession, records of felons seeking sanctuary became more numerous and reached their apogee in the decade between 1525 and 1535. This half century of expansion, by the end of which sanctuary seemed well embedded indeed in the processes of English felony prosecution, very suddenly ceased, the numbers of seekers in the records falling steeply from 1535 and becoming a small trickle by mid-1540s. Both chartered sanctuary and the more traditional abjuration from parish churches had come to flourish in the early Tudor regime because of a particular coalescence of interests: the emphasis on redemption and mercy in contemporary English Christianity; the ambitions of jurisdiction-expanding religious houses; the embedding of sanctuary into local interests through its integration into the economy of Tudor office-holding and perquisites; the widespread conviction that the draconian English law of felony needed tempering, especially for high-status offenders; continued distrust of the legal system; and a crown that found it more convenient than not to support sanctuary, for all of those reasons.

While clearly the practice of sanctuary drew power from the ideology that underpinned it, the ideology also in turn gained force from the way sanctuary manifested the power of God's mercy and the claims both of ecclesiastical institutions and the crown as the vehicles through which those divine qualities were exercised. More pragmatic issues intersected with that ideology: sanctuary rights became one of the means by which religious houses made claims to broader jurisdictional powers, including other seemingly unrelated economic rights to hold markets or allow unguilded tradesmen to manufacture and sell at retail. Conversely, urban governments seeking to expand their own jurisdictions and to curtail the independent corporate entities in their areas, especially religious houses, seized upon arguments that sanctuary encouraged crime as an oblique way of attacking the economic rights the liberties in their regions possessed.

Amongst the developments over the period between 1400 and the 1530s was a shift in the rhetoric of sanctuary-seeking: through the fifteenth century, sanctuary seekers and those who supported their rights emphasized the 'tuition and protection of Holy Church' and the ancient and universal Christian basis of their claims.[1] In the 1530s, by contrast, sanctuary-seekers invoked their claim to 'the *king's* privilege' of sanctuary, emphasizing its foundation in royal grants and royal mercy.[2] If rhetorically the idea of sanctuary had come to depend less on appeals to a universal Christian principle and more on its foundation in a specifically English Christian monarchy, in more practical ways it had also moved away from its clerical and ecclesiastical roots. Most strikingly, the administration of the sanctuaries in the reign of Henry VIII had become laicized. In the few cases from the fifteenth century where we can unravel the internal governance of sanctuaries, it was, not surprisingly, abbots and deans, monk-bailiffs, and collegiate church canons, who administered the sanctuaries, as we saw in Chapter 3. By contrast in the 1530s, as shown by the examples of St Martin le Grand and Knowle explored in Chapters 5 and 6, it was laymen who performed virtually all the administrative functions associated with receiving and regulating the sanctuary-seekers. Sanctuary administration had moved with the times. Government bureaucracy—and paragovernmental bureaucracies such as ecclesiastical institutions and aristocratic estate management—had seen a significant shift in personnel between 1400 and the reign of Henry VIII; not only had changes in education of male elites deprived the clergy of their monopoly of posts requiring advanced literacy, but larger institutions such as religious houses seem increasingly to have moved to a model of contracting out management of properties and services to laymen rather than performing them in-house. This meant that the administration of sanctuaries entered into the larger realm of offices and perquisites from which many Tudor men of middling and elite status made at least part of their living.

---

[1] A few examples: TNA, KB 9/201/4, m. 12; KB 9/297, m. 3; KB 9/408, m. 24; KB 27/986, rex m. 6; C 1/226/44.
[2] See, for instance, TNA, KB 27/1112, rex m. 9; SP 1/130, fol. 179r.

Another key factor in sanctuary's success in the early Tudor era was its functional utility for a particular population, the aristocracy. Many of the decision-makers at the royal court, in the law courts, and in parliament—including not only the county gentry who sat as Justices of the Peace at peace sessions and gaol delivery, but also the professional judges—would have known men who had taken sanctuary, and (excluding here the professional judges) might themselves have employed it in their own or their retainers' entanglements with felony indictments. Not all those in positions of power and influence regarded sanctuary positively: urban elites may not have been unanimously hostile towards sanctuary (some employed the safety of the sanctuaries as debtors), but certainly the predominant mood amongst civic leaders was anti-sanctuary, particularly in relation to felony. This reflected not only the jurisdictional challenges sanctuaries posed to urban corporations, but also the different valences of bourgeois and aristocratic elite cultures: if the prevalence of violence as a tool in aristocratic strategies conditioned the landed elites to find sanctuary useful (and for some indispensable), bourgeois culture—where competition took commercial rather than martial form—made merchants much less likely to need a shelter to protect them from a homicide conviction. Thus the religious houses whose precincts served as sanctuaries were opposed by civic governments, but found alliances and support amongst the aristocracy. In some cases that alliance was close indeed: for instance, as we saw in Chapter 6, the Raynsfords, a leading Essex gentry family, had a close relationship with St John's Abbey in Colchester over several generations, which not only involved substantial financial donations to the abbey and a close relationship with the abbot, but the sheltering of the Raynsford heir and a number of retainers who needed asylum while a pardon was pursued to wipe out an indictment for homicide. It was handy to have a sanctuary in one's pocket.

Seen from this angle—sanctuaries as tools useful, not least to men of the elite, for mitigating the harsh capital penalties of English law of felony; sanctuaries as underscoring the merciful nature of the king's justice and as royally-granted bulwarks against over-reaching civic leaders and other subjects needing a reminder who held the real power; sanctuaries as institutions increasingly integrated into the complex world of Tudor office-holding—it is possible to imagine that sanctuaries could have evolved further towards secularization. As such, sanctuary could have developed into an incarceration system, where felons who qualified for the mitigation were held indefinitely or for a period of time as an alternative to hanging. It might, in other words, have gone the same way as benefit of clergy, a once-ecclesiastical right turned into an entirely common law mechanism of mitigation of capital penalties, only very loosely related to its earlier medieval origins. But it did not.

THE STATUTE OF 1540 AND SANCTUARY'S PRECIPITOUS DECLINE

Sanctuary for felony virtually (if not entirely) ceased in the 1540s. As multivalent as the forces contributing to its success were, sanctuary was vulnerable: it was a house of cards, liable to collapse if one of the cards was pulled out. And that is precisely what happened: the closing of religious houses in England as a key part of the English Reformation robbed the sanctuary system of its infrastructural underpinnings. Although in many ways sanctuary-seeking had evolved to respond to the new circumstances of Tudor England in 1530, it had evolved always with a fundamental dependency on the religious house as its institutional base. This was not so much the actual physical infrastructure of the religious house and its precinct, as the example of Knowle shows: a manorial town with a distant relationship with an ecclesiastical institution would do. But the success of such a derivation of the concept would depend, at least in the form sanctuary had taken by the 1530s, on a franchisal economy that encouraged local men to participate. With the dissolution of the monasteries and the dispersal of their franchises, sanctuary was lost in the shuffle.

It might have gone a different way. A 1540 statute, 32 Hen. VIII, c. 12, 'Concerning Sanctuaries', attempted to provide an alternative basis for the privilege.[3] The preamble to the statute, to be sure, decried the 'idle and evil-disposed persons' whose 'great sundry and detestable murders, robberies, as also other great and heinous offences' were encouraged by the refuge offered to such malefactors by the 'licentious privileges' of sanctuaries. It also declared, however, that the king did not wish for the 'utter abolishing [and] extinguishment of all sanctuaries and the privileges of the same', since they were 'very expedient and convenient to be had and continued in every common wealth by the laws of mercy for some causes and offences'.[4]

By the provisions of the statute, forty-day sanctuary in parish churches and churchyards was to remain intact in accordance with the 1531 statute, whereby abjurers were to proceed to chartered sanctuaries following their oath to the coroner. Sanctuary seekers, as before, could also directly proceed themselves to a sanctuary to seek the privilege. The chartered sanctuaries, however, were no longer to be associated with the now-dissolved religious houses, and instead were to be replaced by eight sanctuary towns scattered throughout the realm, at Wells, Westminster, Manchester, Northampton, Norwich, York, Derby, and Launceston. The only one of these that had a prior history with sanctuary was, notably, Westminster, although it was now the town, rather than the abbey per se, which was to host the sanctuary precinct (although it seems highly likely that the location of the sanctuary remained in the close around the abbey church).[5] The removal of sanctuary from association with religious houses and its roots in specifically ecclesiastical immunity appears as a secularization of the privilege, but it is also worth noting that the sanctuary towns had an Old Testament precedent: Thomas de' Mazzinghi pointed out in the nineteenth century that the statute reflected the Old Testament cities of refuge Moses

---

[3] *SR*, vol. 3, pp 756–8; McGlynn, 'Use and Abuse'.   [4] *SR*, vol. 3, pp 756–8.
[5] Westminster Abbey was dissolved 16 Jan. 1540, but it may be better to say that it was converted rather than dismantled, as on 17 Dec. 1540 it became the cathedral church of a new (short-lived) diocese of Westminster. The quondam abbot became the dean of the cathedral chapter; some of the monks became canons. The keeper of the sanctuary, William Webbe, remained in that position until at least 1544. There is no precise indication that I have found about where the sanctuary was located, but later indications that continued to tie it to the administration of the former abbey suggest that it remained in the same place.

designated, where those who unintentionally killed their neighbours could seek asylum without fear of reprisal.[6] Each of the sanctuary towns was to have no more than twenty privileged persons; if that number had already been reached when a new arrival sought refuge, that sanctuary seeker's request was to be recorded in the sanctuary town's register and the seeker sent onwards, in the custody of constables, to another of the sanctuary towns. Those already in the former chartered sanctuaries were to retain their privilege and could continue to live there for the terms of their lives if they wished.

Another important change the statute brought was in the offences for which sanctuary could be sought. Perhaps in imitation of the Mosaic law that restricted the Old Testament refuges to those who had committed manslaughter, by the 1540 statute the privilege of sanctuary was henceforth not to be available for the most serious felonies: those who had committed intentional murder, ravishment of women, burglary, robbery of a house in which the owner and his household were put in fear of their lives, arson of houses and corn barns, and robbery of churches were all to be barred. This was a significant tightening of restrictions for entry to sanctuary and indeed a shift away from the notion that no sin was too heinous to be redeemed; henceforth mercy was to be shown only to certain kinds of felons.

These were not wholly novel distinctions, however, especially for homicide; through the later medieval period jurors, lawyers, judges, and felons themselves used different categories of killing to denote variable levels of culpability and thus excusability. Self-defence killings had long been pardonable, for instance. The extent of premeditation and intention were also held to be important in describing homicides in late medieval indictments and other legal records, albeit in somewhat imprecise ways. The first statute to make a formal distinction between premeditated murder and a killing by 'chance medley' or manslaughter was in fact one of the early sanctuary statutes, that of 1530.[7] A homicide by 'chance medley' was a killing in hot blood, where a man (and this was an almost paradigmatically masculine form of homicide) slew another in response to provocation or spontaneous rage.[8] Many homicides—including, importantly, those that arose from quarrels between gentlemen—fit the category of chance medley, and indeed even before the statutory definition, many sanctuary seekers at least claimed that the homicides they had perpetrated had come about spontaneously and in the heat of a quarrel, rather than through 'prepensed malice' as the contemporary records put it. In the only extended set of records where the felons themselves described their own offences, the Durham sanctuary register, more than half those who sought sanctuary in the sixteenth century explicitly claimed that they had responded in self-defence or to provocation, or that they had killed accidentally; presumably many more (if asked) would have described the homicide as chance medley, the spontaneous expression of violence

---

[6] Deut. 4:43; Mazzinghi, *Sanctuaries*, pp 84–6.

[7] By the 1530 statute, seekers could only claim sanctuary a second time for a homicide if that killing was a 'manslaughter by chance-medley', implying that they could not have it for a premeditated murder. 22 Hen. VIII, c. 14; *SR*, vol. 3, p. 334.

[8] Bellamy, *Criminal Trial*, pp 60–6; Baker, *Oxford History, 1483–1558*, pp 553–62; Walker, *Crime*, pp 113–58; Kesselring, 'Bodies of Evidence'.

arising from hot-blooded rage. Notably, none explicitly confessed to having committed a premeditated, cold-blooded murder.[9] In other words, at least by their own self-presentation (obviously very biased), many sanctuary seekers before 1540 would likely have fit the requirements of the statute. (This is a hypothetical, given that, as we will see, the 1540 statute's provisions were never fully implemented, and thus we have little sense of how the limitations on felonies would have affected them.)

The 1540 statute thus did not in itself dismantle sanctuary per se and arguably nor did it drastically decrease the numbers of those who would have been eligible for it. Although the 1540 statute has sometimes been seen as the culmination of Thomas Cromwell's campaign for the 'utter destruction of Sanctuaries'[10] (as he put it on a to-do list in 1536), it did not actually seek to destroy the privilege. Indeed, given Cromwell's own extremely shaky position at the point when the bill passed through parliament—the bill was given its three readings in the House of Lords between 3 and 7 June, and Cromwell was arrested and charged with treason on 10 June—this was not likely to have been a 'Cromwellian' bill and it certainly does not seem to have been in accord with his views.[11] As the landed aristocracy made up a significant proportion of parliamentarians, they might well have been resistant to any plans Cromwell might have had to dismantle the privilege altogether. Indeed, at least four former sanctuary seekers were amongst the MPs in the House of Commons for the parliament of 1539–1540: Richard Southwell, Robert Southwell, George Cornwall, and (likely) John Raynsford. In addition, other MPs had seen those close to them employ sanctuary effectively, as for instance Sir John Daunce, who had been closely involved in a mid-1530s homicide case for which one of his servants, Henry Andrew, sought sanctuary before Andrew was pardoned.[12] The statute that was passed certainly significantly modified but by no means demolished sanctuary, and it is significant that the kinds of homicides for which the landed elite tended to need sanctuary—those that came about spontaneously in the midst of a swordfight—were still available for the privilege.

---

[9] Of 166 men who claimed sanctuary at Durham for homicide between 1500 and 1524 (when the records break off), 91 claimed some lesser degree of culpability (it was self-defence, the seeker had responded to an attack, the death was unintentional, etc.). For 75 of the cases, the extent of premeditation was not stated: the homicides could have been the result of spontaneous encounters or of planned ambushes. Entirely missing is the term 'murder' and the language of 'precogitated malice' and 'lying in wait' that peppers indictments of this same period when the jurors intended to convey that the homicides were planned and intentional. See McSheffrey, 'Sanctuary Seekers', and *SDSB*, pp 32–90.

[10] TNA, SP 1/102, fol. 5v; *L&P*, vol. 10, p. 93. Somewhat more ambiguously (although arguably meaning the same thing) he similarly wrote himself a note in 1540: 'For a determynatyon of the Saintwaries'. BL, Cotton Titus MS B I, fol. 476; *L&P*, vol. 15, p. 180. For the view that the 1540 statute was the culmination of these ambitions, see Baker, *Spelman*, vol. 2, p. 346 (intro).

[11] The bill received royal assent on 24 Jul. 1540. *Journal of the House of Lords, vol. 1, 1509–1577* (London: HMSO, 1767), pp 141–2, 161–3; Howard Leithead, 'Cromwell, Thomas, Earl of Essex', *ODNB* (2004), doi:10.1093/ref:odnb/6769. 'Cromwellian' is Baker's term for the act. Baker, *Spelman*, vol. 2, p. 346 (intro). G. R. Elton thought that an original bill Cromwell had presented was modified by the Commons in parliament. G. R. Elton, *Reform and Renewal: Thomas Cromwell and the Common Weal* (Cambridge, 1973), p. 138.

[12] See the MPs' biographies in *HPO*, and McSheffrey, 'Sanctuary Seekers' for details of their sanctuary seeking.

The act mandated commissions to establish boundaries and other details for the operations of these new sanctuaries. In February 1541, about six months after the statute was enacted, letters patent were sent to commissioners for each of the proposed sanctuary towns, requiring them to designate 'such places within the towns...as might be convenient for twenty sanctuary men, the least noisome and incommodious for the said towns'.[13] For two of the towns, some of the work of those commissioners survives. At Norwich, Robert Leche, the mayor, along with Sir Roger Townesend, Sir William Paston, and Robert Townesend, serjeant at law, met and submitted to the king a large parchment map of the city which must have been rather beautiful when it was made but which is now sadly faded and damaged. The map shows a green line demarcating an area encompassing the church of St Stephen and a small neighbourhood of tenements between St Stephen's and the church of St Peter Mancroft. A similar map also survives for the city of York, which indicates a complicated zig-zag outline of an area lying between St Helen's and St Sampson's parish churches, both of which were included within the proposed sanctuary boundaries.[14]

Not everyone was happy with the new plan for sanctuary towns, in at least some cases the designated towns themselves. Manchester vociferously protested in 1542 that harbouring sanctuary seekers was injurious to its cloth industry, as the sanctuary men were by their idleness leading servants and workers astray. Chester was thus substituted for Manchester, but then Chester promptly protested and was replaced by Stafford.[15] It is possible that none of the new sanctuary towns, perhaps with the exception of Westminster, wanted the status imposed upon them. The new statute had, in fact, placed the new sanctuaries in precisely the milieu where they were most likely to be resented, in larger towns and cities. The urban governments charged with administering and implementing the new system had long found sanctuaries an infringement of their franchises and were likely not at all inclined to be cooperative. The planned new sanctuaries would have been a burden to them and they must have viewed the plan as yet another attempt to carve out a geographical chunk of their jurisdiction. As civic authorities were the most vocal and active opponents of sanctuary, the plan to situate these new secular sanctuaries in the midst of towns was a poor one if the system's designers actually wanted it to work. We do not, of course, know whether they actually did want it to work, whether the placement in towns was intentional sabotage or unthinking ignorance on the part of the MPs, royal councillors, and civil servants behind the new plan. On the whole, incompetence is the more likely answer. It is improbable that the statute's rather elaborate provisions were specifically designed to fail; had the king

---

[13] Nicolas, *Proceedings*, vol. 7, pp 134–5.
[14] TNA, MPI 1/221; MPB, 1/49/1 and/2. On these, see brief discussion in P. D. A. Harvey, *Maps in Tudor England* (Chicago, 1993), pp 68–9. As Harvey notes, the York civic records indicate payment to the 'hermit of the King's Manor' for the making of the map; Angelo Raine, ed., *York Civic Records*, Yorkshire Archaeological Society, 8 vols (Wakefield, 1939–1953), vol. 4, p. 63; Harvey, *Maps in Tudor England*, p. 68.
[15] 33 Hen. VIII, c. 15, *SR*, vol. 3, pp 850–951; Hughes and Larkin, *Tudor Royal Proclamations*, vol. 1, pp 311–13; Chester Archives and Local Studies Service, MS ZA/B/1/75, Chester Assembly Book I, fol. 75.

and parliament wished for sanctuary to be fully abolished in the 1540 statute, then surely it would have been more straightforward simply to enact abolition.

We know that ultimately the new plan did not become fully operational, but we are in the dark about precisely how thoroughly it failed. Evidence of resort to these sanctuary towns is scanty, yet not altogether absent. Manchester's complaint to parliament suggests that 'sundry' malefactors—and by implication of the statute's provisions for removal of the sanctuary seekers, perhaps its full complement of twenty—had sought refuge in the town during the year in which it had been in operation. More oblique evidence for its continued operation comes from a statute in Edward VI's first parliament which slightly changed the list of felonies excluded from sanctuary (adding horse theft),[16] a measure that it seems unlikely would have been undertaken had the privilege been thoroughly moribund. Yet we do not know how often the new system was employed, as few seekers after 1540 have individually left marks on surviving records. Evidence is most plentiful for Westminster, where records indicate that as late as the reign of Mary, the precinct hosted sanctuary seekers, although those records clump into two periods, the early 1540s, and 1556–1557, suggesting that the later evidence indicates a revival rather than continuous employment.[17] As David Loades has noted, the later records were generated closely following, and in some cases directly deriving from, the Marian revival of Westminster Abbey as a monastic establishment under Abbot Feckenham. The abbot, like his predecessors, evidently saw the exercise of the traditional sanctuary privileges as an important demonstration of the abbey's rights and immunities.[18] Even after Mary's reign, the sanctuary appears to have continued to function for about a half century or so, although exactly in what sense is unclear, except that there is no direct evidence it was used other than for debt.[19]

Evidence is even less visible for the other new sanctuaries, for which I have found only two records of felons seeking asylum, both in the early 1540s. In 1541 William Cripps, a fisher from Rye, Sussex, took sanctuary in the parish church of Bledlow, Buckinghamshire; after admitting to the coroner that he had stolen a horse in Oxfordshire, he was branded, assigned the 'liberty of the City of Norwich', and given a cross to hold in his right hand 'as is the law and custom of England'.[20] In 1542, William Arthur, a weaver, took to the parish church of Culmington in Shropshire, also for horse theft; the coroner who took his confession reported that Arthur 'following the form of the statute issued and provided in such a case chose

---

[16] 1 Edw. VI, c. 12 and reiterated in 2 & 3 Edw. VI, c. 33; *SR*, vol. 4, pp 20–1, 74.

[17] Westminster sanctuary seekers in the early 1540s: Robert Mere, 1541; Robert Whitfeld alias Johnson, 1541; Thomas Sybbell, 1542. Apart from the evidence for Anthony Spencer, apparently still in sanctuary at Westminster in 1544 (see Ch. 7 at n.50), the other Westminster sanctuary seekers came from the reign of Mary: a debtor who allegedly sought sanctuary about 1554 (TNA, C 1/1369/71), and eight men who were said to have been in sanctuary for felony or escape from custody at Westminster in 1556 and 1557. See McSheffrey, 'Sanctuary Seekers', for details and references on the cases from the 1540s and 1550s.

[18] Loades, 'The Sanctuary', 82–92.   [19] Loades, 'The Sanctuary', 92–3.

[20] 'Et assignavi prefatum Willelmum suo concensu ad libertatem civitatis Norwic' in comitatu Norff', et cruce in sua dextera manu posita, prout lex est Anglie et consuetudo'. TNA, KB 9/550, m. 52; see also KB 29/174, m. 31.

for himself the sanctuary and privilege of the town of Wells'.[21] With the exception of the flurry of references to sanctuary at Westminster in 1556–1557 during Mary's reign, almost nothing clear survives thereafter regarding resort to sanctuary for felony.

It was not until the reign of James, however, that sanctuary was officially abolished by statute: first in 1603, in James's first parliament, all the statutory provisions regarding sanctuary and abjuration were repealed, and then in 1624, all privilege of sanctuary for felony, statutory and non-statutory, was disallowed.[22] Yet certain liberties, especially attached to the sites of former religious houses, such as Whitefriars or Alsatia in London, continued to exercise jurisdictional immunities. Although debtors fleeing from prosecution and imprisonment were the main refugees, as in the medieval period the fuzzy lines between debt and criminality gave these sites—still often called 'sanctuaries'—some of the same valences as medieval asylums for felony.[23]

SANCTUARY, LAW, AND POLITICS IN ENGLAND, 1400–1550

The law of sanctuary in practice was a complicated and sometimes internally contradictory amalgam of ad hoc application on the one hand and strict adherence to arcane rules on the other. Idiosyncrasies, contingencies, and inconsistency marked its handling and use in some cases, while the application of precise rules and procedures, checklists of technical requirements, or literal observance of particular boundaries or touching of walls were at other points crucial factors. In one situation a particular space could be judicially declared not to be a sanctuary, while in another later ruling, that same space might be successfully employed as sanctuary and even recognized as such by the courts. In other words, the practice of sanctuary in England was neither systematic nor neatly defined in law, even though it was unquestionably a legal, rather than extra-legal, mechanism, and many different kinds of laws, rules, and regulations shaped how it could be used. Sanctuary was formed in the broad contexts of Christian religion, English felony prosecution, struggles over jurisdiction, and fears about tyranny and corruption; and it was shaped by the individual particularities of contingent circumstances, through the choices made by individuals—felons themselves, their patrons, the administrators of sanctuaries, and the functionaries of the legal system (sheriffs, coroners, jurors, judges). A sanctuary seeker made a choice to claim the privilege of the church, and others allowed him or her to make that choice, conditioned by the larger cultural framework of law, religion, and politics. For the seeker it was always an uncertain

---

[21] 'Predictus Willelmus secundum formam statuti in tali casue [sic] edito et proviso, abjuravit se et sanctuarium et privilegio [sic] ville de Wellys se elegit'. TNA, KB 9/554, m. 90; TNA, KB 29/176, m. 3d.

[22] 1 Jas. I, c. 25 and 21 Jas. I, c. 28, *SR*, 4:1051, 1237.

[23] Mazzinghi, *Sanctuaries*, pp 21–2; Levin, 'Alsatia'; James R. Hertzler, 'The Abuse and Outlawing of Sanctuary for Debt in Seventeenth-Century England', *The Historical Journal* 14 (1971): pp 467–77, doi:10.1017/S0018246X00007512; Stirk, 'Arresting Ambiguity'.

option, at some times more so than others: he or she could not know in advance whether the privilege would work, and thus to a greater or lesser extent it was always a risk (whether it was a *calculated* risk no doubt depended on the seeker). Yet each of those times when sanctuary was taken, the privilege became more and more embedded in the structures of the law—until, quite suddenly, it wasn't, as the framework that had supported the seeking of sanctuary collapsed like a house of cards.

Sanctuary's fundamental untidiness—the contingency of its application; the susceptibility to influence and favour; the disagreement and confusion about what rules and procedures should apply; the evolution in its boundaries (both literal and figurative) in response to changes in politics, law, and religion; its evident fragility—was not unique to this somewhat anomalous and boundary-crossing legal practice. It was in fact broadly characteristic of law and legal processes generally in this period. To understand late medieval and early modern law, we must allow for contradiction and inconsistency, for unevenness and variegation, for flexibility and pragmatism rather than strict interpretations.[24] This is not to discount the importance of law and legal thinking in late medieval and early modern culture, but instead to acknowledge how deeply embedded law was in the messiness of human life itself.

---

[24] Carpenter, 'Law, Justice and Landowners', 212; Brooks, *Law, Politics and Society*, 20; Benton, *Search for Sovereignty*, 30–2; Johnson, 'Law, Space, and Local Knowledge', 34–6.

Bibliography

ARCHIVAL SOURCES

Chester, Cheshire Archives and Local Studies Service
  MS ZA/B/1/75, Chester Assembly Book I
Kew, National Archives (TNA)
  C 1, Early Chancery Proceedings
  C 4, Chancery Pleadings
  C 24/3, Chancery, Town Depositions (Sundries)
  C 49, King's Remembrancer: Parliamentary and Council Proceedings
  C 54, Close Rolls
  C 66, Patent Rolls
  CHES 3, Palatinate of Chester, Various Inquisitions
  CP 40, Court of Common Pleas, Plea Rolls
  E 13, Exchequer Plea Rolls
  E 101, King's Remembrancer, Various Accounts
  E 135, Exchequer, Miscellaneous Ecclesiastical Documents
  E 136, King's Remembrancer, Escheators' Particulars of Account
  E 179, King's Remembrancer, Lay and Clerical Taxation Accounts
  E 326 and 328, Exchequer, Augmentation Office, Ancient Deeds
  JUST 2, Coroners' Rolls
  KB 9, Court of King's Bench, Indictment Files
  KB 15, Court of King's Bench, Miscellaneous Books
  KB 27, Court of King's Bench, *Coram Rege* Rolls
  KB 29, Court of King's Bench, Controlment Rolls
  MPI and MPB, Maps and Plans
  PROB 11, Prerogative Court of Canterbury: Will Registers
  REQ 2, Court of Requests, Pleadings
  SC 8, Ancient Petitions
  SP 1, SP 3, SP 7, State Papers
  STAC 2, Court of Star Chamber, Proceedings, Henry VIII
London, British Library (BL)
  Additional MS 14848, Registrum Willelmi Curteys
  Cotton Nero MS E VI, Cartulary of the Knights Hospitaller
  Cotton Titus MS B I, Records and Papers, temp. Henry VIII
  Harley MS 2278, John Lydgate, Lives of Saints Edmund and Fremund
  Lansdowne MS 170, A Collection of Records and other Papers transcribed for Sir Julius Caesar
  Lansdowne MS 639, King's Council in Star Chamber
London, London Metropolitan Archives (LMA)
  COL/AD/01, Letter Books, City of London
  COL/CA/01/01, Repertory Books of the Court of Aldermen, City of London
  COL/CC/01/01, Journals of the Court of Common Council, City of London
  DL/C/B/043/MS09064/011, Act Book of the Commissary Court of the Diocese of London, vol. 11, 1511–1516

DL/C/0206, Deposition Book of the Consistory Court of the Diocese of London, 1511–1516
London, Westminster Abbey Library and Muniments (WAM)
Deeds, Leases, etc. (MSS 13165, 13191, 13293, 13294, 13315, 13318, 13319)
Muniment Book 5, Registrum Collegii Sancti Martini Magni, London
Westminster Abbey Register Books I, II, and III (typescript calendars)

PRINTED AND ONLINE PRIMARY SOURCES

Anno XXIIII Henrici VIII. Actis Made in the Session of This Present Parlyamente (London, 1533).
Anno XXVII Henrici VIII. Actes Made in the Session of This Present Parlyament (London, 1536).
Baker, J. H., ed. *The Reports of Sir John Spelman*. 2 vols. Selden Society 93–94 (London, 1977).
Baker, J. H., ed. *The Notebook of Sir John Port*. Selden Society 102 (London, 1986).
Baker, J. H., ed. *Reports of Cases by John Caryll*. 2 vols. Selden Society 115–116 (London, 1999).
Barker, Eric E., ed. *The Register of Thomas Rotherham, Archbishop of York, 1480–1500*. Canterbury and York Society 69 (Torquay, 1976).
Beachcroft, Gwen, and Arthur Sabin, eds. *Two Compotus Rolls of Saint Augustine's Abbey, Bristol, for 1491–2 and 1511–12*. Bristol Record Society 9 (Bristol, 1938).
Bickley, W. B., ed. *The Register of the Guild of Knowle in the County of Warwick, 1451–1535* (Walsall, Staffordshire, 1894).
Brewer, J. S., James Gairdner, and R. H. Brodie, eds. *Letters and Papers, Foreign and Domestic, of the Reign of Henry VIII*. 21 vols in 35 parts (London, 1862–).
Brown, Rawdon, ed. *Four Years at the Court of Henry VIII*. 2 vols (London, 1854).
Brown, Rawdon Lubbock, George Cavendish Bentinck, Horatio Forbes Brown, and Allen Banks Hinds, eds. *Calendar of State Papers and Manuscripts Relating to English Affairs, Existing in the Archives and Collections of Venice*. 5 vols (London, 1864).
Calendar of the Charter Rolls Preserved in the Public Record Office. 6 vols (London, 1903).
Calendar of the Patent Rolls Preserved in the Public Record Office, 1232–1509. 53 vols (London, 1891–1961).
Caley, John, and Joseph Hunter, eds. *Valor Ecclesiasticus Tempore Henrici VIII*. 6 vols (London, 1810).
Carpenter, John. *Munimenta Gildhallæ Londoniensis: Liber Albus, Liber Custumarum, et Liber Horn*. Edited by Henry Thomas Riley. 2 vols (London, 1860).
Davis, Norman, ed. *The Paston Letters and Papers of the Fifteenth Century*. 2 vols (Oxford, 1971).
The Enquirie and Verdite of the Quest Panneld of the Death of Richard Hune Wich Was Founde Hanged in Lolars Tower (Antwerp, 1537).
Erasmus, Desiderius. *Erasmus and Cambridge*. Edited by Douglas F. S. Thomson (Toronto, 1963).
Fabyan, Robert. *The New Chronicles of England and France*. Edited by Henry Ellis (London, 1811).
Fuller, E. A. 'Pleas of the Crown at Bristol, 15 Edward I'. *Bristol and Gloucestershire Archaeological Society* 22 (1899): pp 150–78. https://archive.org/details/transactionsbris22bris.
Fitzherbert, Anthony. *The Newe Boke of Iustyces of Peas* (London, 1538).

Gairdner, James, ed. *Letters and Papers Illustrative of the Reigns of Richard III and Henry VII*. 2 vols. Rolls Series (London, 1861).

Given-Wilson, Chris, ed. *The Parliament Rolls of Medieval England* (London, 2010). http://www.british-history.ac.uk/no-series/parliament-rolls-medieval.

Glover, Robert, et al. *The Visitation of Cheshire in the Year 1580*. Harleian Society 18 (London, 1882).

Grafton, Richard. *Chronicle or History of England*. 2 vols (London, 1809).

Hall, Edward. *Hall's Chronicle*. Edited by Henry Ellis (London, 1809).

Harriss, G. L., and M. A. Harriss, eds. 'John Benet's Chronicle for the Years 1400 to 1462'. In *Camden Miscellany*. Camden Fourth Series 9 (London, 1972).

Hector, L. C., and Barbara F. Harvey, eds. *The Westminster Chronicle, 1381–1394* (Oxford, 1982).

Hilton, R. H., ed. *The Stoneleigh Leger Book*. Dugdale Society 24 (Oxford, 1960).

Holinshed, Raphael. *Chronicles of England, Scotland, and Ireland* (London, 1587). The Holinshed Project, http://www.english.ox.ac.uk/holinshed/.

Horner, Patrick J., ed. *A Macaronic Sermon Collection from Late Medieval England: Oxford, MS Bodley 649* (Toronto, 2006).

Horstmann, Carl, ed. *Nova Legenda Anglie*. 2 vols (Oxford, 1901).

Hughes, Paul L., and James Francis Larkin, eds. *Tudor Royal Proclamations*. 3 vols (New Haven, 1964).

Hunnisett, R. F., ed. *Calendar of Nottinghamshire Coroners' Inquests 1485–1558*. Thoroton Society 25 (Nottingham, 1969).

Ives, E. W., ed. *Letters and Accounts of William Brereton of Malpas*, Record Society of Lancashire and Cheshire 116 (Old Woking, Surrey, 1976).

Jones, Philip E., ed. *Calendar of Plea and Memoranda Rolls, 1458–1482* (Cambridge, 1961).

Journal of the House of Lords. Vol. 1, 1509–1577 (London, 1767).

Kingsford, Charles Lethbridge, ed. *Two London Chronicles from the Collections of John Stow*. Camden Third Series 18 (London, 1910).

Klarwill, Victor von, ed. *The Fugger News-Letters*. Translated by Pauline De Chary. London: Bodley Head, 1928.

Lang, R. G., ed. *Two Tudor Subsidy Rolls for the City of London, 1541 and 1582*. London Record Society 29 (London, 1993).

Leland, John. *The Itinerary of John Leland in or about the Years 1535–1543*. Edited by Lucy Toulmin Smith (London, 1907).

Lindley, Phillip, Miriam Gill, and Alex Moseley. *Seven Deadly Sins and Seven Corporal Works of Mercy* (2001). http://www.le.ac.uk/arthistory/seedcorn/contents.html.

Loengard, Janet Senderowitz, ed. *London Viewers and Their Certificates, 1508–1558: Certificates of the Sworn Viewers of the City of London*. London Record Society 26 (London, 1989).

Lydgate, John. *The Life of St. Edmund, King and Martyr: John Lydgate's Illustrated Verse Life, Presented to Henry VI*. Edited by A. S. G. Edwards (London, 2004).

Lydgate, John. *John Lydgate's 'Lives of SS Edmund & Fremund' and the 'Extra Miracles of St Edmund'*. Edited by Anthony Bale and A. S. G. Edwards. Middle English Texts 41 (Heidelberg, 2009).

McGlynn, Margaret, ed. *The Rights and Liberties of the English Church: Readings from the Pre-Reformation Inns of Court*. Selden Society 129 (London, 2015).

Mackman, Jonathan, and Matthew Stevens. 'Court of Common Pleas: The National Archives, CP40, 1399-1500'. *British History Online* (2010). http://www.british-history.ac.uk/no-series/common-pleas/1399-1500.

McSheffrey, Shannon, ed. *Consistory: Testimony in the Late Medieval London Consistory Court*, http://www.consistory.ca.

Magrath, John Richard. *The Obituary Book of Queen's College, Oxford* (Oxford, 1910).

Marshall, Anne. *Painted Church* (2002). http://paintedchurch.org.

Mason, Emma, Jennifer Bray, and Desmond J. Murphy, eds. *Westminster Abbey Charters, 1066–c.1214*. London Record Society 25 (London, 1988).

Matheson, Lister M., ed. '"Warkworth's" Chronicle: The Chronicle Attributed to John Warkworth, Master of Peterhouse, Cambridge'. In *Death and Dissent: Two Fifteenth-Century Chronicles*, pp 61–124 (Rochester, NY, 1999).

More, Thomas. *The History of King Richard the Third*. Complete Works of St. Thomas More, vol. 2 (New Haven, 1963).

Nicolas, Nicholas Harris, ed. *Proceedings and Ordinances of the Privy Council of England*. 7 vols (London, 1835).

Oakes, Catherine. *Ora Pro Nobis: The Virgin as Intercessor in Medieval Art and Devotion* (London: Harvey Miller Publishers, 2008).

Page, William, ed. *Letters of Denization and Acts of Naturalization for Aliens in England, 1509–1603* (Nendeln, Liechtenstein, 1969).

Palmer, Robert. *The Anglo-American Legal Tradition*. http://aalt.law.uh.edu.

Pepys, Samuel. *The Diary of Samuel Pepys: A New and Complete Transcription*. Edited by Robert Latham and William Matthews. 11 vols (London, 2000).

Philips, Ambrose. *A Collection of Old Ballads*. 3 vols (London, 1725).

Pronay, Nicholas, and John Cox, eds. *The Crowland Chronicle Continuations: 1459–1486* (London, 1986).

Raine, Angelo, ed. *York Civic Records*. 7 vols, Yorkshire Archaeological Society 98, 103, 106, 108, 110, 115, 119 (Wakefield, 1939–).

Ralph, Elizabeth, ed. *The Great White Book of Bristol*. Bristol Record Society 32 (Bristol, 1979).

Sanctuarium Dunelmense et Sanctuarium Beverlacense. Surtees Society 5 (London, 1837).

Seipp, David J. 'An Index and Paraphrase of Printed Year Book Reports, 1268–1535' (2008). http://www.bu.edu/law/seipp/index.html.

Sharpe, Reginald R., ed. *Calendar of Letter-Books of the City of London*. 11 vols (London, 1899–1911).

Sharpe, Reginald R., ed. *Calendar of Coroners Rolls of the City of London, A.D. 1300–1378* (London, 1913).

Stamp, A. E., et al., eds. *Calendar of Close Rolls*. 47 vols (London, 1900–1963).

Stevenson, W. H. 'An Old-English Charter of William the Conqueror in Favour of St. Martin's-Le-Grand, London, A. D. 1068'. *The English Historical Review* 11 (1896): pp 731–44. doi:10.1093/ehr/XI.XLIV.731.

Stow, John. *A Survey of London*. Edited by Charles Lethbridge Kingsford. 2 vols (Oxford, 1908).

Thomas, A. H., and Isobel Thornley, eds. *The Great Chronicle of London* (London and Aylesbury, 1938).

Vergil, Polydore. *Three Books of Polydore Vergil's English History*. Edited by Henry Ellis (London, 1844).

Vergil, Polydore. *The Anglica Historia of Polydore Vergil, A.D. 1485–1537*. Edited by Denys Hay. Camden Series 74 (London, 1950).

Weaver, F. W., ed. *A Cartulary of Buckland Priory*. Somerset Record Society 25 (London, 1909).

Whitney, Isabella. 'The Maner of Her Wyll, & What She Left to London'. In *A Sweet Nosgay, or Pleasant Posye* (London, 1573).
Worcester, William. *William Worcestre: The Topography of Medieval Bristol* (Bristol, 2000).
Worde, Wynkyn de. *The Crafte to Lyue Well* (Westminster, 1505).
Wriothesley, Charles. *A Chronicle of England During the Reigns of the Tudors, from A.D. 1485 to 1559*. 2 vols. Camden New Series 11, 20 (Westminster, 1875).

SECONDARY SOURCES

Allen, Elizabeth. '"As Mote in at a Munster Dor": Sanctuary and Love of This World'. *Philological Quarterly* 87, no. 1/2 (2008): pp 105–33.
Allen, Elizabeth. 'Once and Future King: Sanctuary, Sovereignty, and the Politics of Pity in the Histories of Perkin Warbeck'. *Journal of Medieval and Early Modern Studies* 47 (forthcoming 2017).
Appleford, Amy. *Learning to Die in London, 1380–1540* (Philadelphia, 2015).
Archer, Ian W. *The Pursuit of Stability: Social Relations in Elizabethan London* (Cambridge, 1991).
Archer, Ian W. 'Responses to Alien Immigrants'. In *Le Migrazioni in Europa: Secc. XIII–XVIII*, edited by Simonetta Cavaciocchi, pp 755–74 (Florence, 1994).
Arthurson, Ian. 'Tuchet, James, Seventh Baron Audley (c. 1463–1497)'. *ODNB* (2004). doi:10.1093/ref:odnb/27576.
Ashdown-Hill, John. *Richard III's 'Beloved Cousyn': John Howard and the House of York* (Stroud, 2012).
Baker, J. H. 'The English Law of Sanctuary'. *Ecclesiastical Law Journal* 2 (1990): pp 8–13. doi:10.1017/S0956618X00000788.
Baker, J. H. *An Introduction to English Legal History*. 4th edn (London, 2002).
Baker, J. H. *The Oxford History of the Laws of England, Volume VI, 1485–1558* (Oxford, 2003).
Baker, J. H. 'Croke, John (1489–1554)'. *ODNB* (2004). doi:10.1093/ref:odnb/6732.
Baker, J. H. 'Fitzherbert, Sir Anthony (c. 1470–1538)'. *ODNB* (2004). doi:10.1093/ref:odnb/9602.
Baker, J. H. 'Fyneux [Fenex], Sir John (d. 1525)'. *ODNB* (2004). doi:10.1093/ref:odnb/10261.
Baker, J. H. 'Hales, John (1469/70–1540?)'. *ODNB* (2004). doi:10.1093/ref:odnb/11912.
Baker, J. H. 'Southwell, Sir Robert (c. 1506–1559)'. *ODNB* (2004). doi:10.1093/ref:odnb/26063.
Baker, J. H. *The Men of Court 1440 to 1550*. 3 vols. Selden Society, Supplementary Series 18 (London, 2012).
Barron, Caroline M. 'The Government of London and Its Relations with the Crown 1400–1450'. PhD, University of London (1970).
Barron, Caroline M. *London in the Later Middle Ages: Government and People 1200–1500* (Oxford, 2004).
Barron, Caroline M., and Marie-Hélène Rousseau. 'Cathedral, City and State'. In *St. Paul's: The Cathedral Church of London, 604–2004*, edited by Derek Keene, Andrew Saint, and Arthur Burns, pp 33–44 (New Haven, 2004).
Beaven, Alfred B. *The Aldermen of the City of London, Tempore Henry III to 1908* (London, 1908).
Bellamy, John G. *The Tudor Law of Treason: An Introduction* (Toronto, 1979).

Bellamy, John G. *The Criminal Trial in Later Medieval England: Felony Before the Courts from Edward I to the Sixteenth Century* (Toronto, 1998).
Bellamy, John G. *Strange Inhuman Deaths: Murder in Tudor England* (Stroud, 2005).
Benton, Lauren A. *A Search for Sovereignty: Law and Geography in European Empires, 1400–1900* (Cambridge, 2010).
Bernard, G. W. *The Late Medieval English Church: Vitality and Vulnerability Before the Break with Rome* (New Haven, 2012).
Bietenholz, Peter G., ed. *Contemporaries of Erasmus: A Biographical Register of the Renaissance and Reformation* (Toronto, 1985).
Blickle, Peter, ed. *Resistance, Representation, and Community* (Oxford, 1997).
Bolton, J. L., ed. *The Alien Communities of London in the Fifteenth Century* (Stamford, 1998).
Bolton, J. L. 'La répartition spatiale de la population étrangère à Londres au XVe siècle'. In *Les étrangers dans la ville: minorités et espace urbain du bas moyen âge à l'époque moderne*, edited by Jacques Bottin and Donatella Calabi, pp 425–37 (Paris, 1999).
Boyer, Marjorie Nice. 'A Day's Journey in Mediaeval France'. *Speculum* 26 (1951): pp 597–608. doi:10.2307/2853052.
Braddick, M. J. *State Formation in Early Modern England, c. 1550–1700* (Cambridge, 2000).
Braddick, Michael. 'State Formation and the Historiography of Early Modern England'. *History Compass* 2 (2004): pp 1–17. doi:10.1111/j.1478-0542.2004.00074.x.
Brigden, Susan. *Thomas Wyatt: The Heart's Forest* (London, 2012).
Brooks, Christopher W. *Law, Politics and Society in Early Modern England* (Cambridge, 2008).
Brooks, Peter. 'Narrative Transactions: Does the Law Need a Narratology?' *Yale Journal of Law and the Humanities* 18 (2006): pp 1–28. http://digitalcommons.law.yale.edu/yjlh/vol18/iss1/1.
Brown, Alfred L. *The Early History of the Clerkship of the Council* (Glasgow, 1969).
Burton, John Richard. *A History of Bewdley; with Concise Accounts of Some Neighbouring Parishes* (London, 1883).
Carlin, Martha. *Medieval Southwark* (London, 1996).
Carpenter, Christine. 'Law, Justice and Landowners in Late Medieval England'. *Law and History Review* 1 (1983): pp 205–37. doi:10.2307/743850.
Carrel, H. 'Disputing Legal Privilege: Civic Relations with the Church in Late Medieval England'. *Journal of Medieval History* 35 (2009): pp 279–96. doi:10.1016/j.jmedhist.2009.06.001.
Cassidy-Welch, Megan. *Imprisonment in the Medieval Religious Imagination, c. 1150–1400* (Basingstoke, 2011).
Cavill, P. R. *The English Parliaments of Henry VII, 1485–1504* (Oxford, 2009).
Certeau, Michel de. *The Practice of Everyday Life*. Translated by Steven Rendall (Berkeley, 1988).
Chrimes, S. B. *Henry VII* (London, 1972).
Clanchy, M. T. *From Memory to Written Record, England 1066–1307*. 2nd edn (Oxford, 1993).
Clark, Linda. 'Bourchier, Thomas (c.1411–1486), Cardinal and Archbishop of Canterbury'. *ODNB* (2004). doi:10.1093/ref:odnb/2993.
Clark, Linda. 'Tiptoft, John, First Baron Tiptoft (c. 1378–1443)'. *ODNB* (2004). doi:10.1093/ref:odnb/27470.
Collinson, Patrick. 'The Monarchical Republic of Queen Elizabeth I'. *Bulletin of the John Rylands Library* 69 (1987): pp 394–424.

Cormack, Bradin. *A Power to Do Justice: Jurisdiction, English Literature, and the Rise of Common Law* (Chicago, 2009).
Cox, J. Charles. *The Sanctuaries and Sanctuary Seekers of Mediaeval England* (London, 1911).
Cross, Claire. *Church and People, 1450–1660: The Triumph of the Laity in the English Church* (London, 1976).
Davies, R. G. 'Stafford, John (d. 1452)'. *ODNB* (2004). doi:io.ioi7/Sooi8246Xo999o033.
Davies, Rees. 'The Medieval State: The Tyranny of a Concept?' *Journal of Historical Sociology* 16 (2003): pp 280–300.
Davis, N. Z. 'Les conteurs de Montaillou'. *Annales: économies, sociétés, civilisations* 34 (1979): pp 61–73. doi:10.3406/ahess.1979.294022.
Davis, Natalie Zemon. *Fiction in the Archives: Pardon Tales and Their Tellers in Sixteenth-Century France* (Stanford, 1987).
Davis, Virginia. 'The Rule of Saint Paul, the First Hermit, in Late Medieval England'. *Studies in Church History* 22 (1985): pp 203–14. doi:10.1017/S0424208400007956.
Dodd, Gwilym. 'The Rise of English, the Decline of French: Supplications to the English Crown, c. 1420–1450'. *Speculum* 86 (2011): pp 117–50. doi:10.1017/S0038713410003507.
Donlan, Seán Patrick, and Dirk Heirbaut, eds. *The Laws' Many Bodies: Studies in Legal Hybridity and Jurisdictional Complexity, c. 1600–1900* (Berlin, 2015).
Donno, Elizabeth Story. 'Thomas More and Richard III'. *Renaissance Quarterly* 35 (1982): pp 401–47. doi:10.2307/2861202.
Duffy, Eamon. *The Stripping of the Altars: Traditional Religion in England 1400–1580* (New Haven, 1992).
Dupont-Bouchat, Marie-Sylvie. 'Guilt and Individual Consciousness: The Individual, the Church and the State in the Modern Era, Sixteenth-Seventeenth Centuries'. In *The Individual in Political Theory and Practice*, edited by Janet Coleman, pp 123–48 (Oxford, 1996).
Dykstra, Robert R. 'Lies, Damned Lies, and Homicide Rates'. *Historical Methods* 42 (2009): pp 139–42. doi:10.1080/01615440903259434.
Edwards, A. S. G. 'Introduction'. In *The Life of St. Edmund, King and Martyr: John Lydgate's Illustrated Verse Life, Presented to Henry VI*, by John Lydgate (London, 2004).
Elton, G. R. *Policy and Police: The Enforcement of the Reformation in the Age of Thomas Cromwell* (Cambridge, 1972).
Elton, G. R. *Reform and Renewal: Thomas Cromwell and the Common Weal* (Cambridge, 1973).
Elton, G. R. 'The Sessional Printing of Statutes, 1484–1547'. In *Wealth and Power in Tudor England*, edited by E. W. Ives, R. J. Knecht, and J. J. Scarisbrick, pp 68–86 (London, 1978).
Elton, G. R. *The Tudor Constitution: Documents and Commentary* (Cambridge, 1982).
Emden, A. B. *A Biographical Register of the University of Oxford to A. D. 1500*. 3 vols (Oxford, 1957).
Everett, Michael. *The Rise of Thomas Cromwell: Power and Politics in the Reign of Henry VIII* (New Haven, 2015).
Federico, Sylvia. *New Troy: Fantasies of Empire in the Late Middle Ages* (Minneapolis, 2003).
Fleming, Peter. 'Conflict and Urban Government in Later Medieval England: St Augustine's Abbey and Bristol'. *Urban History* 27 (2000): pp 325–43. doi:10.1017/S0963926800000316.
Forrest, Ian. 'The Archive of the Official of Stow and the "Machinery" of Church Government in the Late Thirteenth Century'. *Historical Research* 84 (2011): pp 1–13. doi:10.1111/j.1468-2281.2009.00528.x.

Forrest, Ian. 'The Transformation of Visitation in Thirteenth-Century England'. *Past & Present* 221 (2013): pp 3–38. doi:10.1093/pastj/gtt013.
Fowler, Joseph Thomas, ed. *Acts of Chapter of the Collegiate Church of SS. Peter and Wilfrid, Ripon, A. D. 1452 to A. D. 1506*, Surtees Society 64 (Durham, 1875).
Freeman, Jessica. 'And He Abjured the Realm of England, Never to Return'. In *Freedom of Movement in the Middle Ages: Proceedings of the 2003 Harlaxton Symposium*, edited by Peregrine Horden, pp 287–304 (Donington, 2007).
French, Katherine L. *The People of the Parish: Community Life in a Late Medieval English Diocese* (Philadelphia, 2001).
Gaskill, Malcolm. *Crime and Mentalities in Early Modern England* (Cambridge, 2000).
Gauvard, Claude. *'De Grâce Especial': Crime, état, et société en France à la fin du moyen âge* (Paris, 1991).
Genet, Jean-Philippe. 'Cartulaires, registres et histoire: l'exemple anglais'. In *Le métier d'historien au moyen age: Études sur l'historiographie médiévale*, edited by Bernard Guenée, pp 95–138 (Paris, 1977).
Gervers, Michael. *The Hospitaller Cartulary in the British Library (Cotton MS Nero E VI)* (Toronto, 1981).
Gewirtz, Paul. 'Narrative and Rhetoric in the Law'. In *Law's Stories: Narrative and Rhetoric in the Law*, edited by Peter Brooks and Paul Gewirtz, pp 2–13 (New Haven, 1996).
Gilchrist, Roberta. *Norwich Cathedral Close: The Evolution of the English Cathedral Landscape* (Woodbridge, 2005).
Goheen, Robert B. 'Peasant Politics? Village Community and the Crown in Fifteenth-Century England'. *The American Historical Review* 96 (1991): pp 42–62. doi:10.2307/2164017.
Goldie, Mark. 'The Unacknowledged Republic: Officeholding in Early Modern England'. In *The Politics of the Excluded, c. 1500–1850*, edited by Tim Harris, pp 153–94 (New York, 2001).
Gowing, Laura. 'The Haunting of Susan Lay: Servants and Mistresses in Seventeenth-Century England'. *Gender & History* 14 (2002): pp 183–201. doi:10.1111/1468-0424.00262.
Gray, Douglas. 'Lydgate, John (c. 1370–1449/50?)'. *ODNB* (2004). doi:10.1093/ref:odnb/17238.
Green, Thomas A. 'Societal Concepts of Criminal Liability for Homicide in Mediaeval England'. *Speculum* 47 (1972): pp 669–94. doi:10.2307/2856634.
Griffiths, Ralph Alan. 'Public and Private Bureaucracies in England and Wales in the Fifteenth Century'. *Transactions of the Royal Historical Society*, Fifth Series 30 (1980): pp 109–30. doi:10.2307/3679005.
Griffiths, Ralph Alan. *The Reign of King Henry VI: The Exercise of Royal Authority, 1422–1461* (Berkeley, 1981).
Gunn, S. J. *Charles Brandon, Duke of Suffolk, c. 1484–1545* (New York, 1988).
Guy, John A. 'Tudor Monarchy and Political Culture'. In *The Oxford Illustrated History of Tudor and Stuart Britain*, edited by John S. Morrill, pp 219–38 (Oxford, 1996).
Harben, Henry A. *A Dictionary of London* (London, 1918).
Harvey, Barbara F. *Living and Dying in England, 1100–1540: The Monastic Experience* (Oxford, 1993).
Harvey, Barbara F., and Henry Summerson. 'Islip, John (1464–1532)'. *ODNB* (2004). doi:10.1093/ref:odnb/14492.
Harvey, P. D. A. *Maps in Tudor England* (Chicago, 1993).
Hayes, Rosemary C. E. 'Alnwick, William (d. 1449)'. *ODNB* (2004). doi:10.1093/ref:odnb/421.
Helmholz, R. H. *The Ius Commune in England: Four Studies* (Oxford, 2001).

Hertzler, James R. 'The Abuse and Outlawing of Sanctuary for Debt in Seventeenth-Century England'. *The Historical Journal* 14, no. 3 (1971): pp 467–77. doi:10.1017/S0018246X00007512.

Hicks, Michael A. 'The Yorkshire Rebellion of 1489 Reconsidered'. *Northern History* 22 (1986): pp 39–62. doi:10.1179/174587009X391411.

Hicks, Michael A. 'Stillington, Robert (d. 1491)'. *ODNB* (2004). doi:10.1093/ref:odnb/26528.

Hindle, Steve. *The State and Social Change in Early Modern England, c.1550–1640* (New York, 2000).

History of Parliament Trust, 'Members, 1509–1558', *The History of Parliament: British Political, Social, and Local History* (London, 1964), http://www.historyofparliamentonline.org/research/members/members-1509-1558.

Honeybourne, Marjorie B. 'The Sanctuary Boundaries and Environs of Westminster Abbey and the College of St. Martin-Le-Grand'. *Journal of the British Archaeological Association* 38 (1932): pp 316–34.

Horst, Irvin Buckwalter. *The Radical Brethren. Anabaptism and the English Reformation to 1558* (Nieuwkoop, 1972).

House, Anthony Paul. 'The City of London and the Problem of the Liberties, c.1540–c.1640'. DPhil, Oxford University (2006).

House, Seymour Baker. 'More, Sir Thomas'. *ODNB* (2004). doi:10.1093/ref:odnb/19191.

Houston, R. A. 'People, Space, and Law in Late Medieval and Early Modern Britain and Ireland'. *Past & Present* 230 (2016): pp 47–89. doi:10.1093/pastj/gtv057.

Hyams, Paul R. *Rancor and Reconciliation in Medieval England* (Ithaca, 2003).

Ives, E. W. 'Crime, Sanctuary, and Royal Authority under Henry VIII: The Exemplary Sufferings of the Savage Family'. In *On the Laws and Customs of England*, edited by Morris S. Arnold and et al., pp 296–320 (Chapel Hill, 1981).

James, Mervyn. *English Politics and the Concept of Honour 1485–1642*. Past & Present Supplement 3 (Oxford, 1978).

Johnson, Tom. 'Law, Space, and Local Knowledge in Late-Medieval England'. PhD, Birkbeck College, University of London (2014).

Jordan, William C. 'A Fresh Look at Medieval Sanctuary'. In *Law and the Illicit in Medieval Europe*, edited by Ruth Mazo Karras, Joel Kaye, and E. Ann Matter, pp 17–32 (Philadelphia, 2010).

Jordan, William C. *From England to France: Felony and Exile in the High Middle Ages* (Princeton, 2015).

Kaeuper, Richard W. *Chivalry and Violence in Medieval Europe* (Oxford, 1999).

Kaufman, Peter Iver. 'Henry VII and Sanctuary'. *Church History* 53 (1984): pp 465–76. doi:10.2307/3166117.

Kaufman, Peter Iver. *The 'Polytyque Churche': Religion and Early Tudor Political Culture, 1485–1516* (Macon, Georgia, 1986).

Keene, Derek. 'Du seuil de la Cité à la formation d'une économie morale: l'environnement hanséatique à Londres, entre XIIe et XVIIe siècle'. In *Les étrangers dans la ville: minorités et espace urbain du bas moyen âge à l'époque moderne*, edited by Jacques Bottin and Donatella Calabi, pp 409–24 (Paris, 1999).

Kempe, Alfred John. *Historical Notices of the Collegiate Church or Royal Free Chapel and Sanctuary of St. Martin-Le-Grand, London* (London, 1825).

Kesselring, K. J. 'Abjuration and Its Demise: The Changing Face of Royal Justice in the Tudor Period'. *Canadian Journal of History* 34 (1999): pp 345–58. doi:10.3138/cjh.34.3.345.

Kesselring, K. J. *Mercy and Authority in the Tudor State* (Cambridge, 2003).
Kesselring, K. J. 'Felony Forfeiture and the Profits of Crime in Early Modern England'. *The Historical Journal* 53 (2010): pp 271–88. doi:10.1017/S0018246X10000014.
Kesselring, K. J. 'Bodies of Evidence: Sex and Murder (or Gender and Homicide) in Early Modern England, c.1500–1680'. *Gender & History* 27 (2015): pp 245–62. doi:10.1111/1468-0424.12124.
Kincaid, Arthur Noel. 'The Dramatic Structure of Sir Thomas More's *History of King Richard III*'. *Studies in English Literature, 1500–1900* 12 (1972): pp 223–42. doi:10.2307/449891.
Knighton, C. S. 'Benson [name in Religion Boston], William (d. 1549)'. *ODNB* (2004). doi:10.1093/ref:odnb/2146.
Lacey, Helen. *The Royal Pardon: Access to Mercy in Fourteenth-Century England* (York, 2009).
Lambert, T. B. 'The Evolution of Sanctuary in Medieval England'. In *Legalism: Anthropology and History*, edited by Paul Dresch and Hannah Skoda, pp 115–44 (Oxford, 2012).
Leach, Arthur Francis. *Report on the Manuscripts of the Corporation of Beverley*. Royal Commission on Historical Manuscripts (London, 1900).
Lehmberg, Stanford E. *The Reformation Parliament 1529–1536* (Cambridge, 1970).
Lehmberg, Stanford E. 'Southwell, Sir Richard (1502/3–1564)'. *ODNB* (2004). doi:10.1093/ref:odnb/26062.
Leithead, Howard. 'Cromwell, Thomas, Earl of Essex'. *ODNB* (2004). doi:10.1093/ref:odnb/6769.
Leland, John L. 'Tresilian, Sir Robert (d. 1388)'. *ODNB* (2004). doi:10.1093/ref:odnb/27715.
Levin, John. 'Alsatia: The Debtor Sanctuaries of London'. http://alsatia.org.uk/site/.
Loades, D. M. 'The Sanctuary'. In *Westminster Abbey Reformed: 1540–1640*, edited by C. S. Knighton and Richard Mortimer, pp 75–93 (Aldershot, 2003).
Lobel, Mary S. *The City of London from Prehistoric Times to c.1520* (Oxford, 1989).
Logan, F. Donald. *Runaway Religious in Medieval England, c.1240–1540* (Cambridge, 1996).
Luu, Lien Bich. 'Aliens and Their Impact on the Goldsmiths' Craft in London in the Sixteenth Century'. In *Goldsmiths, Silversmiths, and Bankers: Innovation and the Transfer of Skill, 1550 to 1750*, edited by David Mitchell, pp 43–52 (Stroud, 1995).
Luu, Lien Bich. *Immigrants and the Industries of London, 1500–1700* (Aldershot, 2005).
Lyons, Mary Ann. 'Rawson, John, Viscount Clontarff (1470?–1547?)'. *ODNB* (2004). doi:10.1093/ref:odnb/23199.
MacCulloch, Diarmaid. *Suffolk and the Tudors: Politics and Religion in an English County, 1500–1600* (Oxford, 1986).
McCune, Pat. 'Justice, Mercy, and Late Medieval Governance'. *Michigan Law Review* 89 (1991): pp 1661–78. doi:10.2307/1289496.
McGlynn, Margaret. 'The Use and Abuse of Sanctuary in Henrician England'. Presentation at the American Society for Legal History, Philadelphia (2010).
McIntosh, Marjorie K. *Controlling Misbehavior in England, 1370–1600* (Cambridge, 1998).
McKinley, Michelle A. 'Standing on Shaky Ground: Criminal Jurisdiction and Ecclesiastical Immunity in Seventeenth-Century Lima, 1600–1700'. *University of California Irvine Law Review* 4 (2014): pp 141–74. doi:10.1037/a0031304.
McSheffrey, Shannon. 'Sanctuary and the Legal Topography of Pre-Reformation London'. *Law and History Review* 27 (2009): pp 483–514. doi:10.1017/S0738248000003886.
McSheffrey, Shannon. 'The Slaying of Sir William Pennington: Legal Narrative and the Late Medieval English Archive'. *Florilegium* 28 (2011): pp 169–203. https://journals.lib.unb.ca/index.php/flor/article/view/21566/25053.

McSheffrey, Shannon. 'Residents of St. Martin le Grand, c. 1500–1550' (2013). https://shannonmcsheffrey.wordpress.com/research/.
McSheffrey, Shannon. 'Stranger Artisans and the London Sanctuary of St. Martin Le Grand in the Reign of Henry VIII'. *Journal of Medieval and Early Modern Studies* 43 (2013): pp 545–71. doi:10.1215/10829636-2338599.
McSheffrey, Shannon. 'William Webbe's Wench: Henry VIII, History, and Popular Culture'. In *The Middle Ages on Television: Critical Essays*, edited by Meriem Pagès and Karolyn Kinane, pp 53–77 (Jefferson, North Carolina, 2015).
McSheffrey, Shannon. 'Sanctuary Seekers in England, 1390–1557' (2016). https://shannonmcsheffrey.wordpress.com/research/.
Maddern, Philippa. *Violence and Social Order: East Anglia, 1422–1442* (Oxford, 1992).
Masschaele, James. *Jury, State, and Society in Medieval England* (New York, 2008).
Matthew, H. C. G., and B. Harrison, eds. *The Oxford Dictionary of National Biography* (ONDB) (Oxford, 2004–). http://www.oxforddnb.com.
May, Evan F. 'For the Good Order to Be Had Thereby: Civic Archives and the Creation of Conformity in Late Medieval London'. PhD, Concordia University (2010).
Mazzinghi, Thomas John de'. *Sanctuaries* (Stafford, 1887).
Merback, Mitchell. *The Thief, the Cross and the Wheel: Pain and the Spectacle of Punishment in Medieval and Renaissance Europe* (London, 1999).
Musson, Anthony. *Medieval Law in Context: The Growth of Legal Consciousness from Magna Carta to the Peasants' Revolt* (Manchester, 2001).
Musson, Anthony. 'Jurisdictional Complexity: The Survival of Private Jurisdictions in England.' In *The Laws' Many Bodies: Studies in Legal Hybridity and Jurisdictional Complexity, c1600–1900*, edited by Seán Patrick Donlan and Dirk Heirbaut, pp 109–26 (Berlin, 2015).
Musson, Anthony, and W. M. Ormrod. *The Evolution of English Justice: Law, Politics, and Society in the Fourteenth Century* (London, 1999).
Nicholson, Helen J. *The Knights Hospitaller* (Woodbridge, 2001).
Nightingale, Pamela. 'Money and Credit in the Economy of Late Medieval England'. In *Medieval Money Matters*, edited by Diana Wood, pp 51–71 (Oxford, 2004).
Norris, M. M. 'Brydges, John, First Baron Chandos (1492–1557)'. *ODNB* (2004). doi:10.1093/ref:odnb/3807.
O'Malley, Gregory. *The Knights Hospitaller of the English Langue, 1460–1565* (Oxford, 2005).
Orridge, B. Brogden. 'Some Particulars of Alderman Philip Malpas and Alderman Sir Thomas Cooke'. *Transactions of the London and Middlesex Archaeological Society* 3 (1865): pp 285–306. https://archive.org/details/transactionsoflo03londuoft.
Page, William, ed. *A History of the County of Lincoln*. 2 vols. Victoria County Histories (London, 1906–).
Page, William, ed. *A History of the County of Essex*. 10 vols. Victoria County Histories (London, 1907–).
Page, William, ed. *A History of the County of Warwick*. 8 vols. Victoria County Histories (London, 1908–).
Page, William, ed. *A History of the County of Huntingdon*. 3 vols. Victoria County Histories (London, 1926–).
Page, William, and J. W. Wills-Bund, eds. *A History of the County of Worcester*. 4 vols. Victoria County Histories (London, 1924–).
Pantzer, Katherine F. 'Printing the English Statutes 1484–1640: Some Historical Implications'. In *Books and Society in History*, edited by Kenneth E. Carpenter, pp 69–114 (New York, 1983).

Parker, K. T. *The Drawings of Hans Holbein in the Collection of His Majesty the King at Windsor Castle* (Oxford, 1945).

Payling, S. J. 'The Ampthill Dispute: A Study in Aristocratic Lawlessness and the Breakdown of Lancastrian Goverment'. *The English Historical Review* 104 (1989): pp 881–907. doi:10.1093/ehr/CIV.413.881.

Pettegree, Andrew. 'The Foreign Population of London in 1549'. *Proceedings of the Huguenot Society of London* 24 (1984): pp 141–6.

Pettegree, Andrew. *Foreign Protestant Communities in Sixteenth-Century London* (Oxford, 1986).

Phillips, Simon. *The Prior of the Knights Hospitaller in Late Medieval England* (Woodbridge, 2009).

Pollard, A. J. *North-Eastern England During the Wars of the Roses: Lay Society, War, and Politics, 1450–1500* (Oxford, 1990).

Powell, Edward. *Kingship, Law, and Society: Criminal Justice in the Reign of Henry V* (Oxford, 1989).

Prestwich, Michael, ed. *Liberties and Identities in the Medieval British Isles* (Woodbridge, 2008).

Pugh, Ralph B., ed. *A History of the County of Wiltshire*. 17 vols. Victoria County Histories (London, 1956).

Pugh, Ralph B. 'The Knights Hospitallers of England as Undertakers'. *Speculum* 56 (1981): pp 566–74. doi:10.2307/2847742.

Rappaport, Steve. *Worlds Within Worlds: Structures of Life in Sixteenth-Century London* (Cambridge, 1989).

Reddan, Minnie. 'The Collegiate Church of St. Martin Le Grand'. In *The Religious Houses of London and Middlesex*, edited by Caroline M. Barron and Matthew Davies, pp 196–206. Victoria County Histories (London, 2007).

Rexroth, Frank. *Deviance and Power in Late Medieval London*. Translated by Pamela Eve Selwyn (Cambridge, 2007).

Richardson, Malcolm. *Middle-Class Writing in Late Medieval London* (London, 2011).

Roberts, Howard, and Walter H. Godfrey, eds. *Survey of London: Volume 22: Bankside* (London, 1950).

Roger, Euan C. 'Blakberd's Treasure: A Study in Fifteenth-Century Administration at St. Bartholomew's Hospital, London'. In *Exploring the Evidence: Commemoration, Administration and the Economy*, edited by Linda Clark, pp 81–107 (Woodbridge, 2014).

Rosenwein, Barbara H. *Negotiating Space: Power, Restraint, and Privileges of Immunity in Early Medieval Europe* (Ithaca, 1999).

Roskell, J. S. 'Sir William Oldhall, Speaker in the Parliament of 1450–1451'. *Nottingham Medieval Studies* 5 (1961): pp 87–112. doi:10.1484/J.NMS.3.13.

Ross, Richard Jeffrey, and Lauren A. Benton, eds. *Legal Pluralism and Empires, 1500–1850* (New York, 2013).

Rosser, Gervase. 'Sanctuary and Social Negotiation in Medieval England'. In *The Cloister and the World: Essays in Medieval History in Honour of Barbara Harvey*, edited by John Blair and Brian Golding, pp 57–79 (Oxford, 1996).

Rosser, Gervase. 'Urban Culture and the Church, 1300–1540'. In *Cambridge Urban History of Britain, Volume I: 600–1540*, edited by David M. Palliser, pp 335–69 (Cambridge, 2000).

Rowlands, John. *Holbein: The Paintings of Hans Holbein the Younger: Complete Edition* (Oxford, 1985).

Sacks, David Harris. *Trade, Society, and Politics in Bristol, 1500–1640.* 2 vols (New York, 1985).
Saul, Nigel. *Richard II* (New Haven, 1997).
Scammell, Jean. 'The Origin and Limitations of the Liberty of Durham'. *The English Historical Review* 81 (1966): pp 449–73. doi:10.1093/ehr/LXXXI.CCCXX.449.
Scarisbrick, J. J. *Henry VIII* (London, 1968).
Schioppa, Antonio Padoa, ed. *Legislation and Justice* (Oxford, 1997).
Scofield, Cora L. 'Elizabeth Wydevile in the Sanctuary at Westminster, 1470'. *The English Historical Review* 24 (1909): pp 90–1. doi:10.1093/ehr/XXIV.XCIII.90.
Shagan, Ethan H. *Popular Politics and the English Reformation* (Cambridge, 2003).
Sharpe, Kevin. *Selling the Tudor Monarchy: Authority and Image in Sixteenth-Century England* (New Haven, 2009).
Sharpe, Reginald R. *London and the Kingdom* (London, 1894).
Shepard, Alan Clarke. '"Female Perversity", Male Entitlement: The Agency of Gender in More's *The History of Richard III*'. *Sixteenth Century Journal* 26 (1995): pp 311–28. doi:10.2307/2542793.
Shoemaker, Karl. *Sanctuary and Crime in the Middle Ages, 400–1500* (New York, 2011).
Simpson, James. *Reform and Cultural Revolution: 1350–1547* (Oxford, 2004).
Smail, Daniel Lord. *Imaginary Cartographies: Possession and Identity in Late Medieval Marseille* (Ithaca, 2000).
Sobecki, Sebastian. *Unwritten Verities: The Making of England's Vernacular Legal Culture, 1463–1549* (Notre Dame, 2015).
Spiegel, Gabrielle M. *The Past as Text: The Theory and Practice of Medieval Historiography* (Baltimore, 1997).
St John Hope, W. H., and Harold Brakspear. 'The Cistercian Abbey of Beaulieu in the County of Southampton'. *The Archaeological Journal* 63, New Series, vol. 13 (1906): pp 129–88. doi:10.1080/00665983.1906.10853026.
Stanley, Arthur Penrhyn. *Historical Memorials of Westminster Abbey.* 2nd edn (London, 1868).
Stansfield, Michael M. N. 'The Hollands, Dukes of Exeter, Earls of Kent and Huntingdon, 1352-1475'. PhD, Oxford University (1987).
Stirk, Nigel. 'Arresting Ambiguity: The Shifting Geographies of a London Debtors' Sanctuary in the Eighteenth Century'. *Social History* 25 (2000): pp 316–29. doi:10.1080/03071020050143347.
Storey, R. L. *Thomas Langley and the Bishopric of Durham, 1406–37* (London, 1961).
Stringer, Keith. 'States, Liberties and Communities in Medieval Britain and Ireland (c. 1100–1400)'. In *Liberties and Identities in the Medieval British Isles*, edited by Michael Prestwich, pp 5–36 (Woodbridge, 2008).
Summerson, H. R. T. 'The Early Development of the *Peine Forte et Dure*'. In *Law, Litigants and the Legal Profession*, edited by E. W. Ives and A. H. Manchester, pp 116–25 (London, 1983).
Sutton, Anne F. 'Malpas, Philip (d. 1469)'. *ODNB* (2004). doi:10.1093/ref:odnb/52271.
Sutton, Anne F. *The Mercery of London: Trade, Goods and People, 1130–1578* (Aldershot, 2005).
Swanson, R. N. 'Peculiar Practices: The Jurisdictional Jigsaw of the Pre-Reformation Church'. *Midland History* 26 (2001): pp 69–95. doi:10.1179/mdh.2001.26.1.69.
Tanner, Lawrence E. 'Nature and Use of Westminster Abbey Muniments'. *Transactions of the Royal Historical Society*, Fourth Series 19 (1936): pp 43–80. doi:10.2307/3678686.

Thompson, S. 'Fitzjames, Richard (d. 1522), Bishop of London'. *ODNB* (2004). doi:10.1093/ref:odnb/9612.
Thornley, Isobel. 'The Destruction of Sanctuary'. In *Tudor Studies*, edited by R. W. Seton-Watson, pp 182–207 (London, 1924).
Thornley, Isobel. 'Sanctuary in Medieval London'. *Journal of the British Archaeological Association* 38 (1932): pp 293–315.
Thornton, Tim. *Cheshire and the Tudor State, 1480–1560* (Woodbridge, 2000).
Thornton, Tim. 'Fifteenth-Century Durham and the Problem of Provincial Liberties in England and the Wider Territories of the English Crown'. *Transactions of the Royal Historical Society*. Sixth Series 11 (2001): pp 83–100. doi:10.1017/S0080440101000056.
Thornton, Tim. 'Savage Family (per. c. 1369–1528)'. *ODNB* (2004). doi:10.1093/ref:odnb/52794.
Thrupp, Sylvia L. 'Aliens in and around London in the Fifteenth Century'. In *Studies in London History Presented to Philip Edmund Jones*, edited by Albert E. J. Hollaender and William Kellaway, pp 251–72 (London, 1969).
Tomlins, Thomas Edlyne. *Yseldon: A Perambulation of Islington* (London, 1858).
Trenholme, Norman MacLaren. *The Right of Sanctuary in England: A Study in Instititutional History*. The University of Missouri Studies (Columbia, 1903).
Tucker, Penny. *Law Courts and Lawyers in the City of London, 1300–1550* (Cambridge, 2007).
Uribe-Uran, Victor M. '"Iglesia Me Llamo": Church Asylum and the Law in Spain and Colonial Spanish America'. *Comparative Studies in Society and History* 49 (2007): pp 446–72. doi:10.1017/SOO10417507000552.
Walker, Garthine. *Crime, Gender and Social Order in Early Modern England* (Cambridge, 2003).
Watt, Diane. 'Barton, Elizabeth'. *ODNB* (2004). doi:10.1093/ref:odnb/1598.
Whittick, Christopher. 'The Role of the Criminal Appeal in the Fifteenth Century'. In *Law and Social Change in British History*, edited by J. A. Guy and Hugh Beale, pp 55–72 (London, 1984).
Williams, C. H. 'The Rebellion of Humphrey Stafford in 1486'. *The English Historical Review* 43 (1928): pp 181–9. doi:10.1093/ehr/XLIII.CLXX.181.
Williams, Penry. *The Tudor Regime* (Oxford, 1979).
Wood, Andy. 'Subordination, Solidarity and the Limits of Popular Agency in a Yorkshire Valley c.1596–1615'. *Past & Present* 193 (2006): pp 41–72. doi:10.1093/pastj/gtl011.
Woolfson, Jonathan. 'Croke, Richard (1489–1558)'. *ODNB* (2004). doi:10.1093/ref:odnb/6734.
Wright, Thomas. *The History and Topography of Essex* (London, 1836).
Wrightson, Keith. 'The Politics of the Parish in Early Modern England'. In *The Experience of Authority in Early Modern England*, edited by Paul Griffiths, Adam Fox, and Steve Hindle, pp 10–46 (New York, 1996).
Wrigley, E. A., and Roger S. Schofield, *The Population History of England: 1541–1871: A Reconstruction* (London, 1981).
Wunderli, Richard M. *London Church Courts and Society on the Eve of the Reformation* (Cambridge, MA, 1981).
Wunderli, Richard M. 'Pre-Reformation London Summoners and the Murder of Richard Hunne'. *Journal of Ecclesiastical History* 33 (1982): pp 209–24. doi:10.1017/S0022046900029596.

Index

Abingdon Abbey 48, 104
  dependent properties offering sanctuary 48–9, 104
abjuration 23, 44, 89, 93, 185
  abjurer caught in the realm 83–4, 92, 107
  chronological pattern 11, 28, 33–41, 57, 189–90
  collapse from c. 1535 23, 38, 142, 166, 189–92
  development in common law 12–13, 17, 28
  from Hospitaller properties 92–4, 97
  from St Martin le Grand, fourteenth century 62
  gendered pattern 19–20
  of the realm, process for 7–8
  statutes regarding 17, 42, 156, 192, 197
  to chartered sanctuary 17, 42, 44, 110, 181, 192
  to post-1540 sanctuary town 196–7
alien workers and sanctuary precincts 9, 21–3, 61, 91, 112–39
Alnwick, William, dean of St Martin le Grand 64–5
Alsatia, early modern debtors' sanctuary 31, 197
Anderson, William 98
Andrew, Henry 194
Anne Boleyn, queen consort of Henry VIII 1–3, 168, 176
apostasy, as grounds for sanctuary 63
appeal of murder 100, 171, 181
Archer, Richard 152–5, 158–61, 164
aristocratic use of sanctuary 1–5, 17–19, 21, 24, 44, 165–88, 191, 194
Arthur, Dominic 94–5
Arthur, Prince of Wales 114, 118
Arthur, William 196
attainder, act of 157, 176
Audeley or Audelegh, George 181
Avery, Thomas 152–6, 158
Avery, wife of Thomas 152, 163

Baddesley, Hampshire, Hospitaller property 107
Bagnall, Thomas 49
Baker, Robert, hermit at Islington 51, 130
Balsall, Warwickshire, Hospitaller property 145
Barnard's Inn, London 61
Barneshurst, William 151, 153, 155, 158–9
Barnet, battle of 45
Barton, Elizabeth 176
battle of St Albans 78
Bayly, William 134
Beaufort, Edmund, duke of Somerset 46, 77

Beaulieu Abbey:
  dependent properties offering sanctuary 104, 144
  sanctuary 11, 23, 33, 45–6, 49, 102, 109, 142, 177
de Benche, Charles 176
benefit of clergy 14, 19, 20, 24, 41, 42, 84, 103, 104, 148, 152, 156, 176, 187, 191
Benson alias Boston, William, abbot of Westminster 127, 173–4
Beverley, St John's Minster, sanctuary 10–11, 21–3, 33–5, 38–40, 75, 94–5, 102, 104, 110, 115, 177
Bewdley, Shropshire or Worcestershire, sanctuary 17, 109, 110, 182
Blackheath, battle of 133
Blakborne, Christopher 70
Blanchappleton, manor of, in London 61, 62, 67
Bland (sanctuary-seeker) 49, 130, 133
Boston, William, see Benson alias Boston
Bosworth, battle of 48
Botolphbridge, Huntingdonshire, Hospitaller property 97
Bottiler, Ralph 72
Bougham, William 95–6
Bourchier, Thomas, dean of St. Martin le Grand, archbishop of Canterbury 46, 52, 63–5
Bradbury, Hugh 105
Bradley, John 106
Brandon, Charles, duke of Suffolk 1–4, 171, 180–1
Brandon, Mary, duchess of Suffolk, daughter of Henry VII 1
Brandon, William 46
Brasebrigge, Michael 185–6
breaches of sanctuary 3, 10, 15, 23, 32, 38, 46–50, 52–6, 58–9, 64, 77–9, 83–7, 92–100, 102, 105, 107, 131–2, 149, 165–6, 169, 173–9, 190; see also plea of sanctuary in royal court
Brereton (married names Cholmeley, Mainwaring), Elizabeth 168
Brereton, William 168
Brewce, George 135, 178
Bristol Temple Fee, Hospitaller property 98, 103, 106, 107–8
Bristol, City of, disputing sanctuary privileges of local religious houses 61, 92–5, 98, 103, 106, 107–8, 128
Broughton, Hampshire, Hospitaller property 92

Browe, John 112
Brutus the Trojan, myth of 74–5
Bull, Maurice 169, 174–7
Bull Head tavern, London 112, 128, 131–3, 136
Burbage, William 102–3
Bury, Robert 150–6
Butler, Robert 143
Button, William 145

canon law regarding sanctuary 6, 12–14, 28, 31, 53, 63, 79–80, 99
Capello, Carlo, ambassador 1
Carpenter, John, common clerk of the City of London 62, 70
Carre, Robert 97
cartularies, ecclesiastical, showing sanctuary rights 9, 66–77, 86, 91–3, 96
Caryll, John, legal reporter 101, 106
Caryon, John 177
Caudray, Richard, dean of St Martin le Grand 51, 56, 58–82, 101, 112, 127, 129, 134, 140
Cayme, William 46, 77
chartered sanctuary, concept of 3, 14, 21–3, 59–61, 66–7, 81–2, 86–7, 90–111, 187–92
  collapse from *c.* 1535 23, 38, 142, 166, 189–92
  origin 8–11, 22, 27–35, 38, 41, 55–7
  see also charters, royal, as basis for sanctuary; liberties, ecclesiastical; sacrality of ecclesiastical space
chartered sanctuaries:
  censuses of seekers in 42–4, 116, 175
  chronological patterns of resort to 35–42
  cost of living in precincts of 21, 38, 43, 188
  length of stay in precincts of 42–4
  precinct boundaries of 10, 127–37
  residing in precincts of 10, 43–4, 115–19
  sanctuary in dependent properties of 48, 90–111, 143–6
  see also Abingdon Abbey; Beaulieu Abbey; Beverley, St John's Minster; Bewdley, Shropshire or Worcestershire; Clerkenwell, Hospitaller priory; Durham cathedral; Glastonbury Abbey; Hospitaller order; Ripon, collegiate church of; St Augustine monastery, Bristol; St John's Abbey, Colchester; St Martin le Grand; St Peter's Abbey, York; Westminster Abbey
charters, royal, as basis for sanctuary 8, 13, 30, 32, 60, 66, 72–5, 77, 81, 101–2, 190
Chester, Cheshire, as post-1540 sanctuary town 195
Chester, Cheshire, port of 8
Cholmeley, Richard 165–80
Cholmeley, Roger 165
church-taking 90

Clarebount, Nicholas 27
Clerkenwell, Hospitaller priory 51, 87–9, 93–4, 98, 100, 178
Clink manor, Southwark 62, 121
'club' sanctuaries 109
Colchester, Essex
  Crutched Friars' priory 174; *see also* St John's Abbey, Colchester
Coly, Henry 121
Colyn, George 112–14, 127, 131–2, 137; *see also* sanctuary parlour
common law, sanctuary as aspect of 2, 7, 11–13, 17, 28–30, 63, 70, 80, 189
Cornwall, George 181–4, 194
Cornwall, Richard 184
coroner, role of in abjuration 7, 34, 36, 41, 62, 93, 97, 109–10, 185, 192, 196
coroner's inquests 25, 27–8, 97, 106, 119, 122–3, 144, 145–6, 166–7, 169–71, 180, 181–2
Courtney, William 184
Cranmer, Thomas, (later) archbishop of Canterbury 147
Crayke, Yorkshire, dependent manor of Durham cathedral 104, 144
Cripps, William 196
Croke, Richard, chaplain to the king 142–59
Croke, Robert 143 57
Cromwell, Ralph, baron Cromwell 72
Cromwell, Thomas, Henry VIII's chief minister 109, 114, 127, 145, 147, 183
  attitude towards sanctuary 2–4, 194
  ordering breaches of sanctuary 165, 169–79
Culham, Oxfordshire, dependent manor of Abingdon Abbey 48–9, 104
Cull, William 143, 150
Curteys, Agnes 92
Curteys, John 132
Curteys, Piers, keeper of the king's wardrobe 48
Curteys, Thomas 64
Curteys, William, abbot of Bury St Edmunds 54, 74

Dalton, William 135
Danby, Henry 8, 92, 107
Daunce, John 194
debt, asylum for
  conceptual relationship to sanctuary for felony 9–11, 15, 21–3, 28–35, 48, 51–2, 57, 62, 81–2, 91, 106, 108, 138
  instances of claims of 41, 62, 64, 70, 74, 92, 116, 135–6, 174, 176, 191, 196–7
Derby, Derbyshire, as post-1540 sanctuary town 192
Dey alias Johnson, Henry 144
Digby, Reginald 49, 142–60
Dinmore, Herefordshire, Hospitaller property 95–6
Docwra, Thomas, prior of the Hospitaller order in England 88, 98, 101

Done, John 170–9, 180, 182
Dover, Kent, port of 7, 8
Durham Cathedral
 dependent properties offering sanctuary 104, 109, 144
 sanctuary at 10–11, 23, 29, 33–5, 38–41, 44, 49, 75, 95, 100, 102, 104, 110, 144, 193–4
Dymmok, Thomas 45

Easterford, Essex, dependent manor of Westminster Abbey 105
Ebesham, William 43
ecclesiastical immunity, concept of 2, 29–30, 110, 192
Edward the Confessor, king of England 75
Edward IV, king of England 14–15, 45, 46, 47, 53, 57, 88, 93, 94, 105, 131
Edward V, king of England 47, 53
Edward, prince, son of Henry VI 45
Edward, prince, son of Henry VIII 168
Edwards, William 167–9, 172, 173–4, 177–8, 179, 180
Elizabeth Woodville, queen consort to Edward IV 45–7
Elliotts, William 145, 146, 150
Essex, Thomas 181–2
Essex, William 181
Estfeld, William, mayor of London 64
Evil May Day riot 124, 135
Eye, Humphrey 181–2

Fabyan, Robert, chronicler 78
Feckenham, John, abbot of Westminster 196
felony forfeiture 147, 149, 164; *see also* stolen goods, right of
Feryng alias Frez or Fryse, Thomas 112
Fitzherbert, Anthony, justice 142–50, 154, 158–60
Fitzjames, Richard, bishop of London 99
Fitzroy, Henry, son of Henry VIII 147
Foteman, Thomas 178
Fowler, Edward 98
Fowler, Gilbert, warden of Knowle College 160
Foyle, William 64
Frognall, Thomas 43
Fyneux, John, chief justice 101–2, 106, 134

Gamlyn, John 122–3
Garratson, Henry 121
gendered patterns of sanctuary-seeking 19, 20, 25, 44, 55
de George, Jerome 176
Glastonbury Abbey, sanctuary at 11, 23, 33–4, 75
Gloucester, Gloucestershire, Hospitaller property at 97
Goat Inn, on the Strand 140–2, 147–8, 150, 154
Goldyng, John 97

Gon, John 42
Good Easter, Essex, dependent manor of Westminster Abbey 104
Gore, John 92–3
governance of sanctuary 8, 13, 16–17, 21, 24, 65, 116, 120, 140–5, 156
 laicization of 16, 139–41, 160–3, 190
Grene, John 144
Griffith, Hugh 167–9, 172, 173–4, 177–8, 179, 180
Gryffyn, Maurice 183–4

Habage, William 97
Hales, John, royal justice 169
Hall, Edward, chronicler 124
Hall, Vincent 93
Hanley, William 100–2, 105
Hardewyn, Andrew 97
Hart, Henry 181
Harvey, Hugh 140–64
Haw, Thomas 143, 145, 150, 152, 157–9
Hawley-Shakell affair 30–1
Henry VI, king of England 14–15, 45, 46, 54–7, 59, 68–9, 72, 75–81
Henry VII, king of England 12, 14–16, 17–19, 47–50, 57, 66, 104, 114, 130
Henry VIII, king of England 1–3, 12, 14–16, 17–19, 57, 85, 122, 138, 142, 147, 181, 184, 187, 190, 192
Hertanger, Richard 64
Heth, John 49
Hexham, lordship of 48–9
Hobbard, Cornelius 131
Hoddesdon, Hertfordshire, dependent manor of Westminster 105
Holbache, Richard 145, 153, 158
Holbache, William 145
Holbein, Hans, the Younger 4–5, 183
Holcroft, Geoffrey 171–2
Holcroft, Ralph 165, 171, 180, 182
Holcroft, Thomas 165, 170–2, 180
Holland, Henry, duke of Exeter 45
Holland, John, earl of Huntingdon, duke of Exeter 65, 68–71
homicide, categories of, and sanctuary 193–4
honour, aristocratic, and homicide 4, 18–19, 180, 185–7
Horkstow, Lincolnshire, Hospitaller property 97
Horley, Henry 145, 149–51, 154–5, 159
Horley, wife of Henry 151, 163
Hospitaller order 9, 83–111
 Hospitaller cartulary and sanctuary rights 9, 85–6, 91–3, 96
 order's role in English criminal justice 85–90
 sanctuary claims in order's properties 9–10, 28, 90–111, 144–5, 178
 St John's cart 89–90
 see also Clerkenwell, Hospitaller priory
Howard, John, duke of Norfolk 46

Howard, Thomas, duke of Norfolk 1–3
Hull, Yorkshire, port of 8
Hunne, Richard 104
Hussey, Edmund, Knight Hospitaller 49, 107–8

Ichener, Thomas 154
Islington, Middlesex 33, 51, 130
Islington, Middlesex, Hospitaller property at 98, 100
Islip, John, abbot of Westminster 126, 173
Isotson, George 51, 130

Jack Cade's Revolt 77
Janyver, William 70
John, duke of Bedford 91
Johnson, John 98
Jones, David 98
Jones, Robert 167–9, 172, 173–4, 177–8, 179, 180
Jones, Thomas 97
Joseph, Charles 104
jurisdiction, *see* liberties, ecclesiastical

Katherine of Aragon, queen consort of Henry VIII 1, 147, 176
Kendall, John, prior of the Hospitaller order in England 88, 97
Kenyngton, John 49
king's privilege, sanctuary as 16, 144, 153, 169, 190
Knevet, William 181
Knight, John 58–9, 65–72, 75–6, 135
Knowle, College of 144, 149, 160
Knowle, Warwickshire, dependent manor of Westminster Abbey 104, 140–64, 192
Kynwolmarsh, William, dean of St Martin le Grand 64

Lastell, Humphrey 185–6
Latin America, sanctuary in 2
Launceston, Cornwall, as post-1540 sanctuary town 192
Lee, Rowland, bishop of Coventry and Lichfield 109, 176–7
Leland, John, antiquarian 109
liberties, ecclesiastical:
  and alien labour 9, 21–3, 61–2, 91, 112–39
  and prostitution 9–10, 62, 121
  freedom from urban labour and market regulation 21–3, 29, 34, 61, 77, 81, 108, 112–39
  intertwining of sanctuary with other franchisal rights of 11, 14–15, 21–3, 28–35, 54–7, 60–4, 73–4, 80–2, 91, 94–5, 105, 109–11, 112–39, 148, 189–91, 192, 197
  see also chartered sanctuary, concept of; chartered sanctuaries; urban governments and hostility to franchisal and sanctuary rights of liberties

Lollard heresy 103–4
London, City of 22
  opposition to sanctuary claims of metropolitan liberties 15, 22, 55–6, 58–82, 94, 112–39
Longstaff, Leonard 144
Lovell, Francis, Viscount 48
Lydgate, John 54–7
Lynn, Norfolk, port of 8

Mainwaring, Humphrey 168
Mainwaring, John 167–9, 172, 173–4, 177–8, 179, 180
Mainwaring, Randall 167–8, 170
Mainwaring, Sir Randall 167–8, 170
Malpas, Philip, sheriff of London 64, 67, 70–1
Maltby, Lincolnshire, Hospitaller property 97
Manchester, Lancashire, as post-1540 sanctuary town 192, 195–6
Marchall, Robert, sheriff of London 64, 67, 71
Margaret of Anjou, queen consort of Henry VI 45
Markes, Robert 107
Marney, Henry 185–6
Marshall, Ralph 143, 149, 153, 155, 159
Marten, John 136
Mary, duchess of Suffolk, *see* Brandon, Mary
Mary I, queen of England 138
Mathew, William 133, 135, 136
Maynard, William 97
Medley, George, chamberlain of City of London 112, 114, 127
mercy, as conceptual foundation of sanctuary 8, 14–16, 19, 30, 45, 50–4, 57, 59, 68, 83–90, 111, 115, 188–93
Minchin Buckland, Somerset, Hospitaller property 97
monastic dissolutions 3, 4, 24, 88, 120, 126, 137, 142, 165, 166, 177, 192
More, Thomas 16, 104
  Historie of kyng Rychard the thirde 52–3
Morsate, William 97
Morton, John, bishop of Ely, archbishop of Canterbury 46, 79, 130
Morys, Richard 70
Morys, Richard, priest of Knowle 153, 160
Myles, Nicholas, canon of St Martin le Grand 122–3
Myles, William 122

Neville, Anne, daughter of the earl of Warwick 46
Neville, Richard, earl of Warwick 46
Newcastle on Tyne, port of 8
Newes, Roger 135
Northampton, Northamptonshire, as post-1540 sanctuary town 192
Norwich, Norfolk, as post-1540 sanctuary town 192, 195–6

Index

Oldhall, William 46, 77–8
ordinances governing chartered sanctuaries 9–10, 80, 91, 156
Orrell, William 181–3

papal bulls, as basis for as basis for religious houses' sanctuary claims 66, 72, 86, 92, 101–2
pardon, royal:
   as merciful mitigation parallel to sanctuary 3–4, 14, 16, 19, 24
   following claim of sanctuary 3–4, 19, 27, 38, 44, 77, 79, 85, 93, 101, 106, 107, 168–9, 177, 179, 180–1, 182, 184, 187, 191, 194
Paris Garden, Southwark, Surrey, Hospitaller property 9–10, 28, 91–4, 107
Parker alias Gerard, John 64
Parker, Robert 98
Paston, John (III) 130
Paston, Sir John (II) 21, 43
Pauncefote, Bridget 100–1
Pauncefote, John 100–1
Payne, Hugh, constable of St Martin le Grand 112, 119–21, 139, 140
Pennington, William 1–3, 168, 183
Pepys, Samuel 118
Peterson, Piers 131
Pickering, Yorkshire, parish church of 51
Pilgrimage of Grace 147
plea of sanctuary in royal court 38–9, 48–9, 84–5, 95–103, 105, 106–7, 132, 169–70, 174–9
Porter, Thomas 122
Portsmouth, Hampshire, port 92
Potter, Thomas 167–9, 172, 173–4, 177–8, 179, 180
Potts, Harry 112, 114
prostitution in sanctuary precincts 9–10, 62, 121
Pulham, Richard 83–90, 110
Purfote, Robert 133, 135–6
Pynchbek, John 91
Pynnock, William 150–2, 158, 164

Rawson, John 83–5, 87, 89
Raynsford, John, the younger 183–6, 191, 194
Raynsford, Sir John 183–6, 191, 194
Rede, John 70
Redshawe, Herbert 48
Redshawe, Thomas 48
registers of sanctuary seekers 10, 35, 39, 104, 144, 153, 174–5
Rich, Richard 169
Richard II, king of England 30–2
Richard III, king of England 46–8, 52–3, 57, 78
Richard, duke of York 53
Richard, duke of York, son of Edward IV 47, 77
Ripon, collegiate church of 41

Roo, Nicholas 169, 174–7
Rotherham, Thomas, archbishop of York 48–9
royal support for sanctuary 14–18, 22–3, 45, 57, 59, 68–9, 75–81, 114, 125–6, 181, 190; *see also* king's privilege, sanctuary as
Ryder, William 171–2

sacrality of ecclesiastical space, as aspect of sanctuary 2–3, 14, 29–32, 44–5, 56, 81, 86, 91, 93, 106, 110–11, 115, 138, 164, 189
St Augustine's monastery, Bristol 94–5, 128
St Bartholomew's Hospital 64, 66
St John's Abbey, Colchester 33, 46, 48, 183–6, 191
St John's Street, Middlesex (Hospitaller property) 93, 99–102, 106
St Katherine by the Tower, hospital of, by London 62, 64, 67, 121
St Keverne, Cornwall, dependency of Beaulieu Abbey 104
St Martin le Grand, collegiate church of, in London 58–82, 112–39
   abjuration from 62
   arguments challenging sanctuary rights of 55–6, 58–82, 112–39
   arguments supporting sanctuary rights of 51–2, 53, 55–6, 58–82, 102, 112–39
   as haven for aliens and non-citizen labour 112–39
   dependent properties of, offering sanctuary 104–5, 144
   early development of sanctuary privileges at 11, 29–35, 189–90
   franchisal liberties of, and sanctuary 21–3, 112–39, 148
   governance of precinct of 119–24
   homicides in precinct of 121–4
   ordinances governing sanctuary (1457) 9–11, 80, 129, 156
   precinct 60, 112
   precinct boundaries 112–15, 127–37
   register (cartulary) of 66–7, 72–6
   residents of precinct 10, 115–19
   royal support of sanctuary privileges at 15, 22–3, 45, 59, 68–9, 75–81, 125–6, 181
   sanctuary sought at 46, 49–50, 51, 58–82, 116, 181
   South Gate, nisi prius and error proceedings at 134
St Mary le Strand church, Middlesex 99
St Mary Spital, hospital of, London 62
St Paul the Hermit, order of 51
St Peter's Abbey, York 31
sanctuary claims
   barred for felonies committed inside the same sanctuary precinct 180
   barred for those stealing from employers 148–58
   in movable objects 83–90

sanctuary parlour, St Martin's Lane, London 131–3, 137
sanctuary seeking
  chronological pattern 6, 11–12, 18–19, 35–44, 47, 108–10, 189
  gendered patterns 19, 20, 25, 44, 55
sanctuary towns ordained by 1540 statute 191–7
  plans for proposed boundaries 195
Sandwich, Kent, port 8, 93
Savage, Anthony 100
Savage, John, the younger 2, 99–106
Savage, John, the elder 100
Selby, William 121
seven works of mercy 50, 111
Seyntbarbe (sanctuary seeker) 49, 133
Skotte, John 49
Slingsby, John 41
Smith, John, commissary of St Martin le Grand 130, 132
Southampton, Hampshire, port of 8
Southwark, Surrey 9, 51, 62, 121
Southwell, Anthony 1–5, 169, 180, 182
Southwell, Richard 1–5, 18, 169, 180–3, 194
Southwell, Robert 1–5, 169, 180–3, 194
Spencer, Anthony 173, 178–9
Stafford, Henry, duke of Buckingham 52–3
Stafford, Humphrey 48, 104
Stafford, John, archbishop of Canterbury 72
Stafford, Thomas 48
Stafford, Staffordshire, as post-1540 sanctuary town 195
state formation 141, 146, 160–3, 189
statute law
  books of 152, 157–8
statute law regarding sanctuary 2, 8, 17, 152–8, 162
  1377 statute (50 Edw. II, c. 6) 30–1
  1529 statute (21 Hen. VIII, c. 2) 156
  1531 statute (22 Hen. VIII, c. 14) 35, 38, 41, 42, 44, 148–9, 156, 175
  1534 statute (26 Hen. VIII, c. 13) 156
  1536 statute (27 Hen. VIII, c. 17) 142, 148–9, 152, 156–7
  1536 statute (27 Hen. VIII, c. 19) 156–7
  1540 statute (32 Hen. VIII, c. 14) 24, 192–7
  1540 statute (32 Hen. VIII, c. 16) 137
  1603 statute (1 Jas. I, c. 25) 197
  1624 statute (21 Jas. I, c. 28) 197
Stillington, Robert, dean of St. Martin le Grand 46, 79
Stokfyssh, Herman 27–8, 33
stolen goods, franchisal right of 10, 62, 79–80, 143, 147–55
Stow, John, chronicler 138

taking church 7, 8, 28, 35, 38, 41–2, 57, 90–2, 102, 106, 192

Talbot, George, earl of Shrewsbury 185
Templar order 87, 96
Tewkesbury Abbey 46
Tewkesbury, battle of 46
Thavie's Inn, London 61
Thornley, Isobel 6, 11–12, 18, 21, 28–9, 52–3, 63, 80
Throckmorton, George 144–6
Tiptoft, John 68–70
Toft, William 96–8
Toker, Ralph 83–90, 110
treason as grounds for seeking sanctuary 7, 9, 13, 32, 46–9, 64, 73, 77–8, 80, 96, 104, 108, 116, 130, 134, 156, 169, 176
Tresilian, Robert, Chief Justice 32
trespass, as grounds for seeking sanctuary 13, 52, 94, 102, 106, 108, 116, 174, 176
Trussell, Thomas 143, 145, 151–5, 159–60
Tuchet, James, Baron Audley 133
Twynne, Ralph 130, 133
Tynhof, Derek 133
tyranny, sanctuary as remedy for 14–16, 47–8, 51–7, 189, 197

urban governments' hostility to franchisal rights of liberties, incl. sanctuary 21–3, 60–4, 70–2, 74–5, 80–2, 94–5, 107–8, 112–39, 174, 191, 195–6; see also Bristol, City of; liberties, ecclesiastical; London, City of

Veale, Leonard 171
de Vere, Elizabeth, countess of Oxford 21, 46
Vergil, Polydore 45, 47–8, 124
Vynes, Richard 184

Walde or Wade, William 177
Waltham, Augustinian priory of 63–4
Warbeck, Perkin 14, 49, 130, 133
Wars of the Roses 15, 20, 21, 29, 44–50, 51, 52, 57, 77–8, 130, 189
Watson, Bartholomew 133
Webbe, William, of Warwick 158–61
Webbe, William, of Westminster 43, 158, 173–4, 178–9, 192
Wells, Somerset, as post-1540 sanctuary town 192, 197
Westminster Abbey 120
  convict house 84
  dependent properties of, offering sanctuary 104–5, 109, 140–64, 192
  dissolution of 159, 192
  early development of sanctuary privileges at 11, 27–35, 189–90
  franchisal liberties of, and sanctuary 21–3, 102, 110
  governance of sanctuary 173
  incorporation of St Martin le Grand (from 1503) 60, 66, 73, 114–16, 120
  residents of precinct 10, 42–3, 175

revival of sanctuary under Mary I 196
sanctuary seekers, censuses of (1532, 1533) 42–3
sanctuary sought at 1–5, 8, 27–34, 42–3, 45–7, 52–4, 106, 136, 165–9, 171–7, 180–1
Westminster, Middlesex, as post-1540 sanctuary town 192, 195–7
Weston, William, prior of the Hospitaller order in England 88, 108
White, John 98
Whitefriars, London, as debtors' sanctuary 197
Whittington, Richard, mayor of London 62
Whorwode, William 170, 178
Wigmore, Herefordshire, 'club sanctuary' 109
William I, the Conqueror, king of England 60, 72–5, 81
Wilton Abbey 23
Winkburn, Nottinghamshire, Hospitaller property 96
Wolfe, Alice 176
Wolfe, John 176
Wolsey, Thomas, Cardinal archbishop of York and chancellor 100, 144, 174, 181
women as sanctuary seekers 19, 20, 25, 44, 55
Woodleke, Francis 112–15, 120, 124, 127, 130–3, 137
Wormelow, Herefordshire, Hospitaller property 95
Wright, Roger 134–6
Wriothesley, Charles, chronicler 88
Wyclif, John 31

Yeoman, Richard 140, 147–8, 150
York, Yorkshire, as post-1540 sanctuary town 192, 195

Printed and bound by CPI Group (UK) Ltd, Croydon, CR0 4YY